THE DIVISION OF THE WORLD, 1941–1955

THE
DIVISION
OF THE
WORLD
1941-1955

WILFRIED LOTH

ST. MARTIN'S PRESS
New York

© Deutscher Taschenbuch Verlag Gmbh & CoKG, 1988

All rights reserved. For information write:
Scholarly and Reference Division,
St. Martin's Press, Inc., 175 Fifth Avenue, New York, NY 10010

First published in the United States of America in 1988

Printed in Great Britain

ISBN 0-312-02045-7

Library of Congress Cataloging-in-Publication Data applied for

Contents

Contents

Contents

Introduction:
Two Interpretations of the 'Cold War'

No other event has had such a lasting impact on the international system emerging out of the Second World War as the confrontation between the two world powers of the USA and the USSR. To this day and for the foreseeable future, the antagonism between these two powers, as well as that between the two power blocs and systems of alliances arising out of their conflict, represents the starting point that renders attempts at *détente* on both sides as necessary as they are difficult. It also represents the starting point from which one must proceed in solving the 'new' international problems, such as the North–South issue, the growth crisis and transnational division conflicts. Since the early nineteenth century, an East–West conflict has often been predicted between 'Asian' and 'Western' civilisation (most impressively and with unequivocal partisanship for the 'West' on the part of Karl Marx). Since the Russian October Revolution and the entry of the United States in 1917 into world politics, this conflict has been variously put forward as the decisive battle between Capitalism and Communism, Pluralism and Totalitarianism, and the Liberal-democratic and the State Socialist systems, as well as being feared, and quite often even provoked. How this conflict has since become politically virulent, emerging out of the war coalition against Hitler's Germany, how in time it was able to take on the existential character of a 'Cold War' embracing almost all spheres of life, why and how it led to the division of Europe and of Germany into two halves, to the crystallisation of two power blocs and to a permanent armament race, have so far never been adequately explained.

None the less there is no lack of literature on the history of the Cold War, or of interpretative models to explain it. In so far as the literature on the Cold War, in dealing with recent historical events, takes the development of the conflict as the starting point, and then proceeds to an interpretation of ideological mobilisation, it in itself forms a part of the conflict. Consistent with the antagonistic character of East–West relations, the literature on the Cold War is marked by two opposing basic positions; the 'traditional' thesis (since this initially predominates in the Western literature) of Soviet expansionism as the cause of the conflict, and the 'revisionist' thesis of the economic imperialism of the USA as

1

the central factor in world politics since the Second World War. Both theses are presented in many variations; both, however, suffer from not being sufficiently empirically documented, and thus all the more from being too emotionally charged.[1]

The traditional view

The traditional thesis was formulated particularly impressively as early as 1946–7 by the then American diplomatic adviser, George F. Kennan.[2] It became definitive for the greater part of the American and West European political public by the end of 1948, subsequently being taken up, especially in comprehensive research into diplomatic history, by such authors as William McNeill, Boris Meissner and Herbert Feis.[3] In the view of these authors, Marxist ideology in its Soviet interpretation with its insistence on world revolution as the outcome of a world-wide class struggle, the historical experiences of the Soviet leadership with an extremely hostile surrounding environment intent on the removal of the Soviet regime between 1918 and 1921, and the concern of the Soviet party oligarchy to retain its power in a mobilisation and development dictatorship were all crucial factors in the origins of the Cold War, setting the Soviet leadership on the path towards a fundamentally hostile policy in relation to capitalist states. Although this policy temporarily, and in a cautious and pragmatic way, served the purpose of peaceful co-operation (the doctrine of coexistence), it simultaneously remained constantly alert for opportunities to weaken the non-Communist powers and to enlarge the Communist area of domination controlled from Moscow. In the Second World War, Stalin initially planned in terms of the self-laceration of the capitalist states. Forced on to the side of the Western powers by German invasion, he sought, by means of the division of the reciprocal spheres of interests in Eastern Europe which had been offered to him by Hitler, as well as through the concerted action of Communist cadres and the Red Army, to transform all the countries of Eastern and Central Europe, and if possible the whole of Germany also, into 'People's Democratic' states structurally dependent on the hegemony of the Soviet Union. He further sought, by means of the encouragement of social unrest in Western Europe, the Mediterranean region and Asia, to extend the area of influence over the long term with the aid

2

of Communist parties linked to Moscow.

The leading powers of the Western world, represented first by President Roosevelt and Hull, his Secretary of State, and then, from April 1945, by President Truman and Byrnes, at first failed to recognise the ambivalent and potentially expansive character of Soviet policy. With a mixture of idealistic hope for the democratisation of the Soviet system and resigned fear that a longer-term American engagement in Europe could not be successfully propounded in the USA in the domestic political climate of the time, they were prepared to view Stalin's efforts in the direction of pro-Soviet neighbour states as a legitimate Soviet security interest, while nevertheless hoping to be able to integrate the Soviet Union into a democratic 'one world' system. Lacking a definite concept for the post-war ordering of states in Europe and the world, and with an unfortunate tendency to divorce issues of military necessity from the consideration of political consequences (a tendency resisted in vain by the British Allied partner), they sought to make co-operation attractive for Stalin by means of generous concessions, by facilitating the forward movement of the Red Army as far as Central Europe, and by ensuring for the Soviet leadership the right to take part in negotiations on the future of Germany, without offering the necessary and possible resistance to the Sovietisation of Eastern Europe. At the end of May 1945, they recognised the provisional government of Poland, which had been dictated from Moscow and expanded by only a few exiled Polish representatives; at the Potsdam Conference, they approved the *de facto* westward shifting of Poland and the plundering by the Soviet government of their occupation zone in Germany by use of their power of occupation; at the Moscow Foreign Ministers' Conference at the end of December 1945, they accepted the Communist alignment of Romania and Bulgaria; and finally, with their ratification of the peace treaty with Romania, Bulgaria, Hungary and Finland at the end of 1946, they relinquished all remaining possibilities for influencing the East European region.

Despite increasing embitterment about the impenetrability of the 'Iron Curtain', as well as about Soviet intransigence in the United Nations, the Truman Administration stood by its original willingness to co-operate with the Soviet Union, offering with the Baruch Plan in June 1946 joint control of atomic weapon production, by seeking to make the Four-Power responsibility for the whole of Germany which had been agreed upon in Potsdam a reality, and by declaring itself ready in July 1946 to conclude a joint pact guaranteeing against any fresh German aggression. In addition, the American leadership invited the Soviet Union in June 1947 to take part, together with its East European allied partners, in a joint rebuilding programme with American support — the Marshall Plan.

Only with Soviet refusal to agree to any of these offers of co-operation did a split in Europe and the formation of two power blocs become inevitable. In order to prevent the further expansion of the Soviet area of control, the American leadership decided in the course of 1947 to meet the threat of economic collapse in the remaining European states with generous economic aid and by furthering its integration, whilst simultaneously incorporating the three Western occupation zones of Germany into this rebuilding process, thus accepting under pressure of necessity the previous division of Germany. The Soviet leadership reacted to this American decision to turn its back once and for all on isolationism with a brutal intensification of the Sovietisation process inside its zone in Germany and Eastern Europe, culminating in the dramatic assumption of Communist power in February 1948 in Czechoslovakia, which had by then enjoyed a partly bourgeois-democratic form of government for a considerable time. It similarly attempted to sabotage the consolidation process of the West by means of Communist-linked strike movements in Western Europe from November 1947, a blockade of all access routes to West Berlin from June 1948, and finally with an offer of negotiations on the reunification of a neutralised Germany in March 1952. In this respect, those Europeans remaining outside the Soviet power zone saw themselves as being dependent upon American support and protection against Soviet aggression; this led to the creation of the OEEC in 1948, the founding of NATO in 1949 and, after the shock-like experience of Communist aggression in the Korean War from July 1950, to the arming of the Federal Republic, which had emerged from the West German territory meanwhile, as well as its entry into the Western Defence Alliance. In this way, Soviet expansion could be halted at least in Europe, although the Soviet will to expand was still by no means extinguished.

The revisionist thesis

The revisionist thesis has evolved in a permanent state of disagreement with the Western interpretation. It started by way of a tendency among internal American opponents of Truman's foreign policy, among them former Vice-President Henry A. Wallace,[4] and European opponents of Western integration into the 'neutralist' movement of the end of the 1940s;[5] then it developed systematically in connection with the articulation of the secular context of American policy, as put forward in numerous works by the American historian William A. Williams;[6] finally, it has developed with the research of the 'New Left', which has dominated public discussion and been influenced by protest against American conduct of the war in Vietnam at the end of the 1960s and beginning of the 1970s — particularly the research of Williams's student Gabriel Kolko, as well as and to some extent in mutual criticism with authors such as Lloyd C. Gardner, Barton J. Bernstein, David Horowitz, Gar Alperowitz and Thomas G. Paterson.[7] The Soviet Union, according to the critique of these authors on the traditional thesis, cannot be held responsible for the origins of the Cold War; it only barely escaped military catastrophe in the Second World War, suffered infinite losses in terms of human life and resources, and stood virtually helpless before the economically prosperous, traditionally anti-Soviet world power of the USA, which had atomic weapons at its disposal. Soviet policy, which since Stalin's assumption of power was clearly more interested in securing the Russian state than in fulfilling the demand for world revolution, evidently aimed at the creation of a security buffer-zone of states that were not hostile to the Soviet Union, particularly in the East European region, as well as at ensuring complete protection against fresh German attack. These aims, however, were not linked *a priori* with the concept of outward-oriented Sovietisation; indeed outside the immediate area of Soviet influence, they presented themselves in an exceptionally conservative manner (in order to avoid unnecessary provocation of their American opponents), which had a decidedly inhibiting effect on socialist movements in Western and Southern Europe at the end of the war, thus rescuing European capitalism from decline long before the Marshall Plan appeared.

The causes of confrontation are rather to be found in the structure of the politico-economic system of the United States. In order to avoid fundamental crises, the liberal-capitalist society of the USA had from its very beginnings been oriented towards a perpetual opening-up of new trade and sales markets, and thus indirectly towards the extension of its political sphere of influence. This led, after the closing of the 'open frontier' in the American West, to a world-wide Open Door policy, to the demand for equality of treatment and opportunity on all foreign markets, to the abolition of protective tariffs and preferential customs systems, to the abrogation of all forms of autarchism, bilateralism or regionalism in trade politics, to a struggle for unhampered access to all raw materials, as well as for unlimited freedom of investment and the free exchange of products and services — a policy that would ensure world-wide dominance for the strongest economic power, the USA, under the cloak of formal equality of opportunity. The 'one world' of war propaganda was no mere idealistic utopia, but an expression of a realistic and resolute war policy on the part of the American leadership, which had grasped the essentials of its social system. Its policy aimed at the 'one world' of the Pax Americana.

The desire to protect and extend American opportunities for influence in the world economy was a decisive factor in its entry into the war against Japan and Germany, which were in fact on the verge of creating autarchic empires in Asia and Europe respectively. The same desire, however, was similarly directed against the two main Allies in the struggle against the German–Japanese coalition: in the first case, because it was economically much more important, this desire was directed against Great Britain; and in the second, and this is a decisive factor in the origins of the Cold War, it was directed against the Soviet Union. Throughout the whole of the Second World War, the struggle for the dissolution of the sterling bloc and the struggle against the signed agreement of Ottawa in 1932 for a preferential tariff system for the British Empire remained in the forefront of US diplomatic activities. Throughout the lengthy negotiations about the Anglo-American agreement on the Lease and Loan law, the founding of the World Bank and the World Currency Fund, finally agreed upon in 1944 at Bretton Woods, as well as on the loan granted by the American government to Great Britain in November 1945, the British were forced to open up their commercial–political empire to American influence piece by piece. At the same time, the USA took advantage of the weakness of Great Britain as a result of the war to take over British export markets in Latin America and to threaten British crude oil companies in the Near East with fierce competition. From 1945 onwards, the confrontation with the Soviet Union over the future of Eastern Europe increased in significance. Although the politico-commercial interests of the USA in Eastern Europe were comparatively limited, the American leadership believed that even in this region it could not afford to relinquish an Open Door policy, which was intended to secure the liberal-capitalist order and American influence in the long term.

The Soviet leadership could not afford to accept such a threat to its basic security interests, especially since the Open Door policy in Eastern Europe, as indeed also in Germany, Italy, Greece, China, Korea and Japan, largely went hand in hand with the encouragement of capitalist-authoritarian and mostly milit-ant anti-Soviet forces. While it was offering its resistance to this, giving the social-revolutionary movements in the power zone of the Red Army a free hand and attempting to shield the liberated territories from the unhindered grasp of American capitalism by means of treaties of alliance, the Truman Administration attempted with a series of blackmail tactics somehow to force an Open Door on Eastern Europe. First, it exerted economic pressure: it deliberately procrastinated over the Soviet attempt to obtain credit in January 1945, by abruptly bringing all deliveries from the Lease and Loan law to an end immediately after the conclusion of the war negotiations, by refusing at Potsdam to grant reparation out of German production in the amounts required for the rebuilding of the destroyed Soviet Union, and by stopping all reparation payments from the American zone of occupation in May 1946. Secondly, the US leadership sought to make the Soviet leadership more compliant by drawing attention to its own monopoly of atomic weapons; it postponed the start of the Potsdam Conference until the first atomic bombs against Japan were operational; and, in addition, it sought by means of the Baruch Plan to ensure its monopoly of atomic weapons for decades ahead and to take control of industrial development in the Soviet Union. Thirdly, with the Marshall Plan in June 1947 it developed an investment and liberalisation programme for the whole of Europe, which was intended not only to lay the econ-omic foundation for an 'informal' American 'empire', to include Eastern Europe, but which was also directed in terms of its politi-cal repercussions against the very substance of the ruling circles in the Soviet Union.

Inasmuch as the power zone of the Red Army showed itself to

be resistant to these blackmail attempts, the American leadership settled under duress for consolidating the Pax Americana in the non-Communist world; the division of Germany and Europe was thus bargained over deliberately and executed systematically from the beginning of 1946. The resistance of the remaining isolationists in the American Congress and of national capitalist and socialist forces in Western Europe was broken by the creation and propagation of the mythology of the Soviet Union's desire for global expansion. The way for the Marshall Plan was paved politically by means of the Truman Doctrine in 1947, and the Berlin blockade of 1948/9 accomplished the creation of the NATO alliance. During the Korean War from 1950 onwards, it was possible for even the domestic political parallelogram of power in the USA and its allied countries to be shifted to the right for the long term. Only in reaction to American blackmail attempts and the formation of a Western bloc did the Soviet leadership begin to exert pressure on the 'people's democratic' transformation process of the countries in its sphere of influence, in order to coerce their governments into unified courses of action and to secure its own dominance in this region by the use of police-state methods. Although it thereby undoubtedly contributed to an entrenchment of the East–West confrontation, such action was clearly only carried out under duress and in the hope of possibly reaching some settlement with the Western powers in the future.

The aim of this book

The contradictions inherent in these interpretations of the Cold War are thus considerable. On the other hand, they are only increased by the tendency of revisionist authors to accuse traditional historiography of inadequate theoretical basis, and of traditional authors to accuse revisionists of inadequate academic solidity,[8] and by the fact that in both camps there is considerable uncertainty as to whether the Cold War is the virtually inevitable result of a collision between two diametrically opposed social systems, or whether it originated as a result of an avoidable escalatory mechanism of mutual errors of judgement and panic reactions.[9] The situation is not entirely hopeless, however. Using the 'traditional' scenario as a starting point, 'realistic' authors, such as Marshall D. Shulman, Hans J. Morgenthau, Arthur M. Schlesinger, Adam B. Ulam, Roger Morgan and to a lesser extent also

8

Louis J. Halle, have uncovered a range of discrepancies between the predominant Western interpretation and the power realities of the conflict.[10] The authors of the 'New Left' began their main research at a time when more material was gradually becoming available in the American archives; this brought to light a wealth of hitherto unknown information, leaving aside the question of the relative comprehensiveness of a number of global attempts at explanation. Building on this new basis, a series of 'post-revisionist' authors, such as John L. Gaddis, George C. Herring, Martin J. Sherwin, Geir Lundestad and above all Daniel Yergin, have undertaken an analysis of American foreign policy in the war and post-war eras that is saturated with an empiricism no longer characterised by a single partisan view.[11] Similarly, with the gradual availability of European archives, it has become possible to comprehend a number of events in the European region without being caught up in the one-sided mythological bias, which as a rule often pertains to the public statements and reminiscences of those involved at the time. In other words, there has been a degree of progress in historical understanding which has only become possible in the era of *détente* politics; the further perfecting of this 'post-revisionist' understanding, moreover, represents in itself an important contribution to the continuance of these *détente* endeavours.

It is in this context that this study can best be understood; it does not take upon itself the task of setting against the two antagonistic interpretative models of the Cold War a third thesis of equal stringency. Such an undertaking, however desirable, would not only require more comprehensive research of sources, but also better acquaintance with the factors linking human awareness and the course of events, economy and policy, as well as with individual interests and causal chains, than we at present possess — an endeavour which could possibly only be accomplished as a collective effort. What can be achieved in the current state of research, and what is attempted here, is, first, an account of the controversial debate so far, testing the proposed theses for their plausibility and explanatory capacity; secondly, a preliminary sketch of connections that have either so far not been taken into consideration *in the course of* the debate, or that as a result of an inadequate availability of sources, could not be taken into consideration; and thirdly, an attempt to weigh up the hitherto discernible factors of the 'Cold War' phenomenon.

Methodologically, this attempt is not based *a priori* on *one* explanatory model, nor does it postulate a single interpretation by way of a heuristic principle; rather, it seeks to reconstruct the salient structural elements of the Cold War, and test them against both the ascertainable historical data and the various interpretative postulations of political economy, the history of ideas and power and behaviour theory. Although this procedure has the disadvantage of lacking theoretical conclusiveness, it does on the other hand run less risk of simply shutting the door on connecting factors essential to the account. This procedure recommends itself all the more in the case of a theme such as the Cold War, since, as will be shown, none of the explanatory models developed so far is competent to comprehend adequately the constituent elements of the conflict and its development, nor (and this is closely connected) has there even once been a remotely satisfactory explanation of what the fundamental character of this conflict in fact consists of.[12] At the conclusion of this analytical process, an attempt will be made to define the Cold War as a historical phenomenon; it is to be hoped that, as a result of this definition, the manner of selection and presentation of the information will have been justified. Although in the light of the inadequacy of our theoretical and empirical knowledge this conclusion can only at best be a preliminary and inconclusive one, it is nevertheless hoped that it may point the way for future academic progress on this theme.

Note on the English edition

In the seven years which have elapsed since the German edition of this book first appeared, numerous gaps in knowledge have undoubtedly been bridged. A whole series of specialised field studies have been carried out on American policy, relations in Europe have been brought into clearer view as a result of the releasing of British documents, and there has even been fresh information in connection with Soviet policy.[13] It has been possible in the course of this to confirm the basis and enhance the detail of events and connections which were only outlined here. On some individual questions, there have been fresh discoveries, although no new total picture has emerged as a result; the necessity for a division of work, and pleasure at freshly obtained source material, have tended, rather, to allow the totality of the Cold War in many respects to slip from view. As a consequence of this, increased precision of detail has often been achieved at the price of loss of clarity of the overall view, the results of detailed research remaining to a large extent manipulable. Inasmuch as the 'traditional' or 'revisionist' global theories were quashed, they were often used only to bolster the current counter-theory.

In the context of this situation, the English edition of this book represents an attempt to pull together once again the threads of this proliferated discussion and to revert the debate on the Cold War back to its basic issues.[14] It presents the text of the German edition largely unaltered, but nevertheless takes account of progress in the research findings of recent years and mentions in the footnotes new publications, which permit the interested reader to carry out further work on separate issues. This edition may therefore be read either as an introduction to the history of the Cold War or as a holistic analysis of it, both encouraging an examination of hitherto current concepts and facilitating a placing of detailed research in its context.[15]

In view of the relevance of the topic to contemporary political life, it would not presumably be superfluous to point out that it is not the intention of this book to pass moral judgement from the self-satisfied position of the better-informed descendant, but rather to achieve a better grasp of the historical connections from which the present has emerged. The author is quite willing to admit that such an undertaking is not without its political implications: as always, the critical work of the historian reveals responsibilities in this case too, as well as dismantling traditional justifications and executing an examination of time-honoured ways of dealing with the issues. The acceptance of such an analysis presupposes a willingness to open one's own political positions to question, inasmuch as they have been affected by our emergence from the era of the Cold War. This is indeed no easy matter, even forty years after the formulation of the Truman Doctrine and the Zhdanov thesis, but it is unavoidable, if the historical inheritance of the Cold War is to be analysed and a realistic approach found towards overcoming the current urgent problems of the East–West conflict. If this book is able to make a contribution towards this, it will have achieved its purpose.

Notes

1. On the revisionist debate, see the bibliography of E. David Cronon and Theodore D. Rosenhof, *The Second World War and the atomic age, 1940–1973* (Northbrook, Ill., 1975); the commemorative volume of Richard S. Kirkendall (ed.), *The Truman period as a research field. A reappraisal 1972* (Columbia, Mo., 1974); and the research report of Wilfried Loth, 'Der "Kalte Krieg" in der historischen Forschung', in Gottfried Niedhart (ed.), *Der Westen und die Sowjetunion* (Paderborn, 1983), pp. 155–75.

2. In his famous 'long telegram' of 22 February 1946 (published in George F. Kennan, *Memoirs 1925–1955* (Boston, 1967), pp. 547–59) and in his anonymous ('Mr. X') article in the journal *Foreign Affairs*, 25 (1947), pp. 566–82; compare John L. Gaddis, 'Containment: a reassessment', *Foreign Affairs*, 55 (1977), pp. 873–87.

3. William H. McNeill, *America, Britain and Russia, their co-operation and conflict 1941–1946* (London, 1953); Boris Meissner, *Russland, die Westmächte und Deutschland*, 2nd edn. (Hamburg, 1954); Herbert Feis, *Churchill, Roosevelt, Stalin, the war they waged and the peace they sought* (Princeton, NJ 1957); also by the same author, *The atomic bomb and the end of World War II*, 2nd edn. (Princeton NJ, 1966); *From trust to terror. The onset of the Cold War 1945–1950* (New York, 1970). For comprehensive accounts based on these works, compare John Lukacs, *A history of the Cold War 1945–50* (New York, 1970; Garden City 1961), and André Fontaine, *Histoire de la guerre froide* (2 vols, Paris, 1965–7).

4. See chapter 5, note 7.

5. See chapter 10, note 14.

6. Essential reading; William A. Williams, *The tragedy of American diplomacy* (New York, 1959; 3rd edn, 1972); in addition, a series of articles in his *History as a way of learning* (New York, 1973). Donna F. Fleming stands somewhere between contemporary liberal critique and scientific revisionism: *The Cold War and its origins, 1917–1960* (2 vols, Garden City, 1961).

7. Gabriel Kolko, *The politics of war, the world and United States policy, 1943–1945* (New York, 1968); Joyce and Gabriel Kolko, *The limits of power, The world and United States policy, 1945–1954* (New York, 1972); Lloyd C. Gardner, *Economic aspects of New Deal diplomacy* (Madison, 1954) and also *Architects of illusion, Men and ideas in American foreign policy 1941–1949* (Chicago, 1970); Barton J. Bernstein (ed.), *Politics and policies of the Truman administration* (Chicago, 1970); and also *The atomic bomb, the critical issues* (Boston and Toronto, 1976); David Horowitz, *The free world Colossus, A critique of American foreign policy in the Cold War* (New York, 1965); Gar Alperowitz, *Atomic diplomacy; Hiroshima and Potsdam, The use of the atomic bomb and the American confrontation with Soviet power* (New York, 1965); Thomas G. Paterson, *Soviet–American confrontation, Postwar reconstruction and the origins of the Cold War* (Baltimore, Md, and London, 1973); as a short account; Walter LaFeber, *America, Russia and the Cold War*, 3rd edn. (New York, 1976).

8. For the last accusation especially, Robert J. Maddox, *The New Left and the origins of the Cold War* (Princeton, NJ, 1973); by contrast, Warren

Introduction

F. Kimball, 'The Cold War warmed over', *American Historical Review*, vol. 79 (1974), pp. 1119–36.

9. Michael Leigh reviews the most important differences in 'Is there a revisionist thesis on the origins of the Cold War?' *Political Science Quarterly* vol. 89 (1974), pp. 101–6.

10. Marshall D. Shulman; *Stalin's foreign policy reappraised* (Cambridge, Mass., 1963); Morgenthau and Schlesinger, *Origins of the Cold War*(Waltham, Mass., 1970), see also A. Schlesinger, Jr (ed.), *The dynamics of world power, A documentary history of the United States foreign policy 1945–1973,*' (5 vols, New York, 1973); Adam B. Ulam, *Expansion and coexistence, The history of Soviet foreign policy 1917–1967*, (London, 1968; 2nd edn, 1974) and also *The rivals, America and Russia since World War II* (New York, 1971; 2nd edn., London, 1973); Roger Morgan, *The unsettled peace, A study of the Cold War in Europe* (London, 1974); Louis J. Halle, *The Cold War as history* (New York, 1967).

11. John L. Gaddis, *The United States and the origins of the Cold War 1941–1947* (New York, 1972; 2nd edn, 1976); George C. Herring, *Aid to Russia 1941–1946; Strategy, diplomacy, the origins of the Cold War* (New York, 1973); Martin J. Sherwin, *A world destroyed, The atomic bomb and the grand alliance* (New York, 1975); Geir Lundestad, *The American non-policy towards Eastern Europe 1943–1947* (Troms, New York, 1975; 2nd edn, 1978); Daniel Yergin, *Shattered peace, The origins of the Cold War and the national security state* (Boston, 1977).

12. The attempt by Ernst Nolte to offer a comprehensive explanation (*Deutschland und der Kalte Krieg*, Munich, 1974) offers historically based contributions to the categorisation of the ideological dimension of the Cold War, but omits to consider in detail the relationship between ideological demands and real events, thus remaining in many respects limited to a reiteration of the 'traditional' self-perception, allowing the conflict and the course it takes to appear historically inevitable. See also the discussion of the Nolte outline in Wilfried Loth, 'Der "Kalte Krieg" in deutscher Sicht', *Deutschland-Archiv*, 9 (1976), pp. 204–13.

13. See the reports on publications in the early 1980s contained in Wolfgang Michalka (ed.), *Ost-West-Konflikt und Friedenssicherung* (Stuttgart, 1985).

14. A central element of the argument developed below can also be found in Wilfried Loth, 'Die doppelte Eindämmung. Überlegungen zur Genesis des Kalten Krieges 1945–1947', *Historische Zeitschrift*, 238 (1984), pp. 611–31.

15. For her committed support in the preparation of this edition, I should like to thank Susanne Dismer. Her determination and sensitivity have made it possible to give the numerous English quotations in their original version, rather than in re-translation.

1

Pax Americana: The Limits of the 'One World'

During the joint war coalition against the National Socialist empire there was intensive discussion in the decision-making centres of the two future world powers about the formation of a peacetime order and the development of their mutual relations. Both powers came out of the war well-armed with prognoses, programmes and strategies — well-armed, that is, for overcoming the crises they had experienced; the survival crisis of the young Soviet state, the world economic crisis, and the threat posed by National Socialism. They were by no means adequately prepared, however, to find solutions to the new problems that had emerged as a result of their joint victory over Hitler's Germany and its allies. They were thus not prepared for a confrontation between two different, and in many respects antagonistic social systems, nor for the problem of accustoming their own populations to the now inevitable contact with their foreign allies without endangering their own system, nor for the problem of the power vacuum in devastated Europe. The fact that the post-war planning of the two world powers was more oriented towards past than present problems (which is of course much easier to discern in hindsight than it was for contemporaries) was one of the initial decisive factors that rendered the co-operation of the USA and the USSR unsuccessful, although, as will be shown, the leading circles of both powers had an interest in its continuance after the end of the war coalition.

Learning from the mistakes of the past was the imperative which at first dominated American war policy discussion, however disparate the positions thereby represented may have been. Never again, according to the basic demands of this imperative, should it become possible for a pre-democratic, militaristic

15

Germany to threaten world peace; never again should the play-ing-out of uncontrolled power politics be permitted to take over sovereign nation states; never again should the jumble of numer-ous customs barriers hamper the advancement of the general good; never again should the United States stand idly by and watch crises building up to the point where the country was faced with a direct threat to its security. Was it possible, however, to do justice to demands that implied a radical break with the past?

The German question

As far as the future of defeated Germany was concerned, it seemed easy to answer yes to this question. In the view of Ameri-can planners, the rise of Hitler and the execution of his plans for conquest were essentially attributable to two factors; on the one hand, to the manifest contradiction between the pledges of the '14 points' of President Wilson and what was for Germany the bitter reality of the Versailles Treaty and, on the other hand, to the legend propagated by internal enemies of the Weimar Republic that the German army of the First World War, 'unde-feated on the field', had only been compelled to capitulate as a result of the treachery of the 'November criminals'. This time, the Advisory Committee on Post-war Foreign Policy of the State Department recommended, there should be no room for doubt as to the defeat of Germany, nor for German hopes for a return to the pre-war *status quo*: Germany — and likewise Japan — were to be fought to the point of unconditional surrender. President Roosevelt discussed this demand with his Commanders-in-Chief as well as with Churchill, and came to a final decision; the world will only have peace, he announced to the public in January 1943, on the eve of the conference at Casablanca 'by the total elimination of German and Japanese war power'.[1]

In the view of many Americans, similar radicalism should also be applied to the future treatment of Germany. In order to avoid a repetition of the German urge to expand, as Treasury Secretary Henry Morgenthau, in particular, never tired of reiterating, it would not suffice to destroy the German war machine; in addi-tion to this, its entire industrial capacity should be destroyed, and the German Reich dissolved into individual provinces, which should retain the character of predominantly agriculturally-oriented regions. In particular, the American occupation troops

16

should not undertake responsibility for the German economy, but make the Germans fully conscious of the material consequences of defeat by means of 'organised chaos'.[2] In this respect also, Roosevelt, who was himself lastingly affected by negative experiences in Wilhelmine Germany in his youth, largely agreed. 'We have got to be tough with Germany', he assured Morgenthau in August 1944, as the latter's basic memorandum (the 'Morgenthau Plan') began to circulate in the US Administration, 'and I mean the German people not just the Nazis. We either have to castrate the German people or you have got to treat them in such manner so they can't just go on reproducing people who want to continue the way they have in the past.'[3]

The desire to nip German evil in the bud drove the USA into a close alliance with its Soviet coalition partner, helping to diminish Stalin's fear of an overturning of alliance relations, that is, of a coalition of the capitalist powers against the Soviet Union. It also seemed the best basis for the continuance of the alliance after the war was over. However, given the tradition of American history, the question had to be asked, and was asked, whether this desire would be able to stand its ground in the face of the long-term interests of American society, or whether in fact it was merely the superficial, emotionally-determined expression of bitterness over the sufferings brought about by the war. Was the destruction of Germany compatible with the values of Western civilisation, against the perversion of which American society felt itself to be a protector? Was it compatible with the interest in a prosperous European trading partner and export market? Was it compatible with the attempt to contain the growth of power of the Soviet Union? The same Advisory Committee of the State Department that had developed the 'unconditional-surrender' strategy presented in September 1943 a German plan that outlined the encouragement of democratic institutions in Germany as the best guarantee of future peace, to be achieved by means of a peacetime regulation sufficing itself with a 'minimum of bitterness' towards the Germans, by a limitation of Allied occupation to a purely security function, by the rebuilding of the economy until 'a tolerable standard of living' for the German population had been reached and, as was also to be intoned by the authors of the plan, of course by the avoidance of revanchism-encouraging experiments with plans for division and with intolerable reparation burdens.[4] These views soon gained support in the State Department; indeed, they attained such wide circulation that

Roosevelt felt compelled five weeks after his encouragement of Morgenthau to criticise the plan of his Treasury Secretary. 'No one,' he assured the enraged Chief of the State Department, Cordell Hull, 'wants to make Germany a wholly agricultural nation again.'[5]

Post-war American policy towards Germany thus bifurcated into the following: on the one hand, a lasting peacetime order for Germany could only be achieved in co-operation with the Soviet Union, a co-operation which in turn could only be based on the concerted will to eliminate the forces that had brought National Socialism into existence; on the other hand, self-knowledge, as well as the economic and power–political interests of the USA, lent themselves to a peace involving the integration of the future community of nations. Doubly undecided which of the two concepts of Germany being discussed in his Administration to prefer, and whether to give priority to an understanding with the Soviet Union or to America's own interests in Germany, Roosevelt opted for a 'policy of postponement', for the prorogation of all political problems connected with Germany until such time as there was a definite peacetime order.[6] The renunciation of an active policy towards Germany led effectively in the end to the supremacy of long-term American interests. In the meantime, however, Soviet uncertainty about the course of US policy towards Germany was sufficient in itself to shake the military alliance.

From isolationism to universalism

Just as general as the desire of the public conscience of the United States definitively to eradicate German expansionism was the desire to turn its back on isolationism. The Japanese attack on Pearl Harbor and the German declaration of war had made it clear to a public which had been prevaricating for a long time that it was an illusion to continue believing that the USA could be safe from outside attack, protected by two oceans, or that the USA was potentially far more threatened by military isolation — namely, as Nicholas J. Spykman had written in a much-quoted book in 1942, when the transatlantic and transpacific regions were united in the hands of a single power or group of powers.[7] To this realisation was added the guilty conviction that the American disengagement after the First World War (even if it was only superficial in the political sense, never economic and thus very partial)[8] had contributed decisively to the failure of the first attempt at establishing an order of world peace. As early as in the summer of 1942, the Gallup Institute carried out 'a profound change in viewpoint on international affairs' and in May 1943 74 per cent of Americans asked were in favour of the participation of the United States in a future international police force which would safeguard peace. Foreign policy was no longer a matter for party political controversy, but was taken on more and more by Congress and the Executive, by the ruling Democrats and the opposing Republicans together. Having had a majority in favour of isolationism before the war, the Republican Party, under the influence of John Foster Dulles, spoke out in favour of world-wide American engagement from 1943 at the latest; Arthur Vandenberg, chief foreign policy spokesman of the Republican Senate party group, made his change of party and the change of policy of his party abundantly clear from 1944/5.[9]

The renunciation of isolationism meant a break with American tradition, which would likewise prove difficult to see through. Throughout the whole war, Roosevelt was greatly concerned that the American people might relapse into an isolationist position, and that they would, to say the least, be unwilling to pay the necessary price for the new universalism. The growing 'Bring the Boys Home' movement towards the end of the war, which drove Roosevelt at the Yalta conference to make the resigned statement that the stationing of American troops on the European continent might have to be maintained for two years after the end of the war, justified these fears.[10] By way of an antidote to isolationist tendencies, Roosevelt hoped to reactivate old Jeffersonian and Wilsonian ideals as war aims and, in doing so, reinforced the already massive onset of a neo-Wilsonite movement. Since the isolationism of the inter-war years had not least also been the expression of disappointment in a power state system, as well as in the principle of the right to self-determination and in an international system based on a postulation of equality, now with the return to universalism the world order in the sense of Wilsonian ideals was postulated anew. The 'four freedoms' proclaimed before Congress as aims of the war by Roosevelt on 6 January 1941 in fact paraphrased the traditional American concepts of the coexistence of men and states: freedom of speech and to express an opinion; freedom of religion; freedom from fear; and freedom from want, the latter two being understood both as individual rights and rights of peoples; and the last of the freedoms was defined as 'economic understandings which will secure to every nation a healthy peacetime life for its inhabitants'. Similarly, albeit with stronger emphasis on collective rights, Roosevelt and Churchill proclaimed in the Atlantic Charter, signed on 14 August 1941, the right of all nations to self-determination and the right to equal access to trade and to the raw materials of the world; they demanded the 'fullest collaboration' of all nations in economic life and renounced 'all aggrandisement' be it of territory or of other aspects of power.[11]

Traditional missionary zeal, and insight into the new vulnerability of American security, were blended in the consciousness of American post-war planners into the option for world-wide application of these principles and the world-wide political engagement of the USA. 'In this global war', wrote Roosevelt in October 1944 to Stalin, 'there is literally no question, political or military, in which the United States is not interested', and when Churchill travelled to Moscow in the same month, to come to some arrangement with Stalin over contentious issues, Roosevelt informed him that his ambassador in Moscow would be taking part in the discussions.[12] Spheres of influence that were closed to American access should no longer exist, any more than there should be a separation of the world into mutually exclusive power blocs, or a secret diplomacy concealed from the world — and, in particular, from the American public. This universalist thinking found its most consistent expression in a new movement for the creation of a world peace organisation, a world organisation that, unlike the League of Nations, would be truly global and equipped with full powers, and that, with the participation of all nations on the basis of equal rights, would be able to guarantee the right of self-determination of all nations. This movement was supported in particular by the left-progressive wing of the Democratic Party; its representative, Roosevelt's many years' Secretary of State for Foreign Affairs, Cordell Hull, saw the setting-up of a world peace organisation as the goal of his life's work, and he had instructed the State Department to draw up plan after plan for such an organisation since 1941.[13] Obviously here also the question needed to be asked whether the vision of 'one world' in freedom and equality would stand up against reality. Was the United States capable of offering itself up to the judgement of a world organisation and of opening up its own, long exclusive, sphere of influence (particularly in Latin America) to world-wide access? Would the other nations, in particular the Soviet alliance partner, be willing to bestow their trust on the world organisation to a sufficient degree to be able to do without the customary means of national state power politics? Would the USA have the wherewithal to impose the principle of the right to self-determin-ation, even in the face of opposition? Roosevelt himself was one of the first to realise the untenability of the 'American Dream'. Formerly a convinced proponent of the League of Nations concept, he had since 1935 developed an aversion to the principle of peace achieved through a world organisation. True peace, he stated when, in spring 1943, the journalist Forest Davis described his 'Grand Design', needed to be much more based on the 'factor of power'. 'Aspirations toward a better world' were legitimate enough, but the decisive factors were 'the cold, realistic tech-niques or instruments' needed to make those aspirations work. Peace thus depended on the might of the victorious powers and on their understanding of the appropriate application of that power.[14] The 'better world', achieved by traditional means such as the politics of spheres of influence, the agreements of the powerful, and by political and economic pressure, in effect implied the retention of the traditional state system, and would be oriented towards state power categories, albeit now cut according to the cloth of the two new world powers. Giving more concrete expressions to his principles shortly after the Japanese attack on Pearl Harbor, he stated that world peace would depend on there being 'four policemen in the world — the United States, Great Britain, Russia and China — charged with the responsibil-ity of keeping peace. The rest of the world would have to disarm ... Russia would be charged with keeping peace in the Western Hemisphere, and the United States and China would be charged with keeping the peace in the Far East. Two of the world police-men, the USA and Great Britain, would in addition control the atomic weapon monopoly, and thus be able to force the co-oper-ation of the other superpowers.'[15]

It is thus not surprising that Roosevelt removed his Secretary of State for Foreign Affairs, along with the latter's plans, made 'in the stratosphere', at the earliest possible moment, and continued his political war diplomacy from then on without the help of the State Department.[16] Although he had to take into account — in order, in the first instance, to avoid the lapse of the American people back into isolationism — the movement in favour of a new world organisation, he did so in such a way as to retain the substance of the 'four-policemen' concept. After initially rejecting a series of outlines from the State Department, he finally agreed in June 1944 to a world organisation plan that formally unified the Wilsonian peace principle (a general conference of nations with the exception of former enemy states) with the principle of the 'four policemen' (a security council with the USA, Great Britain, the Soviet Union and China as permanent members). In fact, however, by introducing a veto right for these permanent members, he made peace dependent upon the agreement of the world powers.[17]

Roosevelt thus followed two foreign policy lines simultaneously, an 'outward foreign policy' of understanding between the two world powers and an 'inner foreign policy' of universal principles, which was clearly intended to mobilise the American people in favour of the power-political engagement of the USA. Obviously he could not help it if the 'internal' foreign policy occasionally broke through the 'external' one, particularly in the case of the demand for the realisation of the right of self-determination for the Eastern European nations; or that, with the ambivalence of the American world policy which was actually realised, the mistrust of their Soviet partner grew; or that, as a result, 'inner' policy expectations were awakened in the American public which would lead to a great deal of disappointment, should the reality of the 'outward' policy be discovered. All this was to shake permanently Roosevelt's endeavours towards an understanding with the Soviet leadership.

Liberalism and imperialism

On the other hand, the economic aspect of this universalism was not at all incompatible with the long-term interests of American society, and it thus rendered by no means ambivalent, and all the more effective, the economic war policy of the USA. For all the planners of the Roosevelt Administration, it was a self-evident conviction that the world economic crisis had made Hitler's rise to power, and thus the war itself, possible, that new depressions would bring new dictatorships into being, and that this crisis had been created above all by the politico-economic nationalism of the European states. 'To me,' attested Hull in retrospect, 'unhampered trade dovetailed with peace, high tariffs, trade barriers, and unfair economic competition, with war. Though

22

realizing that many other factors were involved, I reasoned that, if we could get a freer flow of trade — freer in the sense of fewer discriminations and obstructions — so that one country would not be deadly jealous of another and the living standards of all countries might rise, thereby eliminating the economic dissatisfaction that breeds war, we might have a reasonable chance for lasting peace.'[18] Hull put forward this view with persistent stubbornness and, since it was in any case *communis opinio* in the external economic policy both of the Foreign and Finance State Departments, he also put it into effect.[19] The argument that the opening-up of markets prevented depressions was lastingly reinforced by an analysis of the domestic economic situation. Roosevelt and his advisers were well aware that the New Deal Program had by no means solved the American unemployment problem permanently, and that this problem had in fact rather been camouflaged by the wartime need for a large number of men to enlist in the army and, above all, by the wartime increase of production, and that at the end of the war a serious crisis of overproduction threatened to bring a new depression in its wake — if, that is, new markets, particularly new external and sales markets, could not be opened up for the American economy. In the autumn of 1944, Roosevelt calculated in terms of 4.5 million unemployed in the case of an abrupt end to war-financed production. 'While we shall not take advantage of any country,' he wrote to Hull, 'we will see that American industry has its fair share in the world markets.'[20]

'While we shall not take advantage of any country': what lent the American will to open up world markets its moral dynamic, and led it to become an integral component of humanitarian universalism, was a belief in the classic liberal conviction that the lifting of customs barriers and other hindrances to trade would not only make it possible to avoid an American depression, but at the same time would noticeably increase goods production and trade, thus also increasing the standard of living in all countries — the belief, in fact, that American interest was identical with global interest. The fact that this assumption was partly illusory, and that unhindered access to all markets would be to the unilateral benefit of the economically most competitive nation (this being by the end of the war the USA without any doubt) was not, and indeed could not, be perceived by the majority of 'one world' ideologists. In the same way as the internal New Deal from 1933 entailed the attempt to overcome the deeply-rooted class divisions

23

in American society not by redivision, but by an extension of production, whereby eventually everyone was intended to become somewhat richer, so now the world-wide New Deal entailed the attempt to pre-empt international class redivision processes by means of a world-wide increase in prosperity. This attempt was not consciously planned as such in the context of the first, nor was it staged with any cynical intention, corresponding as it did rather with the practical experience of the American leading elite in the national framework, and then being trans-ferred as a matter of course to the elements of international policy.

When, therefore, American politicians encountered unantic-ipated opposition to the implementation of the 'Open Door' principle, they were nonplussed. Negotiations with the British Allied partner, which were conducted from Washington at a very early date on account of the economic importance of Great Britain in the pre-war world, turned out to be an endless series of American demands for liberalisation, British refusals, American threats of the most brutal nature and eventual British capitul-ation out of their concern for the indispensable support of the Americans during both the war itself and the subsequent recon-struction. During the working out of the British–American aid agreement in the context of the Lend–Lease terms, there was hard bargaining over Article VII, the arrangement which was finally signed in February 1942, according to which the British had for their part to undertake, in return for the material aid they received, to fight discriminatory practices and to adopt a policy of universal liberalisation. Even in the Anglo–American preliminary negotiations for the International Finance and Currency Confer-ence, which later took place in the summer of 1944 in Bretton Woods, the American negotiators had their way in spite of stub-born British resistance. The World Currency Fund was founded on the condition that all future members were obliged to agree to the mandatory free convertibility of their currencies; only for a transition period of five years could the exchange of their curren-cies still be subject to limits — the days of the sterling zone were thus numbered. At the same time, with the establishment of the International Bank for Reconstruction and Development, an instrument was created which enabled private (and once again this means in the first instance American) investors to make world-wide investments with state backing. In practice, the extent of the obligation to open up markets remained at first a moot issue between Great Britain and the USA, and a source of continuing quarrels. In the negotiations for an American post-war loan for Great Britain in the autumn of 1945, however, the British were obliged to make definite material concessions: within a year of the granting of the loan they had to dissolve the accumulated 'Dollar Pool' of the sterling-bloc countries and establish free convertibility of the pound for all current transactions. Import restrictions were henceforth possible only in strictly specified cases; Great Britain entered the World Trade Organization and committed itself to further bilateral negotiations with the USA leading to 'definite measures for the lifting of all trade barriers'. In return, the British received a loan of 3,750 million dollars at a 2 per cent rate of interest, although the British chief negotiator, Keynes, had originally asked for 6,000 million.[21]

The results of the negotiations were sharply criticised by the British public. 'There are two main objectives underlying the agreement which we are being asked to approve', commented Conservative MP Robert J.G. Boothby in December 1945, 'The first is to get back as quickly as possible to the economic system of the 19th century — the system of *laissez-faire* capitalism. The second is to break up, and prise open, the markets of the world for the benefit of the United States of America, who have an intense desire to get rid of their surplus products, which will be enormous, at almost any cost ... This is our economic Munich ... But there is one mandate which His Majesty's Government never got from the people of this country, and that was to sell the British Empire for a packet of cigarettes.'[22] Nevertheless there was no way of avoiding ratification, and thus here in the economic sector it was predetermined what would soon become evident in the political sector also: the abdication of Great Britain as an independent world power in favour of a role as the junior partner of the USA.

In exactly the same matter-of-course manner as the Roosevelt Administration prepared itself for the breaking-up of the sterling zone, it hoped also to be able to co-opt the East European states and the Soviet Union into a multilateral free trade system. Although the economic interests of the USA in Eastern Europe were not great — before the Second World War about 2 per cent of American exports went to Eastern Europe, 3.5 per cent of imports came from Eastern Europe, and 5.5 per cent of external investments were localised there — it was worth protecting those interests, and moreover it was worth retaining Eastern Europe as a complementary agrarian region for the industrialised European West, in the prosperity of which the USA certainly had a primary interest. It was also worth encouraging the prosperity of the Eastern European nations, and thus their independence: in short, it was worth not permitting any exceptions to the principle of free trade.[23] The Soviet Union was also to be incorporated into this multilateral system, if only to prevent a unilateral Soviet hold on the economy of its East European neighbours and to ensure its participation in the investments of the 'Open Door', and also to remedy the considerable Soviet reconstruction problems. At Bretton Woods, Secretary of the Treasury Morgenthau consequently exerted himself for weeks on end to ensure Soviet participation in the World Currency Fund, and did not hesitate to offer the Soviet government, in return for relinquishing its restrictive attitude, the prospect of massive loans for the reconstruction of its war-devastated country.[24] The fact that Soviet difficulties in the face of the American liberalisation campaign were bound to be even greater than the problems of Great Britain, which after all was attached to the USA by virtue of its shared cultural traditions and basically common economic system, was no less evident to him than it was to his colleagues. Nevertheless, precisely this fundamental American–Soviet conflict of interests was to become relevant to the future development of East–West relations.

The relationship towards the Soviet Union

All the impulses for American post-war policy resulting from the experiences of the inter-war years — the striving for the destruction of the German potential for aggression, political universalism in its 'idealistic' and its 'realistic' versions, and economic multilateralism — motivated US post-war planners to seek an understanding with their Soviet wartime partner, even making such an understanding an indispensable precondition for the success of their policies; at the same time, however, they set political developments into motion that in the long term worked against that understanding. Thus the question arose of what the relationship with their Soviet partner in fact consisted, a question that did not originally emerge directly in the centre of American planning, but which very soon arose in the centre of American politics.

The relationship of the Soviet state with American society had been ambivalent since the October Revolution.[25] On the Soviet

26

side, people had marvelled at the radical democratic tradition of the USA and the high performance of its industrial economy, while at the same time fearing the latent aggressiveness and ever greater power of capitalism. On the American side, there was both enthusiasm about the modernisation of the former Russian feudal society and horror at the methods of this modernisation and at the prospect of them being transferred to the Western world. At the beginning of Roosevelt's period of office the first of these basic attitudes was predominant — diplomatic recognition by the USA of the Soviet government ensuing in 1933; the second predominated by the outbreak of the Second World War, not only as a result of the German–Soviet pact, but because many supporters of an understanding with the Soviet Union had in the meantime undergone a process of disenchantment, which now led them to doubt the possibility of any understanding being reached with a Soviet Union which, as they saw it, was fundamentally committed to world-wide expansion.

Among those holding this view was the first US Ambassador to Moscow, William C. Bullitt, who was from 1935 concerned to warn against the machinations of the Communist International, and subsequently concerned to commit the Western nations to a policy of quarantine with regard to the Soviet state, as had already once been the case since 1917. After the Soviet Union and the USA had been compelled by necessity to become coalition partners, President Roosevelt swore that he would demand from Stalin, in return for American material assistance, written assurances with regard to Soviet war aims, thereby salvaging the independence of the European states after the war. A group of Russian political experts of the State Department also subscribed to this view, which was decisive for post-war policy. Some of these experts were settled in Washington, the majority of them prior to taking up diplomatic positions at observation posts in Riga, and later at the US Embassy in Moscow. They initially established relations with Russians by means of contact with representatives of the exiled former Russian *grande bourgeoisie* and aristocracy, later giving the impression in the Moscow Embassy, after preliminary scenes of fraternisation, of being in a besieged stronghold in the midst of a hostile and profoundly suspicious country, particularly as they were having to live through the period of Stalin's purges. Robert F. Kelley, Director of the Eastern Europe section of the State Department, should be mentioned here, as well as Loy Henderson, George F. Kennan, Charles Bohlen and

Elbridge Durbrow. These men all saw themselves as 'realists', were mistrustful of ideologies and directed their efforts at analysing the realities of power. It was precisely as 'realists', however, that they placed emphasis on the aggressiveness of Soviet policy, marked by centuries of experience and given added motivation by the demand for world revolution, a policy to which the Soviet leadership had devoted great care and which, as a result of the pragmatic skill developing out of this, was in the long term concerned not only with the continuance of the tsarist urge for expansion, but also with the encouragement of Communist movements throughout the world. One could not approach a partner who was at one and the same time suspicious and aggressive with cosy offers of compromise, which would only be interpreted as weakness, but should much rather stand on one's own interests and power; only in this way could reliable arrangements be reached.[26] The political weight of this group of experts within the Roosevelt Administration was reinforced by the arguments of powerful groups of a more ideological, traditionally anti-Communist nature, such as by the US Ambassador to London, Joseph C. Kennedy, who had supported the British policy of appeasement on the basis of his anti-Soviet attitude; by the leader of the Republican Party, Robert Taft, who had opposed the entry of the USA into the war out of traditional isolationism; by anti-Soviet groups of mostly East European origin, and involved with these on many levels by the Catholic Church in the USA.[27]

After the German attack on the Soviet Union, the fundamentally critical attitude towards the Soviet government clearly had initially to take a back seat, and the optimistic version defined the discussion. Bullitt's successor as Ambassador to Moscow, Joseph Davies, whose book *Mission to Moscow* attained spectacular success after the beginning of the war, making no small contribution to the definitive swing of the American public away from isolationism after it was filmed in 1943, became the most important spokesman for this line. According to Davies's interpretation, world revolution was for the Soviet leadership now only of secondary interest. The Soviet Union, he explained, had already departed from the Communist principle, and was on the way to becoming a capitalist state like any other, with an economic life once again based on the profit motive, with a new upper class, a return to traditional state power methods in foreign policy, and a progressive social policy considerate of the lot of ordinary people. It was appropriate to this 'Americanisation' of Soviet society that the Soviet leadership should have predominantly friendly sentiments towards the USA; it was therefore worth working on this tendency and establishing a lasting alliance. Davies found support especially in the democratic Left, from such as Vice-President Henry A. Wallace, who pleaded in November 1942 for a joint 'Third Way' somewhere between American political democracy, with its anti-social tendencies, and Soviet economic democracy with its repressive bureaucracy. In addition, however, Davies also had support from the 'One World' movement, which was furthered by official propaganda and convinced of the possibility of being able to build a world on the basis of democratic ideals in co-operation with the Soviet Union.[28]

President Roosevelt refused to allow himselt to be infected by this hope for an inner convergence of systems. 'The Soviet Union, as everybody who has the courage to face the fact knows', he stated in February 1940, 'is run by a dictatorship as absolute as any other dictatorship in the world.' He described the differences in political culture, ideology and economic structure as considerable. Thus far, therefore, he was in agreement with the 'Riga' group. What distinguished him from his experts, however, were four similarly 'realistic' fundamental convictions. His first conviction was that the Soviet Union, unlike its national socialist counterpart, was not fundamentally committed to expansion. Consequently it must be possible to bring the Soviet Union to relinquish its support of external Communist movements by fulfilling its legitimate security needs. Secondly, he believed that the Soviet Union would emerge from the war in ruins and have to devote its energies to reconstruction for years ahead. If one could succeed under these circumstances in removing the mistrust of Soviet leaders towards the surrounding capitalist world, then the development from expansive centre of the Communist International towards a Soviet state that could be saturated would have been taken one definite step further. Thirdly, he believed that an understanding under these conditions would certainly not be easy, but, he was convinced, since the hearty welcome that Stalin had prepared for his trusted Harry Hopkins in July 1941 in Moscow, that it could be made to succeed by dealing with the Soviet leadership at the highest level, circumventing all short-sighted bureaucratic apparatus, and bringing the structural superiority of the USA into play, including its enormous production capacity and, as he hoped since the start of the 'Manhattan Project', soon also its monopoly of atomic weapons. Finally, such an understanding was, whether one wanted it or not, indispensable, since the only conceivable alternatives were the formation of blocs, world armament and thus eventually also war. Another war, however, was as unthinkable for American society as it was intolerable.[29]

When, at the first meeting of the 'Big Three' — Roosevelt, Stalin and Churchill — at the end of November 1943 initially informal talks took place about the post-war order, it seemed as if the realisation of Roosevelt's 'Design' was being set into motion: Stalin was assured the restoration of the Soviet western frontier of 1941 (thus the incorporation of Eastern Poland, the Baltic States, Bessarabia and Northern Bukovina) and, in addition, a certain westward shift of the Polish frontier and the relinquishing of the demand for a new *cordon sanitaire* against the Soviet Union in the form of a central-eastern or Danube federation. Roosevelt and Churchill heard in return from Stalin that it was no easy matter to force Communist regimes on the world, and that he had other problems to consider.[30] 'We really believed in our hearts that a new day had dawned', Harry Hopkins recalled of the mood that emerged around Roosevelt after the conference in Tehran, and that was to last until the conference in Yalta in February 1945, 'We were absolutely certain that we had won the first great victory of the peace — and by "we", I mean *all* of us, the whole civilized human race. The Russians had proved that they could be reasonable and foreseeing and there wasn't any doubt in the minds of the President or any of us that we could live with them and get along with them peacefully for as far into the future as any of us could imagine.'[31] Of course, the Europeans, at least the East Europeans, would have to become accustomed to the Soviet Union as the sole remaining major power in the old continent, but they would no longer be threatened by Sovietisation, and the Soviet Union would co-operate in the United Nations for the world-wide safeguarding of peace.

A belief in the potential realisation of co-operation and the results of co-operation in the American sense was absolutely essential for the Roosevelt Administration. If it did not bring the desired results, then the non-co-operative fundamental line in American Soviet policy would re-emerge and the numerous tendencies pushing for a break would strengthen decisively. It was just this that occurred from the spring of 1945 onwards.

Notes

1. Foreign relations of the United States, diplomatic papers (hereafter cited as FRUS), Casablanca, p. 727. Compare Robert E. Sherwood, *Roosevelt and Hopkins* (Hamburg, 1950), pp. 569–71; Gunter Moltmann, 'Die Genesis der Unconditional-Surrender-Forderung', in Andreas Hillgruber (ed.), *Probleme des Zweiten Weltkreiges*, (Cologne, 1967), pp. 171–98; Raymond G. O'Connor, *Diplomacy for victory; FDR and unconditional surrender*, (New York, 1971); Maxime Mourin, *Reddition sans conditions* (Paris, 1973).

2. Ernest F. Penrose, *Economic planning for peace* (Princeton, 1953), pp. 245f.; John Morton Blum, *From the Morgenthau diaries; years of war 1941–1945* (Boston, 1967), p. 342; compare with this and the following John L. Snell, *Wartime origins of the East–West dilemma over Germany* (New Orleans, 1959), ch. 1; Warren F. Kimball (ed.), *Swords or ploughshares? The Morgenthau plan for defeated Nazi Germany, 1943–1946* (Philadelphia, 1976).

3. Blum, *Morgenthau diaries*, p. 342.

4. Text of the memorandum of 23 September, 1943, in Harley Notter, *Postwar foreign policy preparation 1939–1945* (Washington, 1949), p. 559; further accounts in John L. Gaddis, *The United States and the origins of the Cold War 1941–1947* (New York, 2nd edn, 1976), pp. 97–9.

5. Roosevelt to Hull, 29 September, 1944, FRUS Yalta, p. 155.

6. Essential reading on the 'policy of postponement' is Hans-Peter Schwarz, *Vom Reich zur Bundesrepublik, Deutschland im Widerstreit der aussenpolitischen Konzeptionen in den Jahren der Besatzungsherrschaft 1945–1949* (Neuwied, Berlin, 1966), pp. 105–19.

7. Thus in the case of the German–Japanese coalition, but also in that of the excessive extension of power in the Eurasian Soviet Union, Nicholas J. Spykman, *America's strategy in world politics, The United States and the balance of power* (New York, 1942).

8. Compare amongst others Werner Link, *Die Amerikanische Stabilisierungspolitik in Deutschland, 1921–1932* (Düsseldorf, 1970); Hans-Jürgen Schröder, *Deutschland und die Vereinigten Staaten 1933–1939. Wirtschaft und Politik in der Entwicklung des deutsch-amerikanischen Gegensatzes* (Wiesbaden, 1970); Detlef Junker, *Der unteilbare Weltmarkt, Das Ökonomische Interesse in der Aussenpolitik der USA 1933–1941* (Stuttgart, 1975).

9. Compare with impressive documentation of Daniel Yergin, *Shattered peace* (Boston, 1977), pp. 46f.

10. FRUS Yalta, p. 627, that the American War Department failed during the war, in spite of numerous attempts, to lay down the conditions for the continuance of universal military service (the theme of being ready to defend themselves against the Soviet Union appearing in discussion for the first time only from 1944) is shown by Michael S. Sherry, *Preparing for the next war, American plans for postwar defense, 1941–45* (New Haven, Conn., London, 1977).

11. Text of the Atlantic Charter in FRUS 1941, I, pp. 368f.

12. In fact, however, Ambassador Harriman was only present for parts of the talks. Roosevelt to Stalin, 4 October, 1944, FRUS Yalta, p. 6; Winston Churchill, *Triumph and tragedy* (Boston, 1953), p. 219.

13. Compare overviews of various phases of UN planning until 1944

in Gaddis, *United States and the origins*, pp. 24–9, and Walter Lipgens, *A history of European integration 1945–1947* (Oxford, 1982), pp. 65–6, 73–6.

14. Forrest Davis, 'Roosevelt's world blueprint', *Saturday Evening Post*, 10 October, 1943, quoted by Daniel Yergin, *Shattered peace*, p. 43. The significance of Roosevelt's 'idealism' has long been overestimated in the literature; compare among others William H. McNeill, *America, Britain and Russia* (London, 1953), pp. 761–3; Louis J. Halle, *Der Kalte Krieg* (Frankfurt, 1969), pp. 46–53; Schwarz, *Vom Reich zur Bundesrepublik*, pp. 41–6. Thinking in terms of power politics in fact took priority with Roosevelt; compare Yergin, *Shattered peace*, pp. 43–6, and Robert Dallek, *Franklin D. Roosevelt and American foreign policy, 1932–1945* (New York and London, 1979).

15. Formulation of 13 November, 1942, text by Franklin Delano Roosevelt, *His personal letters, 1928–1945*, vol. II (New York, 1950), pp. 1366f. Compare Robert A. Divine, *Roosevelt and World War II* (Baltimore, 1969), pp. 57–9; Willard Range, *Franklin D. Roosevelt's world order* (Athens, Ga., 1959), pp. 172–6; Louis Fischer, *The road to Yalta. Soviet foreign relations 1941–45* (New York, 1972), pp. 103–5; on the role of the atomic bomb in Roosevelt's calculations, Martin J. Sherwin, *A world destroyed. The atomic bomb and the grand alliance* (New York, 1975).

16. Roosevelt on Hull, after Byrnes, letter of 5 May, 1945, quoted together with other documentation by Yergin, *Shattered peace*, p. 422.

17. Compare Notter, *Postwar foreign policy preparation*, p. 93, 127–9, 533f; here is also documentation of previous, more universalistic-oriented planning stages. On the contradictions in which Roosevelt thereby became caught up, compare Lloyd C. Gardner, *Architects of illusion, Men and ideas in American foreign policy 1941–1949* (Chicago, 1970), pp. 50–3.

18. *The memoirs of Cordell Hull*, 2 vols, (New York, 1948), vol. 1, p. 81. Essential reading on this is Lloyd C. Gardner, *Economic aspects of New Deal diplomacy* (Madison, 1964); for detail see Alfred E. Eckes, 'Bretton Woods: America's New Deal for an open world', unpublished dissertation, University of Texas (1969); for a general overview, Gabriel Kolko, *The politics of war* (New York, 1968), pp. 243–8; Gaddis, *United States and the origins*, pp. 18–22.

19. In this respect Yergin's (*Shattered peace*, p. 57) criticism of an alleged overestimation of Hull's role in Kolko is unjustified.

20. Roosevelt to Hull, 17 October, 1944, quoted after Gaddis, *United States and the origins*, p. 21.

21. Department of State, *Anglo-American financial agreements, December 1945* (Washington, DC, 1945). Essential reading on Anglo-American negotiations: Richard N. Gardner, *Sterling–Dollar diplomacy; Anglo–American collaboration in the reconstruction of multilateral trade*, (Oxford, 1956; 2nd edn., New York, 1969). Complementary reading: Penrose, *Economic planning*; Gardner, *Economic aspects*, pp. 275–91; Kolko, *Politics of war*, pp. 248–50, 255–8; also G. Kolko, *The limits of power, The world and United States policy 1945–1954* (New York, 1972), pp. 59–69; Thomas G. Paterson, *Soviet–American confrontation, Postwar reconstruction and the origins of the Cold War* (Baltimore, Md., London, 1973), ch. 8.

22. *Parliamentary debates*, Fifth series, vol. 417, House of Commons, 12 December 1945, pp. 455–69.

23. Compare Thomas G. Paterson, 'The economic Cold War; American business and economic foreign policy, 1945–1950, unpublished dissertation, University of California (1968), pp. 266–8; Geir Lundestad, *The American non-policy towards Eastern Europe 1943–1947* (Tromsö, New York, 2nd edn., 1978), pp. 61–6.

24. Compare with Blum, *Morgenthau diaries*, pp. 245–65, 275f.

25. Ernst Nolte, *Deutschland und der Kalte Krieg* (Munich, 1974), pp. 123–30, 144–56.

26. Essential reading on the 'Riga' group is Yergin, *Shattered peace*, pp. 18–41; on Bullitt, also see Gardner, *Architects*, pp. 3–25, and Nolte, *Deutschland*, pp. 146–9; a particularly impressive document is George F. Kennan, *Memoirs, 1925–1950* (Boston, 1967), ch. 3.

27. Compare collection of documents on same theme in Gaddis, *United States and the origins*, pp. 42–6, 52–6.

28. Joseph E. Davies, *Mission to Moscow* (New York, 1941 and elsewhere); Rede Wallace's numerous further accounts of 8 November 1942, quoted in Gaddis, *United States and the origins*, pp. 37, 34–42.

29. Roosevelt quotation, according to William C. Bullitt, 'How we won the war and lost the peace', *Life*, 30 August 1948, pp. 83–97, quotation p. 91. Best sketch of Roosevelt 'Grand Design' in Yergin, *Shattered peace*, pp. 55–8; on the role of the atom bomb, additional account in Sherwin, *A world destroyed*, pp. 90–114.

30. Compare Herbert Feis, *Churchill, Roosevelt, Stalin* (Princeton, NJ, 1957), pp. 240–87; Averell Harriman and Elie Abel, *Special envoy to Churchill and Stalin 1941–1946* (New York, 1975), pp. 256–83; Alexander Fischer, *Sowjetische Deutschlandpolitik im Zweiten Weltkrieg 1941–1945* (Stuttgart, 1975), pp. 68–75; Vojtěch Mastný, *Russia's road to the Cold War, Diplomacy, warfare and the politics of Communism, 1941–1945* (New York, 1979), pp. 122–33.

31. Robert E. Sherwood, *Roosevelt and Hopkins: an intimate history* (New York, 1948), p. 870.

2

No *Pax Sovietica*

The leading Soviet circle around Stalin went about its considerations for the creation of the post-war order on the basis of past
experience, in much the same way as US decision-makers.
Although the problem of a confrontation between two opposing
great powers figured more prominently in their attention than
was the case with the USA, they nevertheless interpreted this
problem less in the light of a realistic analysis of the actual
current conduct of the USA than in that of their experience of
Western anti-Soviet policy since 1917. The profound mistrust of
the 'capitalist' states arising out of this orientation led them to
methods for securing their interests which considerably limited the
scope of those forces within the Roosevelt Administration that
were committed to co-operation, and distinctly strengthened
those aspects of the policies of their American partners tending
towards a break with the Soviet Union.

Precarious victory

When planning for the post-war period, the Soviet leadership had
to start from the assumption that although its country was victorious, it would nevertheless emerge from the war widely devastated, and indeed shaken to the very core. The Soviet Union had
only narrowly escaped military defeat after the unexpected
German attack of 1941, and had subsequently had to bear the
major brunt of the land war on the European continent.[1]
Between 1941 and 1945, at least 20 million Soviet citizens had lost
their lives, either in the war itself or as a result of the effects of
war, a loss representing more than 10 per cent of the pre-war

population. Some 25 million people had lost their homes, 1,710 towns and 70,000 villages had been destroyed and 65,000 km of railway track had been damaged. The agricultural economy, which in 1941 had just begun to recover from the effects of collectivisation, was largely in disarray as a result of battles on Soviet soil and of German occupation, and industrial production was considerably below the expectations of the five-year plans. Thus, for example, instead of the 22.4 million tons of steel anticipated in 1941, a total of only 10.6 million tons were produced in 1945.[2] Soviet military strength was similarly exhausted. At the time of the German surrender, the strength of Soviet troops still amounted to 11 million men, while the US fighting forces (without their allies!) numbered 12 million men; by 1948, Soviet troops had had to be reduced to 2.8 million.[3] The levels of loss and destruction in general were so enormous that a concentration of all remaining forces on reconstruction became literally essential for the survival of the Soviet Union; new military developments were to be out of the question for years to come.

Another war was even more out of the question, since the present war had severely shaken the Soviet system of government. The Soviet population had reacted to German occupation not with resistance, but with defeatism, indifference and, on occasion, particularly in the non-White Russian regions, even with open relief. It was thus later to prove difficult to restore Soviet authority in former occupied regions. Similarly, the efforts that the population had had to exert during the war itself had created considerable pressure in terms of expectation: it was widely believed that as a 'reward' for the sacrifices of the war, a visible improvement in living conditions, an increase in personal freedom and of rights to be consulted in the political sphere could now be demanded. The effects of this disorganisation and these demands were so far-reaching that it was not sufficient to re-emphasise in propaganda, for the first time since 1917, the pre-revolutionary traditions of the Russian people, and to concede greater room for manoeuvre to the Orthodox Church; the Soviet leadership believed itself compelled, in addition, to resort to police-state terror. The system of penal and forced labour camps was extended to such an extent that soon 10 million Soviet citizens were permanently interned, among them a large number of demobilised soldiers who had fought in the West, and whole population groups from territories formerly occupied by German troops. Stalin himself lived in constant fear of betrayal, and his

35

entourage lived in latent fear of him. During the course of the war, the power of army leaders and industrial managers had increased considerably; against these people, Stalin mobilised once again the Communist Party, which had remained entirely in the background throughout the war, with the result that from the middle of 1945 the party was able to bring the leadership monopoly itself into dispute. The Supreme Soviet dissolved a whole series of national districts and regions in 1944 and 1945, creating new administrative systems with new personnel. Nevertheless, the Ukrainian Nationalists, for example, were able to continue their partisan struggle into 1947.[4] All this points to the fact that the Soviet leadership needed a considerable amount of breathing space and concerted deflection of outside influences in order to restabilise its power.

Soviet leaders saw the economically and politically unstable Soviet state confronted at the same time by the economically and politically strongest world power, the USA, whose power had increased even more during the war, whose troops now stood on the European and Asian continents, and with whose leaders they now had to reach an agreement about the setting-up of the post-war order. Soviet planners certainly registered crises *in* the capitalist system, but no crisis *of* capitalism and, unlike at the end of the First World War, had no doubt that international capitalism would continue for a long time under American hegemony. Analyses of the probable development of the capitalist economy in the after-effects of the war, prepared by members of the Soviet Academy of Sciences under the direction of Eugen Varga, in fact indicated that at the end of the war the European countries would have to suffer the effects of the destruction of their industries, the shortage of raw materials and a general reduction in buying power, and that the USA, the sole country whose production had substantially increased during the war, would now have to reckon with a crisis of overproduction in the change-over from a wartime to a peacetime economy. On the other hand, it became clear that precisely the concurrence of these two crises would lead to a concentration of capitalist power; in order to reduce the unemployment and sales market stagnation resulting from overproduction, the US economy would try to open new sales and investment markets in impoverished Europe, which in turn would lead to a world-wide expansion of American capitalism.[5]

The Soviet leadership did not remain impervious to such analyses by its economic experts. At first, however, it even hoped to be able to profit from US interest in capital export for its own reconstruction. Numerous requests for high credit were addressed to the US government, without showing the slightest sign of any concomitant willingness to negotiate about conditions of any kind which the American side might wish to attach to the granting of such loans. From this we may conclude that the Soviet leadership believed that, in the context of its crisis strategy, the US economy must have a long-term interest in such capital export, even to the Soviet Union. This hope was of a limited nature, however, and was basically only an expression of the desperate situation in which the Soviet leadership felt itself to be. More far-reaching and of more lasting effect on Soviet post-war policy was the fear that the expansion of American capitalism on to the European continent and into other parts of the world would necessarily assume an imperialist character, thus strengthening anti-Soviet forces in all these places, particularly in the Central and East European regions. Roosevelt's statement at the Yalta Conference, that he would not keep US troops in Europe longer than two years, was not taken seriously by Stalin; he was all too aware of the economic realities.

The foreign policy strategy developed by Stalin and his advisers, which we can analyse here only indirectly by looking retrospectively at its political repercussions, was based on three basic ideas. First, all forces must be mobilised that had any prospect of successfully offering unified resistance to the expansion of American capitalism, but that could not at the same time for their part become dangerous to the security of the Soviet Union. This meant, depending on the situation, socialist forces, radical democratic forces and also (sometimes instead of the above-mentioned) the national capitalist forces of the old continent. Secondly, the remaining power means at the disposal of the Soviet Union, chiefly the coercion of the Red Army and the influence of external Communist parties, must be engaged to the limits of their potential in order both to secure and extend Soviet power. Thirdly, account should be taken in this process of differences in range of these Soviet means and the varying strengths of the respective opposing forces, such as in the East European countries, Western Europe, or in Germany, in order to avoid both a waste of their own forces and any unnecessary provocation of the USA.

These strategic principles found their ideological expression in calls for a Socialist International of a new kind, developing out of the People's Front idea of the 1930s. In the same way that in the 1930s all 'progressive' and 'patriotic' forces were to be mobilised in an 'anti-fascist' resistance front under the leading participation of the Communists, with the aim of stemming fascist movements and at the same time (the two being mutually related) breaking the power of monopoly capitalism, or at least setting some preliminary limits on it, so now, especially since the dissolution of the Comintern in May 1943, 'peace-loving', 'democratic' and 'anti-fascist' forces were called upon to work together for the construction of a 'democracy of a new type' and for 'friendship and understanding of the peoples'. What precisely was meant by such a 'people's democratic' order was not clearly expressed and was hardly theoretically thought out — and indeed could not be so. The decisive factors in it were the obligation of Communist parties to co-operate at the broadest level under the condition of relinquishing revolutionary vocabulary and insurrectional tactics, as well as that of maintaining co-operation with the Western allies, in so far as this was possible without endangering vital security interests. The form to be taken by this co-operation and the direction in which it was intended to lead depended on the evaluation of the current distribution and strength of pro- and anti-Soviet forces, and could not therefore be generally laid down in advance for all countries and regions of co-operation. Little as these creeds on the theme of a 'new democracy' can be understood as representing a turning towards liberal-pluralist concepts of democracy in the Western sense of the term, so equally little should they be misinterpreted as a purely tactically intended means, directed at seizure of power, arising out of a Leninist action model. To the extent that the revolutionary struggle for socialism was now defined as the struggle for the securing and preventive extension of Soviet power, so the Soviet urge for security also determined the content of the 'socialism' that was in the process of being brought about. How the 'new type of democracy' would turn out to be in the end depended not least on the reaction of opposing forces, and in particular on the reaction of the world power of the USA, to Soviet strategy.

In accordance with the varying distributions of power, the implementation of the 'people's democratic' strategy led to three different action models. (1) In the immediate western-front zone of the Soviet Union and extending into the sphere of influence of the Red Army in Europe and Asia (North Korea), an attempt was made to ensure a decisive share of political power for the Communist parties and to encourage social reform movements to the point where a friendly attitude towards the Soviets was guaranteed in the future. (2) In the putative primary sphere of expansion of American capitalism (that is, in Western and Southern European countries and China), an attempt was made to stabilise political and economic relations in the framework of the existing order, even if the development of socialist movements was thereby inhibited. (3) In the region of direct co-operation with the Western powers (that is, jointly occupied Germany), an attempt was made both to retain guarantees for a future friendly attitude towards the Soviet Union, and to prevent the handing over of German industrial potential to Anglo-Saxon capitalism. Within the range of these three models of action there were numerous further variations according to country and level of development, as well as intermediary regions in which elements from various models were applied, such as Finland, Austria, Persia and Turkey. Actual Soviet post-war policy was thus highly stratified — so highly stratified in fact that it would inevitably prove difficult for the American Allied partners to analyse, with the result that mistrust and misunderstanding increased.[6]

Hegemony in Eastern Europe

Within the sphere of influence of the Red Army, Soviet post-war policy evolved from the tradition of pre-revolutionary imperial Russia, both in the endeavour to reverse the ceding of territories that had been compelled by the weakness of the young Soviet state in connection with the peace treaties concluded in Brest–Litovsk in 1918 and in Riga in 1921, and in the attempt to ensure the hegemony of the Soviet Union over the East European region. The experience of the inter-war period made a hegemonic role in Eastern Europe appear to be an absolute condition for Soviet security; the East European states that had been designated as the *cordon sanitaire* against the expansion of Bolshevism had become in the intervening time a hotbed of constant unrest. In the disruption caused by far-reaching social conflicts and national minority problems, their bourgeois-democratic regimes had been transformed into authoritarian, in some cases semi-fascist state forms, and extreme anti-Communist groups hostile to the USSR had been brought to power almost everywhere. Democratic Czechoslovakia, with its still moderate foreign policy, had been broken with the co-operation of Slovak fascist forces; authoritarian-ruled Poland had frustrated Soviet endeavours towards the formation of a security pact against National Socialist expansion; Hungary, Romania and Bulgaria had not only co-operated with National Socialist Germany, but had later even entered the war on the side of the Axis powers. The destruction of the *cordon sanitaire* and the guaranteeing of a pro-Soviet orient-ation in the Eastern European region were thus necessarily to become the most urgent aim of Soviet foreign policy.

Stalin had attempted to bring this aim about even in his co-operation with Hitler from 1939 to 1941. In the secret additional protocol to the German–Soviet non-attack pact of August 1939, he had agreed with the German government about the deline-ation of the boundaries of their respective spheres of interest to the extent that Finland, Estonia, Latvia, Lithuania, Eastern Poland to the line of the rivers Narew, Vistula and San, as well as the Bessarabian part of Romania, should remain open for the Soviet government to take them into its state administration. Until August 1940, therefore, the Baltic states, East Poland with the exception of the Vilna region, Bessarabia and North Buko-vina — that is, essentially those regions that had been in the possession of tsarist Russia prior to the First World War — were occupied by Soviet troops and incorporated into the Soviet Union by means of manipulation of elections. After a Soviet attack, Finland had to relinquish a number of disputed frontier territo-ries to the Soviet Union; in addition, the Soviet government demanded Hitler's agreement to the annexation of the whole of Finland and South Bukovina, as well as the extension of the Soviet sphere of interest into Bulgaria, Hungary, Yugoslavia, Greece and West Poland. Even after the German invasion of the Soviet Union in June 1941, there was no lack of attempts to reach a separate peace agreement with Germany on the basis of this definition of interests.[7]

After the failure of the attempt to achieve a pro-Soviet orient-ation in Eastern Europe by means of a German–Soviet condomi-nium, the possibility of a British–Soviet condominium over the European continent came to the forefront of Soviet policy. In Moscow, then besieged by German troops in December 1941, Stalin called on Eden, the British Foreign Secretary, to recognise the Soviet annexations of 1939, and in addition the incorporation of the Memel region, Tilsit, the Finnish region of Petsamo, and his agreement to set up Soviet bases in Romania, offering him in return Soviet agreement to the stationing of British fighting forces in France, Belgium, the Netherlands, Norway and Denmark.

Poland was to be compensated for the loss of its eastern regions by means of East Prussia and other German regions, possibly as far as the Oder; the remaining part of East Prussia north of the Niemen was to be incorporated into Soviet Lithuania. Efforts towards separation in the Rhineland and in Bavaria were to be encouraged, while in the remainder of Europe the boundary system of Versailles was to be substantially adjusted.

The British government was not fundamentally averse to such a division of interests. Although Churchill was in favour of federation plans for Eastern–Central Europe and the Danube area, for which the extension of the Soviet sphere of influence would present significant obstacles, he was primarily concerned with limiting the future *German* possibilities for influence in Eastern Europe, and he pursued the opening of a 'Second Front' on the Balkan (rather than the Atlantic) coast, since he believed this to be more effective from the military point of view — not, as was long asserted according to an ex-post interpretation, in order to prevent the advance of the Soviet Union into south-east Europe. At the conference in Tehran at the end of November 1943, he thus proved willing to accept the Curzon Line (the dividing line delineated according to the nationality principle, which the British Foreign Secretary of 1920, Lord Curzon, had suggested) as the new eastern frontier of Poland, and to recognise the Soviet extension of territory in general. During his visit to Moscow in October 1944, he suggested to Stalin a delineation of boundaries in their joint areas of influence in south-east Europe; Romania should remain open to Soviet influence to a level of 90 per cent and 10 per cent to British influence, Greece with the opposite ratio of 90 per cent for the British and 10 per cent for the Soviets, Bulgaria with a ratio of 75 : 25 for the Soviets, and Hungary and Yugoslavia with 50 per cent each for the Soviets and British. Stalin agreed with this in principle (at least Churchill reports as much), but the following day he had Molotov demand a revision of the percentages (75 : 25 instead of 50 : 50 for Hungary, and 90 : 10 instead of 75 : 25 for Bulgaria). The delegations parted without reaching any clear agreement on either the figures or what this division of interests should mean in reality; nevertheless a far-reaching British–Soviet understanding about the principle of zones of influence in Europe seemed to have been set in motion.[8]

With the increase of US influence within the war coalition and the decline of the British position in the world power structure, however, such an agreement inevitably lost significance, whilst the necessity of securing Soviet interests in the East European region in fact even increased in Soviet eyes. If one now took into account the newly-emerged disparity of American–Soviet power, then renewed anti-Soviet orientation in the East European states could develop into a fatal threat to the Soviet regime. Stalin was thus determined to proceed with the pro-Soviet restructuring process in the East European region, even if otherwise desirable American–Soviet co-operation might be damaged in the process.

In addition to the extension of Soviet territory, the essential elements of this policy of restructuring were the expurgation of the minority problem by means of forced resettlement, the destruction of the material base of anti-Communist forces by means of land reform and collectivisation, the creation of mass anti-fascist organisations, the occupation of strategic key positions by trusted Communists, the unification of political parties into an anti-fascist democratic united front with the Communists, and the conclusion of bilateral friendship and mutual support agreements with the Soviet Union; all of these elements were guaranteed by the presence of Soviet troops, or by the threat of their presence. According to local conditions, the intensity of Soviet security interest and the reaction of the countries affected, these elements were nevertheless applied in various combinations and with varying intensity. Within the ideological framework of the 'people's democracy' concept, therefore, the possibility existed at first of distinct variations in development in the East European countries.

Poland received the harshest treatment compared with the other East European countries, since it occupied geographically and in terms of size a central position in Soviet security interests in Eastern Europe, and its population was traditionally anti-Russian in its orientation. The Poles were obliged to accept not only the westward shifting of their boundaries, but also the physical liquidation of part of their leadership. Possibly to deprive anti-Soviet policy of its social base, almost 15,000 officers of the 217,000 Polish soldiers captured as Soviet prisoners of war in the previous winter were shot in the spring of 1940. Both these acts, the policy of the westward shift of the boundaries and the murder of the officers, made Stalin's attempts to create a non-anti-Soviet leadership in Poland more difficult. Although the Polish exile government, formed from previously moderate opposition parties under General Sikorski, was keen on the prospect of German territorial acquisitions, it refused to discuss the pre-war Polish–

Soviet boundary and proved at first to be firmly against negotiations when some of the murdered officers were discovered in the
mass graves of Katyn in spring 1943. When the Sikorski government approached the International Red Cross for a statement on
the responsibility for Katyn (the Soviets and the Germans both
blamed the crime on each other), the Soviet government severed
diplomatic relations with Poland. Stalin nevertheless continued
to hope that he would find leaders in the exile government who
were ready to compromise; a take-over of power by Polish
Communists seemed to him for a long time to be an unacceptable alternative in view of their notorious weakness. Pro-Soviet
Polish emigrants who had formed an 'Association of Polish Patriots' in Moscow, as well as Communist Resistance forces who
declared a revolutionary 'National Council of the Homeland'
towards the end of 1943, were held off by Stalin until the middle
of 1944. It was only when Sikorski's successor Mikolajczyk proved
equally reluctant over the boundary issue in renewed negotiations, when the US Ambassador, Harriman, showed a certain
amount of sympathy for the emissaries of the 'National Council',
and when the establishment of the 'Second Front' in Normandy
meanwhile offered the certainty of the Red Army being able to
march into Poland, that Stalin pursued the solution of a Soviet-
controlled minority regime. On 22 July 1944, the 'Lublin
Committee' formed the core of a Communist-dominated government, after vigorous disagreements about the future western
frontier of Poland: Stalin initially insisted on the Oder Line, whereas
the Communists wanted the region as far as the western Neisse.
When the leaders of the non-Communist Resistance in Warsaw
initiated an uprising in August 1944, still before the arrival of
Soviet troops (with the intention of securing a definitive share of
power, but without knowledge of the change in Soviet policy that
had just taken place), Stalin at first refused the rebels any help
from the Soviet army and even prevented the landing of British
and American aid planes; after massive British pressure, he
reluctantly agreed in September to offer support — however, with
the effect that, as a result of the prolongation of fighting in
Warsaw, the greater part of the Resistance had already been
successfully wiped out by German occupation troops. Nothing
now stood in the way of the take-over of the administration of the
liberated regions by the Lublin Committee; in January 1945 it
was officially recognised by the Soviet government as the provisional Polish government.[9]

Unlike the Polish exile government, which had been intransigent until the last, the Czechoslovak exile government, formed in London under former President Beneš, was disposed to securing a share in the determination of the post-war order of *Czechoslovakia* by means of a policy of flexibility and a readiness to make concessions. After the experience of the Munich Agreement and the shift in the balance of power during the war itself, Beneš had come to the conclusion that his country should now turn to the Soviet Union rather than to France as a protective power in order to safeguard its independence. Since there had never been a fundamentally anti-Soviet attitude in Czechoslovakia comparable with the situation in Poland, it was possible for him to pursue a policy of compromise with the Soviet Union on the basis of this calculation. After Soviet objections he gave up plans for a Polish–Czech federation, and in December 1943 decided instead (against the will of the Western powers) on a treaty of friendship and support with the Soviet Union, which allowed the latter to be the sole protective power of Czechoslovakia. For his part, he called on the Soviet government to root out the 'feudalism' in Hungary and Poland, and in return for his diplomatic assistance in the creation of a Soviet security zone he asked for Soviet support in driving the Germans out of the Sudetenland and in the elimination of fascist forces in Slovakia. With the exiled leadership of the Czech Communists in Moscow, he agreed on the formation of a 'National Front' composed of Communists, Social Democrats, National Socialists and the Catholic People's Party as the power behind the future government. Beneš showed a distinct lack of interest in the Carpathian Ukraine, which belonged at that time to the Czechoslovak state, with the result that Stalin, in order to obtain a direct border with Hungary, was able from October 1944 to bring about its incorporation into the Soviet Union without any risk. Beneš in general proved himself to be such a stalwart supporter of Soviet interests that Stalin did not even remotely consider replacing his government with a satellite regime. The fact that the Czech and Slovak Communists were able to obtain a disproportionate number of cabinet posts in the definite formation of the 'National Front' government in March 1945 in Moscow was by no means the result of Soviet pressure, but rather of the astonishing negligence of Beneš, who believed himself able to adopt the position of an arbitrator 'above party politics' without having to involve himself in negotiations. Nevertheless in this way basic democratic structures were retained, a far-reaching consensus with regard to the future democratisation of Czechoslovak society emerged among all partners in the government coalition, and in December 1945 the country was evacuated by the Red Army (as well as by American troops).[10]

In *Romania*, which had fought on the side of the Axis powers under the authoritarian regime of Marshal Antonescu, Stalin first set up a group of conspirators around King Michael, the conservative generals and opposition politicians. This group carried out the coup on 23 August 1944, although it largely avoided the Romanian Communists; only one Communist minister (Pătrăşcanu) was permanently taken into the cabinet formed by the military. Although the country, with the co-operation of the new regime, was now liberated by the Red Army, Stalin resisted the pressure of his Romanian party comrades for a greater share of power. A first attempt on the part of the Communists to change the political structure by means of mass action was unsuccessful in December 1944; a second, in February 1945, triggered substantial unrest among the anti-Bolshevik peasant population. The Soviet chairman of the Allied Control Council for Romania subsequently demanded from King Michael on 27 February 1945 the dissolving of the Radescu government in favour of a more strongly pro-Soviet-oriented cabinet under the Peasants' Party politician, Groza. Conservative forces in the Peasants' Party (around Maniu) and among the Liberals (around Brătianu) continued to retain considerable support in the country, but they were no longer able to obtain direct access to the apparatus of government.

In *Bulgaria*, too, which was at war with the Western powers, but not with the Soviet Union, the Soviet leadership hoped at first for an arrangement with the representatives of the old order; until the end of August 1944 Stalin refused to arrange a truce between the Bulgarian government and the Western powers. When the revolution in Romania surprisingly opened the way for a military conquest of the country by the Red Army, the opposition 'Fatherland Front', which was composed of Communists, Socialists, the Peasants' Party and the Zveno group of the military, organised a *putsch* in September, and after Soviet troops had occupied the country, the Communists were able in the course of the first half of 1945 to gain dominance in this coalition. In January 1945 the General Secretary of the Peasants' Party, Dimitroff, had to resign under Soviet pressure, and in July the Peasants' Party leader, Petkoff, left the government under protest. What

45

remained was the willingness of the government to take account of some of the demands of the opposition in order to obtain recognition from the Western powers.

In *Hungary*, Stalin strove at first to co-operate with Admiral Horthy; only when the latter hesitated to act on the side of the Allies in the war against his former German allies did he have a government coalition set up at the end of December 1944, under the protection of the Soviet troops who had marched into the country in the meantime. This coalition consisted of the Small Landowners' Party, the Socialists and the Communists, although there were three generals from the Horthy regime still at the head. The new regime pursued a conservative and cautious policy for the elimination of fascism, coming under Soviet pressure only comparatively late — from autumn 1946 onwards — in spite of the presence of Soviet troops and increasing reparation burdens.

In contrast with this, Soviet influence in Yugoslavia and Finland remained limited. In *Yugoslavia*, this was because the Communist partisan movement under Tito took power in the country on the basis of its own strength, and initially it was distinctly against the will of Stalin. In *Finland*, Soviet influence remained limited for three reasons: first, the Finnish army brought the Soviet advance successfully to a standstill on two occasions, in 1939/40 and in 1944; second, the USA displayed a manifest interest in the retention of a democratic order in Finland throughout the whole of the war; and finally, the Paasikivi government responded to Soviet security interests after the war with a markedly sympathetic policy.[11]

Different as the methods for securing Soviet interests and their results were for the internal order of the East European countries, in all cases by the end of the war the Soviet leadership had nevertheless successfully set up a western zone that was initially guaranteed not to be hostile to the Soviet Union. How lasting this guarantee would prove to be, however, was uncertain: both the development of the politico-social conflicts in the countries of the Soviet sphere of influence, and the attitude of the Western powers towards the events in Eastern Europe could in the meantime shake the pro-Soviet balance and lead to a change in the political balance of power there, be it either towards more democracy or more repression.

The Stabilisation of Western Europe

Whereas the policy of the Soviet leadership in the sphere of influence of the Red Army consistently showed itself to be on the offensive, in relation to the putative American sphere of influence it was, by contrast, of a defensive nature from the outset. Here, it was concerned with setting limits on the forward pressure of American capitalism, if at all possible, while at the same time re-stabilising the countries disorganised as a result of the war as quickly as possible. For the Communist parties in this region, the new version of the 'People's Front' strategy likewise entailed a commitment to anti-fascist associations at the broadest level, as well as to the extension of Communist influence in all areas of public life. It did not, however, as the majority of Communist Resistance fighters had expected during the war, entail preparation for fundamental social change; rather, as the party leadership returning from Moscow at the end of the war soon made abundantly clear, it guaranteed the handling of the reconstruction of the devastated countries on the basis of their own strength. All means were to be employed to mobilise the masses for raising industrial and agricultural production; patriotic traditions were to be revived everywhere; movements for social reform were only to be encouraged to the extent that they could contribute to the production process, and were to be banned whenever they threatened to view productivity in only a short-term light; traditional national power elites were to be respected and as far as possible were to engage in a policy of independence.

In *France*, the most important country of the European continent to have been liberated by exclusively Anglo-Saxon troops, the Communist Party made use of its comparatively large amount of influence, gained in the inner Resistance movement, to mobilise workers for the struggle for production. 'The battle on the barricades is won, the battle for economic rebirth has begun', wrote the party organ *L'Humanité* three days after the liberation of Paris, on 28 August 1944. As a coalition partner in the 'tripartisan' cabinet (essentially with the Socialists and Christian Democrats), the Communists boycotted the demands of the Socialist Party for the nationalisation of all major industries, economic planning and participation. They themselves took over, in particular, the ministries for industrial production, work, social welfare, economy, armaments and reconstruction, pursuing there a policy of rigorous raising of production and yield levels with

47

concomitant steady or even falling real earnings. Strike movements against this pro-industry policy were combated by the Communist-dominated union organisation, the CGT. After the head of the provisional government, General de Gaulle, had concluded a long-term treaty of friendship and mutual support with the Soviet Union in December 1944, and the Communist General Secretary, Maurice Thorez, had returned from exile in Moscow, the party stripped of power the same administrative organs created by the Resistance in which they had previously secured themselves a dominant role. In terms of foreign policy, the Communists supported de Gaulle's demands for the transference of large parts of West German industrial potential to France by means of the internationalisation of the Ruhr, the secession of the Rhineland, and by massive reparation payments. Even in colonial politics, the Communists supported the endeavours of the French government to reverse the incipient emancipation of the colonised peoples and to bind them firmly to the French motherland, in spite of the tactical concession of greater participation. 'As far as Thorez is concerned,' asserted de Gaulle in retrospect, 'he served the public interest nevertheless, in all his efforts to further the cause of the Communists on several occasions.'[12]

The same applied to Togliatti's efforts in *Italy*. Here also, the Communist Party was, next to the Socialists and the Christian Democrats, the third authoritative political force. In Italy too, the Communist Party involved itself in the coalition government with these parties in the struggle for national reconstruction in the framework of the capitalist system. At first there were still some aspects of a radical-democratic programme involved: at an antifascist congress in Bari in January 1944, the Communists united with other parties of the Left in the demand for the immediate abdication of the King and the handing over of state legitimacy to the organs of the Resistance. Three months later, however, Togliatti went so far as to declare the willingness of his party, like the Liberals, but unlike the Socialists, to postpone the problem of future institutions until the end of the war, thus indicating at the same time his willingness to co-operate with the more conservative forces in the economic and political spheres in the reconstruction of the country. The Communists accepted the disarming of the partisans in the north of the country in the spring of 1944, as well as the stripping of power in the course of 1945 from the local councils which they had set up. As Minister

48

of Justice, Togliatti even assisted with the removal of 'leftist' forces in the Administration. The joint base of the three parties was in this case even greater than in France. In the course of its period of illegality, which lasted for many years, the Italian Communist Party was never Bolshevised to the same extent as its European sister parties: on the contrary, its joint underground struggle with the Socialists, Christian Democrats and Liberals had strengthened its awareness of their shared democratic ideals. The strategic interest of the Moscow party leadership in a swift stabilisation of the West European states coincided here with an autonomous anti-fascist base movement emphasising community with the Democrats; both these factors led the Italian Communist Party to become a totally loyal coalition partner, and to accept the abolition of anti-monopoly legislation, pro-industrial economic policies and a constant deterioration of the Communist position from one cabinet to the next, without in any way adjusting the party's course. This degree of co-operation was so great that the Italian Communists declared themselves on the issue of foreign policy — in this case *against* the interests of the Soviet leadership — in favour of the principle of 'co-operation and increasingly close political, economic and cultural ties with all European democracies'.[13]

The same may be said of the Communist Party of *Belgium*, which after its involvement in the Resistance succeeded in winning itself a place in the first post-war Belgian cabinets; the same too of the small Communist Parties that struggled in vain for a share of power in the remainder of the countries liberated by Anglo-Saxon troops. In *Greece*, Stalin not only refused any help to the national movement of uprising against the regime in Athens, a movement to a large extent carried by Communist leaders, but even held back when the British government engaged troops there in December 1944 for the pacification of the rebels. Soviet policy towards the Communist led partisan movement of Tito in *Yugoslavia* was similary reticent; Stalin not only hesitated for a long time before recognising Tito as head of state and government, but also even exercised his veto when Tito's troops set about securing the region of Trieste in the battle with British and American fighting forces. In *China*, the Soviet government recognised Chang Kai Shek, leader of the corrupt Kuomin Tang regime and arch-enemy of the Chinese Communist Party, as head of state and of the government. Mao Tse Tung's party was invited to form another national united front with the Kuomin

Tang, in order to prevent a unilateral American political line taking hold in the country.[14]

Consistent with this general defensive strategy, the Soviet government took up American plans for a world peace organisation in 1944, much to the surprise of the US government. In this case it was a question of preventing the United Nations from developing into an anti-Soviet system as a result of Soviet non-participation. Finally, the diplomatic efforts of the Soviet leadership in the Mediterranean region and in the Near East must also be seen in this light. In 1944, the Soviet government took up diplomatic relations with Egypt, Syria, Lebanon and Iraq, sought to use the presence of Soviet troops in northern Iran to exert political influence, and asked Turkey in 1945 for permission to establish Soviet military bases in the straits; in addition, it sought from the Western Allies the mandate of former Italian Libya. This certainly linked up with former traditions of Soviet power politics, but now it was also clearly related to the concern not to allow the Mediterranean region to fall entirely into the hands of the British and the Americans after the decline of the French and Italian colonial powers.

The prospects for the success of this anti-American blocking-off policy were considered to be extremely slight even by the Soviet leadership itself. Part of the Soviet leadership regarded France as early as 1944 as being definitely lost to the Anglo-Saxon sphere of influence, and thus demanded the abandonment of the co-operation that had taken place so far with de Gaulle in favour of extreme caution. Only after appropriate persistent pleading on the part of Thorez did Stalin become convinced 'that the weakness of France did not represent an unalterable fact and that one could, if not prevent Anglo-Saxon influence, than at least limit it by helping France to pursue a policy of independence'.[15] Precisely because the prospects for success were so slight, however, the commitment of the Communist parties to the stabilisation of their countries through their own strength had to be total. Until the foundation of Cominform in September 1947, the Communist parties indeed held faultlessly firm to this policy.

In fact, the limits of this stabilisation strategy soon became clear. To the extent that the internal political situation after the end of the war began to normalise again, traditional bourgeois forces also began to threaten to exclude Communists from the government, in France mainly through the Christian Democrat Party and in Italy in connection with corresponding initiatives from the Vatican. The political weight of these demands was decidedly increased by calls of a similar nature from the US Administration. At the same time, dissatisfaction was increasing among the Communist Party rank and file with the policy of sacrifice being put forward by Moscow. This double pressure could only successfully be resisted, if at all, as long as co-operation with the Western powers could be maintained at the global level. This was one more reason for the Soviet leadership to be interested in the continuation of this co-operation.[16]

Indecisive policy towards Germany

The imperatives of Soviet policy towards Eastern Europe and those of the different policy towards Western Europe converged in Germany. On the one hand, the German Reich had almost destroyed the Soviet state: care must therefore be taken to ensure that such a threat to Soviet security could never be repeated. This was to be done, as in the East European countries, by means of fundamental social change and by a definitive share of power for the Communists. On the other hand, the German Reich had only been rendered defeatable with the help of Western troops; therefore the subsuming of German industrial potential into the sphere of influence of American capitalism must be prevented, but at the same time a solution must be sought to the problem of Germany that could be brought about in co-operation with the Western powers. Unlike the case of the East and West European countries, however, no clear strategy for the post-war order of Germany could be derived from these imperatives. Should the Soviet government try to secure social transformation, which in view of the previous strength and expansive character of German capitalism would have to be particularly radical, thus also risking a break with the Western powers, which could bring about another rise of Germany? Should it try to keep German industry from the grasp of the USA, thus running the risk, however, of not fostering social transformation sufficiently? Should it attempt to restrain the expansion power of the German Reich by dividing it into individual states, thereby risking that a proportion of these states would become the junior partners of the USA? Or should it alternatively settle for a unified Germany, thereby taking the chance that Western ideas would penetrate the whole of Germany? Should it hold back its own initiatives until an understanding had been reached among all the occupying powers, thus risking the mobilisation of opposition forces? Or should it further the process of transformation at least in its own zone of occupation, thereby risking the limitation of Soviet possibilities for influence in the other zones? In view of all these imponderables, the answer could essentially only be not to settle for *any* political concept for Germany *a priori*, but rather to explore all conceivable possibilities in an *ad hoc* way in order to discover which combination would prove closest to Soviet imperatives. Soviet policy towards Germany during the war and in the post-war period was thus characterised by a fundamental polyvalence — a polyvalence which allowed the Western powers considerable room for manoeuvre in their decisions over the actual post-war order of Germany.[17]

The polyvalence of Soviet policy towards Germany at first clearly included the possibility of the Soviet Union dispensing with the Allies' demand for 'unconditional surrender'. Repeated informal diplomatic contacts with the German government in 1942, and particularly after the Soviet victory at Stalingrad and before the Soviet breakthrough at Kursk (that is, between February and July 1943), were certainly *also* tactical, being intended to threaten the Western Allies to step up their efforts to form a 'Second Front' on the European continent. Similarly, the establishment of a 'National Committee of Free Germany' under a black, white and red emblem in July 1943 also served the purpose of quashing the fighting morale of German troops on the Eastern Front. Both initiatives, however, sprang mainly from the fear of an understanding being reached between the Western powers and Germany, and additionally made it abundantly clear that the Soviet government did not intend to let German potential fall into the hands of the Western Allies, even if this meant coming to an arrangement with an insignificant and limited German Reich. Some hope along these lines can be especially discerned behind the intensive appeals of 1943–4 for an overthrow of the National Socialist regime from within. This hope grew dimmer, however, in the course of 1944, as the Soviet leadership was obliged to admit how weak the internal German resistance movement actually was.[18]

Stalin had talked with the Western powers on numerous occasions during the war of the possibility of dividing Germany up, but he had always left unanswered questions about his future plans for a solution of the German problem. In December 1941, he suggested to Eden the 'restoration of Austria as an independent state, the detachment of the Rhineland from Prussia as an independent state or protectorate and possibly the constitution of an independent State of Bavaria', as well as the secession of East Prussia and other German regions to Poland, the incorporation of the Tilsit region into the Soviet Union and the return of the Sudetenland to Czechoslovakia.[19] At the conference of Teheran at the end of November 1943, he showed a certain amount of sympathy towards Roosevelt's plan for a division of the German Reich into five state divisions, but at the same time he warned against the revanchism that such a division could bring about, proposed the setting up of permanent strategic 'security areas' on German territory, and urged Churchill first to 'change ... the specific relations of Germany with its Junker class and its large armaments concerns'.[20] At the Yalta Conference in February 1945, he requested, again without putting forward any plan of his own, the execution of the now generally recognised principle of the division of Germany and (not without a sideward glance at possible German attempts to reach an agreement with the Western powers alone) now attempted to commit the Western powers publicly to this principle. At the same time, he demanded clearly for the first time the recognition of the western Neisse as the western frontier of Poland, and announced his claim to reparation payments from German production to the value of 10,000 million dollars. He asserted (probably rightly!) that the rest of the war victim states could receive a further 10,000 million dollars without any damage being sustained to the German peace economy.[21] As long as the Western powers showed themselves willing to use extensive sanctions against Germany, it seemed possible to break German power in this way without at the same time delivering German potential into American hands. The reduction of German potential by means of reparation commitments and social transformation could offer additional guarantees here.

Soviet proposals for the breaking of the agrarian–industrial complex had met with little response in Teheran, whereas demands for reparation payments, the establishing of the Oder–Neisse frontier, and even the demand for the definite signing of division plans in Yalta met with the resistance of Churchill in particular, so that initially only formulary compromises could be aimed at on these questions.[22] These disappointments caused the Soviet leadership to consider the danger of an 'Americanisation' of Germany as being now even more likely. It consequently regarded Soviet rights of consultation and control over the future of the whole German Reich as being of urgent importance. The motive of security in relation to Germany lost importance, however, as soon as the Red Army crossed the Oder in the spring of 1945, thus securing the *de facto* realisation of envisaged Soviet plans for what was, from the military-strategic point of view, an acceptable eastern German frontier. There subsequently followed in March 1945 a spectacular adjustment of course in official Soviet policy towards Germany: Stalin made it known that he no longer wished to insist on the principle of the division of Germany, and in reports divulged after the German capitulation he was quoted as saying that the Soviet Union was able to distinguish between fascism and the German people.[23]

The necessary guarantee against a new rise of the German economy and against a possible association between German and American capitalism had nevertheless not yet been achieved. Although the Soviet leadership permitted the leading circles of the German Communist Party that had returned with the Red Army out of exile in Moscow to begin to set in motion immediately the process of 'democratic transformation', by means of the de-nazification of administration, land reform and the expropriation of the property of capitalists in the Soviet occupation zone of Germany, it could find no means of extending this process into the other occupation zones; on the contrary, the necessity of securing the Communist Party leadership a determining role in this process had given rise very early on in the Western zones of occupation to a fear of Bolshevisation, which made the Soviet demands for transformation seem unacceptable.[24] The fact, however, that the Soviet leadership made no further progress with its envisaged plans for Germany as a whole from the summer of 1945 did not cause the Western Allies to halt or reverse the process of transformation which they had initiated in their own zone of occupation. Still undecided among the various imperatives of their Germany policy, they had made one preliminary decision leading to the actual division of Germany.

Soviet post-war planning as a whole, therefore, unlike that of the USA, had no global vision for the post-war order of Europe and the world. A definite series of essentials and options in relation to Soviet security now existed, and a range of methods had been developed in order to bring about these essentials in various conditions. How the post-war order would turn out in reality, however, remained an open question, being dependent upon the reaction of the Allied partners to Soviet conceptions. Considerable room for manoeuvre thus in fact remained open to the American leadership for deciding upon a future world order. It was hardly able to discern this room for manoeuvre at the time, however, since Soviet conduct in Eastern Europe conveyed an impression of great decisiveness and certainty on the part of the Soviet power.

Notes

1. On the Soviet Union in the war, the official *Geschichte des Grossen Vaterländischen Krieges der Sowjetunion*, 6 vols (East Berlin, 1962); perceptive, but not always reliable is Alexander Werth, *Russland in Krieg 1941–1945* (Munich, Zurich, 1965); on foreign policy, a summary of the traditional interpretation in Adam B. Ulam, *Expansion and coexistence* (London, 2nd edn., 1974), pp. 280–377; Louis Fischer, *The road to Yalta* (New York, 1972), and Andreas Hillgruber, *Sowjetische Aussenpolitik im Zweiten Weltkrieg* (Königstein, 1979), as well the most complete, and as a rule very differentiated evaluation of the American, British and the Eastern sources available at that time, Vojtěch Mastný, *Russia's road to the Cold War* (New York, 1979).
2. On the effects of the war, compare among others Maurice Dobb, *Soviet economic development since 1917* (New York, 1948), pp. 279ff.; Alex Nove, *An economic history of the USSR* (Harmondsworth, 1972), pp. 284ff,; Richard Lorenz, *Sozialgeschichte der Sowjetunion, volume 1: 1917–1945* (Frankfurt, 1976), pp. 265ff.
3. Declarations about the strength of Soviet troops according to Nikita S. Kruschev, *Über die Aussenpolitik der Sowjetunion 1960* (East Berlin, 1962), pp. 32f.
4. Compare, in addition to the by-now classical accounts of Roy A. Medvedev, *Die Wahrheit ist unsere Stärke* (Frankfurt, 1973) and Alexander Solzhenitsyn, *Der Archipel Gulag*, 3 vols., (Berne, Munich, 1974–6), the collection of information available earlier in Zbinyev Brzezinski, *The permanent purge* (Cambridge, Mass., 1956), and Merle Fainsod, *How Russia is ruled* (Cambridge, Mass., 2nd edn, 1963); on the internal political situation as a whole at the end of the war, see William O. McCagg, Jr., *Stalin embattled, 1943–1948* (Detroit, 1978), pp. 73–146.
5. Compare Lászlo Tikos, *E. Vargas Tätigkeit als Wirtschaftsanalytiker und Publizist* (Tübingen, 1965), pp. 65–79. On Soviet post-war planning in general, see Dietrich Geyer, 'Von der Kriegskoalition zum Kalten Krieg', in *Sowjetunion Aussenpolitik, Volume 1: 1917–1945 (Osteuropa-Handbuch* (Cologne, Vienna, 1972), pp. 343–81; additional thoughts in Wilfried Loth, 'Frankreichs Kommunisten und der Beginn des Kalten Krieges', in *Vierteljahrsheft für Zeitgeschichte*, 26 (1978), pp. 7–65, here pp. 13–16. Mastný, *Russia's road*, unfortunately entirely omits the problem posed by Anglo-Saxon capitalism for the Soviet Union at the end of the war, thus reaching in spite of all differentiation of detail theses about Stalin's 'maximal

goals' which are empirically untenable ('Hegemony over the whole of Germany', pp. 257, 290 and elsewhere and 'Influence in Europe as a whole', pp. 110, 283, 306 and elsewhere) as well as Walrab von Buttlar, *Ziele und Zielkonflikte in der sowjetischen Deutschlandpolitik 1945–1947* (Stuttgart, 1980).

6. The multiplicity and flexibility of Soviet post-war planning are also emphasised (with to some extent different classification) by Wolfgang Diepenthal, *Drei Volksdemokratien, Ein Konzept kommunistischer Machtstabilisierung und seine Verwirklichung in Polen, der Tschechoslowakei und der Sowjetischen Besatzungszone Deutschlands 1944–1948* (Cologne, 1974); Geir Lundestad, *The American non-policy towards Eastern Europe 1943–1947* (Tromsö, New York, 2nd edn, 1978), pp. 435–65; and Mastný, *Russia's road*.

7. Compare J.E. McSherry, *Stalin, Hitler and Europe*, 2 vols (Cleveland, Ohio, 1968–70); Vojtěch Mastný, 'Stalin and the prospects of a separate peace in World War II, *American Historical Review*, 77 (1972), pp. 43–66; also Mastný, *Russia's Road*, pp. 73–85; Bernd Martin, 'Verhandlungen über separate Friedensschlüsse 1942–1945. Ein Beitrag zur Entstehung des Kalten Krieges', *Militärgeschichtliche Mitteilungen*, 7 (1976), pp. 95–113.

8. Compare accounts of the 1941 negotiations in Anthony Eden, *The Eden memoirs*, vol. 2 (London, 1965), pp. 289ff.; Winant on Hull, 19 January 1942, *Foreign relations of the United States* (hereafter FRUS) (1942), III, pp. 494–503; Winston Churchill, *The Grand Alliance* (London, 1950), pp. 628ff,; using British documents, Mastný, *Russia's road*, pp. 41–3 and pp. 108f. for Churchill's Eastern European policy. For 1944, Winston Churchill, *Triumph and tragedy* (Boston, 1953), pp. 227f; and for evaluation of British documents in Albert Resis, 'The Churchill–Stalin secret "percentage" agreement on the Balkans, Moscow, October 1944', *American Historical Review*, 83 (1978), pp. 368–87; and Mastný, *Russia's road*, pp. 207–12.

9. Compare the *Documents on Polish–Soviet Relations 1939–1945*, 2 vols. (London, 1961–7); Mastný, *Russia's road*, pp. 53–5, 76f., 167–90; J.K. Zawodny, *Zum Beispiel Katyn, Klärung eines Kriegsverbrechens*, (Munich, 1971); also *Nothing but honour, The story of the Warsaw uprising* (Stanford, Ca, 1977); George L. Bruce, *The Warsaw uprising* (London, 1972), (strong criticism of Soviet conduct); Jan M. Ciechanowski, *The Warsaw uprising of 1944*, (Cambridge, Mass., 1974) (emphasises the contributory responsibility factor of illusionary resistance policy).

10. Compare E. Táborský, 'Beneš and Stalin — Moscow 1943 and 1945', *Journal of Central European Affairs*, 13 (1953/4), pp. 154–81; Vojtěch Mastný, 'The Beneš-Stalin-Molotov conversations in December 1943; new documents', *Jahrbücher für Geschichte Osteuropas*, N.F. 20 (1972), pp. 387–402; also Mastný, *Russia's road*, pp. 133–43, 227–9, 260f.; H. Gordon Skilling, 'Revolution and continuity in Czechoslovakia, 1945–1946', *Journal of Central European Affairs*, 21 (1961), pp. 357–78; Diepenthal, *Drei Volksdemokratien*, pp. 24–7, 45–67.

11. Compare the comparative overview in Lundestad, *The American non-policy*, especially to Romania; Lynn Etheridge Davis, *The Cold War begins, Soviet–American conflict over Eastern Europe* (Princeton, NJ, 1974), pp. 256ff,; McCagg, *Stalin embattled*, pp. 168–173; Mastný, *Russia's road*,

pp. 196–9, 255–7; 199–203 (on Bulgaria), pp. 205–7 (on Hungary); and McCagg, *Stalin Embattled*, pp. 313–16 (accounts of the Hungarian Communist Party leader Erno Gero).

12. Charles de Gaulle, *Mémoires du guerre, vol. 3, Le Salut* (Paris, 1959), p. 101; compare Wilfried Loth, 'Frankreichs Kommunisten und der Beginn des Kalten Krieges', *Vierteljahrshefte für Zeitgeschichte*, 26 (1978), pp. 12–24; for detail, also see Alfred J. Rieber, *Stalin and the French Communist Party 1941–1947* (New York/London, 1962), pp. 126–91, 212–37, 270–357; Ronald Tiersky, *Le mouvement communiste en France 1920–1972* (Paris, 1973), pp. 100–30; Jean–Jaques Becker, *Le parti communiste veut-il prendre, le pouvoir?* (Paris, 1981), pp. 125–207.

13. Declaration of the Italian Communist Party of November 1944, quoted after Wilfried Loth, 'Die Schwäche-Situation Italiens, Belgiens und der Niederlande', in Walter Lipgens, *Die Anfänge der europäischen Einigungspolitik 1945–1950, Vol. 1; 1945–1947* (Stuttgart, 1977), pp. 241–263, quotation, p. 250; compare Giuseppe Vaccarino, 'Die Wiederherstellung der Demokratie in Italien (1943–1948)', *Vierteljahrshefte für Zeitgeschichte*, 21 (1973), pp. 285–324; Harald Hamrin, *Between Bolshevism and Revisionism. The Italian Communist Party 1944–1947* (Stockholm, 1975), Paolo Spriano, *Storia di PCI*, vol. 5 (Turin, 1975), ch. 11–12.

14. Compare on China, Jaques Guillermaz, *History of the Chinese Communist Party* (New York, 1972), pp. 50ff., and Joyce and Gabriel Kolko, *The limits of power* (New York, 1972), pp. 246–76; on Yugoslavia, Walter R. Roberts, *Tito, Mihailović and the Allies, 1941–1945* (New Brunswick, NJ, 1973); on Greece, Christopher F. Woodhouse, *The struggle for Greece, 1941–1949* (London, 1976), pp. 95ff.; on Soviet reticence as a whole, see also McCagg, *Stalin embattled*, pp. 31–71, although it is obviously based on the misleading assumption that Stalin saw greater chances for the successful assertion of Communism in the 'democratic method'.

15. According to the account of Jean Richard Bloch, who accompanied Thorez in December 1944, reprinted in *Le Monde*, 26 November 1969, quoted after Loth, 'Frankreichs Kommunisten', p. 15.

16. That the model used for safeguarding Communist hegemony in Eastern Europe 'was *a priori* not based on any geographical limitations with regard to Western Europe' (according also to Detlef Junker, 'Die Vereinigten Staaten und die Ursprünge des Kalten Krieges 1945–1947', in Oswald Hauser (ed.), *Weltpolitik III 1945–1953* (Göttingen, 1978), pp. 13–38, here p. 31) ranks among the central myths of the Cold War which cannot be upheld by evidence of actual Soviet policy towards Western Europe.

17. This polyvalent structure in Soviet policy towards Germany was first pointed out by Hans-Peter Schwarz, *Vom Reich zur Bundesrepublik* (Neuwied, Berlin, 1966), pp. 203ff., and was first demonstrated in terms of documentation using Soviet sources by Alexander Fischer, *Sowjetische Deutschlandpolitik im Zweiten Weltkrieg 1941–1945* (Stuttgart, 1975). After the report of the Soviet Reparation Administrator Vladimir Rudolph, the majority of the Politburo feared at the end of 1944 that the Soviet Union would not be able to gain any advantage at all from participation in the occupation of Germany; compare Robert Slusser, *Soviet economic*

policy in postwar Germany; a collection of papers by former Soviet officials (New York, 1953), pp. 19, 41.

18. Compare Fischer, *Sowjetische Deutschlandpolitik*, pp. 33–59; Mastný, *Russia's road*, and Martin 'Verhandlungen'. The thesis propounded in the American literature, that Stalin had never really been interested in a separate peace with Germany (e.g. in Adam B. Ulam, *The rivals, America and Russia since World War II*, 2nd edn, London, 1973, p. 14) thus needs to be revised accordingly.

19. Churchill, *The grand alliance*, p. 412; compare above, note 8.

20. Valentin Berežko, *Teheran 1943* (Moscow, 1968), p. 110, quoted after Fischer, *Sowjetische Deutschlandpolitik*, p. 70; ibid., pp. 69–75 for a complete analysis of the Teheran Germany talks.

21. On the Yalta Conference compare Herbert Feis, *Churchill, Roosevelt, Stalin* (Princeton, 1957), pp. 497–558; Diane S. Clemens, *Yalta* (New York, NY, 1970); John Wheeler-Bennett and Anthony Nicholls, *The semblance of peace, The political settlement after the Second World War* (London, 1972), pp. 188–250; Fischer, *Sowjetische Deutschlandpolitik*, pp. 120–31; Mastný, *Russia's road*, pp. 239–53. For a discussion of Soviet reparation demands, cf. chapter 3 below.

22. For a fuller account, see chapter 3 below.

23. Compare with the different interpretation of motive in Fischer, *Sowjetische Deutschlandpolitik*, pp. 131–5 (in addition to the issue of security following the crossing of the Oder, also the fear of losing reparations to France, and the hope for an early American disengagement) and Mastný, *Russia's road*, pp. 233, 237, 242, 261f. (Hope for dominance over the whole of Germany was only postponed at Yalta in order to prevent a separate capitulation of Germany to the Western powers, by the revival of the division formula.)

24. On the allocation of tasks to the German Communist Party in 1945, see Fischer, *Sowjetische Deutschlandpolitik*, pp. 136–53; Arnold Sywottek, *Deutsche volksdemokratie. Studien zur politischen Konzeption der KPD 1935–1946* (Düsseldorf, 1971), pp. 148–207; on the beginning of the 'anti-fascist-democratic swing', see in particular Dietrich Staritz, *Sozialismus in einem halben Land, Zur Programmatik und Politik der KPD/SED in der Phase der antifaschistisch-demokratischen Unwalzung in der DDR* (Berlin, 1976), pp. 12–59, 84–154.

3

Conflicts in the War

The co-operation between the USA and the Soviet Union could be attributed to a range of mutual interests: first and foremost, it was based on the shared concern to bring about the military defeat of the Axis powers as quickly as possible. Closely linked with this was the mutual interest in the material aid of the USA to the Soviet Union, not only to foreshorten the war itself, but also to render the effects of the war — the extensive devastation of the Soviet Union and the crisis of overproduction in the USA — more tolerable for both sides. Similarly, there was a common interest in definitively blocking the path to a renewed expansion of Germany, this time in a different way from that used after the First World War. Even the guaranteeing of regimes in the East European region that were not hostile to the Soviet Union could be regarded as a common interest: Roosevelt at least had become convinced that such a guarantee was a legitimate Soviet security interest, and that for the sake of future peaceful co-operation in the safeguarding of world peace this interest must be taken into account. Lastly, embracing all the above and reinforced by internal political exigencies, this co-operation between the USA and the Soviet Union was based on their mutual interest in avoiding military entanglements in the future. Both sides exerted efforts to bring about this co-operation: Stalin, in spite (or because) of his fear that American capitalism would eventually turn its attention to his own country, by constantly reiterating the theme of US–Anglo-Soviet friendship and by urging common agreements; and Roosevelt, by staking his entire personal prestige on the attempt to remove Stalin's fundamental mistrust. Nevertheless, by the end of almost four years of co-operation in the war, Soviet–US friendship had not been strengthened in any respect; indeed, the mutual sense of mistrust was even stronger than ever before. What could have led to this state of affairs?

Establishing the 'Second Front'

Allied relations had been strained from the very beginning over the question of whether, and if so when, American and British fighting forces would open up a Second Front in the west of the European continent, thus relieving the Soviet army, which was fighting in the east.[1] Here at first, however, there seemed to be every indication of an identity of interest. Stalin was not alone in wanting an early engagement of American land forces on the European continent in order to foreshorten the war; Roosevelt was also interested in an early invasion of the North Atlantic coast, in order to counteract the mistrust of the Soviet leadership, to reduce the chances of a separate peace agreement between the Germans and the Soviets, to be involved in decisions concerning war activity on the continent, and not least in order to bring the seriousness of the situation to the attention of the American public, despite the latter's isolationist tendencies. When Molotov, the Soviet Minister for Foreign Affairs, travelled to Washington at the end of May 1942 to try to commit Roosevelt to the speedy setting-up of a Second Front, Roosevelt assured him that 'we expect the formation of a Second Front this year'. In the communiqué, formulated by Molotov, arising from this consultation, both sides were precise about this declaration to the extent of stating their recognition of the urgent necessity of the 'creation of a Second Front in Europe in 1942'.[2] In adopting this course, Roosevelt was in fact carrying out his resolve, against the prior wishes of the British government to begin with an invasion of North Africa, to have an Anglo-American invasion army transferred from the British Isles to the continent as soon as possible.

In practice, military exigencies soon presented obstacles to these politically motivated declarations of intent. The American military had already informed Roosevelt in the spring of 1942 that an invasion of this kind could take place only in the spring of 1943 at the earliest: Great Britain's armaments production could not reach the necessary level before then. When the War Department subsequently suggested, for the sake of political effect, at least landing smaller contingents of troops on the French coast in the autumn of 1942 ('Operation Sledgehammer'), the British government exercised its veto, fearing substantial human and material losses as a result of a premature attack, as had happened in the First World War. Under pressure, Roosevelt accepted Churchill's alternative plan to launch an offensive against the Germans at least in North Africa in the autumn of 1942.[3] Stalin accepted the news of the postponement of the Second Front in August 1942 with outward reserve, but later lost no opportunity to remind his Western Allies, in propaganda and in bilateral negotiations, of their unkept promise.

Even the intention of opening the Second Front in the spring of 1943 could not be realised, however. British and American troops in North Africa encountered the unexpectedly tough resistance both of the troops of the Vichy regime and of those of the Germans. It took until May 1943 for German troops to surrender Tunisia alone. After the victory in North Africa, Roosevelt and Churchill subsequently decided in Casablanca to launch an offensive against Sicily, in order to pull Italy out of the front of the Axis powers. In the course of 1943, an invasion of the French Atlantic coast consequently became increasingly unlikely and, without any formal resolution about fresh postponement being made, it took until the spring of 1944 for the preparations for 'Operation Overlord' to begin. Churchill even urged his American allies to extend military engagement in the Mediterranean region and to land in the Balkans — a strategy undoubtedly intended to re-secure the British position in the Mediterranean and the Near East and to limit the extension of the Soviet sphere of influence in South-East Europe, but which at the same time was bound to delay even further the establishment of the Second Front on the French coast. Although Roosevelt and his American military forces hesitated to agree to these demands, or to take considerations of the post-war power division in Europe into account in their strategic planning in general, they nevertheless for their part held back the invasion of Normandy until there were sufficient material resources to hand to guarantee the success of the operation and to keep the loss of men to as low a level as possible. They believed that they could not expect the American public to tolerate a game of hazard in which substantial losses of men in the US army would be risked: in reality, such a hazard would hardly have been accepted under any circumstances.[4]

The fact that the Second Front, which had been agreed for 1942, had not even been realised in 1943 decidedly increased the mistrust of the Soviet leadership towards its Western allies. This fundamental mistrust was undoubtedly older than the war alliance, being based on the experience of the anti-Soviet policy of the Western powers since 1918[5] and ideologically underpinned by certainty about the imperialistic character of the capitalist states. It is questionable whether the opening of the Second Front as early as 1942/3 would, in spite of all the risks connected with it, have reduced Soviet mistrust sufficiently to be able to establish enduring co-operation. It nevertheless remains clear that the lengthy delay of the Second Front acted against the simultaneous attempts of Roosevelt to obtain Soviet goodwill. Between June 1941 and June 1944, Roosevelt granted the Soviet government 10 million tons of material aid, without any provisos as to the use to which they should be put or any demands for political concessions·in return. He also twice travelled halfway round the world in order to convince Stalin in person of the correctness of his policies, additionally taking upon himself considerable domestic political risk by showing understanding for Soviet security policy towards Eastern Europe. All this was in vain, however: after the failure of the establishment of a Second Front in 1942, Stalin reacted from the spring of 1943 by placing considerable hopes on reaching an agreement with Hitler or with de-nazified Germany, and responded to Roosevelt's urging for a summit conference of the Big Three with some reticence. Only from 1943, when the Germans had failed to react in the way that had been hoped they would, did Stalin once again seek to reach an understanding with the Western powers. The fear that the Western powers could reach an agreement with the Germans behind his back nevertheless continued to pursue him until the spring of 1945.[6]

The consequences for the post-war order of Europe of the unintended delay of the Second Front were formulated with adequate clarity by the US Commanders-in-Chief in a memorandum of September 1943; the USA, they declared, could not win either the war against Germany or the war against Japan without Soviet assistance. Consequently, Soviet influence in Eastern and Central Europe would increase substantially until the end of the war.[7] In fact Soviet military successes helped the US army to defeat Germany and Japan with less than half the divisions that had been estimated would be necessary for such a victory in the strategic calculations of the pre-war years. At the beginning of the invasion of June 1944, US and British fighting forces in France and Italy were confronted by less than 90 enemy divisions, whereas the Soviet army on the Eastern Front still had over 250 divisions to combat after three years of war. Compared with 20 million war dead on the Soviet side, the Americans and British together could claim less than one million.[8] Stalin thus not only wanted US and British recognition of the Eastern European region being ordered according to the conception of 1939–41, but also the moral justification for the victor to create such an order. An American demand for the right to consultation over Eastern Europe, after the Western powers had denied him a similar right with respect to Western Europe, must have seemed completely incomprehensible to him. Neither the British government of 1942 nor the US government of 1943/4 had been prepared to pay the necessary price in order to retain the power-political basis for such a right to consultation.[9]

American credit for the Soviet Union?

Another cause of the divergence of the coalition partners during the war lay in the unfolding of their bilateral economic interests, although here also at first everything pointed to a harmony of interests.[10] The USA had developed a huge level of war production, not only for its own needs, but also for those of its allies, and therefore needed to open up substitute markets for the time when the war would be over, in order to prevent a crisis of overproduction with a high level of unemployment and recession. The USSR, on the other hand, was in need of a considerable supply of industrial goods and equipment, in the first instance to overcome the effects of war devastation, but also to be able to match the population's new material expectations, which had arisen during the war with an increase in consumption. These two interests complemented each other; assuming that the USA would provide the USSR in the first place with the appropriate loans, the Soviets would be able to meet their import requirements with American products. The opening-up of Soviet markets that would accompany this process would coincide with the US interest in a world-wide multilateral system of trade, whilst in order to cancel its trade deficit in relation to the USA, the Soviet government could make its unavailable stocks of raw materials accessible to American industry.

Considerations of this kind were widely circulated in the US business world, and conspicuously encouraged by the Soviet leadership. Eric Johnston, the dynamic president of the American Chamber of Commerce, spent eight weeks in the Soviet Union in the summer of 1944, and was able to go round Soviet industrial facilities without any restriction. Stalin explained to him in a long conversation his interest in the export of raw materials and in heavy industry imports.[11] On his return, Johnston published enthusiastic reports about the possibilities for Soviet–American economic co-operation, and American industrial and trade circles began to envisage the future 'Russia business' with great optimism. Over 700 American companies had their names put in a catalogue intended for Soviet buyers, banks prepared for the formation of a consortium for the financing of trade with the Soviet Union, and a campaign was conducted for the abolition of the ban on loans to the Soviet Union which had been in existence since 1943. The Secretary of the Treasury, Henry Morgenthau, made efforts towards the granting of a credit facility of 10,000 million dollars to the Soviet Union. Experts estimated the future level of American exports to the Soviet Union at a value of between 1,000 and 2,000 million dollars per annum.[12]

There was, however, no lack of warning voices, not only from the quarter of the American crude oil and mining companies, who feared competition from Soviet raw materials, but also from experts within the Roosevelt Administration, such as Elbridge Durbrow, who regarded it as impossible for the Soviet trade deficit with the USA ever to be balanced, or George Kennan, who feared that the Soviets would not commit themselves to any conditions, but would take advantage of the USA's dependence on Soviet orders, to the detriment of US interests.[13] Roosevelt, however, leaving aside considerations of viability, decided on political grounds to present the Soviet leadership with the prospect of an extensive post-war loan. After the delay in establishing the Second Front, he hoped at least with this offer to be able to demonstrate American goodwill. This calculation indeed seemed to be hopeful: when the new (from October 1943) US Ambassador in Moscow, W. Averell Harriman, who was himself an enthusiastic supporter of the loan idea, intimated to the Soviet leadership at Roosevelt's bidding the possibility of extensive American post-war credit, the Soviet Foreign Trade Commissar, Mikoyan, immediately suggested a credit level of a 1,000 million dollars over 25 years, repayable only from the seventeenth year at a 1.5 per cent rate of interest.[14]

In reality, however, two obstacles stood in the way of the

planned economic co-operation, although they were of a different kind from those feared by the sceptics; first, there was the refusal by US Congress to grant funds for post-war loans during the war itself; and secondly, the hope, widely prevalent in the US Executive, of being able to negotiate political concessions from the Soviet leadership in return for credit. The funds of the US Export–Import Bank, which was empowered to grant credit without the specific agreement of Congress, were almost exhausted, and it seemed to Roosevelt too risky in terms of domestic politics to approach Congress, only a few months before the presidential elections of 1944, for the abolition of the legal restrictions of 1934, or even for a massive foreign-state loan. Against the urging of Harriman to grant a swift credit facility, the Roosevelt Administration therefore decided in May 1944 initially to extend the material war aid of the lend-lease agreement by encouraging the Soviet leadership to request material aid, which would also serve it for future reconstruction. In order to pay for this, credit was to be extended, repayable from the third year at an interest rate of 3.375 per cent — an offer far below the expectation awakened by Roosevelt's original talks with the Soviet leadership, but which, like previous lend–lease grants, was still free of political conditions of any kind.[15]

Although the Soviet government began by negotiating on the basis of the offer, it broke off talks in September 1944 as a result of a deadlock over the interest rate. Molotov informed Harriman by way of an alternative on 3 January 1945 that the USSR would buy industrial equipment in the USA worth 6,000 million dollars, if the USA was prepared to offer appropriate credit for a period of 30 years, repayable from the tenth year at an interest rate of 2.25 per cent.[16] Evidently the Soviet leadership still hoped that economic self-interest would coerce the USA into an agreement on Soviet terms. In contrast to 1944, the political conditions for credit had changed: Congress announced its unwillingness to extend lend–lease allowances for so much as a day longer than the end of the war. Pressure had meanwhile increased among the American public to adopt a 'hard' stand in relation to Soviet demands, and Harriman, whose commitment to credit for the Soviet Union had been based on the conviction that it would prevent Soviet hegemony over Eastern Europe, now believed that Soviet good conduct in Eastern Europe could be brought about by dilatory handling of the credit request. Under pressure from Congress, the public and his ambassador, Roosevelt at first decided to postpone the response to the Soviet credit request. The agreement of Congress could only be obtained if the Soviet Union showed itself to be 'co-operative' in other areas. Consequently Soviet good conduct would have to be a condition for credit to be given, as Harriman maintained.

Roosevelt, however, did not make this connection clear to the Soviet leadership, but only informed it (on 27 January 1945) that long-term post-war loans, however important for bilateral relations, nevertheless necessitated time-consuming legislative preparation.[17] Nothing could have been more calculated to foster Soviet illusions about the priorities of American credit interest, or Soviet mistrust of incomprehensible US tactics. Credit to the Soviet Union, in Roosevelt's view a means for obtaining Soviet co-operation, had now become dependent upon prior Soviet co-operation. As a weapon for coercing the USSR into good conduct, however, it was entirely unsuitable, as was to become clear after the end of the war. The experience of the unforthcoming US credit that had been promised was not least among the factors which in the meantime made the Soviet leadership more inclined to rely on its own strength in the reconstruction of its country.

Negotiations on Germany

A further substantial dampening factor in Soviet–American relations arose out of the inability of the two sides to reach an understanding about the post-war order of Europe, and in particular the future destiny of Germany. Both sides were aware that the problem could only be resolved in co-operation, and therefore they had a fundamental interest in reaching such an understanding. Both, however, were in their respective ways to some extent unsure and undecided about the future of Germany, which rendered timely and specific agreements impossible.

The British government, in particular, urged the conclusion of such agreements. As early as 1 July 1943 — that is, shortly before the landing of Western troops in Sicily, while the Red Army was still fighting far in the interior of the Soviet Union — it suggested to the US and Soviet governments the setting up of a 'United Nations Commission for Europe' for the joint surveillance of liberated territories and of territories now administered by their former liberators. At the Moscow Conference of Foreign Ministers in October 1943, Eden specified this suggestion in terms of a plan for a 'European Advisory Commission' (EAC), which was not only intended to prepare truce negotiations with the defeated enemies, but also to advise on all problems which the 'Big Three' would wish to have worked out, in particular the problems of the future peacetime order. When the EAC subsequently met in London in January 1944 with reluctant Soviet and American agreement, the British delegation presented the first drafts for the handling of Germany at its capitulation. The country was first to be divided into three zones of occupation: a Soviet zone in eastern and central Germany, a British zone in the north-west, and an American zone in southern Germany and Austria, with a joint Allied administration of the capital Berlin. In addition to this, upon capitulation they should take upon themselves the complete disarmament of Germany, the arrest of all Nazis in authority and a strict control of political life.[18]

Although the Soviet government showed considerable interest in the institutionalisation of co-operation, as the British government had proposed, it did not show corresponding enthusiasm about extensive specific agreements on the German post-war order. As long as the Soviet government was uncertain whether the Western powers might after all reach an understanding with the German Reich, it had to employ all possible means to prevent a separate capitulation and to commit the Western powers to a joint occupation regime. As long as the Second Front was not forthcoming and the Red Army was consequently unable to aim for a definitive breakthrough, it was in Soviet interests to prevent settlements for the post-war order that reflected the current unfavourable military situation. As long as the Western powers made no firm statements about their conceptions of German policy, it was bound to be difficult for the Soviet leadership to make a choice from among the many hazardous potential directions of Soviet policy towards Germany. It consequently reacted to the British initiative of 1 July 1943 only at the end of August, when Marshal Badoglio had already offered the Western powers the capitulation of Italy. Instead of a planning and steering committee for the activity of the occupation authorities of the time, the Soviet government demanded a 'military–political commission' of the three Allies to take over direct executive power in the liberated areas. In order to ensure a right to be consulted on all questions concerning the post-war order, the Soviet Union was prepared to accept a right for the Western Allies to be consulted even in those areas that.had been liberated by the Red Army.[19] (The Western powers did not grant such a right to consultation: the 'military–political commission' was set up in September 1943 in Algiers, but was subordinate to the Allied Commanders-in-Chief of the time — in the case of Italy, the British and the Americans.) In the EAC, the Soviet delegation seized gratefully upon the suggestion of the British on zones of occupation, being less interested in the method of territorial division than the principle of joint responsibility for capitulation and occupation. In other respects the Soviet members were sparing with suggestions and aimed at gaining time; only with regard to the right of the victor to reparations did the Soviet Union demand precise settlements.[20]

No progress could be made even on this issue, however, since the American representative to the EAC, John G. Winant, had been directed not to enter into discussion on general political questions, and also, in spite of almost desperate efforts, no competence of any kind had been given to him to discuss capitulation terms or the general occupation organisation.[21] There were numerous reasons for the American decision to refuse general post-war planning: a traditional mistrust of all 'secret diplomacy' (which Wilson had made so difficult in 1919); the concern of Hull that the new institution might be in competition with the universal world organisation; a general tendency in the State Department towards wanting to resolve problems of the peacetime order only after the conclusion of war negotiations at a comprehensive peace conference; Roosevelt's fears that his own room for manoeuvre in sovereign negotiations with Stalin might be restricted by a bureaucratic apparatus; and, above all, the absence of a clear conception on the part of the Roosevelt Administration on the subject of the peacetime order — the German question.

As long as the State and Treasury Departments were unable to agree whether Germany should be retained as an economic power and state, or be 'agrarianised' and divided, the War Department was able to carry out its plans for the defeat and occupation of Germany unhampered by political considerations about the future of Germany. Winant was expressly forbidden to handle questions concerning the future of Germany, beyond the solution of occupation questions. The EAC was thus able to work out a basic plan for the division of Germany into three zones of occupation (including the tripartite division of Austria urged by the Soviet Union) essentially according to the British suggestion.

When the State Department and Winant, however, set about discussing the problem of German reparation payments with the Soviet leadership, Roosevelt prevented such a discussion in October 1944.[22] The Soviet leadership was obliged to wait until the Yalta conference of February 1945 until it was able to discuss the problem of reparation with the Allies.

Even by that time, however, the internal US process of decision-making was still no further forward. In order not to leave US troops completely without directions in the case of a collapse of the German Reich (which now 'threatened' to take place at the end of 1944), the US Commanders-in-Chief had issued a provisional directive in September 1944 which in fact favoured Morgenthau's conception of 'organised chaos' in its concern not to burden the army with political tasks and not to pre-empt future political decisions. Germany was to be treated as a defeated, not as a liberated nation, and responsibility for economic life was not to be taken on by the occupation authorities, but to be left to German officials; on the other hand, all Nazi and pro-Nazi officials (meaning almost all officials) were to be arrested. If with this directive, issued under the registered number JCS 1067,[23] it seemed that a German policy in Morgenthau's sense of the term was being set in motion, then on the other hand the representatives of the State Department gained credence during the direct preparations for the Yalta conference. In the papers prepared as conference documents for Roosevelt's Yalta trip by experts of the State Department for Foreign Affairs, papers which, now that Stettinius had taken over from Hull as Secretary of State in November 1944, were even more respected by Roosevelt than previously submitted documents, the 'assimilation — on a basis of equality — of a reformed, peaceful and economically non-aggressive Germany into a liberal system of world trade' was put forward, together with a joint economic policy in the three zones of occupation, as being the aim of American policy towards Germany. In order this time to avoid the indirect financing of German reparations through the USA that had followed the First World War, German reparation payments were to be arranged only in the form of payments in goods and services, and not as money transfers. The period of the reparation obligation was to be determined beforehand — ten years at the most, but preferably five. The total sum of the payments was not to be fixed beforehand, however, in order to take the development of German productive capacity into account.[24] Without explicitly adopting these ideas, Roosevelt nevertheless decided to take Stettinius, but not Morgenthau, with him to Yalta.

In Yalta, Roosevelt in fact kept to some of the recommendations of the State Department, but in doing so contributed to the further postponement of vital German policy issues.[25] On the question of reparations, some progress towards *rapprochement* seemed to have been made when the Soviet delegation agreed to the principle of limiting them to ten years and drawing the payments from production. A request to fix the total sum of reparation payments to a value of 20,000 million dollars also seemed acceptable: the direct damage alone sustained by the Soviet Union amounted, according to US estimates, to 35,700 million dollars (according to Soviet calculations of 1947 they totalled 128,000 million dollars' worth, plus 357,000 million dollars' worth of damage resulting from the war). After the First World War, the Allies had fixed the total indemnities of the German Reich at 55,000 million dollars (at the Conference of London of 1921; this figure was adjusted to the dollar value of 1945), and in the 'Briefing Book' for Yalta the State Department quoted German payments to a value of 6,500 million dollars per year as recommendable. Fearing a unilateral strengthening of the Soviet Union at Germany's expense, however, Churchill voiced his objection to the reparation level demanded by Stalin. In order to avoid being suspected by his own public of submitting to another financing of German reparations by the US taxpayer (as had happened after the First World War), Roosevelt hesitated to fix a sum. Reluctantly, he at last declared himself prepared to recognise a sum of 20,000 million dollars as a 'basis for future negotiation', but then the British delegation refused to agree, so that the Soviet representatives were once again without firm guarantees.

On the question of the division of Germany, Roosevelt was at first prepared to acquiesce to Soviet demands to agree now to division in principle. This was consistent with his basic view since Teheran, which went against State policy; he took for granted, however, that Churchill and Eden, with the support of Stettinius (an advocate of the State line), would enforce a formula in the capitulation document agreed on in Yalta which, although it did not rule out a possible division of Germany, could also be interpreted in the sense of simple decentralisation.[26] This question thus remained open. On the issue of the eastern frontier of Germany, the third essential item on German policy that Stalin wanted settled at Yalta, the agreement 'in principle' to a western shifting of Poland, which had been settled in Teheran, was upheld, but a fixing of the Oder–Neisse line demanded by Stalin did not take place, after Churchill argued that a westward shifting of the Polish border across the Oder would involve substantial resettlement of Germans, a question that would need to be considered at greater leisure. Roosevelt was influenced by this argument.

In reality, the fundamental conflict dividing the world powers over the issue of Germany only became clear for the first time in Yalta: US interest in integrating German potential into the economic alliance of the 'One World', against Soviet interest in not allowing this potential to fall into the hands of the British and the Americans — a contradiction of which Churchill and Stalin were certainly aware, but Roosevelt was not. The fact that at the second conference of the 'Big Three' no efforts were undertaken to deal with this conflict, so that all crucial questions were put off, was essentially due to American indecisiveness.[27] When the Soviet leadership presented its demands relating to German policy at Yalta, the US delegation showed itself in the final analysis to be inadequately prepared. American planners, whether those of the Morgenthau group or the State Department, had never paused to consider what kind of policy concepts the Soviet leadership might have in relation to Germany, or how these might be brought into line with their own concept at that time. When the US delegation was suddenly confronted with the problem in Yalta, therefore, they had even less idea how to deal with it, since they were not even clear about their own objectives.

After Yalta there was a similar lack of necessary decision-making. The reparation policy of the State Department, accepted by Roosevelt, tended towards a future integration of Germany, thus pushing Morgenthau's plans more and more into the background, but the JCS 1067 directive favoured by the War Department was set in motion in May 1945 without the State Department's efforts at modification leading to any appreciable changes.[28] Even now Soviet interests were not taken into account in planning for German policy. Faced with this American refusal to make specific agreements, the Soviet leadership concluded that its distrust of the intentions of its capitalist allied partners was justified, and that it must consequently rely on its own potential alone, regardless of Western perceptions, to effect its policy essentials. In this way, the chances for a *rapprochement* over bilateral

71

interests in the German question — albeit to some extent contradictory interests — were lost before they could even be explored.

Tension over Eastern Europe

The most significant conflict for future Soviet–American relations developed over the issue of the post-war order of Eastern Europe. In this case, unlike that of the German question, the Roosevelt Administration had quite a clear idea of what it wanted. On the one hand, as was constantly reiterated by experts of the State Department,[29] the East European nations were to be organised according to the principle of self-determination and integrated into the multilateral system of the 'One World', if only to vindicate the principles for which they had gone into the war to avoid a repetition of those conflicts of nationality that had contributed to the destruction of the peacetime order after the First World War, and not least to convince the American public of the possibility of the 'One World' concept, thereby winning them over to the idea of a world peace organisation. On the other hand, as Roosevelt at least was quite well aware, pro-Soviet regimes needed to be set up in Eastern Europe in order to do justice to Soviet security interests, to meet Soviet claims as a victorious power, but above all to secure the necessary co-operation of the Soviet Union in the creation of the world peace order.[30] The fact that they could not have both these things at once, that free elections according to democratic principles, for example, and the establishment of pro-Soviet regimes in large parts of Eastern Europe were mutually exclusive, was not, however, realised by the Roosevelt Administration — neither by the State Department which, exactly as in the case of its planning for its German policy, never took into account the situation regarding Soviet interests in Eastern Europe; nor by Roosevelt himself who, in his only vague cognisance of East European relations, hoped that the principles of the Atlantic Charter and Soviet security interests in Eastern Europe could 'somehow' be made compatible, thus resolving the contradictions between the 'internal' and the 'external' aspects of his foreign policy.

By wanting self-determination for Eastern Europe and Soviet friendship at the same time, the US leadership lost both in the gamble: Roosevelt was unable to convey to the Soviet leadership his fundamental agreement with a pro-Soviet orientation in Eastern Europe. Although he had always spoken along these lines in his personal contacts with Stalin, his efforts were nevertheless cancelled out by the State Department policy of postponing the settlement of territorial questions until the conclusion of war negotiations, and as far as possible avoiding altogether the official delineation of spheres of influence. When the British government urged the Roosevelt Administration in February 1942 (that is, shortly after Stalin's division offer to Eden) to recognise officially Soviet territorial claims, at least in principle, in order to obtain in return the commitment of the Soviet Union to the principles of the Atlantic Charter, Roosevelt not only rejected this suggestion, according to the relevant statements of the State Department, as 'provincial', but even went so far as to approach the Soviet leadership unilaterally in order to postpone the settlement of its territorial claims until the time of the peace negotiations. In response to Soviet attempts to sign a settled agreement with Great Britain on its claims, Roosevelt voiced the strongest objections, managing finally to make Molotov settle at the end of May 1942 for a purely military Anglo-Soviet agreement, in return for a promise to open up a Second Front in that year after all. When Churchill, after failed attempts to draw the USA into an arrangement, finally in October 1944 reached an understanding on his own with Stalin on the division of spheres of influence in the South-Eastern European region, the US government refused to give official recognition to this agreement.[31] The result of this policy was that the Soviet government placed no faith in Roosevelt's affirmations of *rapprochement* and, without regard for Western perceptions or, to be more precise, without any effort to assist Roosevelt in the safeguarding of his policy of *rapprochement* in the domestic political sphere, proceeded to create the necessary guarantees for the development of Eastern Europe in its understanding of the term. The arrangement with Beneš, the break with the Polish exile government, the negotiation of capitulation terms with Romania, Bulgaria and Hungary, the refusal to give assistance to the Warsaw uprising, and finally the recognition of the Lublin Committee as the provisional Polish government, all occurred without the Soviet leadership attaching any appreciable importance to possible Western reactions.

As was only to be expected, unilateral Soviet action in the sphere of influence of the Red Army encouraged anti-Soviet circles in the American public, which created new opportunities for influence within the Administration for the critics of Roosevelt's *rapprochement* line. From the spring of 1943, the US government was under pressure in particular from the seven million Americans of Polish origin. Alarmed by the break of Moscow with the Polish exile government and the silence of official Moscow and Teheran reports on all questions of a territorial nature, Poles, Catholics and Republican representatives of the Mid-West, who were dependent upon Polish votes, sought with a wave of press appeals, as well as congressional and parliamentary enquiries, to pin the President down to an integral application of the Atlantic Charter in Eastern Europe. The movement was so strong that at one time it threatened to jeopardise the re-election of Roosevelt in November 1944. It was known that the Poles would decide the voting pattern in Illinois and Ohio, and perhaps also in New York and Pennsylvania. In addition, the whole concept of the world peace organisation threatened to collapse, if the minds of the minorities of East European origin could not be put to rest. Senator Vandenberg of Michigan, himself dependent on Polish votes, and now the most influential Republican spokesman on foreign policy, soon informed the government that the Senate would only permit the entry of the United States into the organisation envisaged at Dumbarton Oaks, if world-wide respect of the Atlantic Charter were secured. All this now compelled the President to make the 'internal' foreign policy, which had only been intended as rhetoric, the actual foreign policy.[32]

Roosevelt, on the one hand, sought to evade the dilemma of having to do something for the self-determination of East Europeans while in fact hardly being in a position to do anything, by trying to convince representatives of the exile governments of the necessity of reaching some arrangement with the Soviet government; on the other hand, he sought to win Stalin over to solutions that would enable all those involved to save face. In the first case, Roosevelt's efforts were without success: although the Polish exile premier Mikolajczyk was won over to the idea of *rapprochement* with the Soviet Union at least on the border question, he was not able to convince his colleagues and resigned in November 1944. Under his successor, Arciczewski, the exile government went into complete isolation. Neither Churchill nor Roosevelt saw any chance of being able to present this government to the Soviet Union as an acceptable negotiating partner. In the second case, success was equally limited, although Roosevelt at first regarded it as considerable. Stalin finally reacted to constant pressure from

Roosevelt for 'some public declaration (which) would be helpful for him personally' by agreeing at the conference in Yalta in February 1945 to the publication of a joint 'Declaration on Liberated Europe', which affirmed once again the principles of the Atlantic Charter.[33]

In the text, which was based on an American presentation, the three allied governments committed themselves 'to concert' their policies 'in assisting the peoples liberated from the domination of Nazi Germany and the peoples of the former Axis satellite states of Europe to solve by democratic means their pressing political and economic problems', and in particular to assist them 'to form interim governmental authorities broadly representative of all democratic elements in the population and pledged to the earliest possible establishment through free elections of governments responsive to the will of the people' and 'to build ... a world order under law, dedicated to peace, security, freedom and the general well-being of all mankind'. In total, like the rest of American rhetoric, it was as emphatic as it was open to multiple interpretation (what was meant, for example, by 'democratic elements in the population'?). The *de facto* decisions on Eastern Europe made at the Yalta conference alone made it sufficiently clear just how little weight the text really carried. The Polish provisional government, which had emerged from the Lublin Committee, was to be reorganised on 'a broader democratic basis' by the inclusion of representatives of other 'democratic leaders' — not, as Roosevelt and Churchill had requested, to be replaced by a new government appointed proportionally from the Lublin and London representatives. The government was to organise free elections as soon as possible, but not, as Roosevelt had demanded, under the joint supervision of the Allies.[34] Once Soviet agreement to the 'Declaration on Liberated Europe' had been obtained, Roosevelt himself did not show the slightest interest in creating either institutions or controls that could have helped to bring about the 'concerting policies' that had been heralded. Even before the conference, he had rejected the urgent recommendation of the State Department to pursue the creation of a 'High Commission for Europe' for this purpose; he now stood by with increasing impatience while Churchill tried to clarify a range of detailed questions concerning the problem of Eastern Europe. He himself, however, against the advice of the State Department, undertook no efforts to clarify the areas of competence of Western representatives in the Allied Control

Commissions for Romania, Bulgaria and Hungary, on the grounds that the *rapprochement* with the Soviet Union was not to be jeopardised, and the USA was not to be drawn too much into the postwar quarrels of the old continent.

After his return from Yalta, Roosevelt immediately used the results of the conference to restore the faltering balance in the foreign policy consensus of the USA. Yalta, he declared before both houses of Congress on 1 March 1945, would form the basis for a lasting peace 'based on the sound and just principles of the Atlantic Charter'. Compromises had been necessary, but nevertheless in general the agreements of the unfortunate spheres-of-influence policy of previous years had been brought to an end.[35] The glowing Wilsonianism of this speech was persuasive. The Yalta agreements met with optimistic approval amongst almost the whole of the American public, and even a sceptic such as Vandenberg, who immediately recognised the limited value of the agreements, no longer dared to oppose the President publicly. The ideals for which they had fought seemed to have been secured, and the dream of the 'One World' seemed, in spite of all the recently experienced perils, still to be realisable. A general air of auspicious 'Roosevelt weather' reigned,[36] even with the President himself, who was visibly relieved at his domestic political success and spared little thought for how long the agreements would in fact last.

If the Americans interpreted the European declaration of Yalta as a guarantee for peace in the sense of the Atlantic Charter, then Stalin was obliged, after all that Roosevelt had said and done, to construe it for what it really was: a verbal concession to the American public, which was of little significance for actual policy. From the Soviet viewpoint, the balance-sheet from Yalta was, if anything, a negative one. Although the Curzon line had been recognised as the eastern border of Poland, and the 'Lublin' government had been assured a substantial share in the future regime of Poland, these results had nevertheless never been in any serious doubt since the Red Army had reached almost as far as the Oder.[37] The Soviet government had not only agreed to the 'Declaration on Liberated Europe', but had also committed itself, as was equally important for the American side at least, to enter the war against Japan two or three months after the conclusion of the European war negotiations, and to co-operate in the founding of the United Nations Organisation. In return for these co-operative gestures, the Soviet Union had been assured the restoration of Russian rights in relation to China from the time before the Russian–Japanese war of 1904/5 (the return of South Sakhalin, the internationalisation of the harbour of Dairen, the leasing of Port Arthur, and joint Sino-Soviet administration of the Chinese Eastern Railway and the South Manchurian Railway). The secession of the Japanese Kuril Islands to the Soviet Union had also been agreed. In relation to the post-war order of Europe, the Soviet delegation had not been able to have its way, however. On all the crucial questions of German policy, the Western Allies had prevented firm agreements; as a result of the inclusion of France as the fourth occupation power in Germany, with a seat and a vote in the Allied Control Council of Germany (at the urging of Churchill), the weight of the Western powers in policy towards Germany had been strengthened, and after three years of the war coalition the Soviet leadership still knew nothing about actual American intentions in Europe. What could be more likely to suggest itself after such conference results than renewed concentration on the securing of its own sphere of influence — independent of the framework of the 'Declaration on Liberated Europe', which was, after all, broad enough?

The *rapprochement* of Yalta had thus only been an apparent one: each side interpreted the results in its own way. The American public clung to its dream of the liberal–democratic principles of the 'One World', without ever seriously weighing up Soviet security interests, and without wishing to pay any real price for its engagement in world politics. Even Roosevelt, who had been realistic in his estimation of the possibilities of world politics, like most of his compatriots did not succeed in keeping foreign policy sufficiently separate from the implications of the Wilsonianism necessary for his domestic policy. The Soviet leadership did not perceive the contradiction between the USA's world-wide pretensions and its limited readiness for action, seeing in its idealistic 'One World' ideas merely the cynical expression of expanding American imperialism, and interpreting its own security interests extensively as a result. With regard to Eastern Europe, the Soviet leadership regarded the guarantee of pro-Soviet orientation as being even less compatible with liberal and democratic principles as long as this guarantee in fact gained for the American public a symbolic value in terms of the rightness of having entered the war. The conflict over Eastern Europe was thus momentarily suspended, and would have to reappear later. The unpleasant experience for both sides, that unity had been in appearance only, now rendered final the break which had been set in motion during the war coalition years.

Notes

1. Compare with the following: John L. Gaddis, *The United States and the Origins of the Cold War 1941–1947* (New York, 2nd edn, 1976), pp. 66–80; and Mark A. Stoler, *The politics of the Second Front: American military planning and diplomacy in coalition warfare 1942–1943* (Westport, Conn., 1977).

2. Recod of the Roosevelt–Molotov conversation in *Foreign Relations of the United States*, diplomatic pages (hereafter FRUS) (1942), III, pp. 577 and 582f.; general communiqué ibid., p. 594.

3. Compare Maurice Matloff and Edward L. Snell, *Strategic planning for coalition warfare: 1941–1942, (United States Army in World War II: The War Department)* (Washington, DC 1953); Forrest C. Pogue, *George C. Marshall; Ordeal and hope, 1939–1942* (New York, 1966), pp. 305ff.

4. Compare with overview in Gaddis, *The United States and the origins*; Maurice Matloff, *Strategic planning for coalition warfare, 1943–4 (United States Army in World War II: The War Department)* (Washington, DC, 1959); Gordon A. Harrison, *Cross-Channel attack (United States Army in World War II: The European theater of operations)* (Washington, DC, 1951).

5. On more than just a Russian 'national character' affected by centuries of fear, as George F. Kennan (telegram of 22 February, 1946, *Memoirs 1925–1950* (Boston. 1967), pp. 547–59; and after him Louis J. Halle, *Der Kalte Krieg*, (Frankfurt, 1969), pp. 25–33, asserted, with rather superficial use of deep psychological interpretative models.

6. Compare Vojtěch Mastný, *Russia's road to the Cold War* (New York, 1979), *passim*; from the Soviet viewpoint as a whole, see also Viktor Issraelian, *Die Antihitlerkoalition, Die diplomatische Zusammenarbeit zwischen der USSR, den USA und England während des Zweiten Weltkrieges 1941–1945* (Moscow, 1975).

7. JCS 506 of 18 September, 1943, quoted by Matloff, *Strategic planning*, pp. 292f.

8. Quoted after the summary in Gaddis, *The United States and the origins*, pp. 75f.

9. There can, therefore, be no question of Eastern Europe having been 'offered up to Bolshevism', as Karl Dietrich Erdmann, *Das Zeitalter der Weltkriege* (= Gebhardt, *Handbuch der Deutschen Geschichte*, 9th edn, vol. 4) (Stuttgart, 1976), p. 600, sums up an interpretation put forward by 'traditional' authors. The fundamental political decisions had been made by the Western powers in 1942/3.

10. Compare with the following: George C. Herring, Jr, 'Lend–Lease to Russia and the origins of the Cold War, 1944–1945', *Journal of American History*, 56 (1969), pp. 93-114; also by the same author, *Aid to Russia 1941–1946* (New York, 1973), as well as based on more limited sources, but with the same conclusions, Gaddis, *The United States and the origins*, pp. 174–97.

11. Eric Johnston, 'My talk with Joseph Stalin', *Reader's Digest*, 45 (October 1944), p. 1410; in addition, after Harriman to Hull 30 June, 1944, FRUS (1944), IV, pp. 973f.

12. After a report in the journal *Fortune*, 31 (January 1945), pp. 153ff., quoted in Gaddis, *The United States and the origins*, p. 188.

13. Memorandum of Durbrow on 29 November, 1943 in FRUS (1943), III, pp. 722f.; Memorandum of Kennan on September 1944 ('Russia after seven years') in Kennan, *Memoirs*.

14. Gaddis, *The United States and the origins*, pp. 176–8; Herring, *Aid to Russia*, pp. 149f.

15. Herring, *Aid to Russia*, pp. 150-9; compare W. Averell Harriman and Elie Abel, *Special envoy to Churchill and Stalin 1941–1946*, (New York, 1975), pp. 366–87.

16. After a report by Harriman to Stettinius, 4 January, 1945, FRUS (1945), V, pp. 942–4.

17. Grew to Kennan, 27 January, 1945, FRUS, V, pp. 968–70.

18. FRUS (1944), I, pp. 112–54; compare Bruce Kuklick, 'The genesis of the European Advisory Commission', *Journal of Contemporary History*, 4 (1969), pp. 189-201; Keith Sainsbury, 'British policy and German unity at the end of the Second World War', *English Historical Review*, 94 (1979), pp. 786-804.

19. Correspondence between the Chairman of the Council of Ministers of the USSR and the Presidents of the USA and the Prime Ministers of Great Britain during the Great Patriotic War of 1941–1945; correspondence with Franklin D. Roosevelt and Harry S. Truman, Moscow, 1957, p. 84; FRUS (1943), I, p. 786; compare Mastný, *Russia's road*, pp. 106f.

20. FRUS (1944), I, pp. 173–9; compare Mastný, *Russia's road*, pp. 145–53.

21. Compare Hull to Winant, 23 December, 1943, FRUS (1943), I, p. 812; and in general Gaddis, *The United States and the origins*, pp. 105–14.

22. Roosevelt to Hull, 20 October, 1944, FRUS Yalta, p. 158; on the discussion of the demarcation of the occupation zones, see Tony Sharp, *The wartime alliance and the zonal division of Germany* (Oxford, 1975), pp. 3–119.

23. Text of the directive of 22 September, 1944 in FRUS Yalta, pp. 143-54; compare Paul Y. Hammond, 'Directives for the occupation of Germany: The Washington controversy', in Harold Stein (ed.), *American civil-military decisions*, (Birmingham, Ala, 1963), pp. 311–464, here pp. 371–7 and 390f.

24. Yalta briefing book papers, FRUS Yalta, pp. 178–97, quotation p. 191.

25. Compare literature in chapter 2, note 21; on the reparation question, additionally see John H. Backer, *The decision to divide Germany, American foreign policy in transition* (Durham, 1978), pp. 34-8 and 61-72.

26. 'Dismemberment' measures were agreed 'in order to secure peace and security of Europe' — FRUS Yalta, pp. 565f.

27. Not, as Gabriel Kolko asserts in *The politics of war* (New York, 1968), p. 353, an American tactic to avoid firm agreements in view of the momentary military strength of the Soviet Union in Germany.

28. Compare Hammond, 'Directives', pp. 422–7; Gaddis, *The United States and the origins*, pp. 129–31; Backer, *The decision*, pp. 38-41. As Hermann Graml shows, 'Zwischen Jalta und Potsdam, Zur amerikanischen Deutschlandplanung in Frühjahr 1945,' *Vierteljahrshefte für Zeitgeschichte*, 24 (1976), pp. 308–24, the War Department now also began to interpret the JCS 7067 directive in terms of a future integration of Germany. The promulgation of the reparation concept of the State Department in the first months of 1945 is analysed in detail by Bruce Kuklick, *American policy and the division of Germany, The clash with Russia over reparations* (Ithaca, NY/London, 1972). Kuklick's thesis, that this change of position was part of a comprehensive anti-Soviet strategy, has no documentary basis in the sources, however.

29. Compare the assessment of the East European planning of the State Department in Lynn Etheridge Davis, *The Cold War begins* (Princeton, NJ, 1974), *passim*, and esp. pp. 62–88; this account, however, overestimates the influence of state planning on the American East European policy that was actually put into effect.

30. Cf. chapter 1, above.

31. 'Provincial': conversation on 20 February, 1942, FRUS (1942), III, p. 521; in general, Davis, *The Cold War begins*, pp. 24–37 and 143–59; on the Anglo-Soviet agreement, see also Gaddis, *The United States and the origins*, pp. 15–17.

32. Substantial evidence of internal political pressure in Gaddis, *The United States and the origins*, pp. 139–57; on American Polish policy in general, see Richard C. Lukas, *The strange allies, The United States and Poland, 1941–1945* (Knoxville, Tenn., 1978).

33. Thus as early as at Teheran; FRUS Teheran, pp. 594f.

34. Text of the Yalta communiqué in FRUS Yalta, pp. 971ff.; the 'Declaration on Liberated Europe' contained in it is quoted here after the German translation in *Europa-Archiv*, 1 (1946), p. 212. Compare in addition to note 21 in chapter 2 above, also literature quoted on the treatment of the Eastern Europe question in Yalta, especially Davis, *The Cold War begins*, pp. 172–201.

35. Samuel I. Rosenman (ed.), *The public papers and addresses of Franklin D. Roosevelt*, vol. 13 (New York, 1950), pp. 570–86.

36. Daniel Yergin, *Shattered peace*, (Boston, 1977), p. 67. The best description of the American euphoria of early spring 1945 is given by Gaddis, *The United States and the origins*, pp. 165–71.

37. See note 9 above.

4

1945: The Turning-point

In 1945, the same year in which the Allies achieved their military goals with the capitulation of Germany (8 May) and Japan (14 August and 2 September), the war coalition effectively broke up, and the confrontation between the two new world powers began to determine the course of international politics. In the final communiqué of Yalta, the Allies had announced their intention 'to maintain and strengthen in the peace to come that unity of purpose and of action which has made victory possible and certain for the United Nations in this war'. Yet only a year later, Molotov could speak openly of 'insatiable imperialists' and 'warmongering groups of adventurers' among the 'ruling classes' abroad who 'foster far from harmless talk about a "Third World War"'. Churchill responded with the image of the 'Iron Curtain', which the Soviet Union had drawn across the continent 'from Stettin in the Baltic to Trieste in the Adriatic'.[1] The fact that the conflicts had been masked at Yalta would soon reassert themselves was as predictable as the fact that, after the disappointment on both sides, they would now take a more acute form. After the removal of the most important common interest, the defeat of the Axis powers, indeed, they were able to threaten the continuation of the alliance itself. What needs to be explained, however, is how these conflicts were able, as early as the year in which the war ended, to take on such compelling dimensions that they proved to be insurmountable, in spite of the fact that both sides were at first interested in continuing their co-operation.

Transformations in Eastern Europe

The starting-point of the East–West crisis of 1945 consisted of Soviet efforts to consolidate the sphere of influence that had been created by the Red Army. These efforts were necessary in the Soviet view after the failure to obtain from their capitalist allies sufficiently far-reaching guarantees with regard to the post-war order of Europe. All this was now possible, since the substance of what was meant by the 'democratic forces' to be encouraged in the Soviet sphere of influence had not been clarified at the Yalta conference. Such efforts were all the more urgent for Stalin, since in the meantime, within the Soviet hegemony system, the weight carried by those forces of the party with a sceptical stance towards co-operation with the Western powers had substantially increased.[2] 'This war,' as Stalin elucidated the principle of this consolidation policy to Tito's representative, Milovan Djilas, in April 1945, 'is not like those in the past; when someone occupies a region, he imposes his own social system on it. Everyone introduces his own system as far as his army is able to advance. It cannot be any other way.'[3]

The extent to which Soviet mistrust of the Western powers had increased, in spite of the semblance of Yalta, emerged as early as during negotiations over the capitulation of the German fighting forces in northern Italy. When German SS General Wolff went to Berne at the beginning of March 1945 in order to negotiate with British and American Commanders-in-Chief about a possible capitulation of his troops, the Soviet government demanded to be included in these negotiations. The US government, however, refused to permit Soviet participation in the purely military preliminary negotiations, referring its Soviet partners to the forthcoming formal capitulation negotiations at the Allied Headquarters for Italy. Stalin, enraged, consequently surmised that the Berne negotiations had led to a secret agreement: that in return for assurances of mild peace terms, the German army command had opened the Western Front to the British and Americans, so that they could advance as far as possible to the east, whilst the Germans would fight with reinforcements on the Eastern Front. At first Roosevelt regarded this accusation as monstrous and saw his efforts towards US–Soviet conciliation as being seriously open to question; later, however, he decided not to permit the incident to develop into a serious crisis in bilateral relations.[4]

This by now unsurpassable mistrust increased the tendency of the Soviet Union, in the absence of other means, to resort to police-state methods for securing its influence in what were for the most part the pre-industrial and pre-democratic regions of Eastern Europe. In Bulgaria, for example, in the first months of 1945, bloody purges took place to which over 2,000 leading anti-Communists from all levels fell victim. In a spectacular intervention in Romania, at the end of February 1945, as has already been described, the Soviet government forced on King Michael the dissolution of the openly anti-Communist government of Radescu. In Poland, at the end of March, sixteen Resistance leaders, who had abandoned illegality in order to negotiate with the Soviet authorities, were arrested and deported to Moscow. There was uncertainty for more than two months as to their whereabouts, until it was heard that they had received sentences of between eighteen months and ten years' imprisonment on 21 June for 'subversive activity behind the back of the Red Army'. (In reality, the internal Polish Resistance had resolved not to give in to the Communists without a fight.) In all the 'liberated' countries, the domestic ministries were entrusted to Communist ministers, and potential opponents of pro-Soviet regimes were arrested on the pretext of the 'punishment of fascist forces'. Pro-Soviet forces controlled the press and the army, whilst the Communists sought to establish unified 'anti-fascist' electoral lists, in order to conceal their relatively poor backing among the population. Czechoslovakia alone remained to a large extent unaffected by this police-state interference: Beneš was solely obliged to accept the fact that, with the advance of the Red Army, Communists often took over key positions in the newly-created administrative organs.[5]

The partial police-state atmosphere in the occupied regions was intensified by measures used by the Red Army. Numerous abuses of the civil population by Soviet soldiers, especially in Romania and Hungary, but also in the occupied regions of the German Reich, Czechoslovakia, Poland and even in Yugoslavia, their ally, although not politically planned, nevertheless aroused a feeling that there was considerable bias on the part of the administration, thus intimidating potential opponents of pro-Soviet policy. Similarly uncoordinated war booty actions led to an enormous transfer of goods into the Soviet Union: heavy industrial plant, railway rolling stock, supplies of produce and livestock, and stores of raw materials and goods; even private consumer goods and art treasures were taken into the Soviet Union, in order to assist with the most elementary needs of reconstruction. Some 2,000 million dollars' worth of goods was transported out of Romania alone in August/September 1944, industrial plant worth 500 million dollars out of the eastern territories of Germany up to July 1945, and from Czechoslovakia goods and capital to a value of 390 million gold dollars. Of more long-lasting significance, however, were the considerable reparations that the former enemy states, Romania, Hungary and Bulgaria, had to pay to their East European neighbours and above all to the Soviet Union (37.5 per cent of the Romanian and 26.4 per cent of the Hungarian state budgets respectively of 1946/7), as well as the setting-up of mixed-nationality concerns under Soviet management, working towards the alignment of former national industrial production and commercial policy according to the needs of Soviet reconstruction. Soviet economic policy in the sphere of influence of the Red Army showed every sign of a reorientation from Western markets to the Soviet market and the exploitation of Eastern Europe in the interests of a swift recovery from the severe setbacks the industrial process in the Soviet Union had suffered during the war.[6]

The factor that had the greatest direct repercussions on future Soviet–US relations was the Soviet policy of *faits accomplis* with regard to the Polish question. Even during the Yalta conference, Bierut, the Polish premier, had proclaimed the taking of Silesia and East Prussia under Polish administration. Moreover, although the Western Allies had deliberately left open the question of the western shifting of Poland across the Oder frontier to the Oder–Neisse boundary, on 14 March 1945 four Polish *woiwods* were set up in the hitherto eastern territories of Germany up to the Oder–Neisse line. The German population, where it had not already fled, was largely resettled there. Meanwhile in Moscow, the commission for the reorganisation of the Polish government, consisting of the Foreign Minister, Molotov, and the British and US ambassadors, split up in disagreement over the issue of which Polish representatives should be invited to negotiations on the reshuffling of the government, and whether there should at first be an initial round of talks with the 'Lublin' Poles alone. After these discussions reached a deadlock at the end of March, the Soviet government concluded a friendship treaty on 21 April with the former provisional Polish government alone, which legitimated the shift of territory and power on the basis of international law. As a mark of protest, the Western powers refused the unreshuffled government entry to the founding conference of the United Nations, which began on 25 April in San Francisco.[7]

The Soviet Union in a new light

The methods used to secure Soviet interests in the sphere of influence of the Red Army led in the spring of 1945 to a turnabout in the American attitude towards the Soviet Union, which took effect at four levels simultaneously.

First, many Americans, from simple soldiers to the Secretary of State, all of whom had since come into direct contact with Soviet citizens for the first time, experienced the profound qualitative difference of Soviet civilisation. They now reinterpreted it, as the disappointed diplomats of the 'Riga School' had already done in the inter-war years, as evidence of the dominance of non-European traditions and ways of life in the Soviet Union. Thus Ambassador Harriman spoke in April 1945 of how the USA stood before a 'barbarian invasion of Europe' and how Hitler's greatest crime had been 'in opening the gates of Eastern Europe to Asia'. Stimson, the Secretary of War, found the Soviet booty actions 'rather oriental'; General George S. Patton reported that Soviet officers gave the impression of being 'recently civilised Mongolian bandits', whilst Kennan, now Harriman's representative in Moscow, found during a flight over East Prussia that 'they had swept the native population clean in a manner that had no parallel since the days of the Asiatic hordes'.[8]

Secondly, these emotional impressions, and to an even greater extent the Soviet policy of *faits accomplis*, strengthened the position of the 'hardliners' among the American public and in the Republican factions in Congress, who had already criticised Roosevelt's policy of *rapprochement* in 1944. Disappointed in their hopes for Yalta, they blamed the Soviet leadership for massive infraction of the provisions made at Yalta, and demanded the honouring of these pledges as they interpreted them. Senator Vandenberg, whom Roosevelt had invited to take part in the UN founding conference in order to secure US entry into the new world organisation from the point of view of domestic politics, used the conference in San Francisco as a forum for the denunciation of Soviet infringement of the Atlantic Charter. 'I don't know whether this is Frisco or Munich,' he wrote in his diary. 'We must "stand by our guns" ..., This is the point ... to win and end this appeasement of the Reds now before it is too late.'[9] How the 'American Dream' was to be realised, he was obviously not able to say. The founding conference of the United Nations thus exhausted itself in vigorous polemic between the US and Soviet delegations. This polemic was well suited to the need of large sections of the American public for a demonstration of its own strength. In public opinion in the rest of the world, however, it aroused substantial anxiety about the possibility of the collapse of the war coalition.

Thirdly, US diplomats now also insisted on a clarification of the Yalta agreements in the sense of the interpretation predominating among the American public. The critics of the 'Riga School', who had accused Roosevelt of insufficient power-political decisiveness over the Soviet Union, now had a hearing; diplomats of Hull's ilk, who had hoped that Soviet security interests would be satisfied by the creation of a world peace organisation, now saw their hopes disappointed. They were not prepared, however, to relinquish their ideals concerning Eastern Europe. Roosevelt for his part was unable to find his way back from the 'internal' to the 'external' foreign policy. The Soviet urge towards expansion was now as overestimated as the exigencies of Soviet security interests had previously been underestimated: one irrational perspective had replaced the other. 'Russian plans for establishing satellite states,' Ambassador Harriman, the most important spokesman of this diplomatic turnabout, declared in April 1945 in front of State Department officials, 'are a threat to the world and to us. The Soviet Union, once it had control of bordering areas, would attempt to penetrate the next adjacent countries.' Soviet demands to set up military bases in the Dardanelle Straits in Turkey and for a protectorate over former Italian Libya (in fact a preventive attempt to contain Anglo-Saxon capitalism), as well as Yugoslav claims to Trieste, were all taken as proof of the correctness of this 'domino theory'. At the end of May, Joseph C. Grew, the Under-Secretary of State, noted that the result of the Second World War had been 'the transfer of totalitarian dictatorship and power from Germany and Japan to Soviet Russia, which will constitute in future as grave a danger to us as did the Axis'. What had happened in Eastern Europe represented 'the future world pattern' which the Soviet Union wanted to bring about, step by step, first in Europe, then in the Near East and finally in the Far East. A war with the Soviet Union 'is as certain as anything in this world can be certain'. Even Stimson, the Secretary of War, otherwise known for very cautious and sober analyses, warned that the economic chaos in Western and Central Europe could lead to 'political revolution and Communistic infiltration'. Analyses of this type increased in the spring and summer of 1945 within the US Administration, and the conclusions always ran in the same direction: insistence on the 'fulfilment' of the Yalta agreements, no new 'concessions', and the stabilisation of those regions not occupied by the Red Army.[10]

Fourthly, the difficult balance between the 'internal' and the 'external' foreign policies was all the less successfully maintained because President Roosevelt died on 12 April 1945, during this crisis in Soviet–American relations. His successor, Harry S. Truman, who had only become Vice-President in November 1944 as a compromise candidate between Wallace and Byrnes, and who by his own admission knew nothing about foreign policy, initially had some trouble finding his way among the contradictions of Roosevelt's policies. Although a thoroughly convinced Wilsonian, Truman nevertheless decided very quickly on a policy of 'realistic' firmness towards the Soviet Union. In order to gain authority as President, he showed a great willingness to make decisions, but remained dependent for those decisions on the advice of those around him. Since those among the Administration who were in favour of a change of course in foreign policy had by now grown in both numbers and influence, he found himself further and further along the path towards confrontation, in spite of his stated intention to continue Roosevelt's policy unchanged. 'The Soviet Union needed us more than we needed them', he declared one week after entering office to a surprised and relieved Harriman. Seen from this point of view, there was good reason to suppose that if not 100 per cent, then 85 per cent of American ideas on the East European question could be put into effect.[11]

He immediately made his decision on the carrying out of the American interpretation of the Yalta agreements clear to Molotov, as the latter visited him on 23 April on his way to the conference in San Francisco. Molotov sought in vain to explain to him that the Soviet government was adhering correctly to what had actually been agreed; Truman cut him short and pronounced in drastic American style that the 'one-way street' in Soviet–American relations would have to come to an end. Molotov was speechless: 'I have never been talked to like that in my life,' was all that passed his lips, to which Truman countered laconically that he should stick to his agreements in future, and then no one would speak to him like that.[12] In fact Roosevelt would not have said anything very different on the matter, but the form of this first meeting with the new President convinced the Soviet government that Truman had broken with the (from the Soviet viewpoint, still inadequate) co-operation policy of Roosevelt, and that a Western 'roll back', an encroachment of the USA into the Eastern European security zone, now definitely threatened.

Co-operation and coercive measures

In reality, the turnabout in the American attitude towards the Soviet Union by no means signified a definite change in American Soviet policy. Although Truman and his political mentor Byrnes, whom he now appointed as Secretary of State for Foreign Affairs, were determined to arrest the Sovietisation process in Eastern Europe, and at least to some extent reverse it, American foreign policy was at first nevertheless still determined by other factors. There were still some influential Roosevelt supporters, however, who attached a high intrinsic value to peaceful co-operation with the Soviet Union. Truman himself still hoped, with sufficient firmness, to be able to reach some arrangement with the Soviet leadership, but he was also occasionally dogged by doubts as to whether an unyielding attitude was really in harmony with Roosevelt's approach. All resources were still necessary for the overthrow of Japan, and it was still hoped that there would be Soviet support against the Japanese. Furthermore, in the complex machinery of the US Administration the traditions of non-interference in the political developments of Europe and a fear of peacetime military engagement still lived on. Above all, however, the American public was still not ready to make appreciable sacrifices for the leading world role now under consideration: even the President was powerless in the face of increasingly vociferous demands, as the war drew to an end, for the speedy demobilisation of conscripts ('Bring the boys home').

Churchill, in terms of *his* conception of containment policy, found as little of an ally in Truman as he had found in Roosevelt. Shortly before Roosevelt's death, the British premier had urged that British and American troops should press ahead of the Russians towards Berlin in their forward march into Central

Europe. The US Commander-in-Chief in Europe, General Eisenhower, had argued against this, however, saying that such a strategy would spin out the war negotiations unnecessarily; his argument prevailed. Churchill now requested Truman to let his troops remain at the Elbe and not retreat at once to the boundary of the American occupation zone in Germany, as had been agreed at the EAC. In addition, they should advance towards Vienna and Prague. Eisenhower countered this with the argument he had used previously, and Truman decided that the agreements on the zones of occupation should be adhered to. When British Commander-in-Chief Field Marshal Montgomery accepted on 4 May the partial capitulation of the Doenitz government for the Western Front only, Eisenhower forced total capitulation on 7 May. Churchill at first held firm to the Doenitz government, not without the idea at the back of his mind that, in the case of a Soviet advance on the North Sea, German troops could be used against the Soviet army; however, under considerable American pressure, he was obliged to abandon it on 23 May.[13] Even among the British public, Churchill was unable to find the necessary support for such an anti-Soviet pawnbroking policy. This became clear when the Labour Party surprisingly won the general election of 25 July, having fought the election with the argument that a 'socialist' government had a better chance of achieving *rapprochement* with the Soviet Union than the Conservative war prime minister.

The contradiction between the declared intention of organising Eastern Europe according to liberal principles and the lack of opportunity to carry out this intention led American diplomacy in the first instance to a contradictory policy of threatening *and* wooing, of denial *and* concession. The Truman Administration thus refused to recognise the Soviet interpretation of the Yalta agreements, but at the same time also refused to take specific steps towards a forceful implementation of its own ideas. In order to break the deadlock which had been reached in bilateral negotiations, Truman sent Roosevelt's close friend Harry Hopkins to Moscow at the end of May. The latter succeeded in reconjuring the spirit of co-operation and, much to Churchill's displeasure, began to negotiate a preliminary compromise solution for Poland. Stalin and Hopkins agreed on the names of four representatives of the London exile group and the internal Resistance, among them former premier Mikolajczyk, who were invited to negotiate a new cabinet formula with representatives of the

'Lublin' government. This Polish committee in fact did then agree at the end of June on an extension of the existing government by four representatives of the Peasants' Party and one socialist, and the Truman government then bestowed diplomatic recognition of this extended government at once.[14] Free elections in Poland were thus clearly as little guaranteed as a democratic orientation in the rest of the Eastern European countries. Truman's diplomats continued to exercise 'diplomatic pressure' without becoming materially involved in the East European countries.[15]

The way seemed to be paved for an escape route for American self-confidence out of this scarcely tolerable situation in the deliberate use of American strength against the Soviet Union — that is, both its economic superiority, as Harriman had been urging since autumn 1944, combined with the Soviet need for credit, and, since the detonation of the first atomic bomb on 16 July 1945, the American monopoly of atomic weapons, which now entered into the discussion for the first time. Byrnes, who regarded himself as heir to Roosevelt, and who from the middle of 1945 manoeuvred as high-handedly as the latter round the State Department with regard to US foreign policy, sought with Truman's support to make use of this double superiority of the USA, in order to coerce a revision of the *faits accomplis* that had been brought about in Eastern Europe.

Even before Byrnes took office, Truman had twice attempted to use the economic superiority of the USA as a lever. On the advice of Harriman, who wanted to force a turn in the Poland negotiations in Moscow, and simultaneously, under pressure from Congress, which had voted on 17 March not to agree to any as yet unpaid lend–lease supplies for the reconstruction of Allied countries, he had stopped all supplies to the Soviet Union that were not intended for the war against Japan. Truman had not anticipated that this resolution would be put into effect with such extreme abruptness or so extensively: even cargo ships already at sea were summoned back. After Soviet protests, however, some individual deliveries were made belatedly. In principle, however, the resolution to make the Soviet government feel its dependence on American supplies was upheld. Truman had similarly agreed to a revision of the guidelines for American reparation policy with regard to Germany: deductions from current production should be kept as low as possible; exports from production should be used in the first instance to pay for imported goods from the

West, whilst only what remained over and above that should be at the disposal of the Soviet Union as reparation payments. The most important motive behind this Congressional decision had been the determination not to permit German reparations to be paid for once again — as they had been after the First World War — by the American taxpayer. The State Department and former President Herbert Hoover had moreover stressed to Truman the negative effects of high reparation obligations for the recovery of a healthy German market. Out of a contrasting fear that reparation demands might serve as a pretext for the retention of German industrial potential, the Morgenthau group had also argued in favour of a low level of reparations. Finally, a restrictive attitude in reparation policy was now intended to make the Soviet leadership more compliant. The fact, however, that at Yalta reparations envisaged by the Soviet leadership at a total value of 20,000 million dollars had been accepted as the basis of negotiations was now virtually forgotten.[16]

Byrnes endorsed both these decisions, adhering furthermore to the dilatory treatment of the Soviet request for credit of January 1945. Although Congress passed a law at the end of July permitting the Export-Import Bank to grant credit to a level of 1,000 million dollars (instead of the 6,000 million dollars asked for by the Soviet government), when the Soviet leadership thereupon suggested a first loan at precisely this level on 28 August, Byrnes provisionally forestalled all negotiations with indications of the political concessions required from the Soviet side in return, and allowed the request to lose itself in the convolutions of US bureaucracy.[17] What in the meantime was expected in the way of concessions is shown in the report of a delegation of Congressmen under the chairmanship of William M. Colmer, which visited the Soviet Union in September 1945. On their return, the Congressmen recommended granting extensive credit, both to the Soviet Union and to the East European countries, on the condition that the Moscow government would guarantee not only American property and the propagation of American films, books and magazines, but also that it would ensure everywhere (even in the Soviet Union!) religious freedom, freedom of the press, and free elections, and that it would of course observe the Yalta agreements.[18] Byrnes himself did not voice his own ideas about what should be expected from the Soviet government in return for such credit. Although he certainly did not share the starry-eyed innocence of the Colmer delegation, he was, as the following example indicates, increasingly limited in his room for manoeuvre, even within the domestic sphere.

Byrnes sought with the same dilatory tactics to implement his ideas by using the American monopoly of atomic weapons. Although he never actually threatened to use the atomic bomb against the Soviet Union (an idea which was unthinkable, even in internal politics), he nevertheless did not take up the suggestion of Stimson, the Secretary of War, to offer the Soviet Union a nuclear partnership in return for compliance with the disputed East European question. Instead, he shelved all initiatives towards the internationalisation of the new weapon and demonstrated the atomic superiority of the USA — in the hope that the Soviet leadership would be impressed by this demonstration and be more willing to co-operate with American wishes regarding Eastern Europe. In accord with Byrnes, Truman postponed the beginning of the next conference of the 'Big Three' in Potsdam, which had been requested by Churchill and Stalin, until 16 July, in order to move it closer to the date of the first atomic test detonation. After news of the successful attempt in New Mexico had reached the President in Potsdam on 21 July, he informed Stalin that the USA possessed 'a new weapon of awful destructive power'. From then onwards, as Stimson commented, Byrnes conducted the negotiations 'having the presence of the bomb in his pocket, so to speak, as a great weapon to get through the thing', both in Potsdam and at the following first meeting of the Allied Foreign Ministers' Council, which began in London on 11 September. He also included in his calculations the demonstrative effect of the dropping of the atomic bomb on Hiroshima and Nagasaki, with the intention that it should help finally to resolve the issues under dispute since March in favour of the American view (although the dropping had not been made for this purpose, but clearly rather that of foreshortening the war against Japan and keeping the Soviet share in the victory over Japan as minimal as possible).[19]

The collapse of American pressure politics

In fact, however, both the USA's monopoly of atomic weapons and its economic superiority proved to be useless weapons. The Soviet government was clearly little impressed by the atomic bomb, and did not even insist on its credit requests; indeed, it had good reason for the former reaction: the threat of the atomic bomb was not credible, because it could only be used *in toto* and not progressively. The atomic bomb could deter potential enemies from attacking the USA, but it was entirely unthinkable that it could be used by the American government in order to implement aims that were as peripheral to American security interests as free elections in Romania. The threat of refusing credit was real, but similarly lacking credibility: first, because the USA had an equal economic interest in the credit transaction, and second, because the Soviet government overestimated the direct political weight of this economic interest in the American decision-making process. For the Soviet leadership, the securing of its own buffer zone was of greater importance than economic aid from the USA. If necessary, it could mobilise the resources of Eastern and Central Europe in order to support Soviet reconstruction.

Byrnes's dilatory tactics, therefore, with the obstruction of credit requests, far from leading to greater compliance on the Soviet side, only increased the latter's interest in the economic exploitation of the Eastern European countries and in massive reparations from Germany. The demonstration of the atomic weapon monopoly furthered the concentration of all Soviet resources more than ever on the expansion of its own security sphere (now including pushing through atomic weapon plans of its own). American interference in the relations of Eastern Europe, which in spite of all appearances was finally recognised by the Western powers as a Soviet sphere of influence only in Yalta at the latest, merely increased the number of guarantees that seemed necessary to secure the pro-Soviet orientation of the region.

Since American diplomacy did not want to admit the 'importance of omnipotence',[20] these contradictions conflicted with one another more forcefully than ever at the conferences after the end of the war. These contradictions could be solved by means of a bilateral demarcation of interests, as was indeed attempted on numerous occasions, after atomic and dollar diplomacy had been shown to be useless weapons, and the polemic on both sides had reached a stalemate. Byrnes thus returned to Roosevelt's 'four-policemen' policy, with all its former dilemma: the necessity of having to secure actual political compromises with idealistic domestic rhetoric.

Even at Potsdam (16 July–2 August, 1945), the contradictions between American and Soviet concepts of post-war planning had such a forceful effect on the course of the conference that the delegates were on the brink of open crisis on more than one occasion. A rift discernible even from the outside could only be avoided after two weeks of extensive, but unproductive negotiation by Byrnes putting together a provisional compromise package: with the proviso of a conclusive settlement in the future peace treaty with Germany, the Western powers recognised Polish administration of the former eastern territories of Germany as far as the Oder–Neisse line. In return for this, the Soviet leadership was provisionally to reduce its reparation demands with regard to Germany. Every occupying power was initially permitted to draw reparation payments only from its own zone of occupation. In addition, the USSR and Poland were to receive 15 per cent of 'superfluous' industrial goods from the Western zones, in return for equivalent foodstuffs and raw material supplies from the East, and likewise a further 10 per cent without anything in return. (Prior to this Stalin had attempted in vain to obtain the agreement of the representatives of the Polish government at Potsdam to relinquish the Neisse boundary line in order to be able to negotiate more reparation payments from the Western zones.) In this way these decisions led to a stabilisation of the *status quo*, each side only making concessions where it had hardly any potential influence at its disposal anyway. Soviet demands for the internationalisation of Ruhr industry, access to the Dardanelle Straits and for a mandate over Libya went unfulfilled, as did US demands for the internationalisation of the great European waterways (in particular the Danube). Western efforts towards a greater right of consultation in the East European countries were similarly blocked by the Soviet delegation, with the latter's referral to the complete dominance of Western influence in Italy and Greece. On the issue of Germany, both sides expressed their interest in the continued existence of an undivided nation; they decided to treat Germany economically as a single unit and to hand over responsibility for the administration of Germany to a Four-Power Allied Council consisting of the Commanders-in-Chief of the occupation fighting forces. They did this, however, out of differing motives: the USA for the sake of the future integration of Germany into the multilateral system of free trade, and the Soviet Union precisely to prevent such an integration into a 'One World' ruled by the USA. The essential conflict of the

German question was thus only postponed, the 'provisional' agreements on the reparation question operating along the lines of a division of spheres of influence.[21]

This Potsdam compromise was only acceptable within the USA's internal political scene because the really crucial issues had yet again been left open. Stalin, Truman and the new British premier, Attlee, subsequently agreed, in pursuit of a proposal from Byrnes, to have all outstanding questions cleared up by an Allied Council of Foreign Ministers, in which, in addition to the three great powers, France and China should also take part. The peace treaty with Italy was to be discussed first, then the agreements on the 'recognised democratic governments' of Romania, Bulgaria and Hungary (a classic example of the obscuring of the real controversial points!), and finally the peace treaty with Germany. The final protocol of the Potsdam conference was only published in abbreviated form, which left unmentioned the essential areas of dispute. Byrnes made it quite clear publicly that these could be resolved in accordance with the American 'One World' dream at the forthcoming first Council of Foreign Ministers in London. With the atomic and economic superiority of the USA uppermost in his mind, he himself even still believed this.

In London (11 September–2 October 1945), it became clear, however, that the Eastern European question at least could not be resolved along American lines. Molotov presented written suggestions for peace treaties with Romania, Bulgaria and Hungary that perpetuated the *status quo*, that is, ceding no new possibilities for influence in this region to the USA. Byrnes for his part insisted on the 'Polish formula', that is, the reshuffling of the governments in question on a broad democratic basis, and the earliest possible organisation of free elections as a precondition for peace treaties. Both sides stubbornly clung to their viewpoints during endless meetings — until Molotov, in order to escape threatening isolation, demanded that the French and Chinese foreign ministers be excluded from the East European negotiations, referring to the relevant Potsdam agreements to this effect. (In fact, it had only been decided at Potsdam that the latter two countries should not have a vote.) The conference thus reached deadlock. Byrnes began to realise the limited extent to which American superiority was convertible into political coin, and after a further week of mental struggle finally decided to agree to compromises on the East European question, compromises which left Soviet security interests largely untouched, and which were thus bound to destroy the American dream.

At the last moment, however, he once again shrank from making these compromises a reality. John Foster Dulles, a leading Republican member of the US negotiating delegation, made it clear to him in a private conversation that he and the Republican public would oppose compromises over the East European question as a dangerous appeasement policy: if Byrnes made a settlement with the Soviet leadership without substantial progress in relation to the right to self-determination, then Dulles would attack him publicly as an appeaser. Byrnes bowed to this threat and, since a settlement on Dulles's terms could not be reached, he broke off the conference: not even a joint final protocol was signed.[22] The contradictions had now become publicly visible. The American public was nevertheless pleased with the conduct of its Secretary of State, and President Truman emphasised in a speech the steadfastness to principle of American foreign policy, simultaneously announcing that the United States would not for the time being share the atomic secret, but would preserve it as a 'sacred trust' for the peace of the world.[23]

Despite this, Byrnes was extremely irritated about Soviet conduct, and full of doubts as to the right foreign policy course. Like Roosevelt before him, he sought possibilities for satisfying to an equal degree both American 'One World' concepts and the security concepts of the Soviet leadership. In a speech on 31 October, he indicated to the Soviet government his sympathy 'with ... the effort of the Soviet Union to draw into closer and more friendly association with her Central and Eastern European neighbors', and his full recognition 'of her special security interests in those countries'. At the same time, unaware of the contradiction, he assured his own public of his adherence to the principle of the 'world system', and his rejection of a 'world divided into exclusive spheres of influence'.[24] In order to obtain a more realistic picture of the situation in the East European countries than the constantly anti-Communist-coloured reports of his diplomatic personnel permitted (as he guessed, not without some justification), he sent Mark Ethridge, a noted liberal journalist, known for being in favour of a US–Soviet reconciliation, on an extensive information trip round Eastern Europe. At the same time, he took the initiative for a further meeting of foreign ministers, this time, as Molotov had wanted, without the participation of the French and the Chinese.

At Moscow, where the three foreign ministers met from 16 to

26 December 1945, it became clear that with a mutual respect of security interests compromises were in fact possible, although, as in Potsdam, not compromises establishing common policy, but in fact amounting to a division of the world into spheres of influence. The Soviet government agreed to ensure the appointment of two non-Communist ministers in the governments of Romania and Bulgaria respectively. In return, Byrnes agreed to participate in the speedy preparation of peace treaties with the former allies of Germany. The Soviet government relinquished effective participation in the control of Japan, and permitted the USA to allow its troops to carry out a complete disarming of the Japanese in China. In return for this, Byrnes invited Molotov to take part in a US–Anglo-Canadian initiative for the establishment of a UN control system for atomic weapons. Harmony was even achieved in the attempt to agree on a treaty for the unification of Korea, which was divided into an American and a Soviet zone of occupation. Only the question of the withdrawal of Soviet troops from Iran remained controversial. Byrnes returned from the talks satisfied, and announced to the nation in a radio address on 30 December that the Moscow negotiations had brought the USA nearer to a peace based on 'justice and wisdom'.[25]

Unlike Roosevelt, however, Byrnes did not succeed in convincing the American public of the conformity of the agreements reached by him with the principles of the Atlantic Charter. Moscow was not Yalta, and hardly could be, after the disappointment of the previous spring. The Republicans and the 'realistic' experts of the State Department had followed Byrnes's arbitrary policies with increasing bitterness, and now saw their worst fears confirmed in the results of the Moscow conference. Byrnes, they maintained, *was* an appeaser: he had made too many concessions to the USSR and had not recognised the Soviet Union's urge for world-wide expansion. A broad front was organised against Byrnes: in the State Department, where, as Elbridge Durbrow reports, 'the Russians' "real intentions became more than clear to all who followed developments closely"'; in Congress, whose members were now bombarded with constant criticism of Byrnes by Vandenberg and Dulles; and among public opinion, where the percentage of people who believed in the possibility of long-term co-operation with the Soviet Union fell from 54 per cent in September 1945 to 34 per cent in February 1946.[26]

It was decisive for future US policy towards the Soviet Union that Truman now allied himself with this anti-Byrnes movement.

Since November 1945 the President had grown weary of the quasi-patronage of his political mentor, had been angered during the Moscow conference by lack of information from his Secretary of State, and now, after Moscow, he received Ethridge's report. In contrast with what Byrnes had expected, this report, written after Ethridge's information trip round Eastern Europe, depicted the situation there in the worst possible light and warned against conceding a demarcated Soviet sphere of influence. Such a concession, he argued, was bound to lead to ever-greater extensions of the Soviet sphere of influence in the future. All this led Truman to the decision to bring about a change of course in foreign policy. 'I do not think', he noted down for a serious 'talk' with Byrnes on 5 January 1946, 'we should play compromise any longer. We should refuse to recognize Rumania and Bulgaria until they comply with our requirements; we should let our position on Iran be known in no uncertain terms and we should continue to insist on the internationalization of the Kiel Canal, the Rhine–Danube waterway and the Black Sea Straits and we should maintain complete control of Japan and the Pacific. ... *I'm tired of babying the Soviets.*'[27]

Byrnes accepted this disavowal of his Moscow policy.[28] From now on there were to be no more compromises and no efforts towards co-operation with the Soviet Union for the securing of world peace; instead, there was to be a policy of 'firmness' based on the axiom of potential Soviet world-wide expansion. Byrnes himself nevertheless still hoped for an arrangement with the Soviet Union, but no longer had any room for negotiating manoeuvres. He thus decided in April 1946 to resign from office as soon as the peace treaty procedure negotiated in Moscow had been concluded. Meanwhile he conducted foreign policy along Truman's lines: concessions were in future to come only from the Soviet side. The turnabout in assessment of the Soviet Union had thus now become a turnabout in American policy towards the Soviet Union.[29] Roosevelt's 'Grand Design' now finally had to give way to the 'policy of containment'.[30]

Interim results: 1945

In retrospect, the events of 1945 reveal several crucial factors for the emergence of the Cold War. First, the turnabout of 1945 was in US, not in Soviet policy. Whereas the US government sought to implement its own interests, and expected solutions to conflicts only in the form of concessions from the Soviet side, the Soviet government admitted the priority of consolidating its hegemonic region, but otherwise continued until the autumn of 1947 to make efforts towards bringing about a co-operative relationship with the USA.

Secondly, the turnabout in American policy was undoubtedly triggered by Soviet policy towards Eastern Europe, but it had been made inevitable in the first instance by the illusions the American public had fostered about the exigencies of the Soviet system's security policy. These illusions, however, were already deeply rooted in American policy, and had virtually constituted a precondition for US participation in the Second World War. In this way, the profound structural contradiction between the two world powers and their policies manifested itself in the conflict over Eastern Europe. Against the interest of the expanding capitalism of the USA in world-wide free trade and world-wide implementation of liberal principles stood the interest of the Soviet mobilisation dictatorship in creating a shield against these principles and against the economic forward march of the USA.

Thirdly, this contradiction was bound to lead to a rift, but it was by no means inevitable in the beginning that it would lead to a division of the world into two power blocs in absolute enmity with each other, each feeling threatened by the other.[31] Naturally, the American economic system was working towards an ever-greater orientation of the world economy towards American needs, but the economic interests of the Soviet Union and the USA were at first to a large extent complementary, so that it was not clear from the outset that co-operation gains would work unilaterally in favour of the USA. The expanding capitalism of the USA was all the less unequivocally imperialistic in view of the fact that American leading circles were at first neither willing nor able to undertake long-term political involvement in Europe. Even co-operation with the European Left and the toleration of socialist processes of transformation were by no means ruled out in the beginning.[32] Similarly, although the Soviet government and the Communist parties of other countries adhered to their revolutionary self-image and claims, pragmatism and flexibility nevertheless dominated Soviet methods for securing its interests in Eastern Europe. An extension of the Soviet sphere of influence beyond the region controlled by the Red Army was thus completely out of the question for practical purposes, so that

Soviet and Communist policy was in this regard anything but a threat.[33]

Finally, in view of its structural superiority, the USA had greater opportunities for influencing the actual form of future Soviet–American relations. It lay in its power to reduce the asymmetry existing in the security situation of the two powers, for example by recognising Soviet security interests in Eastern Europe more clearly, by effecting real international atomic-weapon control or by granting aid in accordance with the economic interests of both sides.[34] The US government, however, by failing to recognise the Soviet security sphere, and by attempting, even if in vain, to use its own atomic and economic superiority to revise the situation that had been created in Eastern Europe, in fact set in motion in 1945 a mechanism of mutual false interpretation, and thus an escalation of conflict. American decision-makers mistook the security policy of the Soviet Union as evidence of fundamentally unlimited Soviet expansionism, and reacted by refusing all further co-operation. The Soviet leadership, in turn, mistook this refusal to co-operate as evidence of the necessarily aggressive character of expanding US capitalism, and reacted with a further entrenchment of its security policy. This vicious circle was not broken again in the years after 1945 and thus rendered the formation of power blocs increasingly inevitable.

Notes

1. Text of the Yalta communiqué in *Foreign Relations of the United States*, diplomatic papers (hereafter cited as FRUS) Yalta, pp. 971ff.; Molotov's speech at a voters' meeting in Moscow, 6 February 1946 in Vyacheslav M. Molotov, *Fragen der Außenpolitik, Reden und Erklärungen* (Moscow, 1949), pp. 26–38; Churchill's speech of 5 March 1946 in Fulton in *Vital speeches of the day*, vol. 12, 15 March 1946, pp. 329–32.

2. Thus far we can certainly agree with the conclusions of William D. McCagg, *Stalin embattled, 1943–1948* (Detroit, 1978), pp. 147–260. His attempt, however, to explain Soviet foreign policy in terms of the ascertained international Soviet shifts of power *alone* — that is, as a means used by Stalin to assert himself between the party, the army and the state apparatus — is not convincing. Basing his argument on methodologically unreliable conclusions short-circuiting from long-term internal political trends to particular foreign policy actions, he entirely neglects the specific foreign policy interests of the Soviet state, and thus frequently falls into misleading conclusions regarding Soviet motives.

3. Milovan Djilas, *Gespräche mit Stalin*, (Frankfurt, 1962), p. 146. 'Traditional' authors who see in this quotation evidence of a preconceived

Sovietisation concept overlook the date and motive of the statement; it came *after* Soviet efforts gaining guarantees from the Western powers had failed, and was made before a Yugoslav delegation which was pressing for an intensification of revolutionary politics. In fact it represents *one* method of Soviet foreign policy, but not Soviet foreign policy *per se*.

4. Most information on the 'Berne affair' is in Allen Dulles, *The secret surrender*, (New York, 1966); cf. also Gabriel Kolko, *The politics of war* (New York, 1972), p. 379; John L. Gaddis, *The United States and the origins of the Cold War 1941–1947* (2nd edn, New York, 1976), pp. 92–4; Adam B. Ulam, *The Rivals* (2nd edn, London, 1973), pp. 60–2. There is no evidence to support Kolko's thesis that the Soviet government had been denied direct participation in order to prevent a take-over of power by a people's revolutionary movement in northern Italy.

5. Compare the overviews in Hugh Seton-Watson, *Die osteuropäische Revolution* (Munich, 1956); Geir Lundestad, *The American non-policy towards Eastern Europe 1943–1947* (Tromso, New York, 2nd edn, 1978), pp. 435–65; Kolko, *Politics*, pp. 396–410.

6. Compare compilation of the most important data in Jörg K. Hoensch, *Sowjetische Osteuropapolitik 1945–1975* (Kronberg, 1977), pp. 16–19.

7. Compare Lynn Etheridge Davis, *The Cold War begins* (Princeton, NJ, 1974), pp. 202–12; W. Averell Harriman and Elie Abel, *Special envoy to Churchill and Stalin 1941–1946* (New York, 1975), pp. 426–31.

8. FRUS (1945), V, p. 232; *Forrestal diaries* (New York, 1951), p. 79; Henry L. Stimson and McGeorge Bundy, *On active service in peace and war* (New York, 1948), p. 594; Ladislas Farago, *Patton. Ordeal and triumph* (London, 1963), p. 513; George F. Kennan, *Memoirs* p. 269.

9. Arthur Vandenberg, Jr (ed), *The private papers of Senator Vandenberg* (Boston, 1972), pp. 176–80; compare Kolko, *Politics*, pp. 467–77; Daniel Yergin, *Shattered peace* (Boston, 1977), p. 98f.; on the conference of San Francisco in general, see also Herbert Feis, *Churchill, Roosevelt, Stalin* (Princeton, NJ, 1957), pp. 550–60.

10. Harriman; FRUS (1945), V, pp. 841, 843; Grew memorandum of 19 May 1945, in extracts in Joseph C. Grew, *Turbulent era* (Boston, 1952), pp. 1445f.; Stimson, diary entries of 19 April and 16 May 1945, quoted in Yergin, *Shattered peace*, p. 95 and chs. 4 and 5 for numerous similar statements. For similar thoughts in the War Department, see Melvyn P. Leffler, 'The American conception of national security and the beginnings of the Cold War, 1945–48', *American Historical Review*, 89 (1984), pp. 346–81.

11. FRUS (1945), V, pp. 232f.

12. Harry S. Truman, *Memoirs, years of decisions* (Garden City, NY, 1955), pp. 79–82; FRUS (1945), V, pp. 256–8.

13. Stephen E. Ambrose, *Eisenhower and Berlin 1945*, (New York, 1967), pp. 54ff.; Kolko, *Politics*, pp. 382–8, 411–14; Gaddis, *The United States and the origins*, pp. 206–11; Arthur Smith, *Churchills deutsche Armee. Die Anfänge des Kalten Krieges 1943–1947* (Bergisch-Gladbach, 1978).

14. Gaddis, *The United States and the origins*, pp. 231–6; and Davis, *The Cold War begins*, pp. 234–41.

15. As Davis shows in detail (*The Cold War begins*, pp. 241–87 and

335–68). Davis is mistaken, however, in seeing in this policy the expression of a lack of American interest in Eastern Europe. In fact the realisation of liberal principles in Eastern Europe had by then become the central component of foreign policy thinking in the USA; the lack was in the means with which to put this aim into effect. A reliable overview of Truman's policy until the Potsdam conference is also offered by Lisle A. Rose, *After Yalta* (New York, 1973), pp. 32–51.

16. Gaddis, *The United States and the origins*, pp. 196f., 215–24; George C. Herring, *Aid to Russia, 1914–1946* (New York, 1973), pp. 171–230; Yergin, *Shattered peace*, pp. 93–8; John H. Backer, *The decision to divide Germany* (Durham, 1978), pp. 41–5. Herring's detailed account leads to the thesis of bureaucratic chaos in US economic policy towards the Soviet Union, in the process of which the fact is lost that the manifold internal political pressure on the Administration was exerted not least out of foreign policy motives. It was a question of remaining 'tough' towards the Soviet Union in order to compel its compliance with the Yalta agreement.

17. Herring, *Aid to Russia*, pp. 248–56.

18. Gaddis, *The United States and the origins*, pp. 258–60.

19. This is the main argument against the presentation in Gar Alperowitz, *Atomic diplomacy* (New York, 1965); even less tenable is Alperowitz's thesis that the Truman government had openly threatened use of the bomb. Cf. concurring views in Gaddis, *The United States and the origins*, pp. 247–52; Martin J. Sherwin, *A world destroyed* (New York, 1975), ch. 7, and also 'The atomic bomb and the origins of the Cold War: US atomic energy policy and diplomacy 1941–1945', *American Historical Review*, 78 (1973), pp. 945–68; Lundestad, *The American non-policy*, pp. 359–64; Barton J. Bernstein, 'Roosevelt, Truman and the atomic bomb, 1941–1945; a reinterpretation', *Political Science Quarterly*, 15 (1975), pp. 23–69; Thomas Hammond, 'Did the United States use atomic diplomacy?' in Peter Potichnyi and Jane Shapiro (eds), *From the Cold War to détente* (New York, 1976), pp. 26–56. Rose, *After Yalta*, pp. 52–85, underestimates the role of the bomb in Byrnes's calculations for Potsdam. Stimson, diary entry of 4 September 1945, quoted after Lundestad, *The American non-policy*, p. 363.

20. Gaddis, *The United States and the origins*, p. 244. The experiences that Byrnes had to go through with his atomic and credit diplomacy are evidence of the unsubstantiated nature of Ulam's critique (*Rivals*, p. 52 and elsewhere) as well as of that of Vojtěch Mastný (*Russian's road to the Cold War* (New York, 1979), pp. 310f and elsewhere) that the USA was unaware of its strength by the end of the war and would not have used it.

21. Cf. William H. McNeill, *America, Britain and Russia* (London, 1953), pp. 615–30; Boris Meissner, *Russland, die Westmächte und Deutschland* (Hamburg, 2nd edn, 1954), pp. 60–76; Herbert Feis, *Zwischen Krieg und Frieden. Das Potsdamer Abkommen* (Frankfurt, Bonn, 1962) and also *From trust to terror* (New York, 1970), pp. 36–55; Ernst Deuerlein, *Deklamation oder Ersatzfrieden? Die Konferenz von Potsdam 1945*, (Stuttgart, 1970); and also *Potsdam 1945, Ende und Anfang* (Cologne, 1970); Kolko, *Politics*, pp. 568–93; Davis, *The Cold War begins*, pp. 288–99; Yergin, *Shattered peace*, pp. 111–19; Mastný, *Russia's road*, pp. 292–303.

22. Accounts of the conference in McNeill, *America, Britain and Russia*, pp. 696–704, and Rose, *After Yalta*, pp. 120–6, depict the break-off too onesidedly as the result of Soviet aggressiveness; Joyce and Gabriel Kolko, *The limits of power* (New York, 1972), pp. 37f, attribute to the American delegation an unbroken policy of strength. For the actual process of Byrnes's disillusionment, compare Gaddis, *The United States and the origins*, pp. 263–75; for Dulles's role, see Yergin, *Shattered peace*, pp. 122–32.

23. *Vital speeches of the day*, vol. XII, 15 November 1945, p. 68.

24. Ibid., p. 69.

25. Text of the address in: *Department of State Bulletin*, XIII, 30 December 1945, pp. 1033–6; on the course of the conference, see McNeill, *America, Britain and Russia*, pp. 704–12; Feis, *From trust to terror*, pp. 53–5; Gaddis, *The United States and the origins*, pp. 276–81; Yergin, *Shattered peace*, pp. 147–51.

26. Durbrow, according to Yergin, *Shattered peace*, p. 152; further evidence in ibid., pp. 152–8; opinion polls according to Gaddis, *The United States and the origins*, p. 289; further evidence up to March 1946 in Gaddis, pp. 281–315, as well as in Rose, *After Yalta*, pp. 151–5, 157–62.

27. Harry S. Truman, *Memoirs. Years of decisions* (Garden City, NY, 1955), pp. 550–2.

28. Although there is some evidence of Truman not having given Byrnes *literally* this tirade (Byrnes disputes this in his memoirs; James F. Byrnes, *All in one lifetime* (New York, 1958), pp. 402f.), the intensity of the Truman–Byrnes disagreements around the turn of 1945/6 cannot be doubted: cf. Gaddis, *The United States and the origins*, pp. 287–9; Yergin, *Shattered peace*, pp. 160f; and Robert L. Messer, *The end of an alliance: James F. Byrnes, Roosevelt, Truman, and the origins of the Cold War* (Chapel Hill, 1982).

29. The inconsistency of the phase in which this new American Soviet policy was put into effect has received varying interpretations, as was only to be expected. Feis, and from the opposing viewpoint Kolko, overemphasise the continuity of 1945 policy; Alperowitz overaccentuates the break during the transition from Roosevelt to Truman.

30. Over one year before the official proclamation of this policy. As will be shown in the following chapter 1946 was, in contrast with the opinion of the 'traditional' authors, in fact already a year of 'containment'.

31. The deterministic interpretation that the Cold War, on the grounds of the difference of the systems involved, was 'as inevitable as any event in history' (Ernst Nolte, *Deutschland und der Kalte Krieg* (Munich, 1974), p. 599), cannot be substantiated. The structural opposition of the two world powers only explains the subsequent emergence of competition and disagreement, not the fact that these disagreements then led to the formation of blocs, the division of the world into two halves, mutual threat to security and a condition of siege in internal politics.

32. Werner Link ('Die amerikanische Aussenpolitik aus revisionistischer Sicht', *Neue Politische Literatur*, 16 (1971), pp. 205–20) rightly criticises in Kolko's work the fact that the basic thesis of 'revisionist' literature, 'which asserted an *inevitable* causal relationship between the

American socio-economic order and its counterrevolutionary policies, is unfortunately never *systematically* analyzed' (p. 209). In fact proof of such a connection cannot be produced; compare for the original openness of American policy to transformation processes in Europe, for example, the State Department memorandum for the conference of Yalta: 'Judging from recent indications the general mood of the people of Europe is to the left and strongly in favor of far-reaching economic and social reforms, but not, however, in favor of the left-wing totalitarian regime to achieve these reforms ... These governments (i.e. of Eastern Europe) *must be sufficiently to the left to satisfy the prevailing mood in Europe* [my italics] and to allay Soviet suspicions. Conversely, they should be sufficiently representative of the center and *petit bourgeois* elements of the population so that they would not be regarded as mere preludes to a communist dictatorship.' FRUS, Yalta, p. 103.

33. The thesis of the fundamentally unlimited nature of Soviet expansionism, central to the 'traditional' position, is equally untenable; cf. chapter 2, note 16 above.

34. Cf. also Werner Link, *Das Konzept der friedlichen Kooperation und der Beginn des Kalten Krieges*, (Düsseldorf, 1971), which shows that such symmetry, which would have formed the precondition for friendly cooperation in 1945, was not only not available, but was not even restored by the USA. See also by the same author, 'Handlungsspielräume der USA in der Entstehung der Ost–West-Gegensatzes 1945–1950', *Ausspolitik und Zeitgeschichte*, B 25 (1983), pp. 19–26.

5

Decisions for Division

The mechanism of mutual misinterpretation on the part of the two world powers, which was set in motion as a result of the turnabout in American policy in 1945, came at a time when most of the problems of the post-war order, in fact precisely the most disputed issues, had not been resolved. Six months after the end of the war, negotiations on peace treaties with the former enemy states had not yet begun, whilst discussion on the German question had hardly been touched on. Meanwhile the countries of Europe were suffering the direct consequences of war: setbacks in production, hunger, inflation and debt. The USA could see its feared crisis of overproduction coming, and the Soviet Union scarcely stood on the threshold of its reconstruction. In terms of power politics, the structure of the international system had seen great changes: the USA had risen to the position of leading world power and had developed the atom bomb; Great Britain had become the junior partner of the USA; the Soviet Union had been able to extend its power, especially in Europe, but a power vacuum had emerged in the centre of the European continent and on its periphery. The implications of these changes for the security of individual nations, however, was not yet clear, and general uncertainty still prevailed as to the conditions on which future security would rest.

All these problems were eclipsed by the fundamental conflict between the USA and the Soviet Union. To be more precise, these problems provided the conflict between the two world powers, at first only a surmised, partial and potential conflict, with the material basis on which it was able to develop to increasingly drastic proportions. The problems demanded decisions, and since the prospect of a US–Soviet conflict was ever-present, decisions were now made along the lines of a dismantling of shared elements and a division of spheres of influence.

The 'containment' concept

A decisive factor for American perception at the outset of the East–West conflict from the beginning of 1946 was the doctrine of 'containment', which had already been developed by representatives of the 'Riga School' of the diplomatic service, and which was now propounded extremely forcefully by George F. Kennan. Convinced of an axiomatic and fundamental hostility on the part of the Soviet Union towards the outside world, as well as of the impossibility of lasting co-operation, Kennan had bitterly opposed Roosevelt's policy of co-operation during the war. 'Should the Western world ... muster up the political manliness to deny to Russia either moral and material support for the consolidation of Russian power throughout Eastern and Central Europe,' then he was convinced 'Russia would probably not be able to maintain its hold successfully for any length of time over all the territory over which it has today staked out a claim. In this case, the lines would have to be withdrawn somewhat.' If the West, however, was not prepared 'to go whole hog', then there was nothing left but to divide Germany, divide up the European continent into spheres of influence and to draw the line 'beyond which we cannot afford to permit the Russians to exercise unchallenged power or to take purely unilateral action'.[1] Resignedly, in the winter of 1944/5, he had urged his superior, Ambassador Harriman, to accept the division of the world into spheres of influence and to mobilise the American public against the new enemy.

It was characteristic of the turnabout in American policy that the head of the European Section of the State Department, H. Freeman Matthews, now instructed precisely this diplomat to draw up a fundamental exposé of the main features of Soviet policy and their necessary consequences for US policy.

Kennan's now famous 'long telegram' of 22 February 1946 described Soviet foreign policy, with the now familiar mistrust and aggression of the Soviet leadership, not as the result of current political developments, but as an inherent element of the Soviet system. 'Thus Soviet leaders are driven by necessities of their own past and present position to put forward a dogma which pictures the outside world as evil, hostile, and menacing, but as bearing within itself germs of creeping disease and destined to be wracked with growing internal convulsions until it is given the final *coup de grâce* by the rising power of socialism and yields to a new and better world. This thesis provides justification for that increase of military and police power in Russia state, for that isolation of Russian population from the outside world, and for that fluid and constant pressure to extend limits of Russian police power which are together the natural and instinctive urges of Russian rulers.' In Kennan's view, the dogma of the hostile capitalist world was independent of the actual experiences of the Soviet leadership (which, he maintained, must suggest the opposite). Consequently it was not possible, even by means of such a great willingness, for the Western world to co-operate to free Soviet policy of its aggressiveness. 'In summary, we have here a political force committed fanatically to the belief that with the US there can be no permanent *modus vivendi*, that it is desirable and necessary that the internal harmony of our society be disrupted, our traditional way of life be destroyed, the international authority of our state be broken, if Soviet power is to be secure.' The Soviet leadership would do anything to strengthen the socialist camp and at the same time weaken the capitalist nations and stir them up against one another. With the help of the Communist parties, guided by an 'underground operating directorate of world Communism', a 'concealed Comintern tightly coordinated and directed by Moscow', it would try 'to undermine the general political and strategic potential of the major Western powers', it would exert pressure to remove from office governments, from Turkey, across Switzerland to England, which 'stand in path of Soviet purposes', whilst 'in foreign countries' it 'will, as a rule, work toward the destruction of all forms of personal independence, economic, political, or moral'. To counteract this, he recommended a policy of strength and a gathering of the Western nations: the success of Soviet policy depended 'on the degree of cohesion, firmness, and vigor which the Western world can muster'. Furthermore, 'many foreign peoples, in Europe at least, are tired and frightened by experiences of the past, and are less interested in abstract freedom than in security. They are seeking guidance rather than responsibilities. We should be better able than the Russians to give them this.'[2]

There is no doubt that Kennan overestimated the significance of Soviet ideology for Soviet policy as much as he did the

107

potential influence of Moscow on the Communist parties and the potential influence of the latter on the countries to the west of the Red Army. He compensated knowledge of the weakness of the Soviet union with deep pessimism regarding the future chances of the liberal capitalist system in Europe, attributing a decisiveness and inflexibility to Soviet policy which was beyond the actual elementary needs of the Soviet leadership, and which suppressed every differentiation between the East European security sphere and the rest of the world. He did not say that in his opinion Soviet policy was *not* aimed at the establishment of Communist revolutions in Eastern and Western Europe, but *only* at the securing of Soviet dominance.[3] He left it equally unclear that the policy he recommended, and for which he introduced the concept of 'containment' a year later, amounted to a bilateral division of at least Germany and Europe.

This connection was not immediately understood by contemporaries, but in general Kennan's telegram offered at first sight a brilliant intellectual vindication of the 'domino theory', of fear of the Soviet threat and the feeling of not having been 'tough' enough with the Soviet Union for a long time, all of which had predominated in the US Administration from the New Year of 1946 at the latest. Byrnes saw in the telegram a 'splendid analysis'; Matthews found it 'magnificent'; Forrestal, Secretary of State for the Navy, enthusiastically sent out hundreds of copies to all Navy offices; and the State Department sent copies to all diplomatic missions abroad, as well as to General Eisenhower and to the heads of the War Department.[4] With only a few exceptions, the contents met with total agreement. Kennan had become famous: in April 1946 he was recalled from Moscow in order in future to expound the 'elements of Soviet behaviour' in the academies and planning headquarters of the USA. At the same time, a publicity campaign started which reiterated the core idea of the 'containment' concept in constantly new variations. On 27 February in the Senate, Vandenberg urged toughness in the face of the Soviet drive for expansion ('What is Russia up to now?') and warned of 'fellow-travellers' among their own ranks. On 28 February, Byrnes replied with a confession of resistance against every shift in the *status quo* to the detriment of the USA ('We will not and we cannot stand aloof if force or the threat of force is used contrary to the purposes and principles of the [UN] Charter'). On 5 March, in Fulton, Missouri, Churchill called in the presence of Truman for an Anglo-American alliance against Soviet expansionism ('What they desire is the fruits of war and the indefinite expansion of their power and doctrines'). On 1 April, *Time* published a dossier inspired by Kennan's telegram; it described Iran, Turkey and Manchuria as being 'infected with Communist contagion' and Saudi Arabia, Egypt, Afghanistan and India as being 'exposed'. On 3 and 10 June, Dulles warned in *Life* of a 'Pax Sovietica', and called on his compatriots to show military strength, economic aid to the endangered regions and firmness against the Soviet Union.[5]

With Kennan's 'long telegram', therefore, the policy of 'firmness' towards the Soviet Union finally prevailed in the Truman Administration. When Clark Clifford and George Elsey of the White House requested in July 1946, on the President's instructions, comments from officials of all departments of the Administration for a report on Soviet–American relations, they received memoranda exclusively confirming the threat to American security of the very existence of the Soviet Union, and the necessity for containing the Soviet danger. Clifford's final report, handed to Truman on 24 September, thus recommended 'patience with firmness' and 'the language of military power' in order to secure American interests and the rights of the smaller nations. The United States was to be put into a position where it could counter further Russian expansion. At the same time, all nations 'not now within the Soviet sphere should be given generous economic assistance and political support in their opposition to Soviet penetration ... Military support in case of attack is a last resort; a more effective barrier to communism is strong economic support. Trade agreements, loans and technical missions strengthen our ties with friendly nations and are effective demonstrations that capitalism is at least equal of communism.'[6]

Whoever now clung to earlier convictions, pointing out the weakness of the Soviet Union and its cautiousness, or who did not on principle rule out the possibility of *rapprochement* with the Soviet Union, now belonged to a politically uninfluential minority living on nostalgic memories of the New Deal. For Henry Wallace, former Vice-President and now Secretary of Commerce, who repeatedly sought a more differentiated analysis of Soviet policy and who pointed out the features of American policy that were threatening to the Soviet leadership, there was no longer room in the government. When on 16 September he spoke openly of how '"the tougher we get, the tougher the Russians will get"' and recommended that the West should acknowledge the

Soviet sphere of influence in Eastern Europe, Truman dismissed him from office under pressure from Vandenberg and Byrnes (the latter even theatening his own resignation). Truman regarded his as an inevitable step, although Wallace was still the acknowledged leader of the liberal wing of the Democrats, and Congressional elections were only two months ahead. There was to be no doubt, however, about the new foreign policy orientation of his government.[7]

How was it possible for the 'containment' concept to assert itself in so short a time, in spite of the fact, as can easily be observed in retrospect, that the essential assumptions of the concept did not correspond with the actual state of affairs at the end of the war? Five reasons for this can be discerned. First, historical experience of the expansionist policy of National Socialism suggested a policy of 'firmness' towards the Soviet Union. Churchill's theory that a policy of appeasement had smoothed Hitler's path to world war had been generally accepted. If one now subsumed National Socialism and Soviet Communism under the general heading of totalitarianism, and attributed to the Soviet dictatorship an expansionism similarly inherent to the system, as indeed it had been in the case of the National Socialist dictatorship, then in fact one did have another security threat to fear. The American people had been deceived as to the nature of the Nazi regime and did not want to be deceived again over the nature of the Soviet regime (thus deceiving themselves all the more).

Secondly, an American sense of security had not grown with American power as a result of the war: paradoxically, the feeling of insecurity had increased. The experience of not having been prepared for the attack of the Axis powers now led to a heightened interpretation of security risks. The substantial extension of the American sphere of influence now made world events seem much more relevant to the security of the USA than they had done previously, whilst acceleration in the technological development of weapon systems demanded constant redefinition of the security situation.

Thirdly, uncertainty was decisively increased by fear of a crisis of overproduction as a consequence of the war and of a return to the situation of the world economic crisis, which had scarcely been resolved by the New Deal. Entrepreneurs and trade unionists alike sought ways to avoid the threatening slump. Representatives of bourgeois liberalism saw their social system weakened

110

— in Europe it even appeared to be close to its demise. Deliverance was generally seen in the opening of new markets and in the liberalisation of world trade. If they viewed the Soviet policy of spheres of influence as being incompatible with this opening of markets (which in fact it was not!), then they saw in that policy a threat to American interests, all the more so when they drew a connection between this and the increase in socialist movements in Europe and in nationalist movements in former European colonies.

Fourthly, the economic crisis that threatened to emerge from the war was best avoided by finding politically motivated aims to replace those of the war that would be suitable for mobilising the public for high productivity and for creating new tasks for industry abroad. Although this connection was never made consciously, everything pointed to such a renewed mobilisation, and when Kennan demanded conducting the conflict with the Soviet Union 'with the same thoroughness and care as the solution of a major strategic problem in war, and if necessary, with no smaller outlay in planning effort' the motive for the mobilisation was found.[8] As the Second World War had done, the Cold War was now to be turned to the benefit of the US economy, and was to render possible a continuation of the participation policy of the New Deal.

Fifthly, the military apparatus that had proliferated in the war now found in the alleged Soviet threat a welcome justification for its own existence. This was all the more necessary, and the Soviet threat was consequently brought to attention all the more frequently, since after the end of the war the three organisations of the army, the marines and the air force were to be merged into one department, and each of these clamoured for assurance of its previous importance. It is thus no coincidence that Forrestal, Secretary of State for the Marines, as spokesman for the most threatened of these groups (as a result of technological development) was among the most vociferous advocates of containment policy.

The policy of containment was thus firmly rooted in the direct historical experience and structural exigencies of American politics;[9] it had, so to speak, 'the logic of history' behind it, even if it did *not* represent the only possible American policy after the end of the war.

The beginning of the American policy of containment

Convinced of the necessity of not being able to make any more concessions to the Soviet leadership, and under constant pressure from the Republicans, whose representatives accompanied him on all conferences, Byrnes executed the US foreign policy of 1946 in the sense defined by Kennan. Soviet demands now met with tougher resistance than hitherto; efforts to set up a joint security system along the lines of Roosevelt's 'four policemen' were no longer made; controversies, unlike in 1945, were deliberately brought into the open; and at the same time the first measures for the stabilisation of that part of Europe that was outside the sphere of influence of the Red Army against the Communist 'threat' now began.

The new policy was first practised in February/March 1946, in the Iran crisis. As in many regions of the world, American and Soviet interests also confronted each other here. The Soviet leadership was interested in the existence of crude oil in Iran, and feared an extension of British and American influence in the region, which could ultimately endanger its own oil production in Russian Azerbaijan, on the north Iranian border. The Americans hoped to break the previous British crude oil monopoly in the Near East and to pre-empt Soviet competition, fearing at the same time an extension of Soviet influence across Iran as far as Saudi Arabia. During the war, both British and Soviet troops had occupied the country, in order to prevent the Shah joining the Axis powers: these troops were to withdraw at the latest six months after the end of the war (that is by 2 March 1946). The crisis arose when the Soviet leadership tried in the winter of 1945/6 to make use of the presence of its troops in order to further its own interests. It demanded from the Persian government a favourable concession for the northern provinces now in its occupation, and encouraged the transitional movement for autonomy in North Iran, which now formed a separatist government in Persian Azerbaijan. Concerned that the Soviet Union would not keep to the date for withdrawing its troops, the British government made the Persian government call on the Security Council of the United Nations at the end of January 1946. The Soviet government then began to negotiate a compromise solution with the Persian premier, Qavam, initially leaving its troops in the country over the 2 March deadline, but then even moving in towards the interior, in order to make a show of Soviet power to the Persian government and its Western allies. When new proceedings were pending with the Security Council, the Soviet government announced on 25 March the complete withdrawal of its troops within five or six weeks. The Persian government, however, was prepared to permit Azerbaijan a certain degree of autonomy within the Persian state federation, and to run a joint oil company with the Soviet Union.

In this way the crisis came to an end; the Soviet Union, in the face of British and American superiority in the Near East and in the UN, had to be content with the prospect of a comparatively modest share in Persian crude oil. (In fact, the Persian parliament later failed to ratify the agreement on the oil company, and the Persian government had the leaders of the autonomists executed.) Byrnes nevertheless insisted on new proceedings before the Security Council, where on 27 March he once again, as he had already done repeatedly in the course of the crisis itself, branded Soviet conduct in Iran as an imperialistic policy of brute force. The American public had to see that the Secretary of State was no appeaser, and it was indeed convinced by Byrnes's action. The Iran crisis, in fact a virtually classic case of the collision of interests of great powers, was now interpreted as proof of the correctness of the containment doctrine. Soviet pressure on the Persian government was now looked upon as an attempt to incorporate Iran into the Soviet power zone, and Soviet withdrawal was put down entirely to American threats in the UN. Soviet expansion beyond the sphere of influence achieved in the war now appeared for the first time to be a reality, and US containment policy a success, a factor which contributed considerably to the latter's definitive implementation.[10]

At the second meeting of the Allied Council of Foreign Ministers, which began on 25 April in Paris and was to prepare the peace treaties in accordance with the procedure negotiated in Moscow in December 1945, Byrnes continued the apparently so successful policy of 'firmness' supported by the public. Almost all Soviet demands were thus refused: the demand for high reparation payments from former enemy states; the demand for the setting-up of Four-Power control of the Ruhr; the Yugoslav claim to the Trieste region (which, although populated by an Italian majority, was of central importance to the Yugoslav economy because of its port); and likewise the demand for a mandate of the former Italian colony of Libya. Instead, Byrnes attacked Soviet practice in Eastern Europe and demanded once again the internationalisation of the European waterways, as well as the opening of the former Axis-Power countries to the American market by the abolition of all trade preferences. 'Byrnes has "stood up" 100%', Vandenberg, who had been appointed to the US delegation, wrote to Dulles from Paris, full of satisfaction. He informed *Time* editor, Henry Luce, 'I think we had to do at least one thing at Paris — namely to demonstrate that the "appeasement" days are over ... Paris was Munich in reverse'; US representatives had rejected 'compromise principles', although 'Molotov was in a trading mood.'[11] In fact, however, the first round of negotiations had to be broken off on 15 May without specific results.

During the second round of talks, which lasted from 15 June to 12 July, an element of agreement on the question of peace treaties with the former allies of Germany was only reached by the Soviet delegation relinquishing all essential demands arising from what had thus far been the actual sphere of Soviet influence. The Soviet delegation thus accepted the postponement of the mandate issue until the next UN General Assembly (that is, a *de facto* US veto against Soviet influence in Libya), as well as Italian overseas credit and possessions instead of the 100 million dollars' worth of reparations demanded from Italy, and the establishment of Trieste as an autonomous city under UN supervision. On the other hand, Byrnes did not succeed in writing American Open Door demands into the draft peace treaties, and on the question of Germany, the only one in which both sides still had the potential for influence, their conflicts resounded against one another more than ever, this time in full public view.[12] In general, Byrnes had now grasped how to present the Soviet Union to the American and European public as an expansionist power unwilling to compromise, and thus to attribute to it the blame for a possible breakdown in the peace-treaty undertaking. This was particularly true of the Paris conference, at which, from 29 July to 15 October, the representatives of all 21 Allies against the Axis powers now discussed the treaty drafts of the Council of Foreign Ministers. Byrnes had made sure that all negotiations would be conducted in public, with the result that the conference was often reduced to vociferous showmanship on the part of the smaller nations pleading for the right to self-determination and often also condemning Soviet policy. This conference was even more a publicity ploy than the meeting of foreign ministers had been. The delegates were hardly able to influence the actual form of the peacetime order, which in any case depended on a further report by the

Council of Foreign Ministers. In fact, the third meeting of the Council of Foreign Ministers, held from 4 November to 12 December in New York, passed the peace treaties more or less as had already been decided at the Paris council meeting.[13]

Meanwhile another crisis occurred in US–Soviet relations, this time one that brought the Truman government to the brink of military confrontation. On 7 August, the Soviet government requested Turkey's renunciation of the Montreux Convention of 1936, in which Turkey had been pledged the right to control the passage of warships from states bordering on the Black Sea through the Straits. The Soviet government now wanted to participate in this supervision, and in addition to establish joint Turkish–Soviet defences along the straits. Churchill had already, in October 1944, acknowledged the justification for this traditional Soviet claim, and the Potsdam conference had approved the Soviet claim for revision of the Montreux Convention. Now, however, in the light of the containment doctrine, this claim was regarded as further proof of threatening Soviet expansionism. Recognition of the Soviet demand, explained Under–Secretary of State Dean Acheson to the President, would lead to Soviet control of Turkey, and thus to Soviet control of Greece and the whole of the Near and Middle East, which in turn would significantly help the Soviet Union 'to obtain its objectives in India and China'. The Soviet leadership could only be dissuaded from its intention if it saw that the USA was 'prepared, if necessary, to meet aggression with force of arms'.[14] The Soviet government was sent a strong note of protest, and the Turkish government was warned to defend itself; at the same time, substantial US naval units were despatched to the eastern Mediterranean. One month later, Forrestal authorised long-term stationing of the fleet in this region: containment had now begun to materialise in military form.

Finally, a further decisive step towards containment was undertaken by Byrnes when he revamped American loan policy. The aim of this policy had of course been to open up external markets to American capital and goods exports, in order, in particular, to check the threatening crisis in overproduction. Even the Soviet Union and its neighbours in Eastern Europe were to be included in this multilateral system of free trade. This aim remained, inasmuch as the economic exigencies underlying it did not change, but it was now combined with another aim, that of stabilising 'endangered' regions against Communist influence.

115

Totalitarianism, as one knew since the world economic crisis, emerged out of economic distress: the all-round reboosting of the economy was now carried out in order to help remove the 'susceptibility' to Communism of those nations situated in the potential area of expansion of the Soviet Union. Thus, in contradiction to the economic interest, credit to the Soviet Union and pro-Soviet states was now ruled out, and in the case of a conflict of interests, the containment effect was to take priority over the implementation of Open Door requirements.[15]

This economically absurd combination of market expansion and containment policy had already manifested itself in 1945 in the increasing demands of US politicians for political concessions in return for a loan to the Soviet Union, and the so-far dilatorily handled Soviet credit requests were officially answered with American counter-demands, bringing the US–Soviet credit project to the point of definite failure. Negotiations for credit, the State Department informed the Soviet government on 21 February 1946, should now include claims for the repayment of requisitioned US property in the liberated nations, as well as a greater right of consultation for the USA in the economic reconstruction of the East European states (in accordance with the principles of the Declaration on liberated Europe), as well as the questions of the internationalisation of the waterways, a definitive settlement of lend–lease obligations, a trade and shipping agreement and, finally, general methods for the removal of trade restrictions.[16] The Soviet government could not agree to such conditions, which considerably overstepped the American Open Door interest, and which aimed not at a dovetailing of economies in the interests of both countries, but at the economic penetration of the Soviet Union and East European countries by the USA, and which thus tended to lay the entire Soviet security system in Eastern Europe open to question. Thus, after a few futile rearguard actions, US–Soviet credit negotiations broke down in June 1946.

The funds that had been set aside by the Export–Import Bank for credit to the Soviet Union were now mostly used for a loan to France, which, in spite of US economic aid at 1,675 million dollars in February 1945 and US credit of 550 million dollars in December 1945, showed in the spring of 1946 a budget deficit of 1,800 million dollars; the French government presented as an additional motive for economic aid the strengthening of non-Communist forces in the country. After more than two months of talks, during which US representatives urged on several occasions for the elimination of Communists from the French government (albeit in vain) and the French delegates Léon Blum and Jean Monnet sought to play off the American fear of Communists against Open Door requirements, an agreement package was settled on 28 May, containing a reduction of French war debts from 3,474 million dollars to 700 million dollars, credit of 300 million dollars for buying American surplus at 20 per cent of the revised price, credit from the Export-Import Bank at 650 million dollars and France's relinquishing of former methods of import quotas. If one added to these credit agreements the reconstruction advance of 500 million dollars put forward by the International Reconstruction Bank, however, this only just covered three-quarters of the French deficit.[17]

In general, funds previously envisaged for transactions in the Soviet sphere of influence were now used for the stabilisation of Western Europe. 'I am convinced,' wrote Byrnes to Acheson at the beginning of September, 'that the time has come when we should endeavor by all fair means to assist our friends in Western Europe and Italy in the matter of surplus property sales and such other means as are feasible rather than to continue to extend material aid to those countries of Eastern Europe at present engaged in the campaign of vilification of the United States and distortion of our motives and policies.' Negotiations for a 50 million dollar credit facility to Czechoslovakia for buying American surplus were thus stopped on 28 September, after the Czechoslovak government had applauded Soviet condemnation of American economic imperialism at the Paris conference and thus, Byrnes maintained, demonstrated that it belonged to the Soviet camp. In November, the US government decided, after a basic resolution passed by Congress in 1945, to discontinue by the end of the year its payment for the UN aid organisation, UNRRA, whose budget had thus far been two-thirds disputed by the USA, and whose humanitarian (that is, 'anti-totalitarian') aid had been for the most part for the benefit of East European countries, playing a sizeable role in reconstruction. Applications from Poland, Czechoslovakia and Hungary to be given long-term credit by the World Bank after the UNRRA aid had expired were turned down. Instead, 5,700 million dollars in credit and support were granted to countries outside the Communist sphere of influence as early as 1946; even a loan to Great Britain in December 1945, originally conceived in terms of the global policy of securing exports, was now seen in the light of the containment of Communism.[18]

Decisions on the questions of the atomic bomb and Germany

The US government was still not prepared to undertake a delineation of spheres of influence in the traditional power-political sense, as Churchill, for example, had urged, adhering rather to its universalistic goal of the formation of a world order based on liberal principles. Therefore the efforts towards the containment of alleged Soviet expansion increasingly led to the concentration of American interests in those regions that lay outside the Soviet sphere of influence, and thus to the restriction of a leading world role for the nations in these areas, and to what Kennan had foreseen as a consequence of containment policy, although he had not said as much at the time: the effective division of the world into two parts. Universalism thus became more and more a matter of pure rhetoric for ensuring domestic political and 'world public' support for foreign-policy actions, whilst the US government was in reality beginning to create a Western hemisphere in response to the Soviet security sphere. The demand for consultation over Eastern Europe remained, but American interest really centred on the *de facto* consolidation of Western Europe. The division was not planned and intended as such, but emerged as a consequence of the new definition of American security interests. Two sets of decisions in 1946 demonstrate this development particularly clearly, namely, those on the atomic-weapon question and on German policy, that is, the two problem areas that had the greatest relevance for the future security of the two world powers.

The question of atomic weapons

On the question of atomic weapons, the Truman Administration decided unequivocally in 1946 to place security — by means of retaining its atomic-bomb monopoly — before the avoidance of an atomic arms race. As we have seen, Stimson, the Secretary of War, had argued in the summer of 1945 on behalf of part of the US Administration for offering the Soviet Union an atomic partnership in return for co-operative behaviour, but Byrnes had successfully countered that the partnership offer should be withheld in order to make the Soviet leadership more amenable. After 'atomic diplomacy' had proved ineffective at the London meeting of the Allied Council of Foreign Ministers, the thought of such a direct offer was never taken up again. The Truman Administration now developed a test programme that was intended to try out Soviet co-operativeness over the atomic-weapon question, and that envisaged an internationalisation of atomic weapons only as the result of a lengthy testing process.

The central idea behind this plan, formulated by Vannevar Bush, Director of the National Agency for Science and Development, in November 1945, was to make the internationalisation of the atomic bomb dependent upon the prior establishment of a series of control mechanisms requiring the agreement of all involved, the Soviet Union and the USA in particular. First, there was to be an exchange of all scientific information. Then, if both sides agreed that this stage had been reached, an inspection commission was to be set up under the auspices of the United Nations, to control systematically all scientific establishments concerned with atomic questions. Thirdly, all fission material was to be confined and then controlled to ensure that it was used only for peaceful purposes. Until the setting-up of this control system had been completed, the USA was to proceed with the production of the material necessary for bombs, but not to stockpile any completed atomic bombs.[19] With this plan, applied immediately by Byrnes as the basis for negotiations with the British, Canadian and Soviet governments, the Soviet leadership saw itself faced with a choice: either to trust the USA and to relinquish the development of its own atomic bomb, thereby possibly only losing valuable time in the atomic arms race, or to take on the costly risk of the atomic arms race from the outset. Both risks must have seemed equally great in Soviet eyes, so that the choice at first remained entirely open. In the case of Soviet rejection of the plan, however, the US government effectively settled for the plan for an atomic arms race. The plan thus had the sole function of laying the blame for the collapse of universalism at the door of the Soviet Union in the eyes of public opinion, and possibly (in the case of a rejection after only the second or third stage) of being able to postpone the beginning of Soviet atomic armament.

Before this plan was presented to the forum of the United Nations on 15 June 1946, however, it underwent definite changes in the continuing course of the policy of increasing 'firmness' towards the Soviet Union. First, the entire control system was now not to be carried out by an international commission, but by a supranational 'Atomic Development Authority', under the supervision of the UN Security Council. This authority was at the same time to become the owner of all fission material and to direct the total, peaceful use of atomic energy. Secondly, until the setting-up of the control system was complete, the USA was to reserve the right to decide whether to produce further bombs or not. Thirdly (contrary to Byrnes's intention, but under pressure from Bernard M. Baruch, who was popular with Congress as Director of the Atomic Control Commission), the veto right of the great powers in the Security Council was to be suspended on all questions of atomic-weapon control, and any violation of the restrictions decided upon to be punished. Soviet security was thus *de facto* made dependent upon a UN majority (at that time pro-American), and it surprised no one that the Soviet Ambassador to the UN, Andrei Gromyko, immediately rejected the so-called Baruch Plan, and demanded instead, firstly, the destruction of all existing atomic-weapon and production installations, and then the establishment of a world-wide control system. After months of debate, the UN Atomic Energy Commission finally ratified the American plan on 30 December 1946 with 10 votes to 0 and the abstention of the Soviet Union and Poland; the Soviet Union subsequently blocked all further discussion of the project in the Security Council. The propaganda effect had thus been achieved, and at the same time the age of the arms race had definitely begun.[20]

The question of Germany

On the question of Germany, the US government, in pursuit of the dogmas of the containment doctrine, began to interpret Soviet policy towards Germany as an attempt to draw the whole of Germany into the Soviet sphere of influence. Faced with a supposed choice between losing Germany to the Soviet Union and accepting the division of Germany, the US government decided to give priority to the establishment of a partial West German state over a total German solution.

Here, too, Kennan, who had predicted the division of Germany in 1945 as the consequence of containment policy, pointed the way. Asked by Matthews, he wrote on 6 March to the State Department that the Soviet leadership would only agree to the setting-up of a central German administrative structure (against which the French government at that time, supported by the French Communists, exercised its veto), if it could be sure that it would bring it under its own control. There were thus only two possibilities open to American policy towards Germany, these being

1. to leave remainder of Germany nominally united but extensively vulnerable to Soviet political penetration and influence or
2. to carry to its logical conclusion the process of partition which was begun in the East and to endeavor to rescue Western Zones of Germany by walling them off against Eastern penetration and integrating them into international pattern of Western Europe rather than into a united Germany. I am sure the Russians themselves are confident that if rump Germany west of Oder–Neisse were to be united under single administration, there would be no other single political force there which could stand up against a Left Wing bloc with Russian backing.[21]

One can scarcely say that the Soviet leadership tried in reality to bring the whole of Germany under Soviet hegemony. In its own zone of occupation, it had certainly continued the transformation process for the eradication of the social base of National Socialism — in a pragmatic way, making use of grass-roots initiatives and with an increasingly bureaucratic regimentation. Similarly, as in Eastern Europe, it had arbitrarily dismantled the industrial plant, and from 1945/6 had used these industrial resources in the main for Soviet reconstruction, both by means of high reparation payments and by the conversion of sequestered enterprises into Soviet corporations. On the other hand, the German Communist Party had started out with a programme that was explicitly not aimed at socialist transformation, but pledged to 'make good' the failed bourgeois revolution of 1848. Republican parties were again permitted; a broad alliance of 'anti-fascist' forces striven towards; and the foundation of a 'Unity Front' of political parties was encouraged. This programme was intended to unite Communists and Democrats in joint responsibility for eradicating the social roots of National Socialism. The same policy was to apply in Soviet eyes to the whole of Germany; the Soviet government continued to demand (after the collapse of US–Soviet credit negotiations more intensively than ever) reparations at the level mentioned at Yalta, in addition to the extension of 'democratisation' measures into the Western zones of occupation and Four-Power supervision of the Ruhr. Since the Western powers made no arrangements of any kind to comply with these demands, the securing of the transformation process in the Soviet zone immediately moved to the forefront of Soviet policy towards Germany, and unity slogans acquired more and more the function of providing a propaganda shield for the threatening separation that accompanied this separate information. The Soviet leadership furthermore accepted the fact that its potential influence in the Western zones was rapidly reduced as a result of just this separate transformation. All things considered, we can see that once again the basic strategic aim of the Soviet government was confirmed, namely not to allow Germany to fall into the hands of Anglo-Saxon capitalism, or at least not completely; this basic aim was increasingly masked by direct interest in German assistance in the reconstruction of the devastated Soviet Union. It was certainly consistent with this strategic thinking (as it was on the opposite side) to prefer a division of Germany to the incorporation of its own zone of occupation as well into the 'One World' of the USA, but it was not consistent to incorporate a unified Germany exclusively into the Soviet power zone and to re-shape it according to concepts of a socialist order; Soviet strength was not sufficient for such an undertaking.[22]

The limits of the Soviet position in Germany are typified by the story of the founding of the Socialist Unity Party (the SED). The 'unification of working-class parties' was at first called for by the socialist political base in the summer of 1945, particularly by the Social Democrats. The Communist Party however, turned this down, fearing that it would have to settle for a minority role within a unity party. From October 1945, however, unity was urged by the Communist Party itself, now out of fear that in elections its relatively limited support among the population would be exposed. In the meantime, misgivings had arisen among the Social Democrats. Although a conference of Communist and Socialist delegates decided in principle at the end of December 1945 on the founding of a joint workers' party, German Socialist Party representatives nevertheless ensured that at first there would not be a joint electoral list of candidates, whilst delegates from the leadership of parties in the Western zones rejected the unity offer in January 1946 so as not to jeopardise their own concept of an anti-Communist movement. In West Berlin, the only party district in which a free referendum of the political base took place, on 31 March less than 13 per cent of Socialist Party members voted for direct unification, whereas 63 per cent voted for an action alliance with the German Communist Party. The meeting of the Unity Party on 21 and 22 April proceeded with only minimal participation from the Western zones.[23] There was thus no 'Left Wing bloc' under Soviet control, as Kennan claimed to discern; there was indeed a broad socialist movement which hoped for a reunification of workers' parties without Soviet tutelage.

It is likewise not possible to say that the US leadership could not have come to some arrangement with Soviet policy towards Germany, in spite of contradictory interests. Although there were Soviet–American differences in the Allied Control Council, particularly over the question of the level of German industrial production considered 'necessary for peace', and the point at which reparation payments could be paid, the majority of difficulties in the Control Council did not arise from the Soviet Union, but from France, which blocked all initiatives towards a German central administration. The Soviet representatives in the Control Council, as General Clay, US military governor in Berlin, informed the State Department at the beginning of April 1946, 'could not be accused of violating the Potsdam Agreement'; on the contrary, 'they have been meticulous in their observance', and showed 'a sincere desire to be friendly with us and also a certain respect for the US'. These 'on-the-spot' experiences of Clay's made him one of the few opponents of the Kennan doctrine: 'We have never and still do not believe for a minute in imminent Soviet aggression.'[24]

At first, Byrnes was also not quite ready to believe in Kennan's theory of Germany, and therefore decided to test Soviet co-operativeness over the German question with the proposal of a 25-year Four-Power Guarantee treaty for the demilitarisation of Germany. If Soviet policy towards Germany was really only aimed at its security in relation to Germany, then, he was convinced, the Soviet leadership would accept the proposal; if it rejected the proposal, then this would be proof of an expansionist objective. The alternatives were badly chosen, however; in fact, the Soviet leadership was less interested in security in relation to Germany *per se* than in protecting it from being incorporated into 'One World'. Molotov, confronted at the beginning of the Paris Council of Foreign Ministers with Byrnes's proposal, thus responded with a counter-test: he did not reject the treaty idea outright, but first demanded the fulfilment of Soviet reparation requests (as a component of demilitarisation) in order to test how substantial the American promise of guarantees really was. Both tests proved negative, and the Paris council meeting resulted in the two opponents taking their results in the German issue to the German public. In a press declaration of 10 July, Molotov pleaded for German unity; Byrnes replied on 6 September in his Stuttgart speech with the promise of a speedy return to German self-determination and economic reconstruction, although of course he did not say that he meant only the reconstruction of West Germany.[25]

Under these circumstances, Clay's attempts to put into effect the economic unity agreed upon in Potsdam in order to counter-act threatening economic collapse in the Western zones, and not to allow these zones to fall under Soviet influence, led to a *de facto* division. In order to force France to give up its veto against economic unity, and thus also to be able to persuade the Soviet Union to join, Clay stopped on 3 May all reparation payments out of the American zone until the settlement of a joint export–import plan for the whole of Germany. After Molotov had rejected his treaty proposal, and in addition his British colleague Bevin had threatened complete refusal of reparation payments from the industrially rich British zone, and unilateral stepping-up of production (which would have been disastrous for France especially), Byrnes yielded to pressure from Clay to see at least to an integration of the British and American zones. On 11 July he announced that he was prepared to 'join with any other occupying government or governments in Germany for the treatment of our respective zones as an economic unit'. As expected, only the British government agreed (on 27 July). The way was thus open for the formation of the bizone, which was decided upon in December and took effect from 1 January 1947, after dramatic disagreements over the joint division of obligations. Byrnes had given up hope of a unified Germany that would not fall to Soviet expansion.[26] Even the Soviet offer of 14 October, to supply the Western zones with raw materials in return for reparations at the level they requested, and to ensure the equalisation of the trade balance of a unified Germany, was no longer able to alter the new course of US policy towards Germany.[27]

Consolidation in the Soviet sphere of influence

As US policy concentrated in 1946 on the consolidation of regions allegedly threatened by Soviet expansion, so too Soviet policy concentrated on consolidating a sphere of influence of its own. The experiences of the Soviet leadership with US policy in the first year after the end of the war had amply confirmed the most pessimistic analyses of the situation made before the war had ended. With its campaign for self-determination, the USA had laid open to question the apparently already conceded Soviet security policy in Eastern Europe. The USA had refused the very nearly agreed reparations from Germany, had used its economic superiority as a political lever, had tried to keep the Soviet Union from possessing atomic weapons, and was now trying to present the Soviet Union as an aggressor everywhere in the world. All this now strengthened the conviction, nourished by ideology and experience, that the capitalist states had by no means relinquished their imperialistic character. This led to the conclusion that Soviet power and the security system, after the defeat of the Axis powers, were once again in danger, if not acutely so, then at least potentially and in the long term. This analysis vindicated the correctness of Communist stabilisation policy in Western Europe, making it more necessary than ever, and likewise gave added urgency to the Soviet reconstruction programme. Lastly, however, it limited the room for manoeuvre of the East European nations.

In an assessment of war experiences, which Stalin presented to the Soviet public in an election speech on 9 February 1946, this concentration of all resources on preparation for a new conflict becomes clear. Against all expectations, the Soviet Union would now, after winning the war, find its way back to peacetime conditions; the production of consumer goods and the standard of living would rise, and Stalin announced a fresh mobilisation of the country. In the same way that the vigorous industrialisation of the period of the first Five-year plans, he said, had made the Soviet Union strong enough to repel the onslaught of National Socialism — Stalin celebrated the victory as proof of the efficiency of the Soviet system — now 'three, if not more, new Five-year plans' were once again to transform the Soviet Union into a country of heavy industry; 'only in these conditions will our country be secure against every eventuality'. In the USA, this speech was misinterpreted as a 'Declaration of World War III'; in fact, it was the outward sign that the Soviet Union was adjusting itself to the Cold War.[28]

This was all the more important for the Soviet Union in that the situation in the East European security region was still by no means stabilised. Without any definite concept for the future social order in the countries of this region, the Soviet government had attempted, by means of swift economic stabilisation after its initial plundering, partial democratic reforms (which did not go nearly as far as the socialists wanted, for example) and a definite share of Communists in power, to create guarantees for a policy that would not be hostile to the Soviet Union. It was precisely because of this, however (except in Czechoslovakia, where a broader basic democratic consensus had developed), that the government had called forth opposition forces which, blinded by American self-determination rhetoric, increasingly hoped for US support, and accordingly showed themselves less willing to compromise. The results of this were high internal political tension in the course of 1946/7 and, as a result of this, a firmer grip on the part of the Communists, backed up by the Red Army. A proportion of the non-Communists in the coalition governments (particularly urban people, who were pressing for 'modernisation'), partly out of opportunism, partly out of conviction that this was the only way they could secure the reconstruction of their countries, now joined the Communist leadership. The remainder was increasingly taken up by the opposition movement outside the unity fronts; this was then destroyed by the Communists, who were now stronger, with methods that were often brutal.[29]

Thus in Poland, Stanislas Mikolajczyk, now acting Premier and, as Chairman of the Peasants' Party with 600,000 members, leader of potentially the most powerful group in the country, came into increasing difficulties with the partisan actions and terrorist attacks of the remainder of the still underground anti-Soviet 'Homeland Army'. The strength of resistance to the new regime and hope for support from the Americans led him to shut his eyes to Communist demands after entry into the 'Democratic Front', which was controlled by the Communists and Socialists. The Communists then postponed the elections planned for February 1946 and used terrorist acts as an excuse to cripple the Peasants' Party. Mikolajczyk lost more and more support in the country. After the elections, which took place after all on 10 January 1947, and which were manipulated far more by the Communists than was really necessary (as they themselves admitted afterwards), his party commanded only 28 out of 444 parliamentary seats. The Communists had become the ruling power in the country.

In Bulgaria, the Peasants' Party, influenced by British action against the pro-Communist partisan movement in neighbouring Greece, had left the 'Fatherland Front', which was consequently also crippled by the Communists. The elections of 19 November 1945 brought a majority of 90 per cent for the now Communist-dominated 'Fatherland Front'. In accordance with the Moscow agreements, the Front refused to take opposition representatives into the government, retained 366 out of 465 members of parliament in further elections on 27 October 1946, and then began to smash the defeated Peasants' Party with repressive measures.

In Romania, the National Peasants' Party and the Liberals remained fundamentally opposed to the regime, with the potential support of King Michael, who had attempted at the end of August 1945, in the hope of American support, to force the resignation of the Groza government. One representative of each of these opposition parties was appointed to the government in January 1946, following the Moscow resolutions, but they were unable to exert any influence there. Opposition to the regime grew so strong in the meantime that the results of the elections on 10 November 1946 were catastrophic for the Communists. The election results were consequently rigged, the 'Democratic Parties bloc' obtaining 347 seats, the Peasants' Party 39 and the Liberals three. The Communist-dominated bloc now felt strong enough to make use of the famine in the summer of 1947 for the implementation of currency reform, which removed the material base of the middle classes. After this, it proved easy to destroy bourgeois and peasant opposition politically.

In Hungary, opposition to Soviet hegemony was even stronger than in Romania and Bulgaria, or even Poland. The bureaucracy and army were still the same as they had been under the Horthy regime, and the Catholic Church under Cardinal Primate Mindszenty openly opposed all attempts to alter the pre-democratic conditions of the country. In free elections, to which the Soviet leadership had finally agreed under American pressure, the (predominantly bourgeois Protestant) Small Landowners' Party won 57 per cent of the votes on 7 November 1945, and the Communists suffered a defeat with just 17 per cent. The leader of the Small Farmers, Ferenc Nagy, was accepted by the Soviet leadership as Prime Minister, but he came under increasing pressure from his Cabinet colleagues who, as in Poland, used *putsch* attempts and alleged *putsch* attempts as an excuse visibly to restrict the room for manoeuvre of the Farmers' Party, using 'salami tactics' (according to Communist Party leader Rakósi). In February 1946, twenty 'reactionary' members of parliament had to leave the Small Farmers' faction. In February 1947, a series of further members, among them the General Secretary of the Small Farmers, Béla Kovác, were accused of involvement in an attempted *putsch* and arrested. At the end of May 1947, the most outstanding Small Farmers' representatives were removed from the Cabinet, and Nagy, on holiday at the time, remained abroad. Further elections held on 31 August 1947, in spite of severe obstacles to the Small Farmers, still brought results that were 35 per cent in favour of non-Communist groups. The Communists nevertheless felt sufficiently strong to exclude them completely.[30]

In general, the incipient East–West confrontation intensified the conflict between traditional anti-Soviet forces and the Communist minority in such a way as progressively to reduce the ground for co-operation on the basis of an anti-fascist minimum consensus. Communists responded to potential or actual force on the part of the opponents to their regimes with massive counterforce, thus monopolising power more and more. In contrast to the countries mentioned above, however, there were no such tensions in the two years immediately following the Second World War either in Yugoslavia or in Czechoslovakia. In Yugoslavia, this was because the indigenous Communist Party had been so totally victorious, and defended its victory with such drastic methods, that the representatives of the former London exile government appointed under pressure from the Western Allies had hardly any potential influence left open to them. In Czechoslovakia, there was already a bourgeois-democratic basis for a pro-Soviet policy, the Communists commanding broad support among the population with 38 per cent of the votes in the — free — elections of 26 May 1946. Certainly in Czechoslovakia the activities of the Soviet NKVD made themselves felt. Non-Communist groups were considerably set back, however, only from the summer of 1947 onwards, when serious difficulties emerged in economic reconstruction and, in addition, the confrontation between the world powers had entered a new phase.[31]

Inasmuch as the Soviet government not only endorsed the violent actions of the Communist Parties, but even encouraged them, it furthered the division of Europe in the same way as did the American government. At the same time, it constantly provided the American public with new grounds for seeing the thesis of the aggressive character of international Communism vindicated, thus also furthering the containment policy. Both sides had defined their security interests in such a way that they saw a justification for the correctness of their fears in the action of the other side. In this way the division of Germany, Europe and potentially the whole world, which no one had wanted at first, now became increasingly inevitable and more far-reaching.

Notes

1. Quotation (1) from memorandum of Kennan, May 1945, published in George F. Kennan, *Memoirs 1925–1950* (Boston, 1967), pp. 545f; quotation (2) from a letter of Kennan to his colleague Charles Bohlen in February 1945; for further documentation, cf. Daniel Yergin, *Shattered peace*, p. 75.

2. Text of the Kennan telegram (to Byrnes) on 22 February 1946, in *Foreign relations of the United States* (hereafter cited as FRUS) (1946), VI, pp. 696–706.

3. For which reason he always complained later of having been misunderstood. He said in his letter to Admiral Hill, 7 October 1946, that it was not a question for the Soviet leadership of encouraging 'Communism'; *Forrestal Papers*, quoted by John L. Gaddis, *The United States and the origins of the Cold War 1941–1947* (2nd edn, New York, 1976), p. 323.

4. Byrnes to Kennan, 27 February 1946; Matthews to Kennan, 25 May 1946, *State Department Papers*, quoted after Yergin, *Shattered Peace*, pp. 170f.; for further positive reactions, see Yergin. The 'traditional' thesis, that Kennan's telegram only gradually received positive echoes (e.g. Eric F. Goldman, *The crucial decade: America 1945–1955* (New York, 1955), pp. 70f.) is not tenable.

5. Vandenberg, *The private papers of Senator Vandenberg* (Boston, 1952), pp. 246–9; Byrnes, *Department of State Bulletin*, XIV (10 March 1946), pp. 355–8; Churchill, *Vital speeches of the day*, vol. 12 (15 March 1946), pp. 329–32; no author, '"Communist" contagion. What does Russia want?' *Time*, 1 April 1946, p. 27; *Life*, 3 and 10 June 1946. Alarmed by Stalin's violent reaction to Churchill's speech, Truman and Byrnes refused to identify themselves with the content of the speech in public; in fact, however, they had both read the text before Churchill's appearance and agreed with the contents. Compare, for background to the speech and for further documentation on the publicity campaign of spring 1946, Gaddis, *The United States and the origins*, pp. 290–309, 313–15; Yergin, *Shattered peace*, pp. 171–8.

6. Text in Arthur Krock, *Memoirs: sixty years on the firing line* (New York, 1968), pp. 225–31, 421–82; compare Yergin, *Shattered peace*, pp.

241–5, and Melvyn P. Leffler, 'The American conception of national security and the beginnings of the Cold War, 1945–48', *American Historical Review*, 89 (1984), pp. 370ff.

7. Compare Alonzo L. Hamby, 'Henry A. Wallace, the Liberals and Soviet–American relations', *Review of Politics*, 30 (1968), pp. 153–69; Gaddis, *The United States and the origins*, pp. 338–41; Yergin, *Shattered peace*, pp. 245–55; J. Samuel Walker, *Henry A. Wallace and American foreign policy*, (Westport, Conn., 1976), ch. 11; Richard J. Walton, *Henry Wallace, Harry Truman and the Cold War* (New York, 1976), pp. 99f.; on the background to his political development, see also Edward L. and Frederick H. Schapsmeier, *Prophet in politics: Henry A. Wallace and the war years, (1940–1945*, (Ames, Iowa, 1970); Norman D. Markowitz, *The rise and fall of people's century: Henry A. Wallace and American liberalism 1941–1948*, (New York, 1973).

8. As in his telegram of 22 February 1946; Kennan, *Memoirs*, p. 557.

9. Much material on this structural background can be found in Hans Gunter Brauch, 'Struktureller Wandel und Rüstungspolitik der USA (1940–1950), Zur Weltführungsrolle und ihren innenpolitischen Bedingungen', dissertation, (Heidelberg, 1976); an evaluation of individual factors is nevertheless not forthcoming.

10. American documents on the Iran crisis in FRUS 1945, VIII pp. 388–522 and FRUS (1946), VII, pp. 289–415. Compare J.E. Kovac, 'Iran and the beginning of the Cold War. A case study in the dynamics of international politics', unpublished thesis, University of Utah (1970); Mark H. Lytle, 'American–Iranian relations 1941–47 and the redefinition of national security', unpublished thesis, Yale University (1973); Yergin, *Shattered peace*, pp. 179–90; Garry H. Hess, 'The Iran Crisis of 1945/46 and the Cold War', *Political Science Quarterly*, 29 (1974), pp. 117–46; Bruce R. Kuniholm, *The origins of the Cold War in the Near East* (Princeton, NJ, 1979); Bruce R. Kuniholm, *The origins of the Cold War in the Near East: great power conflict and diplomacy in Iran, Turkey and Greece* (Princeton, NJ, 1980); also the critique of Melvyn P. Leffler, 'From Cold War to Cold War in the Near East', *Reviews in American History*, 9 (1981), pp. 124–30.

11. Vandenberg to Dulles, 13 May 1946, Dulles Papers; Vandenberg to Luce, 28 May, 1946, Vandenberg Papers; both quoted after Yergin, *Shattered peace*, p. 223; the letter to Luce also in Joyce and Gabriel Kolko, *The limits of power* (New York, 1972), p. 48. American documents on the Paris Council meeting in FRUS (1946), II, pp. 88–440 and 493–940; on presentations, see Herbert Feis, *From trust to terror* (New York, 1970), pp. 121–35; Kolko, *Limits*, pp. 46–50; Yergin, *Shattered peace*, pp. 221–3.

12. See beow, pp. 123–4.

13. Documents on the Paris Peace Conference can be found in FRUS (1946), III and IV, *passim*; on the New York Council meeting in FRUS (1946), II, pp. 965–1566.

14. FRUS (1946), VII, pp. 840–7. Compare Dean Acheson, *Present at the creation: my years in the State Department* (New York, 1970), pp. 261–5; Yergin, *Shattered peace*, pp. 233–5; and Jonathan Knight, 'American state craft and the 1946 Black Sea Straits controversy', *Political Science Quarterly*, 90 (1975), pp. 451–75.

15. The 'revisionist' thesis that American loans after the end of the war were effected *only* for the sake of the economic interest and that the USA turned its back on the East European market because it was not able to implement its Open Door policy (e.g. Kolko, *Limits*, p. 197) is not tenable. Open Door demands were not in fact at the forefront of American policy towards Eastern Europe in 1946.

16. FRUS (1946), VI, pp. 828f.; compare George C. Herring, *Aid to Russia, 1941–1946* (New York, 1973), pp. 256–67. The US–Soviet credit transaction thus did not fall through, as Ernst Nolte maintains as a central position in his book (*Deutschland und der Kalte Krieg* (Munich, 1974), p. 180), because of the incompatibility of systems, but because of the decision of the USA now to exaggerate its Open Door demands to a degree, in contrast with 1944, that was no longer consistent with the Soviet system's securing of hegemony hitherto, a decision which was politically motivated.

17. American negotiation documents in FRUS (1946), V, pp. 409–64; analysis in Wilfried Loth, *Sozialismus und Internationalismus, Die französischen Sozialisten und die Nachkriegsordnung Europas 1940–1950* (Stuttgart, 1977), pp. 98–104.

18. Byrnes: FRUS (1946), VI, pp. 216f.; Czechoslovakia; Geir Lundestad, *The American non-policy towards Eastern Europe 1943–1947* (Tromsö, New York, 2nd edn, 1978), pp. 167–71; compare Walter Ullmann, *The United States in Prague 1945–1948* (New York, 1978); UNRRA: Lundestad, *Non-policy*, pp. 394–7; $5,700 million: calculated by Kolko, *Limits*, p. 26.

19. FRUS (1945), II, pp. 69–73.

20. Compare Gaddis, *The United States and the origins*, pp. 331–5; Kolko, *Limits*, pp. 98–110; Yergin, *Shattered peace*, pp. 237–41; Gregg, F. Herken, *The winning weapon, The atomic bomb in the Cold War 1945–1950* (New York, 1981); and Larry G. Gerber, 'The Baruch Plan and the origins of the Cold War', *Diplomatic History*, 6 (1982), pp. 69–95.

21. FRUS (1946), V. pp. 516–20.

22. Compare Dietrich Staritz, *Sozialismus in einem halben Land*, (Berlin, 1976), pp. 84–154; and also *Die Gründung der DDR. Von der sowjetischen Besatzungsherrschaft zum sozialistischen Staat* (Munich, 1984), pp. 75–112; Gregory Sandford, *From Hitler to Ulbricht. The Communist reconstruction of East Germany, 1945–1946* (Princeton, NJ, 1983).

23. Compare (attributing too great Sovietisation intentions to the German Communist Party) Albrecht Kaden, *Einheit oder Freiheit, Die Wiedergründung der SPD 1945/46* (Hanover, 1964); Klaus-Peter Schulz, *Auftakt zum Kalten Krieg, Der Freiheitskampf der SPD in Berlin 1945/46* (Berlin, 1965); Henry Krisch, *German politics under Soviet occupation* (New York, 1974); tending to stray from the essentials, Wolfgang Diepenthal, *Drei Volksdemokratien*, (Cologne, 1974), pp. 112–21; Staritz, *Sozialismus in einem halben Land*, pp. 60–83 and also *Gründung der DDR*, pp. 112–23; and Werner Müller, *Die KPD und die 'Einheit der Arbeiterklasse'*, (Frankfurt/ New York, 1979). The attempt by Gerhard Stuby, in 'Die SPD nach der Niederlage des Faschismus bis zur Gründung der BRD (1945–1949)', in *Geschichte der deutschen Sozialdemokratie 1863–1975*, (2nd edn, Cologne, 1977), pp. 242–306, here pp. 266–73, to represent these events as a vote on the part of the great majority of the German working class as a whole

for the founding of the SED is not convincing.

24. Murphy (Clay's state adviser) to Matthews, 3 April 1946; State Department Records, file 861.00; see Jean Edward Smith, 'The view from UFSET: General Clay's and Washington's interpretation of Soviet intentions in Germany, 1945–1948', in Hans A. Schmitt (ed.), *US occupation in Europe after World War II* (Lawrence, 1978), pp. 64–85.

25. At least not publicly; he confided to a journalist during the Paris negotiations 'that he had rather given up hope of a unified Germany' Mowrer to Pollock, 4 June 1946, Pollock papers, and Yergin, *Shattered peace*, p. 226. Compare in addition to the conference literature given in note 10, also Gaddis, *The United States and the origins*, pp. 328–31; Yergin, ibid., pp. 224–6; Axel Frohn, *Deutschland zwischen Neutralisierung und Westintegration* (Frankfurt, 1985), pp. 63–5, and note 24 above. Vyacheslav M. Molotov, *Fragen der Aussenpolitik, Reden und Erklärungen* (Moscow, 1949), pp. 218ff., Byrnes: *Europa–Archiv*, I (1946), pp. 261–4.

26. Compare John Gimbel, 'Byrnes' Stuttgarter Rede und die amerikanische Nachkriegspolitik in Deutschland', *Vierteljahrshefte für Zeitgeschichte*, 20 (1972), pp. 39–62; also by the same author, 'Die Vereinigten Staaten, Frankreich und der amerikanische Vertragsentwurf für Entmilitarisierung Deutschlands. Eine Studie über Legendenbildung im Kalten Krieg', *Vierteljahrshefte für zeitgeschichte*, 22 (1974), pp. 258–86; also 'The American reparations stop in Germany: an essay on the political uses of history', *The Historian*, 37 (1975), pp. 275–96; also 'Byrnes und die Bizone — eine amerikanische Entscheidung zur Teilung Deutschlands?' in Wolfgang Benz and Hermann Graml (ed.), *Aspekte deutscher Aussenpolitik im 20, Jahrhundert* (Stuttgart, 1976), pp. 193–210; also *The origins of the Marshall Plan* (Stanford, CA, 1976), pp. 67–126. Gimbel describes Byrnes's actions in minute detail, thereby destroying several hallowed legends of Cold War literature, although he himself often loses sight of the strategic connections in the process; certainly Byrnes's draft treaty was *also* intended to offer France a security guarantee against Germany, and thus to cause it to relinquish its obstruction of central authorities, but officials of the State Department had recommended the treaty as a test of the Soviet Union, and Byrnes also saw it in this way. Similarly, the British threat of withdrawing its own zone from the reparation association entirely if necessary was also the 'last straw' for Byrnes, but this still does not prove that he did not foresee the division of Germany as a consequence of his negotiations in July 1946; see for comparison, for example, the quotation in note 25, as well as Bevin's impression of a completely anti-Soviet attitude on the part of Byrnes during this phase of the conference, reported by Rolf Steininger, 'Die Rhein-Ruhr Frage im Kontext der britischen Deutschlandpolitik 1945/6', in Heinrich August Winkler (ed), *Politische Weichenstellungen im Nachkriegsdeutschland 1945–1949*, (Göttingen, 1979), pp. 111–66, esp. pp. 129f. Ultimately Byrnes's Stuttgart speech does *also* contain a warning signal to France, but the decisive factor was the message of this signal; the determination of the USA to involve itself in the reconstruction of Germany in the same way as the Soviet Union. This message was equally directed at the Germans themselves, to balance the positive impression of the Molotov Declaration. As Klaus Schwabe has shown ('Die amerikanische Besatzungspolitik in

Deutschland und die Entstehung des "Kalten Krieges" 1945/46', in *Russland–Deutschland–Amerika*, commemorative publication for the 80th birthday of Fritz T. Epstein, Wiesbaden, 1978, pp. 311–32), Clay's action, including the Stuttgart speech urged by him, were directed in the first instance at not allowing the USA to find itself at a disadvantage in relation to the Soviet Union. Unlike Byrnes, 'the military government was also to a large extent oriented towards cooperation with the four victorious powers in Germany' (p. 324).

27. FRUS (1946), V, pp. 611f., 622–5, 792f.

28. Text of Stalin's speech in *Neue Welt* (Berlin), no. 1 (1946), pp. 3–12; Third World War: William D. Douglas to Forrestal, *The Forrestal Diaries* (New York, 1951), p. 134.

29. Close observation of events in Eastern Europe shows that one cannot attribute to the Soviet Union, as do most 'traditional' authors (e.g. Ernst Birke and Rudolf Neumann (eds.), *Die Sowjetisierung Ost-Mitteleuropas, Untersuchungen zu ihrem Ablauf in den einzelnen Ländern*, vol. 1, Frankfurt/Berlin, 1959), a planned Soviet intention based on a unified concept, but also that one cannot completely deny the existence in its policies of imperialistic characteristics, as some 'revisionist' authors tend to do (e.g. Gabriel Kolko, *The politics of war* (New York, 1972), pp. 176–217). For differences in the processes of transformation in Poland, Czechoslovakia and the Soviet occupation zone of Germany, cf. Diepenthal, *Drei Volksdemokratien*, although it lacks a detailed and objective analysis.

30. Stephen D. Kertesz, *Between Russia and the West, Hungary and the illusion of peacemaking, 1945–47* (Notre Dame, 1984).

31. Martin Myant, *Socialism and democracy in Czechoslovakia, 1945–1947* (New York, 1981).

6

The Emergence of the Marshall Plan

The first year of American containment policy had been 'successful' in terms of its unintended side-effect, the incipient division of the world into two competing spheres of influence, but not at all successful, however, in its central aim, the stabilisation of those regions allegedly threatened by Communist expansion. Too many obstacles stood in the way: economic disruption in Europe was far more extensive than American planners had expected; the US loans that had already been granted were proving insufficient; and a return to protectionism threatened in all European countries. Congress was blocking new, more comprehensive credit: in spite of the popularity of containment policy, the American public was still not prepared to pay an appreciable price for the leading world role it demanded. The French government, moreover, backed by vigorous nationalist feeling among the French public, who wanted to use German resources for the reconstruction of France, was blocking the reconstruction of German industry, the nub of the whole European restoration programme. The Marshall Plan, developed by the US government in spring 1947, was an attempt to overcome these obstacles in one concerted effort — an attempt obviously also intended to uphold the fundamental economic Open Door interest in US calculations, but which at this juncture and with its specific formulation was clearly determined by a politically-motivated interest in the containment of Soviet expansion.

Europe in Crisis?

Inasmuch as the American public concerned itself with foreign policy questions, Byrnes's containment policy, particularly its anti-Communist rhetoric and its uncompromising adherence to the Atlantic Charter, was popular. Critics of the new course, such as Wallace, were only able to collect around themselves a small remnant of New Deal liberals. In any case, those interested in foreign policy represented only a minority among American voters: the majority had slipped into apathy after the exertions of the war. Even among supporters of the Republican Party, whose representatives were urging 'firmness' towards the Soviet Union most decisively, there was a widespread tendency not only not to increase the costs of foreign policy, but even to reduce them substantially. Truman's attempt to introduce a generally binding military training programme in peacetime collapsed in the face of combined resistance from religious, pacifist, agricultural, union and the more educational organisations. A 3,750 million dollar credit for Great Britain was disputed at length in Congress, in spite of its conditions being so favourable to Open Door interests, and it was only pushed through with great efforts on the part of the Administration. The Republicans won the Congressional elections in November 1946 with an election programme envisaging a 20 per cent reduction in income tax and a corresponding reduction in public spending by the government. When Truman presented the new Congress at the beginning of January 1947 with expenditure plans for the fiscal year to begin on 1 July, the Budget Commission initially reduced the budget from 37,700 million to 31,500 million dollars, including a reduction in military expenditure from 11,200 million to a scant 9,000 million dollars. General George C. Marshall, who had in the meantime replaced Byrnes as Secretary of State for Foreign Affairs, feared 'impossible' conditions in the occupied countries as a result of these restrictions.[1]

In fact, the situation in the Western zones of Germany and the West European countries could only be described as catastrophic from the American point of view: the loans of 1945/6 had been far too meagre to institute a process of stabilisation. The 650 million dollar loan to France, together with other supportive measures, had scarcely been sufficient to cover three-quarters of the French budget deficit from 1946. Even the 3,750 million dollar loan to Great Britain was used up far more quickly than expected. When the British government, in accordance with the loan agreement, introduced the free convertibility of the pound on 15 July 1947, the reserves from the loan fell within four weeks to 1,300 million dollars, with the result that convertibility had to be lifted again on 20 August, a round 400 million dollars remaining from the credit. Industrial production in France, Belgium and the Netherlands had reached some 85 per cent of the pre-war level at the end of 1946, and in Italy 60 per cent, whereas in Great Britain and Scandinavia it had slightly exceeded the pre-war level. In Germany, it stagnated at some 36 per cent of the 1936 level, thus holding back the other countries. Taken together, the production index of the sixteen participant countries of the Marshall Plan ran at 83 per cent of the pre-war level. Between the first and last quarters of 1946, production rose by 23 per cent, but gains that could have been used for new investment rose by only 1 per cent. In any case, there were few possibilities for investment: private American investors, because of the high risk, invested in Europe even less than financially weak Europeans in the USA. Europe was living on capital and on imports that it could no longer afford. In 1947, the sixteen countries reached a balance of payments deficit of 7,500 million dollars, whereas the USA in the same year produced a surplus of 10,000 million dollars.[2] The fact that the decline of the European economy had just come to an end, and what was later to be such a spectacular reconstruction process had just begun[3] — not particularly on the basis of American money, but mainly because an excess of skilled workers, soon made high investment levels possible — was hardly perceived by contemporaries. In contrast, the shortage of food after the climatically determined bad harvest of 1946, the shortage of coal in the extremely cold winter of 1946/7, and transport difficulties in war-devastated Germany intensified the impression of an impending crisis which, after all the European countries had experienced in the way of destruction during the war, was bound to have even worse consequences than the world economic crisis.

This crisis, as all American observers were agreed in spring 1947, had to be averted at all costs, not only because the severe plight of the European governments was pushing them once again towards protectionist measures, thus endangering Open Door policy (this argument was hardly mentioned any more at this juncture), but also because a European collapse would deprive the USA, threatened with a crisis of overproduction, of its most important trade and sales outlets, thus precipitating a world-wide recession of unimaginable proportions. Most importantly, this crisis, or at least so it seemed, could be exploited by the Communist movements to seize power for themselves in the interests of Moscow. In the eyes of American planners, memories of the world economic crisis and the dogmas of the containment were fused into nothing short of an apocalyptic vision. Full of 'hunger, economic misery and frustration', as William Clayton, Under-Secretary in the Department of Commerce, expressed it in a note of 5 March to the heads of the Administration, the majority of European countries were standing 'on the very brink and may be pushed over at any time; others are gravely threatened'. One could predict in Greece and France how economic collapse would be followed by a Communist take-over of power. Without American aid of enormous proportions 'such affairs will become so hopeless that the seeds of World War III will inevitably be sown'.[4]

The German political situation must have seemed absolutely hopeless against this background. German industry had always been the heart of the European economy, and its collapse had, if not actually triggered the European crisis, then definitely aggravated it: its rehabilitation, as State Department experts had emphasised since their fight against the Morgenthau Plan, had to be at the centre of efforts towards a reconstruction of the European market. The speedy rehabilitation of Germany, or, when any other alternative seemed impossible, of the Western zones, was all the more necessary since, as the American military government now increasingly suspected, the continuation of deprivation was beginning to make orientation towards the Soviet occupation power seem attractive to the population, thus threatening to push the whole of Germany into the Soviet sphere of influence. In order to open the way for the rehabilitation of West Germany, it was necessary to break the resistance of the French government, which had by its veto in the Allied Control Council hitherto blocked every step towards collective authorities for Germany and towards economic reconstruction, as long as the cession of the Ruhr and the Rhineland from the German federation and its economic co-exploitation with France were not ensured. Clay, with the support of the War Department, which no longer wanted to carry the high financial burden of the occupation, had been urging the State Department since spring 1946 to exert appropriate pressure on France. Experts of the State

Department, however, regarded such pressure as only of limited justification, since they feared that a forced relinquishment by the French of their political demands with regard to Germany would provoke a general national rebellion, from which the French Communists would ultimately emerge the victors — an argument of which they were very skillfully persuaded by representatives of the French government. 'Clay is running a German show', as Charles P. Kindleberger, former head of the German–Austrian section of the State Department, described the problem in August 1946, but 'the State Department tries to tell him from time to time to pay attention to the consequences on third countries. Especially has this been true in France where our policy has been to baby government along, because of fear of Communists capitalizing on our toughness, while the French have stabbed our German policy in the back.' State experts regarded conditions in France as extremely unstable. 'In France', Acheson, for example, declared in February 1947 to leading Congress members, 'with four Communists in the Cabinet, one of them Minister of Defense, with Communists controlling the largest trade union and infiltrating government offices, factories, and the armed services, with nearly a third of the electorate voting Communist, and with economic conditions worsening, the Russians could pull the plug any time they chose.'[5] Efforts to contain Soviet expansion in Germany thus encouraged Soviet expansion in France, and vice versa. If one did nothing, however, the economic crisis would encourage Soviet expansion everywhere — an insuperable dilemma, assuming that one believed in the thesis of Soviet expansionism, but no one in Washington dared to doubt its correctness.

The consciousness of being confronted by a dangerous crisis was further accentuated by the fact that Soviet policy was interpreted as being a deliberate encouragement of the impoverishment of Europe in the interests of a Communist take-over of power. At the fourth meeting of the Council of Foreign Ministers, in Moscow, at which the peace treaty with Germany was negotiated from 10 March until 24 April 1947, and the Soviet leadership persisted with its reparation demands (in Soviet eyes, a test case for American co-operativeness), this interpretation seemed to be confirmed. Molotov proved ready to make concessions in order to prevent a unilateral rehabilitation of Germany, so that it was then possible on 2 and 3 April (albeit in Bidault's absence) to reach an agreement on the creation of a central German administration, a German consultative council and the plan presented by Bevin for the gradual establishment of a provisional German government. All four foreign ministers decided jointly to carry out land reform in the whole of Germany within 1947. After all this had been achieved, however, Marshall caused deadlock in the conference with his categorical refusal to agree to reparations — against Clay's advice to yield somewhat in the matter of reparations in order to salvage German economic unity. Stalin's co-operatively intended request for patient continued negotiation on the reparations issue ('Differences had occurred before on other questions, and as a rule after people had exhausted themselves in dispute they then recognized the necessity of compromise') he interpreted as a deliberate delay of any solution of the German question until there was a collapse in the whole of Europe. 'Disintegrating forces are becoming evident', declared Marshall on the day of his return from Moscow in a radio message to the nation. The patient is sinking while the doctors deliberate. So I believe that action cannot await compromise through exhaustion.'[6]

The contradiction between the unwillingness of Congress to pay out and the crisis into which this forced the Truman Administration in the spring of 1947 had thus escalated to the same vast proportions as the dilemma that had been precipitated by French policy towards Germany. The urgent necessity of a much more comprehensive aid programme, aimed mainly at Western Europe, was now completely beyond question; it was now a matter of finding a way to overcome the resistance first of Congress, and secondly of the French government. The Truman Administration, mainly due to the fact that Marshall's co-ordination abilities were considerably more effective than those of Byrnes, finally accomplished both these things:[7] the former according to plan, the latter under pressure and by improvisation.

The Truman Doctrine

Officials of the State Department had discovered the key to the problem of the internal political implementation of stabilisation policy during the debate in the spring of 1946 on the loan to Great Britain. As long as the necessity of the Open Door policy was invoked, opposition seemed insurmountable. When Dean Acheson presented the loan as aid in order to pre-empt a

Communist threat in Great Britain, however, a breakthrough had been achieved. In order to mobilise Congress for the appropriate granting of aid, therefore, it would be necessary to fall back on anti-Communist tendencies among the American public, in order to present the threat of Soviet expansion in a consciously simplified and exaggerated way.[8] The State Department found grounds for such an operation, which had been urged in a series of memoranda since the beginning of that year, in the announcement by the British government on 21 February that it would have to discontinue its military and economic support of Greece and Turkey by 31 March 1947 because of internal economic difficulties.

This announcement by Hugh Dalton, Chancellor of the Exchequer, carried out against the dogged resistance of his colleague Bevin, certainly came as a surprise at that juncture, but it did not fit the facts. The British and American governments had already agreed in October 1946 to share support for Greece and Turkey because of Britain's shortage of finances: Britain was additionally to supply weapons and the USA to provide other resources and to help out with weapons in case of need.[9] There was no doubt that the Administration was prepared even to take sole responsibility for the stabilisation of the two countries: as Robert Patterson, the Secretary of War, had said, 'the independence of Greece and Turkey were of vital importance to the US strategic position',[10] and both countries looked as though they might fall into the Soviet power zone, if they were not given support.

The fact that the situation in these two countries was by no means so unambiguous was given little thought. The Soviet Union had demanded from Turkey the right to participate in supervision of the Straits, but this had not amounted, until the Potsdam conference, to an attempt to draw Turkey into the Soviet power zone. In Greece, the 'National Liberation Movement' (EAM) of broad-based worker and peasant groups, only partly controlled by elite Communist groups, after their defeat by British troops at the turn of 1944/5 had taken up their partisan struggle again in the summer of 1946, in response to the 'white terror', the brutal persecution of all opposition forces by the authoritarian government. Stalin, however, on the basis of his spheres-of-influence arrangement with Churchill, had kept out of the conflict, and later even severely reprimanded Yugoslavia and Bulgaria for their support of the partisans.[11] Of course Soviet co-supervision of the Straits could not be in the strategic interests of the USA, and a victory of the 'National Liberation Movement', in view of Stalin's orientation towards the contemporary Greek Communist Party, threatened to lead to a change of political course in the direction of the Yugoslav model. Under closer scrutiny, however, neither of these cases could be offered as proof of aggressive Soviet expansionism.

Such closer scrutiny was therefore deliberately avoided, in spite of the doubts of a few liberals in the State Department. Convinced of the fundamental justification of the thesis of Soviet expansionism even in Greece and Turkey, the Executive presented both these cases as Soviet attacks on the free democratic order of the West. To an audience of leading Congressmen called together by President Truman for consultation on the British aid application, Acheson declared on 27 February that 'a Soviet breakthrough' in the Near East was 'highly probable', and that then it 'might open three continents to Soviet penetration'. 'Like apples in a barrel infected by the corruption of one rotten one, the corruption of Greece would infect Iran and all to the East ... likewise Africa ... Italy and France ... Not since Rome and Carthage had there been such a polarization of power on this earth.' Before both houses of Congress on 12 March, Truman then depicted events in Greece and Turkey as part of a global struggle between two alternative ways of life: 'One way of life is based upon the will of the majority, and is distinguished by free institutions, representative government, free elections, guarantees of individual liberty, freedom of speech and religion, and freedom from political oppression. The second way of life is based upon the will of a minority forcibly imposed upon the majority. It relies upon terror and oppression, a controlled press and radio, fixed elections, and the suppression of personal freedoms.' In order not to lose this struggle, it had to be 'the policy of the United States to support free peoples who are resisting attempted subjugation by armed minorities or by outside pressures'.[12]

Even if one believed in the dogma of Soviet expansionism, it was bordering on cynicism to describe Greece as an example of the struggle of totalitarian minorities against a democratic majority, and irresponsible flippancy to make out a blank cheque for American aid to all countries pleading 'outside pressures'. Nevertheless this black and white view of the world and the missionary role attributed to the United States in it exactly suited the historical tradition of the 'New World' and the ideological truism of an

American society convinced of its 'way of life'. Truman and his colleagues accepted the distortions and exaggerations of this 'Truman Doctrine' in order to mobilise Congress and the American public, not only for the support of Greece and Turkey, but also for what was now a financial and material commitment to containment policy.[13] Their success proved them right: within two months Congress had allocated the 300 million dollars requested for Greece and the 100 million dollars for Turkey (not without emphasising that it did not want to issue *any* blank cheques). The Greek government received so much material support that after a further two years of bloody fighting it was able to defeat the partisan movement in the summer of 1949. In future, the Truman Administration was to find not only agreement to its policy of containment, but also a supportive attitude among the bulk of the American population.

Nevertheless, the Truman Administration also paid for this successful 'public relations operation' with a new and considerable restriction of manoeuvrability in its foreign policy, a restriction foreseen at the time of the Truman speech by only a few critics, such as Walter Lippmann and Kennan, the latter being much more discriminating in private than he was in his public remarks.[14] The anti-Communist rhetoric of the Truman Doctrine, with its deliberate simplicity, gave such a boost to the anti-Communist movement in the USA that the dogmas of the containment doctrine soon became part of the basic national consensus, thus in turn inevitably affecting the government, although of necessity in a simplified form. The government had already missed a number of alternative decision possibilities, having become accustomed to viewing all problems of world politics in terms of the Soviet–American conflict: now it was obliged to do without alternative options almost entirely, as it could scarcely any longer afford significant deviations in front of the public from the line prescribed by the Truman Doctrine. Although, therefore, the doctrine had not 'actually' been intended as it had been formulated, the government was increasingly obliged to align itself with it. Thus the Greek example of support for an authoritarian and repressive power in the name of freedom soon found unfortunate imitation (after Iran, mainly in South Korea and Indo-China). At the same time, awareness of the imperialistic features of their own policies, or even of the realities of their own power, was lost to members of the US government as a result of defensive interpretations in relation to the Soviet threat.

Marshall's offer

The second obstacle, France's refusal to agree to a swift reconstruction of the German economy, was only overcome with massive domestic and foreign policy pressure.[15] Clay and the War Department had meanwhile acquired powerful allies in their demand for a swift rehabilitation of the economy, at least in the bizone — the British government and the Republican majority in the new Congress. In the course of their tax-reduction campaign, the Republicans had also homed in on the high costs of American occupation and, in preparing an all-out attack on the 'failure' of the government in its occupation policy since 1945, had demanded the comprehensive self-financing of the occupied zones by means of an increase in production. Impressed by the argument of former President Herbert Hoover, who after an official government information trip round Germany in January/February demanded the liberation of German industry (particularly heavy industry) from all restrictions, 'so as to relieve American taxpayers of the burdens of relief and for economic recovery of Europe',[16] they found it expedient in conjunction with the War Department to dictate a new German policy without regard to the possible endangering of France, while Marshall was away at the foreign ministers' meeting in Moscow. At the same time, the British Foreign Secretary, Ernest Bevin, made it unequivocally clear to his American colleagues that the British shortage of finance would no longer permit prevarication in Germany; annual steel production in the bizone, he declared on 14 April, must be directly raised to 10 million tons (in the industrial plan of March 1946 a level of 7.8 million tons had been agreed for the whole of Germany), otherwise Great Britain would dismantle the bizone and continue to allow only Ruhr industry to operate to finance the British zone.[17]

Marshall was no longer able to resist this double pressure. Under the impression that the Soviet leadership was banking on the further impoverishment of Germany in particular, he agreed on 18 April to Bevin's demand for a general raising of production in the bizone, including the raising of steel production to 10–12 million tons (the military governors were to work out the details), as well as to a more effective and new organisation of bizonal economic administration, and its centralisation at another location. Bevin only had to agree that the new organisation would not lead to the setting-up of a provisional government, and that the public announcement of these decisions would be postponed by about six weeks.[18] The dilemma of American policy towards Germany had thus now been resolved by force: Marshall was no longer faced with the problem of having to choose between the collapse of Germany and the collapse of France and yet not being able to choose either. The convenient reconstruction of West Germany without regard to German unity and French demands was thus decided upon, and there now 'only' remained the problem of how to prevent the collapse of France.

As far as possible, this problem needed to be solved within six weeks. Bidault, France's Minister of Foreign Affairs, had acquired the conviction during the Moscow council meeting that Soviet policy was aimed at expansion as far as the Atlantic. He had given up his demand for mediation between East and West, and now urged 'containment'; thus he was more open to pressure from the American government, although he still remained to a certain extent dependent on nationalist groups, especially the Communists and the growing Gaullist opposition movement. The State Department was convinced that if Bidault were to fall, it would sooner or later lead to a Communist take-over of power.[19] Under pressure from Marshall not to delay, State Department planners, especially those of the political planning staff headed by George Kennan, seized on the previously developed concept, already discussed both among the American public and in the Administration, which now promised to solve the problem of the reconstruction of Germany and France at one stroke: the concept of *joint* economic aid for the European countries, including (West) Germany, combined with extensive integration of the national political economies.

John Foster Dulles may be regarded as the originator of this concept, having like almost no other proponent of containment policy pointed again and again as early as 1946 to the necessity of confronting France with the much too severe demands of its German policy, arising from its internal political instability. As a way out of the impasse into which this policy was leading, he called on the people, in a spectacular speech given on 17 January 1947 in New York, to 'plan the future of Germany' ... more in terms of the economic unity of Europe and less in terms of the Potsdam dictum that Germany shall be "a single economic unit"'. The world, particularly Western Europe, was threatened by a 'Soviet challenge' more dangerous than Soviet expansion as far as the Iron Curtain, namely the revolutionary and subversive challenge presented by 'economic need'. Therefore, as the Founding Fathers of the USA had once done, now also in Europe the victorious power must place 'matters of concern to all under an administration responsible to all. Europe divided into small economic compartments cannot be a healthy Europe. All of Europe's economic potentialities need to be used and European markets should be big enough to justify modern methods of cheap production for mass consumption.'[20] Unlike Churchill's Zurich plea for 'a kind of United States of Europe' on 19 September 1946, this speech was entirely well received by the American public, both on the Republican and the Democratic sides; for example, by Walter Lippmann, who called on 20 March 1947 for a 'European economic union' in order to avoid the threatening collapse of the European political economies, additionally speaking in Congress on 31 March in favour of the 'creation of a United States of Europe within the framework of the UN'.[21] An *ad hoc* committee from the State and War Departments and the Navy Coordination Committee (SWNCC) was formed to examine the necessities and possibilities of new foreign loans, presenting a 'preliminary report' on 21 April — that is, before Marshall's return from Moscow — which not only confirmed yet again that quite substantial aid was in the interests of American security, but which additionally pointed out that the 'cost and duration of United States economic assistance are directly dependent upon the successful integration and coordination of the economic programs in the critical countries both with each other and with similar programs in countries not receiving special US aid'.[22]

A co-ordinated European programme of reconstruction, as was here conceived, had three decisive advantages compared with the hitherto individual loans. First, as was elucidated in planning texts until the end of April, it took better account of the actual independence of European economies, facilitated the rational implementation of American means, not least by means of a more effective division of labour in the European countries, and thus had a better chance of bringing about lasting economic stabilisation in these countries. It also offered better guarantees for the implementation of a multilateral free trade system and against the general tendency towards a relapse into protectionist measures. Secondly, an additional factor after the Moscow decision on the German question was that the programme held out hopes for solving the problem of France, which was still an obstacle to the reconstruction of Germany, the latter in turn being indispensable to the reconstruction of Europe. It did this by offering France new American credit instead of German reparations, thus proposing a recovery of both the French *and* the German economy, which would enable France to buy the German products it required, and thus lead to a certain institutionalisation of the interdependence between the German and French economies, thereby removing the grounds for French fears of repeated German dominance. Thirdly, as was shown by the favourable response among the American public, the programme had the advantage of making the considerable new loans domestically acceptable by combining them with the anti-Communist rhetoric of the Truman Doctrine, offering a potential forward leap with the 'unification' of Europe, which would make future subsidies superfluous, a leap for which there was, however (or at least apparently), an extremely successful parallel in the history of the 'United States' of America.

What had previously been highly desirable now became urgently necessary with the Moscow agreements between Marshall and Bevin, and now even seemed realisable. Immediately after Marshall's return from Moscow therefore, all the personnel of the Truman Administration agreed on the decision to launch the new multilateral aid programme at this point.[23] With an eye to the European public, which, unlike the American public, had characterised the Truman Doctrine very unfavourably, Kennan's Political Planning staff formulated in a memorandum prepared on 23 May the main tactical elements of the operation that was now beginning. The American offer was not to be presented as a programme for combating Communism, but for combating the economic disaster in Europe, 'which makes European society vulnerable to exploitation by any and all totalitarian movements'. It was not to be formulated by the US government, but by the Europeans: 'the formal initiative must come from Europe'; and for political and economic reasons it had to be 'a joint one agreed to by several European nations'. The offer was in principle to be open also to the East European countries, and even the Soviet Union, inasmuch as the (West) European countries wanted it to be, but it then had to be formulated in such a manner 'that the Russian satellite countries would either exclude themselves by unwillingness to accept the proposed conditions, or agree to abandon the exclusive orientation of their economies'.[24]

In his speech of 5 June at Harvard University, Marshall basically kept to Kennan's recommendations, setting off a world-wide debate on what was soon to be described as the 'Marshall Plan'. He depicted the economic misery of Europe as it had been described in State Department analysis, encouraged 'a joint program' for reconstruction 'agreed to by a number, if not all, European nations', and announced in addition (so as not formally to pre-empt the jurisdiction of Congress) merely his willingness that 'the role of this country should consist of friendly aid in the drafting of a European program and of later support of such a program so far as it may be practical for us to do so'. Questioned on this, he specified in a press announcement on 12 June that this offer was valid for 'all countries west of Asia', and that even the Soviet Union was welcome.[25] Europeans and Soviets were thus invited to discuss the new American aid offer.

The significance of the Marshall Plan

Marshall's offer, as is shown by the background to its emergence, was originally thought of as a tactic to make the rehabilitation of (West) Germany, the heart of European reconstruction, acceptable, especially in France, in terms of the domestic politics of the USA,[26] and additionally as a means of using this reconstruction to protect the European region from Soviet expansion and to restore it as an outlet and trading partner of the USA. Both these aims, containment against Communist subversion and economic stabilisation in the liberal sense, were inseparable in the view of the US leadership, and thus also functioned together in fact. In the same way that the interest in the reconstruction of German industry and the integration of the European economy cannot be explained *only* in terms of the fear of an expansion of the Soviet power zone, so too the consequences of economic aid to (Western) Europe and its concentration in the spring of 1947 also cannot *only* be explained in terms of an interest in a multilateral system of free trade. Among the American public, and to some extent also among the American leadership, the securing of free trade was almost seen simply as a means of containing Communism. In fact, containment rhetoric had a similar function in furthering domestic acceptance of loans in the USA and Open Door policy in Europe. Containment policy opened up for the US economy the prospect of penetrating the European market, but also limited it in its room for manoeuvre: the principle for the distribution of state subsidies was no longer namely economic profitableness, but the current degree of (supposed) political threat. (Of course, once the Marshall Plan had been set in motion, the US economy did attempt to implement specific economic interests counter to this political principle of distribution, but as will be shown this was only partially successful.)[27]

The observation that the Marshall Plan was thought of politically as an instrument for the containment of Soviet expansion is not contradicted by the fact that Marshall's offer also applied to the Soviet Union and the East European countries. Furthermore, this offer should not be understood as a mere tactical attempt to shift responsibility for the division of Europe onto the Soviet leadership in the eyes of the public. Clearly it was *also* for this purpose; those responsible for the plan in Washington had developed the suggestion of including Eastern Europe and the Soviet Union with an eye to West Europeans, who at that juncture were for the most part not predisposed to the formation of a Western bloc. Western Europe (including West Germany) had since 1946 been placed at the centre of the reconstruction programme in their order of priorities; they hardly expected Soviet approval and had no intention of making any particular political efforts to obtain such approval. Nevertheless, some of the experts involved in the formulation of the Marshall Plan policy expressly declared the participation of the East European countries to be desirable, taking into account the economic interdependence of Eastern and Western Europe, thus substantially reducing the cost and duration of West European reconstruction.[28] The inclusion of the East European countries would furthermore bring some chance of limiting Soviet influence in the region, and possibly even of reducing it, although only of course if the Soviet Union itself kept out of the programme (this thus appeared in some planning texts as an ideal concept).[29] In any case, the USA had nothing to lose by the participation of Eastern Europe and the Soviet Union, for which reason the American offer contained only one publicly mentioned condition: the co-ordination of the reconstruction programmes of all participant countries and the beginning of their economic integration.

For the Soviet Union, consent to this condition would have meant relinquishing the unilateral pro-Soviet orientation of economic policy in the East European countries, inevitably combined with a loosening of political ties with the Soviet state. Such a decision, after all that had just occurred in the East–West confrontation, was certainly no longer likely. However, in *this* offer (unlike the case of the credit offer of February 1946), it was by no means definite whether it would be aimed at an economic co-operation useful to both sides, or economic penetration in the unilateral interests of the USA. It was at the same time aimed at the West European countries, most of whom at that time did not wish to have economic aid at the price of the political hegemony of the USA; it thus contained the possibility of the Soviet Union finding an ally among the European countries against the political superiority of the USA. The offer was certainly directed at the export of the liberal economic principles of the USA (for the benefit of the Europeans, as was taken for granted, but also of course for the benefit of the USA), but not, however, against the European Left,[30] offering at the same time with European integration an instrument with which Europeans could protect themselves from unilateral measures by the American economic power. The offer was aimed at combating a threat which in reality did not even exist, but coincided in this reality with Soviet strategy, which was also aimed at the economic stabilisation of Western and Eastern Europe. It could not therefore be completely ruled out that economic interests — in American funds, on the one hand, and the inclusion of the Soviet Union and Eastern Europe in a multilateral system of free trade, on the other — would after all prevail over the mutual fear of expansion, and thus put a stop to the escalation mechanism of the East–West conflict.

Contemporaries were by all accounts aware of such a possibility. Liberals and socialists of all shades from Prague to San Francisco saw in Marshall's speech the hope for a unified and independent Europe, which would have a substantial effect on Soviet–American disagreements. Walter Lippmann, for example, described this vision thus:

> But there are reasons for thinking that the Russians will not be able to maintain the iron curtain and that we cannot construct western Europe as a containing wall. They are that the vital needs of the people of Europe will prevail: the economic interdependence of western and eastern Europe will compel the nations of the continent to exchange their goods across the military, political and ideological boundary lines which now separate them. The great virtue of the Marshall proposal is that it has set in motion studies abroad and in this country which will demonstrate conclusively

that the division of Europe cannot be perpetuated. And since the division of Europe came about because the Red Army and the Anglo-American armies met in the middle of Europe, the withdrawal of these armies is necessary if Europe is to be reunited. The Harvard speech calls, therefore, for a policy of settlement, addressed to the military evacuation of the Continent, not for a policy of containment which would freeze the non-European armies in the heart of Europe.[31]

What the Marshall Plan would actually lead to beyond fictive 'containment' — to a definitive division of Europe into two halves, or to the overcoming of such a division, to the Americanisation of Western Europe or to the restoration of the independence of the Continent — did not, however, depend only on how far American policy would be able to release itself from the chains that had been laid on it by the dogmas of the Truman Doctrine, but also, and even more so, on the response of the Soviet leadership and the Europeans to the American offer. It speaks for the openness of the situation in the summer of 1947 that not only did the Europeans debate their response in the sense outlined by Lippmann, but also that the Soviet leadership gave very serious thought to its response.

Notes

1. Quoted from Joseph M. Jones, *The fifteen weeks (February 21–June 5, 1947)* (2nd edn, New York, 1964), pp. 90f.; compare John L. Gaddis, *The United States and the origins of the Cold War 1941–1947* (2nd edn, New York, 1976), pp. 341–6. Jones's account, which originally appeared in 1955, is still seminal on events within the US Administration in the spring of 1947, in spite of the subsequent opening of archives. Also worthy of mention from among the other older works are Warren L. Hickman, 'Genesis of the European recovery program. A study of the trend of American economic policies', dissertation, Geneva (1949), as well as William C. Mallalieu, 'The origin of the Marshall Plan. A study in policy formation and national leadership', *Political Science Quarterly*, 73 (1958), pp. 481–504. For newer works see notes below.

2. Compare the compilation of relevant data in S.E. Harris, *The European recovery program* (Cambridge, Mass., 1948), quoted here pp. 30f., 41–51, 92, 168f., 252–9; also the collection of contemporary impressions (on a study trip made by the author round Europe in the summer of 1947 for the National War College) in Thomas A. Bailey, *The Marshall Plan*

summer. An eyewitness report on Europe and the Russians in 1947 (Stanford, Ca., 1977).

3. As Werner Abelshauser has shown in the extreme case of the particularly devastated, but subsequently particularly successful Western zones of Germany; *Wirtschaft in Westdeutschland, Rekonstruktion und Wachstumsbedingungen in der amerikanischen und britischen Zone* (Stuttgart, 1975); and also 'Wiederaufbau vor dem Marshall-Plan, Westeuropas Wachstumschancen und die Wirtschaftspolitik in der zweiten Hälfte der vierziger Jahre', *Vierteljahrshefte für Zeitgeschichte*, 29 (1981), pp. 545–78.

4. Text for this from Dean Acheson, *Present at the creation* (New York, 1970), p. 226. For further discussion of this seminal memorandum, see Ellen Clayton-Garwood, *Will Clayton: a short biography* (Austin, Texas, 1958), pp. 115–18; numerous similar accounts in Daniel Yergin, *Shattered peace* (Boston, 1977), pp. 279–82; Walter Lipgens, *A history of European integration 1945–1947* (Oxford, 1982), pp. 462f., 468–73; and Imanuel Wexler, *The Marshall Plan revisited. The European recovery program in economic perspective* (Westport, Conn., 1983).

5. Kindleberger to J.K. Galbraith and E. Mason, 13 August 1946; Kindleberger, *Papers*, quoted from Yergin, *Shattered peace*, p. 458; Acheson quoted from Jones, *Fifteen weeks*, p. 140. On French obstruction policy, see Ernst Deuerlein, 'Frankreichs Obstruktion deutscher Zentralverwaltung 1945', *Deutschland Archiv*, I (1971), pp. 455–91; on the aims of French foreign policy, see Walter Lipgens, 'Bedingungen und Etappen der Aussenpolitik de Gaulles 1944–1946', *Vierteljahrshefte für Zeitgeschichte*, 21 (1973), pp. 52–102; on the efforts of Clay and the War Department, John Gimbel, *The origins of the Marshall Plan* (Stanford, Ca., 1976), *passim*; on the motive for the reticence of the State Department, see Wilfried Loth, 'Frankreichs Kommunisten und der Beginn des Kalten Krieges', *Vierteljahrshefte für Zeitgeschichte*, 26 (1978), pp. 56f.

6. Marshall–Stalin conversation on 15 April 1947, in *Foreign relations of the United States*, diplomatic papers (hereinafter cited as FRUS) (1947), II, pp. 337–44; radio speech of Marshall on 28 April 1947, quoted from Department of State, Germany, 1947–1949 (Washington, DC, 1950), p. 57. Soviet declarations in Vyacheslav M. Molotov, *Fragen der Aussenpolitik, Reden und Erklärungen* (Moscow, 1949), pp. 367–495. Conference accounts which appeared before the publication of the FRUS documents only bear out Marshall's interpretation: Boris Meissner, *Russland, die Westmächte und Deutschland* (2nd edn, Hamburg, 1954), pp. 105–31; and Herbert Feis, *From trust to terror* (New York, 1970), pp. 208–20. On the perception of the conference by the US delegation, see Yergin, *Shattered peace*, pp. 296–302.

7. The fact that these difficulties were able to be resolved in spite of the gloomy prospects of spring 1947 made a lasting impression on all those involved. The legend thus arose that this shift of US policy to 'containment' occurred only under Marshall. See the particularly impressive account by Kennan's colleague, Louis J. Halle, *Der Kalte Krieg* (Frankfurt, 1969), pp. 108–37.

8. Seminal on this is Richard M. Freeland, *The Truman Doctrine and the origins of McCarthyism, Foreign policy, domestic politics, and internal security 1946–1948* (New York, 1972). Freeland's later thesis that the Truman

Administration consciously fanned up anti-Communist hysteria in order to promote its foreign policy programme (p. 10), however, is contradicted by the material he himself presents. In fact, the government drew support from an already existing anti-Communist movement, also seeking even to bring it under control with domestic political means, but was none the less unable to prevent it from being further intensified by foreign policy rhetoric. Kolko's argument (*The limits of power* (New York, 1972), pp. 68f., 331, 341, 376–9) that the Truman Administration cynically 'made up' the Soviet threat of expansion in order to implement its Open Door policy is greatly exaggerated. Internal documents show that American politicians did already believe what they uttered more crudely outwardly. Their whole containment practice from the beginning of 1946 would otherwise be incomprehensible.

9. See FRUS (1946), VII, p. 255.

10. FRUS (1947), V, p. 57.

11. Compare George Kousoulas, 'The Truman Doctrine and the Stalin–Tito rift; a reappraisal', *South Atlantic Quarterly*, 72 (1973), pp. 431ff. 'The most well-informed account of the situation is John Iatrides, *Revolt in Athens: the Greek Communist 'Second-Round', 1944–1945* (Princeton, NJ, 1972); and Heinz Richter, *British intervention in Greece. From Varzika to civil war* (London, 1985). For further development of the conflict, see Christopher M. Woodhouse, *The struggle for Greece 1941–1949* (London, 1976); and Lawrence S. Wittner, *American intervention in Greece 1943–1949* (New York, 1982).

12. Acheson: Jones, *Fifteen weeks*, pp. 140f, (cf. note 5 above); Truman: *Public papers of the presidents of the United States: Harry S. Truman 1947* (Washington, DC, 1963), pp. 177ff.

13. Critics of the 'excessive dimensions' of the Truman Doctrine (e.g. Halle, *Der Kalte Krieg*, pp. 124–9) overlook the fact that its main function was domestic.

14. On Kennan, see Jones, *Fifteen weeks*, pp. 154ff.; and George F. Kennan, *Memoirs 1925–1950* (Boston, 1967), ch. 13; on Lippmann, see the collection of his articles from August–September 1947 in the *New York Herald Tribune* in Walter Lippmann, *The Cold War. A study in US foreign policy* (New York, 1947). Ironically, Lippmann wrote his article in disagreement with Kennan's by then famous (although in fact very ambiguous) popularisation of the containment doctrine, the 'Mr X' article in the July 1947 number of *Foreign Affairs* (see Introduction, note 2, above).

15. As Gimbel has shown in his pioneering work on the history of the emergence of the Marshall Plan (*Origins*, esp. pp. 179–206). Gimbel's further thesis that the Marshall Plan was not conceived 'as an answer to the Soviet Union or as an element in the Cold War', but only as an attempt to solve the dilemma of German policy, is clearly not tenable. It omits the fact, as mentioned above, that this dilemma itself only arose from the implications of containment policy, and also fails to take a number of important connections in the spring of 1947 into account, as will be shown below. Compare also Manfred Knapp, 'Das Deutschlandproblem und die Ursprünge des europäischen Wiederaufbauprogramms, Eine Auseinandersetzung mit John Gimbels Untersuchung "The Origins of the Marshall Plan"' *Politische Vierteljahrsschrift*, 19

(1978), pp. 48–65 and Axel Frohn, *Deutschland zwischen Neutralisierung und Westintegration* (Frankfurt, 1985), pp. 98–105.

16. As in the title of the third memorandum submitted by Hoover, dated 18 March 1947, quoted by Gimbel, *Origins*, p. 183. On Hoover's German trip, see Louis P. Lochner, *Herbert Hoover and Germany* (New York, 1960), pp. 179ff.

17. FRUS (1947), II, pp. 315–17, 473–5.

18. FRUS (1947), II, pp. 357f. It seems to me highly significant in terms of interpretation that between Bevin's original demands (on 8 April), his threat of breaking up the bizone (on 14 April) and Marshall's agreement (on 18 April) occurs Marshall's key conversation with Stalin (on 15 April); see above, note 6, a fact which Gimbel, *Origins*, (here pp. 189–92) completely overlooks.

19. Which Gimbel likewise overlooks. Cf. Wilfried Loth, 'The West-European governments and the impulse given by the Marshall Plan', in Lipgens, *History*, pp. 488–507, here p. 497.

20. *Vital speeches of the Day*, 13 (1947), pp. 234–6, this being the third and most essential connection which Gimbel overlooks.

21. Compare with a number of other accounts Lipgens, *History*, pp. 468–71; further evidence in Ernst H. van der Beugel, *From Marshall Aid to Atlantic partnership. European integration as a concern of American foreign policy* (Amsterdam, London, New York, 1966), pp. 100–3; also the whole of Pierre Melandri, *Les Etats-Unis face à l'unification de l'Europe 1945–1954* (Paris, 1980).

22. FRUS (1947), III, pp. 204–13. The SWNCC group subsequently made its ideas more precise; their concluding memorandum of 12 June 1947 (extracts in Jones, *Fifteen weeks*, pp. 149–201 and 243f.) recommended 'a plan for European reconstruction which would help European production and consumption back on its feet by means of the economic and functional unification of Europe'.

23. Although no conference took place which formally took such a resolution, all considerations and activities of the Administration converged at this point, and Marshall's action, which will be discussed below, was not disputed.

24. FRUS (1947), III, pp. 223–9; see also on the emergence of the policy, Kennan, *Memoirs*, pp. 326–42.

25. The text of the Harvard speech has been published many times, e.g. in *A decade of American foreign policy, Basic documents, 1941–49* (Washington, DC, 1950) pp. 1268–70; press announcement in Harvey B. Price, *The Marshall Plan and its meaning* (Ithaca, NY, 1955), p. 21.

26. Thus far we can agree with Gimbel, but this was not the whole of the plan.

27. Every interpretation which bases the Marshall Plan one-sidedly on economic interests, as do most 'revisionists', or political interests, as do the 'traditionalists', falls short of the truth. Such incomplete interpretations, leaving aside function analysis, are also untenable in the area of motivation analysis. In the internal discussion papers for the preparation of the Marshall speech, there are neither 'references to Communism' (in contrast with what Kolko, *Limits*, p. 376, maintains) nor hints of the necessity of an environment in accordance with the interests of American capitalism.

28. This line of argument is most apparent in the memorandum of Van Cleveland, Moore and Kindleberger, three members of the SWNCC *ad hoc* group, of 9 May 1947, in Joseph M. Jones's Papers, Truman Library: information given by Geir Lundestad, Oslo.

29. Particularly in the memoranda of William C. Clayton, FRUS (1947), III, p. 232, 235f., 244, 290f. See for discussion of the Administration on the incorporation of Eastern Europe, Geir Lundestad, *The American non-policy towards Eastern Europe 1943–1947* (2nd edn, Tromsö, New York, 1978), pp. 397–408.

30. There is no evidence to support the corresponding thesis in the 'revisionist' literature (e.g. Kolko, *Limits*, p. 358); it confuses original intentions with subsequent effects. In fact, the social democratic faction of the European Left seemed, at least to the State Department, an ideal partner.

31. Lippmann, *The Cold War*, pp. 56f.

7

The Soviet Response: From the Paris Conference to the Break with Tito

From the beginning of American containment policy the Soviet leadership had repeatedly warned, in the strongest language, of the danger of 'imperialist warmongers' in the West, but had at the same time vigorously emphasised its readiness to co-operate. The Soviet Union attempted to achieve its foreign policy goals (particularly on the reparations issue) by means of patient negotiation, and intensified its efforts at stabilisation in Western Europe. Even the announcement of the Truman Doctrine had done nothing to alter this; on the contrary, *Pravda* had remained silent after a clear warning against 'the realisation of certain plans of a world power'. In an interview with the Republican Harold Stassen, Stalin had once again described co-operation between the Soviet Union and the USA as 'desirable', without once mentioning the Truman speech — although on the condition that each side respected 'the systems approved by the people'.[1] Marshall's offer, which, unlike Greece–Turkey aid, also applied to the countries in the Soviet sphere of influence, was now on the one hand in harmony with the Soviet desire for co-operation aimed at avoiding unilateral American superiority in Europe, but also on the other hand contained a possible threat to the Soviet security system, thus presenting the Soviet leadership with an extremely difficult decision. Should it accept American economic aid as a decisive contribution towards overcoming the immense reconstruction problems of the Soviet Union and Eastern Europe, as well as towards the equally desired stabilisation of Western Europe? Thereby the Soviet leadership risked the possible release of the East European states from their unilateral ties with the Soviet Union, with the whole of the European continent perhaps falling under the hegemony of the USA. Or should the

Soviet Union torpedo the plan as a danger to Soviet security, thereby risking that a West European bloc would emerge under American leadership and with all prospect of American funds and reparations from West Germany thus vanishing, the Soviet Union appearing to be the cause of the split in Europe? This controversial question seems to have been discussed at length in Moscow.

Rejection of the Marshall Plan

At first the Soviet government did not react at all to Marshall's speech of 5 June 1947. Only after eleven days, on 16 June, did *Pravda* comment on the American proposal — and this negatively, the proposal being 'basically the same Truman Plan for interference in the internal affairs of other states'. When, however, Ernest Bevin, the British Foreign Secretary and his French colleague Bidault invited the Soviet Foreign Minister from Paris on 18 June to take part in early talks about Marshall's proposal, Molotov accepted the invitation with the comment that his government was also in favour of the speedy reconstruction of Europe, to which the USA, with its enormous production potential, could certainly contribute decisively. *Pravda* published on 23 June the positive note replying to Bevin and Bidault, and on behalf of the French Communist Party, which as late as 25 June had attacked the Marshall Plan as 'a trap for the West'. General Secretary Maurice Thorez issued on 27 June a denial of this assessment, as being based on the false information of the party's press department: 'We are far too aware of our responsibility to make difficulties under the Allies or to be able to do anything which could damage harmony among the Allies and ultimately also to the reconstruction of our country.' On the same day, Molotov, accompanied by 89 Soviet experts, met Bevin and Bidault in Paris, clearly seriously interested in negotiating with them about the possibilities for joint European utilisation of the American offer.[2]

Bevin and Bidault presented him in Paris with two largely parallel proposals which envisaged (according to the British text) the creation of a 'steering committee' of interested European states 'to work out forthwith a four-way programme for the reconstruction of Europe', with Germany to be represented by the Allied military governors, and self-help to be placed at the centre of the programme, 'in order to create a solvent and prosperous Europe'. Molotov agreed with the principle of such a co-ordination committee, but wanted to be sure that its function would be limited to the collection of the demands of the European states and their 'compilation' into a reconstruction programme to be presented to the USA. He also demanded that Germany be left entirely out of consideration, this lying within the competence of the Council of Foreign Ministers. In essence, these two positions were not so incompatible: Bevin and Bidault were pleading for a co-ordinated programme, 'without the sovereignty of any states or the development of national plans being thereby in the slightest way damaged'. Molotov was not opposed to the reconstruction of Germany *per se*, but merely wanted to ensure that the opportunity would remain open to the Soviet Union to implement its demand for reparations. These points of view could not be reconciled, however. It was precisely in the inclusion of the German zones of occupation that Bevin saw the essential point of the whole undertaking, and 'from a practical point of view' he regarded it as being 'far better to have them definitely out than half-heartedly in'. 'Had the Russians decided to come in, even on our terms, the opportunities which they would have to delay and obstruct would have been almost unlimited' (as he wrote in his concluding report to the British Cabinet). Backed by Bidault, who shared Bevin's evaluation of Soviet intentions, and knew how to propound it in the French Cabinet against alternative interpretations, Bevin therefore aimed 'from the outset on thrashing out the differences of principle between us and making that the breaking point'. Molotov was still unsure in his appraisal of American, British and French objectives and thus held back with concessions in order to leave himself room for retreat. The decision was made in Moscow: on 1 July Molotov received a telegram from Stalin and 'he interrupted his remarks to read it and said nothing more during the remainder of the day's meeting'. The following day he finally rejected the Anglo-French proposal on the grounds that they would lead 'to a denial of their economic independence' and that they were 'incompatible with national sovereignty', and left the conference.[3] Faced with the intransigence of the Western Allies, the Soviet leadership had struggled its way through to seeing the disadvantages of a rejection as less than those of an acceptance, and in order to justify the rift, what were in fact minimal differences over the organisation of the reconstruction programme were exaggerated into an insuperable fundamental conflict.

Bevin and Bidault were visibly relieved at Molotov's departure. Under pressure from the left wing of the Labour party in Great Britain, and above all from the Socialist Party of France (SFIO), both of which set great store by a reconstruction programme for the whole of Europe, they now nevertheless made efforts to achieve the participation of at least the East European states in the programme. On 4 July the 22 European governments (that is, all the governments of the continent apart from the Soviet and the Spanish) were invited to Paris for 12 July to consult on the Marshall Plan with respect to the Anglo-French procedural proposals.[4] To the surprise of most Western observers, the European governments approached reacted almost without exception positively. From the outset, the Czechoslovak government had decided in favour of participation in the Marshall Plan, on account of the necessary west-orientation of its economy. Although it had been informed by the Soviet government on 6 July of the reasons for the Soviet rejection, on 7 July the Czechoslovak executive, under the chairmanship of Gottwald, the General Secretary of the Communist Party, decided unanimously to appoint a representative to go to Paris. At the same time, the Polish Foreign Minister Modzelewski informed the American Ambassador in Warsaw that Poland would be sending a delegation to Paris; the Hungarian press agency similarly reported that the Hungarian government had voted unanimously for participation in the European programme of reconstruction and had requested the Soviet military administration for permission to take part in the Paris conference. The Yugoslav government, which like the Polish government had already announced to the American government at the end of June its interest in an aid programme in accordance with 'the principles of the status of the United Nations', now asked in Moscow how it was to conduct itself with regard to the Anglo-French invitation; the Romanian government did the same. The governments of Bulgaria and Albania also seemed interested in going to Paris.[5]

The readiness of the East Europeans to take part in the Marshall Plan even without the Soviet Union precipitated the Soviet leadership into considerable uncertainty. The negative aspect of the American proposal — the opening of Eastern Europe to Western influence — now threatened to become a reality, with no prospect of its positive potential — specifically the backing of Soviet reconstruction. The East European governments were therefore instructed under massive pressure to withdraw their acceptances for the Paris Conference. The Czechoslovak Prime Minister, Gottwald, and his Foreign Minister Masaryk, who were in Moscow on 8–9 July negotiating on the participation of Czechoslovakia, were threatened with the immediate termination of the Czechoslovak–Soviet treaty of 1943 should they go to Paris. On 9 July, the Yugoslav and Bulgarian governments refused to participate, the latter only after Radio Moscow had already reported this rejection. On 10 July, Czechoslovakia and Hungary followed and on 11 July Romania, Albania, Poland and even Finland, whose government after vigorous internal disagreement preferred to relinquish aid rather than belong to a Western bloc opposed by the Soviet Union. In this way, the European countries' room for manoeuvre was further restricted and the division of the European continent decidedly deepened. Masaryk rightly judged after his return from the Soviet capital: 'I went to Moscow as the Foreign Minister of an independent sovereign state; I returned as a lackey of the Soviet Government.'[6]

With the rejection by the Soviet government of the Marshall Plan and the enforced rejection of the East European governments, what had hitherto been the Soviet strategy of co-operation with the Western powers and the stabilisation of Western Europe had now in practical terms broken down. The establishment of a Western bloc, the prevention of which Soviet strategy had been intended to secure, was now inevitable, not only because the US government was urging the consolidation of Western Europe, but undoubtedly primarily because the Soviet government had decided to regard the realistically required level of co-operation and multilateralism in the European programme of reconstruction as inseparable from the maintenance of its control over the East European region. Those Europeans remaining outside the Soviet sphere of influence, the majority of whom were, as before, still opposed to an East–West division, now felt compelled to co-operate with the *de facto* formation of a West European bloc, in order to benefit from the urgently needed American funds and to further the hoped-for consolidation of their countries.

The Cominform strategy

Alternatives to the failed Soviet stabilisation strategy had been under discussion in Moscow since the end of the war, including a 'policy of isolation' (Stalin in October 1945 to US Ambassador Harriman), a policy of socialist reorganisation on the part of the external Communist parties (favoured by the more dogmatic circles of the Soviet Communist Party around Molotov and Zhdanov), an 'aggressive and uncompromising policy against the great powers of capitalism, England and America, in the form of the creation of a pan-Slavic block, a consolidation of the current strategic situation, a division of Germany into a Western and an Eastern part, and an aggressive diplomacy towards the Anglo-American imperialist bloc' (Stalin in 1946 to Labour leader Harold Laski). It had not been possible to implement these alternatives, however:[7] even now, after the rejection of the Marshall Plan, they could not be implemented directly. The Soviet government remained undecided for the whole of the summer of 1947 about how to respond to the clearly successful American offensive. French, Italian and Belgian Communists hoped in vain for Moscow directives as to how to conduct themselves in the face of the incipient organisation of a West European reconstruction programme. In the absence of instructions to the contrary, they fought for the swift economic stabilisation of their countries and agreed to the Marshall Plan on the condition that the programme be assigned to the UN Economic Commission for Europe (ECE). 'What Frenchman could do otherwise than accept the aid of our American friends with satisfaction?' confirmed Thorez on 23 July. 'We cannot turn down the support which is being offered for the reconstruction of our country'; on 4 September, the Central Committee of the French Communist Party made a statement to the same effect.[8]

Only in the middle of September did the essentials of the Soviet response become clear. The leaders of the Yugoslav, Bulgarian, Romanian, Hungarian, Czechoslovak, French and Italian Communist Parties were invited to the estate of Szlarska Preba, which is today situated in Polish Silesia, for 22 September. They there discovered from Zhdanov, the leader of the Soviet delegation, an assessment of the situation that now prevailed among the Soviet leadership. 'The USA,' according to Zhdanov, had developed into the 'main force in the imperialist camp', its main aim being 'the strengthening of imperialism, preparation for a new imperialist war, a struggle against socialism and democracy, and the support of reactionary and anti-democratic, pro-fascist regimes and movements'. Even the Marshall Plan was an expression of the 'aggressive, naked course of expansion' which had been adopted by American policy since the Second World War, a 'plan for the enslavement of Europe'. The essence of this plan was 'the construction of a bloc of states bound by obligations to the USA, and to guarantee the American loans in return for the relinquishing by the European states of their economic and later also their political independence'. It was a particular perfidy of this plan to give priority to the reconstruction of the 'industrial areas controlled by the American monopolies', thus with the intention of bringing the 'impoverished victorious countries ... into dependence on the restored economic power of Germany and of German imperialism'.

The strategy that should be developed by the 'anti-imperialistic democratic camp' under the leadership of the Soviet Union in view of this American offensive was only outlined in brief by Zhdanov: not underestimating their resources, 'the Communist Parties must place themselves at the head of the resistance against the plans for imperialist aggression and expansion in all regions' — this applied mainly to the West European parties, which were to break with the social democratic parties, the tools of US imperialism: 'they must close ranks, concert all their efforts on the basis of a general anti-imperialist and democratic platform, and gather round themselves all the democratic and patriotic forces of the people — this applied mainly to the East European parties, thereby heralding a more uniform alignment of the Communist parties and the stricter control of their countries as they were at that time.[9] This conjuring-up of an imperialist danger emanating from Germany was intended to immunise the East European countries against further attempted approaches on the part of the Western powers, whilst the appeal to nationalist sentiment was intended to foster the latent contradictions within the Western camp.

The Yugoslav delegates, Kardelj and Djilas, were more unequivocal, passing heavy criticism on the progress reports of the French and Italian delegates, after appropriate consultation with Zhdanov: the two Western parties had not made use of their opportunity after the end of the war, always wanting to remain within the bounds of legality, and had clung opportunistically to ministerial seats. Without recognising the dangerousness of their class enemies, they had even begun seriously to believe in the virtues of parliamentarianism. The Czechoslovak Communists were similarly criticised for their 'bourgeois' role in the National Front. What was required, therefore, was a radical break with the stabilisation strategy which had been followed since 1943, a break with all people's front tactics and a recollection of the 'revolutionary' foundations of the Communist movement. The conference ended with the resolution to set up in Belgrade a joint 'Communist Information Bureau' (Cominform) of the participant parties, to consolidate forces with their own camp, 'to draw up and agree on a common platform to work out its tactics against the chief forces of the imperialist camp, against American imperialism, against its English and French allies, against the Right-Wing Socialists, above all in England and France'.[10]

In accordance with the directives of the founding conference of Cominform, the West European Communist parties now gave up their previous stabilisation strategy. They gave full rein to the considerable social annoyance which had accumulated throughout the previous Communist policy of raising production by foregoing consumption among the workforce, a build-up which the party leadership was in any case now no longer able to resist. They sought to use the strikes now breaking out to bring about the downfall of the Marshall Plan in domestic politics in the West European countries. A wave of strikes started in France on 18 November, which soon began to acquire the character of a general revolt. Two million workers took part in the strike: coal was no longer delivered, food supplies were interrupted, and acts of sabotage were carried out on transport routes. In parliament, there was frequent uproar: on one occasion Communist representatives occupied the tribune for a whole night; the socialist Minister of the Interior, Jules Moch, a Jew and soldier in both world wars, was shouted down with 'Heil Hitler!', whilst in Marseille security forces and strikers battled furiously on the streets.[11] On 9 December, the strikes broke, since they were still without tangible results. In Italy, on the other hand, where unrest had broken out at the same time, it flickered on and off throughout the whole winter of 1947/8.

The result of these spectacular strike actions, however, which the Communist Party leadership had only partly under control, was by no means the collapse of the Marshall Plan in Western Europe, but, on the contrary, a concentration of all non-Communist forces on the reconstruction of Western Europe in the framework of the Marshall Plan and the virtual complete isolation of the Western Communist parties. In the spring of 1947, the Communists were expelled from West European governments: in France, therefore, the Communist Party leadership, under pressure from its rank and file, had provoked a government crisis in order to strengthen its position, but had then emerged from this test of strength as the loser. In Italy, the right and left wings of the *Democrazia Cristiana* had pressed de Gasperi, the Christian Democrat Prime Minister, for the elimination of the Communists, whose attempt to counter pressure to extend the government coalition to include Republicans, Liberals and Social Democrats had failed with the resistance of the Republicans and the Social Democrats; thus once again only a Christian Democrat minority cabinet was able to emerge. In Belgium, the Communists had allowed the coal subsidy policy to bring about a government crisis, during which the hitherto opposing Catholic Party offered itself to the governing Socialists as a coalition partner, thus rendering communist support superfluous. All these, however, were 'normal' crises, albeit intensified by the argument of East–West tension, but ultimately internally determined, and although after the Soviet rejection of the Marshall Plan the number of those who viewed further Communist participation in government as inopportune at that time increased, almost no one imagined until the autumn of 1947 that the Communists would remain in opposition in the long term. Most socialists, in particular, wished for a speedy return of their brother parties, and the Communists still conducted themselves as responsible government parties. It was only after the spectacle of the November strike that the Communist parties were discredited in the eyes of their potential coalition partners as being the tools of Moscow, intent on the collapse of the existing order. The verbal revolutionism was believed, all the anti-Communist fears of the past revived, and the Communists were forced into the ghetto of their 'counterculture'. What the clarion call of Churchill since the spring of 1946 had not been able to achieve was brought about now by the actions of the Communists themselves: only now, at the turn of 1947/8, did the Cold War become an internal political reality in Europe.[12]

It is doubtful whether Soviet leading circles had really counted on some chance of their Cominform policy being able to torpedo the Marshall Plan in Europe. It is certain, however, that they placed the priority of consolidating their power in Eastern Europe before that of the future of the West European Communists. The unexpectedly positive reaction of the East European governments to the invitation of the West Europeans had shown them just how fundamentally at risk the Soviet demand for control in Eastern Europe still was, despite the degree of Communist penetration that had meanwhile been achieved. This led to an interpretation of the Marshall Plan as a deliberate attack on the Soviet security system in Eastern Europe, or rather helped such an interpretation to come to the fore among the Soviet leadership. The consequence of this was now to weld together the countries of their own security zone into a real 'Eastern bloc'.

Whereas the East European Communists had thus far conducted themselves pragmatically, with an ideology of 'new-type democracy' or 'people's democracy' providing an extremely superficial cover for courses of action as diametrically opposed as democratic parliamentarianism and police-state rule, as well as both capitalist and collectivist economic leadership, the Soviet model of society and its interpretation by Stalin was now declared to be the exclusively applicable correct course of all 'People's Democracies'. The remaining organised opposition groups were soon completely eliminated, the social democratic parties being merged with the Communists after extensive purges, all workers' organisations being placed under Communist control and the Communist Party leadership gradually purged of all elements suspected of not being absolutely loyal to Stalin at all times. In accordance with the Soviet pattern, the growth of heavy industry was given universal priority, and in spite of strong opposition, centralised planning methods and the collectivisation of the lowlands were also introduced. Economic production, which in spite of the enforced reorientation of 1945 had aligned itself more and more towards exchange with Western markets, was now reorganised entirely in accordance with the needs of Soviet reconstruction, individual economies being forced to accept far more interference in the form of external *dirigisme*, as would also have been necessary in the case of a co-ordination based on a freely made agreement in the context of the Marshall Plan. The trend was an effort towards an autarchy of the East European bloc, but at all events in addition to its political hegemony the economic dominance of the Soviet Union in the region was also secured. Even in Eastern Europe, therefore, it was only the Soviet response to the Marshall Plan which made the formation of a political bloc definite.[13]

The Sovietisation of Czechoslovakia

These developments in Eastern Europe were not solely the result of a change in Soviet strategy, however. The Sovietisation of Eastern Europe was carried out from 1947 to 1949 only in a complex inter-relationship between the dynamics of internal social conflicts and the increasing bipolarisation of international politics. This is demonstrated most clearly by the case of Czechoslovakia, which emerged within a few months in the winter of 1947/8, under pressure from both internal and external factors, as a 'People's Democracy' in the sense of the term defined by Cominform policy, having previously long seen itself as a parliamentary democracy situated between East and West.

The trigger for the political crisis of that winter was the economic crisis of the summer of 1947, in which both internal and external factors were inextricably interwoven. As a consequence of the inherent weaknesses in the Czechoslovak economy, the results of the reconstruction and transformation process were far below the expectations of 1945; in spite of the persistent exertion of all resources, there was no improvement in the standard of living in sight. On the contrary, as a result of the general drought of the summer of 1947, the consumer goods intended for internal use had had to be exported in order to be able to import a minimum of foodstuffs essential for survival. A general drop in living standards thus set in, the balance of trade showed increasing deficits, and a systematic continuation of socialisation plans was for the time being out of the question.[14] Definite aggravating factors in this crisis — since the urgently needed American aid had fallen through — were that UNRAA aid had run out, the US government had broken off credit negotiations in September 1946, the Soviet government had compelled the rejection of the Marshall Plan and Czechoslovak requests for American support outside the Marshall programme had met with brusque rejection from Washington.[15]

The result of this crisis was a general social discontent, which was directed at the strongest party in the government, the Communist Party. A considerable loss of votes was expected for the Communists in the elections set for spring 1948. With the potential loss of their leading position in sight and the Yugoslav scolding at the Cominform founding conference still ringing in their ears, the Communist Party leadership resorted to the traditional Leninist double strategy: within the police apparatus more

and more key positions were appointed to Communist supporters, cases were prepared against political opponents, 'reliable'
leaders were infiltrated into the opposition parties or obtained
within them, and Communist supporters were rallied in support
of militant action against 'reaction'. Their non-Communist coalition partners reacted to these first signs of extra-parliamentary
strategy on the part of the Communist Party with panic: with an
eye to the violent suppression of non-Communist elements in
Hungary and Bulgaria, they tried to repulse the Communists as
long as it was still possible. This toughening of line on both sides
led to increasing tension in the National Front cabinet, in which
the Communists on the one side and the Catholic People's Party,
the Democratic Party and the People's Socialist Party on the
other, both sides with twelve ministers each, were soon in bitter
conflict, the two Social Democrats visibly isolating the Communists. The Communist Minister of the Interior and the People's
Socialist Minister of Justice waged a mutual war of arrests.
Connections were uncovered between Democratic Party leaders
and plans were discovered to overthrow the government in favour
of Slovak autonomy, and likewise attempted bomb attacks by
leading Communists. In an atmosphere of fear, tension, hostility
and nervousness, the two sides thus fought for power.[16]

In order to find some mass support against this parliamentary
isolation, the Communists propagandised a number of highly
popular measures in the winter: a millionaires' levy for compen-
sation of the failed harvests, the nationalisation of all businesses
with more than 50 employees, an extension of land reform and a
levelling of incomes in the civil service — measures which their
coalition partners bitterly opposed. Police-state measures and a
growing pro-Communist mass movement combined to make the
prospect of free elections, or even the hoped-for victory of the
non-Communists, seem increasingly remote. When the Minister
of the Interior replaced the non-Communist Chief of Police with
supporters of his own choice, the Catholic, Democratic and
People's Socialist ministers felt themselves compelled to make a
definite test of strength. On 20 February 1948 they resigned, in
the hope of thereby toppling Prime Minister Gottwald and swiftly
bringing about new elections.

The two Social Democrat ministers, however, did not follow
them, and confusion reigned about the step even among non-
Communist supporters. Instead, Gottwald organised mass meetings in Prague, had Communist-controlled police units march

into the city on 21 February and ordered a general strike on 24 February. Under pressure from this militant mass movement and the Soviet Union, whose representative Valerian Zorin, who was staying in Prague, was maintaining ostentatious contact with Soviet troops deployed at the Czech border, president Beneš accepted the resignation of the non-Communists on 25 February. Instead of forcing Gottwald to dissolve parliament as the non-Communists had hoped, he accepted a new government of the National Front on 29 February, in which the previous positions of the non-Communists were occupied by 'reliable' supporters. In this way the Communists achieved a monopoly of power — in form quite legally,[17] but in fact under considerable extra-parliamentary and external pressure. On 10 March, Jan Masaryk fell to his death from the window of his office in the Foreign Ministry; whether it was suicide or murder on behalf of the secret service remains a disputed question (although the second of these two possibilities has gained considerable credence).[18] In the elections, 237 out of 300 representatives were elected from lists controlled by the Communists. Beneš was replaced as president and died, and the non-Communist parties were dissolved. Compelled by necessity to gain hold of the economic and internal political crisis, the Communists now resorted to Soviet methods of transformation before they had even been propounded as obligatory for all the East European countries by the Soviet leadership,[19] although the official Cominform policy of the Soviet Union helped to set the new internal political course.

The break with Tito

Nothing shows more clearly than Stalin's break with Tito in the spring of 1948 that the Sovietisation of Eastern Europe was in fact ultimately dependent on an inter-relationship between internal and external power relations, and that Cominform ideology, although a stabilising influence, in the last analysis played only a subordinate role. No one since the end of the war had so consistently urged a 'revolutionary' policy along the lines of the subsequent Cominform doctrine, and no one so inexorably represented the new course at the founding of Cominform than the Yugoslav leadership. Nevertheless, the implementation of this course in Yugoslavia led directly to a conflict between Stalin and Tito which was conducted as passionately as the now full-blown

Cold War between East and West. In spite of all the subjective conviction on the part of the Yugoslav leaders of the identity of the 'revolutionary' interest of the Soviet state and the Yugoslav federation, the contraditions were greater between the latter than was the case with any of the other East European parties. The Yugoslav Communists had been able to obtain power in their country through their own efforts, which effectively made them independent of Soviet backing, and potentially made possible resistance to a strengthened Soviet grip in pursuit of the Cominform policy, without Tito planning it.[20]

There had in fact been latent conflicts between the Soviet Union and Yugoslavia since the war: Stalin had judged the uncompromising precipitate action of Tito's partisan troops to be very imprudent; the Yugoslavs had had to suffer the violence of the Red Army and the spoliation methods of the 'mixed' Yugoslav–Soviet companies; and Tito had complained about inadequate Soviet support over the Trieste question. Stalin for his part had viewed with great concern Yugoslav support for the Greek partisans. Nevertheless, only when the Soviet Union attempted in the winter of 1947/8 to align the Yugoslav economy more with the needs of the Soviet Union in pursuit of the unification of the East European market did this conflict become virulent. Instead of specialising, giving priority to heavy industry and aligning their foreign relations exclusively towards the East European market, the Yugoslavs, in order to be able to raise the standard of living directly, wanted to diversify their production, expand the consumer-goods sector and extend trade relations to include the Western powers — and would not allow themselves to be diverted from this course in spite of Soviet pressure.

In view of this unexpected evidence of Yugoslav independence, Yugoslav efforts towards forming federations in the southern European and eastern-central European region must suddenly have seemed very dangerous in Soviet eyes. Previously Stalin had encouraged the activities of Tito and his Bulgarian colleague Dimitrov, which went back to the 1920s,[21] in the hope of alleviating East European national tensions through the forming of federations, and of thereby being able to stabilise the entire region. A triformation of the Soviet security zone now seemed to be emerging: in the north-west, Poland and the CSR, then a non-Slav central bloc consisting of Romania and Hungary, and finally a southern Slav federation consisting of Bulgaria, Yugoslavia and Albania. When, however, Tito concluded friendship and mutual support treaties with the former enemy states of Bulgaria, Romania and Hungary in November and December 1947, before corresponding treaties had even been negotiated with the Soviet Union, and Dimitrov announced in January 1948 the establishment of a customs union as a prelude to the federalisation of the Balkan states and presented a federation plan which included even Poland and Czechoslovakia, the time seemed right to Stalin to step in to prevent the danger of a power centre emerging in Eastern Europe that was not entirely dependent on the Soviet Union. The party leaders of Yugoslavia and Bulgaria were informed in no uncertain terms that 'relations between people's democracies which exceeded the interests of the Soviet government and which did not have its approval ... were inadmissible', and that the Soviet Union had the right to intervene in the socialist interest in the internal affairs of the People's Democracies.[22] Dimitrov travelled to Moscow to receive this pronouncement; Tito, however, merely sent two representatives, thereby showing that he was not prepared to bow to the Soviet demand for absolute control.

With this the break had become inevitable. Stalin now attempted to replace Tito with a Yugoslav group of leaders loyal to him; convinced that he only needed to lift his little finger 'and then there will be no more Tito',[23] he announced on 18 and 19 March the withdrawal of all Soviet economic experts and military advisers from Yugoslavia and made contact with Zretan Zujovc and Andrija Hebrang, the two most pro-Soviet members of the Central Committee. The majority of the Central Committee nevertheless decided on 12 April to stand firm; Hebrang and his supporters were arrested, and after a vigorous written dispute, in which Tito persistently responded to Stalin's accusations with professions of loyalty on the matter of world Communism.[24] Cominform decided on 28 June to expel Yugoslavia on the grounds that Tito had broken with class war theory out of 'petty-bourgeois nationalism'.

Although Tito continued to campaign against American imperialism in international politics along the lines of Cominform policy, the Soviet Union and the remaining East European states cancelled all trade and friendship agreements with Yugoslavia, broke off diplomatic relations, erected an economic blockade and called on the Yugoslav people in endless tirades to bring down 'the fascist Tito clique'. The Yugoslav leadership, which for its part now repudiated the Soviet system as a state capitalist perversion of socialism, was only able to survive with credit from the Western powers and American military aid. On many occasions, especially from 1950 to 1952, it feared a direct military invasion by the Soviet Union. Only after the death of Stalin did the Soviet leadership suspend its war of nerves. Tito had not allowed himself to be driven out; on the contrary, his prestige had grown enormously because of his resistance.[25]

In the remaining Cominform countries, however, a general hunt for alleged 'Titoists' set in from 1948 which was almost equal to the Soviet purges of 1936–8. Partly the expression of internal party power struggles, partly the result of the massive transformation process in accordance with the Soviet model, and partly a conscious measure by Stalin in order to secure the Soviet demand for control, this wave of purges was directed both against representatives of the 'left' wing of the party, who like Tito and Zhdanov attributed too much importance to revolutionary ideology, and against 'right-wing deviators', party leaders who resisted an unreflected transferral of the Soviet model into the conditions prevailing in their countries. In Poland, as early as 1948/9 Party Secretary Gomulka, together with the closest associates of his departments, was arrested; in Bulgaria the Minister Kostoff was executed; in Hungary, a spectacular show trial was staged against the former Hungarian Minister of Internal and Foreign Affairs, László Raik; in the same way, Enver Hodja in Albania secured power by conducting show trials against the pro-Yugoslav faction of his party. In Czechoslovakia, in 1949/50, Husák, Novomeský and Clementis were the first to fall from power, and then, after a lengthy power struggle with President Gottwald, the Communist Party General Secretary, Slánský, was arrested in November 1951 and executed a year later for 'Zionism and Trotskyism'; almost 150 alleged Slánský supporters received long prison sentences, and some of them were also executed. Finally, in Romania, there were two waves of purges, the first in 1951/2, which eliminated the 'Moscovite' group around Anna Pauker; Pătrășçanu, the former Justice Minister, was executed during the second wave in 1954.[26] Police-state violence, which was decisively intensified by the compulsion towards alignment with the Soviet model from the turn of 1947, had now become the most important characteristic of the East European states.

To sum up, therefore, the Soviet leadership did not take the opportunity for the limitation and gradual overcoming of the East–West conflict which was inherent in the Marshall Plan, regardless of the objectives of its American initiators. On the contrary, it interpreted the Marshall Plan as an attack on the Soviet security system (which it was not intended to be, and which was so in its effects only to a very limited extent), responding to it with close internal adherence to the Soviet 'model' and theatrical hostility directed abroad. As had been the case with the containment doctrine on the American side, so now the Cominform doctrine marked the end of a readiness to negotiate, the 'end of diplomacy'.[27] In addition, with its efforts towards the Sovietisation of Eastern Europe and the turnabout towards a destructive policy in Western Europe, it seemed to provide Western fears of Soviet expansion with belated justification, allowing them to become all the more certain and, as was highly significant for subsequent developments, it allowed them to spread to the European continent, where they were understandably bound to acquire a much more existential dimension than they had hitherto in the USA. The anti-Communist Western bloc against which Cominform policy turned from 1948 onwards thus became a reality in the sense of a 'self-fulfilling prophecy'. An escalation of hostile rhetoric took place in addition to the escalation of mutually preventive measures against the alleged threat from the other side. Free World ideology presented itself defensively in this exchange, although the Western powers in fact certainly had opportunities at their disposal for being effective in the Soviet security zone, whereas Soviet policy, adopting an offensive posture against 'US imperialism', was in reality hardly able to exert any influence in the Western countries.[28] The East–West conflict was now no longer understood solely in terms of a power struggle between two world powers, in which a balance was possible in principle, but more and more as an all-consuming battle for survival between two social systems which could only end in defeat or victory. It is no coincidence that from the turn of 1947/8 the description of this conflict as the 'Cold War' became popular.

In view of everything to which ideology, historical experience and the instinct of self-preservation disposed the Soviet mobilisation dictatorship, such a development in response to the Marshall Plan was certainly likely, and indeed a number of American experts predicted this response.[29] It must be borne in mind, however, that it was not inevitable. At first, the Soviet leadership had a different reaction in mind; it was only the short-sightedness of the Soviet leadership, combined with concern for the unrestricted retention of its dictatorial power system, that made definitive in 1947–8 the process of division in the world that had previously begun in 1945–6 as a result of the short-sightedness of the American leadership, with its desire for the world-wide application of liberal principles.

Notes

1. *Pravda*, 15 March 1947, the Stassen interview in Joseph W. Stalin, *Werke vol. 15 May 1945–October 1952* (Dortmund, 1976), pp. 62. On the continuation of Stalin's *détente* efforts see also William Taubman, *Stalin's American policy: from entente to détente to Cold War* (New York, London, 1982), p. 128f.

2. *Pravda*, 16 and 23 June 1947; *L'Humanité*, 26 and 27 June 1947; see Adam B. Ulam, *Expansion and coexistence*, (2nd ed., London, 1974), pp. 432–5; on the reflection of Soviet indecision among French Communists see Wilfried Loth, 'Frankreichs Kommunisten und der Beginn des Kalten Krieges', in *Vierteljahrshefte für Zeitgeschichte* 26 (1978), p. 59.

3. Collection of conference documents in Ministère des Affairs Etrangères, *Documents de la Conférence des Ministres des Affaires Etrangères de la France, du Royaume Uni et de l'URSS tenue à Paris du 27 juin au 3 juillet 1947*, (Paris 1947); *Pravda*, 28 June–3 July 1947; Vyacheslav M. Molotov, *Fragen der Außenpolitik Reden und Erklärungen* (Moscow 1949), pp. 499–510 and 657–9 (German); FRUS 1947, III pp. 296–309. Bevin's memorandum to the British Cabinet 5 July 1947, CAB 129/19, Public Record Office, see also account of Averell Harriman in Charles L. Mee, *The Marshall Plan* (New York, 1984), p. 136. Molotov's reaction to Stalin's telegram according to Bevin in W. Bedell Smith, *My three years at Moscow*, (Philadelphia, 1950), p. 198; Dean Acheson, *Present at the Creation*, (New York, 1970), p. 234, also attests to this Soviet final declaration of 2 July 1947 in *Documents on American foreign relations,* (Princeton, NJ, 1949), vol. IX, p. 186

4. On the British and French attitudes towards the participation of the Soviet Union and Eastern Europe see FRUS 1947, III, p. 225, pp. 259ff., 292–294, 296, 298, 301–303, 305, 328–330, and Wilfried Loth, 'The West-European governments and the impulse given by the Marshall Plan', in Lipgens, *History*, p. 490f. and 497.

5. It is reported at least by Milovan Djilas, *Gespräche mit Stalin* (Frankfurt, 1962), pp. 163f. that ultimately only the Soviet Union and Yugoslavia were against the inclusion of Eastern Europe in the Marshall programme. See all reports from Eastern Europe in FRUS 1947, III, pp. 313–27, and Vincent Auriol, *Journal du septennat 1947*, (Paris, 1970) Vol. 1, pp. 338f.: on Czechoslovakia the protocols of government sessions in the archive of the presidential office in Prague, as given in Karel Kaplan, *Der kurze Marsch. Kommunistische Machtübernahme in der Tschechoslowakei 1945–1948* (München/Wien 1981) p. 107f; on this and also Poland the report of the then Czechoslovak Minister of Foreign Trade, Hubert Ripka, *Cze-*

choslovakia enslaved, the story of the Communist coup d'etat, (London, 1950), pp. 51–5; on Hungary see Stephen D. Kertecz, *The fate of east central Europe*, (Notre Dame, 1956), p. 239; question by Yugoslavia and Romania from a despatch by Gottwald from Moscow to Prague, 10 July 1947, given in Kaplan, ibid.

6. Quoted in R.B. Lockhardt, *My Europe* (London, 1952), p. 125; on the Moscow trip, Gottwald's despatch of 10 July 1947 and Ripka *Czechoslovakia enslaved*, pp. 56–71; on the rejection, Peter Calvocoressi, *Survey of international affairs 1947–1948* (London, 1952) pp. 37f.

7. Stalin always described Molotov as the exponent of this course to western negotiating partners, and himself as the friend of co-operative policy, which is not particularly significant for the actual course of discussions, offering evidence only for the existence of different positions, Harriman, FRUS 1945, IV, pp. 567ff, and VI, p. 782, as well as W. Averell Harriman, Elie Abel, *Special envoy to Churchill and Stalin 1941–1946*, (New York, 1975), pp. 514f. Molotov/Zhdanov: according to the findings of William D. McCagg, *Stalin embattled, passim*. Laski: to an audience of Labour functionaries, report in archive of the Central committee of the Czechoslovak Communist Party, the Gottwald funds, information given by Karel Kaplan of Munich.

8. Compare, for further evidence Loth, *Frankreichs Kommunisten*, pp. 54–6 and 59f.; the Thorez quotation from *L'Humanité*, 24 July 1947.

9. Text of the Zhdanov report in Information Conference of representatives of a number of Communist parties in Poland at the end of September 1947, Moscow, 1948; extracts in Curt Gasteyger (ed), *Einigung und Spaltung Europas 1942–1965*, (Frankfurt, 1965), pp. 175–81.

10. Text of the final communiqué in *Documents on American foreign relations*, vol. IX, p. 625; attacks on the French and Italian CPs from the report of the Italian delegate Eugenio Reale, *Avec Jacques Duclos au banc des accusés* (Paris, 1958); analyses of the conference in Lilly Marcou, *Le Kominform*, (Paris, 1977), pp. 39–58, and McCagg, *Stalin embattled*, pp. 261–84. It is conceivable that Stalin had intended a different result for the conference, namely the defeat of the Paris party dogmatists (according to McCagg), but this intention completely failed.

11. See the impressive account in Jacques Fauvet, *Histoire du Parti communiste français 1920–1976*, (2nd edn, Paris, 1977), pp. 393–400.

12. On France see Loth, *Frankreichs Kommunsten, passim*; on Italy and Belgium see by same author *Die westeuropäischen Regierungen*, pp. 503f. and 507.

13. See overview in Jörg K. Hoensch, *Sowjetische Osteuropapolitik 1945–1975*, (Kronberg, 1977), pp. 44–72; on change in ideology and its function following the break of 1947 see Heinrich Heiter, *Vom friedlichen Weg zum Sozialismus zur Diktatur des Proletariats, Wandlungen der sowjetische Konzeption der Volksdemokratie 1945–1949*, (Frankfurt, 1977). On how dogmatists prevailed in Moscow, see Werner G. Hahn, *Postwar Soviet politics. The fall of Zhdanov and the defeat of moderation, 1946–53*, (Ithaca/London 1982), pp. 20–5, 67–113.

14. See analyses in Hans Kaiser, 'Sozialökonomische Entwicklungsbedingungen, Ordungspolitik und Klassenkampf in Osteuropa in den Jahren 1945–1948 am Beispiel der Tschechoslowakei', in Lutz Nietham-

mer and Othmar N. Haberl (eds.), (Hrsg.), *Der Marshall-Plan und die europäische Linke* (Frankfurt, 1987), pp. 139–66.

15. Jan Masaryk, social democrat Foreign Minister of the CSR, strongly criticised the USA because of this policy; it helped to prepare the Sovietisation of the CSR; account in Trygve Lie, *The cause of peace* (New York, 1954), p. 233; compare Walter Ullmann, *The United States in Prague 1945–1948* (New York, 1978), *passim*.

16. See François Fejtö, *Le Coup de Prague 1948*, (Paris 1976); Kaplan, 'Der Kurze Marsch'; Peter Heumos, 'Der Februarumsturz 1948 in der Tschechoslowakei', in Bernd Bonwetsch (ed.), *Zeitgeschichte Osteuropas als Methoden- und Forschungsproblem* (Berlin, 1985), pp. 121-35.

17. It is thus not justifiable to speak of a 'state strike' as is usual in the Western literature.

18. See Claire Sterling, *The Masaryk case*, (New York, 1970), based on information which became available during the 'Prague Spring' of 1968.

19. See Kaiser, *Sozialökonomische Entwicklungsbedingungen*, pp. 25ff.

20. Compare this and the following Adam B. Ulam, *Titoism and the Cominform* (Cambridge, Mass., 1952), pp. 69–95; Marcou, *Le Kominform*, pp. 198–236.

21. Compare J. Kühl, *Föderationspläne im Donauraum und in Ostmitteleuropa*, (Munich, 1958), L.S. Stavrianos, *Balkan Federation, A history of the movement toward Balkan unity in modern times*, (Hamden, Conn., 1964)

22. Quoted in the account by Djilas, *Gespräche mit Stalin*, pp. 217–20.

23. From the evidence given by Krushchev at the 20th Party meeting of the Soviet CP, 25 February 1956, quoted in Hoensch, *Sowjetische Osteuropapolitik*, p. 53.

24. See *Tito contra Stalin, Der Streit der Diktatoren in ihrem Briefwechsel*, (Hamburg, 1949).

25. See amongst others B. Farrell, *Yugoslavia and the Soviet Union 1948–1956*, (Hamden, Conn., 1956); Marcou, *Le Kominform*, pp. 230–7.

26. See overview in Hoensch, *Sowjetische Osteuropapolitik*, pp. 58–61; particularly impressive evidence in Jiří Pelikán (ed), *Das unterdrückte Dossier, Bericht der Kommission des ZK der KPTsch über politische Prozesse und Rehabilitierungen in der Tschechoslowakei 1949–1968*, (Vienna, 1970); and Arthur London, *Ich gestehe. Der Prozeß um Rudolf Slánský*, (Hamburg, 1970).

27. See the apt chapter heading on the containment doctrine in Daniel Yergin, *Shattered Peace*, (Boston, 1977), p. 257.

28. The discrepancy asserted by Ernst Nolte, *Deutschland und der Kalte Krieg*, (Munich, 1974), pp. 232–5, between the offensive Soviet policy and the defensive Western policy only applies to the level of ideological requirements; on the level of real possibilities rather the opposite appeared to be the case, and it took both to produce the Cold War.

29. E.g. George F. Kennan; see his *Memoirs 1925–1950* (Boston 1967), pp. 379–89. It was *communis opinio* in Washington at the beginning of 1947 that 'the stopping of the Communist advance of Moscow forces it to strengthen its grip on Eastern Europe', according to a memorandum presented by Marshall to the Cabinet on 7 November 1947; FRUS 1947, I, pp. 770–7.

8

The European Response:
The Hope for a 'Third Force' and its
Failure

In Europe, Marshall's offer had at first raised hopes for quite a different development from that which subsequently material-ised: that the division of Europe would be avoided and a new independent role would be realised for the old continent in inter-national politics, a role consisting essentially of alleviating the conflict between the two world powers, and ultimately of resolv-ing it. This hope effectively became obsolete with the Soviet rejec-tion of the Marshall Plan. However, it was still to be decided whether and to what extent the remaining West European coun-tries would rely closely in the course of the Marshall Plan on American leadership and adopt American economic structures along with American support, thus widening the gulf dividing East and West even further, or whether they would still be able to preserve some room for manoeuvre for independent politics, in spite of American aid, both at home and abroad, and thus be able in the long term to form something resembling a 'third force' between the two world powers. This decision rested in the first instance with the Europeans themselves, giving them to this extent an opportunity to exert an influence on the future course of the East–West conflict. It also depended, however, on Ameri-can policy towards the participating countries of the Marshall Plan, and finally on the effects of Soviet policy on the Europeans.

The concept of the 'third force'

The idea of the 'third force', a Europe which would maintain equal distance in its social order and foreign policy orientation from both the USA and the Soviet Union, thus being able to mediate between the two, was more popular in post-war Europe than any other key idea. Virtually the whole of the non-Stalinist Left, from the Trotskyists through the majority of the social democrats to the reformist Catholics in the newly-emerged Christian parties, lived with the vision of a social system that combined the characteristics of the political democracy of the USA with a socialist economic order, as was believed to have been, at least allegedly, achieved in the Soviet Union. Conservatives of all shades distrusted the technocratic dynamic of American capitalism, hoped for an independent role for their own nations in world politics, or set their sights, to the extent that they perceived the loss of power of their nations, on an independent Europe. Some even thought that their nation would be able to continue to play the lost role of a great power by acting as the leading power of a united Europe, such a Europe sometimes being seen more as a protection against the Soviet threat, sometimes more as a protection against American hegemony, a stance which was nevertheless applicable to both. Such ideas of a separate way for Europe between the two non-European powers were combined with the conviction that only the unification of Europe — objectives here ranging from loose association through regional ties to supranational federation — would be able to guarantee independence. Even the opponents of such unification, however, based their point of view on the argument of independence (in this case national), and their aversion to Soviet and American influence on the old continent was often even more pronounced than that of the supporters of the unification idea.[1]

In France, from the end of the war onwards the socialists around Léon Blum propounded the creation of a West European association under Anglo-French leadership as a preliminary to a united Europe, a 'third force'. The Belgian Social Democrat Foreign Minister, Paul-Henri Spaak, approached the British and French governments with similar ideas, and his Italian Christian Democrat colleague, Alcide de Gasperi, presented himself in the Allied Council of Foreign Ministers in September 1945 as 'the pioneer of a new, federated Europe'. At first these initiatives were not very widespread, leading only in 1947 to France and Great Britain promising close future co-operation in the Dunkirk Treaty of 4 March 1947. Even the opponents of these initiatives, however — above all, General de Gaulle in France and, to a lesser extent, Ernest Bevin, the British Foreign Secretary — were concerned about 'independence', also and mainly from the USA.

In 1944–6, de Gaulle had initiated an ambitious attempt to create a mediating role for France between East and West, a line which his Foreign Minister, Bidault, also pursued in the Christian-Democrat–Socialist–Communist coalition government that succeeded de Gaulle. Bevin's party had entered office in 1945 with the conviction that as a 'socialist force' its members could reach an understanding with the Soviet Union, and although in practice Bevin did not adhere very long to these ideologically all-too-vague concepts, he nevertheless followed with growing scepticism the increasing hardening of the American line towards the Soviet Union, finding cause on more than one occasion to complain about American lack of regard for the interests of Great Britain.

With the announcement of the Marshall Plan, the concept of a 'third-force' was given an enormous boost: on the one hand, because with the American requirement of co-ordination among the European economies, it offered an opportunity of realising the plan for a real integration of European states which was often connected with the 'third-force' idea; and on the other hand, indeed mainly, because the division of Europe and the world into two halves now threatened to become fact. 'We must,' declared Léon Blum, on 1 August 1947, to the French President, Vincent Auriol, 'fight with all our strength, even to the brink of despair, against this situation, the East bloc against the West bloc, becoming permanent.'[2] Blum was not alone among Europeans in the summer and autumn of 1947 in thinking this; the way in which he outlined the basic idea of the 'third-force' concept to the French National Assembly on 21 November reflected the feelings of the most varied political groups:

> In Europe and everywhere in the world there are states, groups and individuals who have grasped that in the present state of economic development none of the great problems can be solved satisfactorily within national boundaries, that without a living solidarity with one another no people can live in prosperity, or survive at all, and that we must group, federate and unite, or go under. They refuse to join one of the camps that seem to be dividing the world, because they see the necessity of this universal solidarity, because they realize the danger to peace inherent in the continuation of the division, and because they have understood what the word *war* means today. The

177

task and mission of France lies in co-operating towards the creation of an *international third force*, a force which will work tirelessly by means of mutual *rapprochement* and persuasion to remove mistrust and suspicion and which ... will not shrink in so doing even from a partial relinquishment of sovereignty of their states for the benefit of the community.[3]

The allegiance to the world peace organisation, the hope for a dissolution of the division of Europe, and the appeal to the mediating function of the European countries — all this was first and foremost an expression of repugnance at the possibility of another world war (a possibility which must have seemed all the more real before the nuclear 'balance of horror' existed) in terms of specific programme content. If one leaves aside in this and other similar texts the degree of verbal promises and the overplaying of the East–West conflict which they contain, there remain three solid foundations for a third-force policy. First, it backed a rationalisation and domestication of the areas of conflict existing between East and West. Without underestimating the force of either American capitalism or Soviet oppression in Eastern Europe, the representatives of the third force indicated, in contrast with what American containment ideologues maintained, that there was no Soviet expansion towards Western Europe and, in contrast with what the Cominform doctrine taught, that US capitalism was not necessarily imperialistic. They concluded from this that the formation of blocs and the conflict between these blocs was not inevitable, and that the conflict could be contained by means of a return to the negotiating table. Secondly, it backed the independence of the non-Communist countries of Europe and the prevention of a Western bloc under American leadership — in spite of the participation of these countries in the Marshall Plan — or even as a result of this programme. The Marshall Plan, they hoped, would lead Europe to economic prosperity and political power, assuming that the participant countries would introduce a community-building process along with aid, an assumption which not only had a long tradition in the third-force movement, but which at the same time represented the only condition which the American government attached to its offer of aid. Disregarding the danger of initially making national markets vulnerable to American superiority, this integration plan contained the chance that through the creation of community organisations a political counterweight to the USA would also be created, thus guaranteeing the independence of Europe. Thirdly, it supported the mediatory effect of such an independent Europe: a strong Europe would remove from the world powers their chances of projecting their differences onto the old continent (as the conservative power theorists hoped), and thus have a balancing effect, as a social system 'combining personal freedom and a collective economy, democracy and social justice' (as the authors of the democratic Left phrased it).[4] Even this hope was not entirely without justification; in fact, the socialists, social democrats and reformist movements were stronger in post-war Europe than they had ever been, and seemed to be rising to the position of the leading political force on the continent. In spite of all its escapist tendencies, the third-force programme contained a number of realistic proposals for the containment of the East–West conflict; the continuation of this conflict depended on the extent to which these proposals would be put into effect.

The emergence of the OEEC

The first decisions concerning the degree to which independence from American influence could be preserved by the Europe of the Marshall Plan were made in Paris in the summer of 1947. Following the invitation of Bevin and Bidault on 4 July, the representatives of sixteen countries met there on 12 July 1947 — Denmark, Belgium, France, Greece, Ireland, Iceland, Italy, Luxemburg, the Netherlands, Norway, Austria, Portugal, Sweden, Switzerland and Turkey, as well as Great Britain. Representatives of the British, American and French military governors in Germany also came, in order after basic clarification of objectives and procedure on 16 July to instigate a 'Committee of European Economic Cooperation' (CEEC) with the task of working out a joint reconstruction programme limited to four years, which was to be presented to the American government as the basis of assistance. The eleven weeks of Paris negotiations were coloured by two conflicting patterns: disagreement over the question of which concerns were to be given priority by which nations, and disagreement over the degree of co-operation and integration deemed necessary for Europe.[5]

Measures for the institutionalisation of economic co-operation, and towards the economic integration of the countries participating in the aid programme, were demanded by the French delegation, in particular. Under pressure from his socialist cabinet colleagues, Bidault had made substantial readjustments to his foreign policy concept. Demands for the territorial cession of the Ruhr and the Rhineland were now put aside in favour of an international (consisting of the participant countries of the Marshall Plan) authority to decide on the distribution of Ruhr production, thus no longer securing French dominance on the continent, but nevertheless preventing German dominance and allowing France to participate in Ruhr profits. Joint planning and shared organisation were otherwise to ensure the success of the reconstruction programme. The socialists, who had developed this concept, also hoped to be able to further the independence of Europe, in the sense of the 'third force', in conjunction with its integration. With the argument 'that the present division of Europe into small economic units does not correspond to the needs of modern competition', Bidault thus offered the first step towards the establishment of a customs union of participant countries.[6]

The Italian delegation took up this proposal immediately, also seeking 'to warmly co-operate' (Count Sforza, the Foreign Minister). Supported by the wide popularity of the unity idea among the Italian public, the Italian government, consisting of Christian Democrats and Liberals, similarly hoped to achieve a prosperous and independent Europe through unity, a Europe which would furthermore not give up the East European countries. The Belgian government, which had been urging for a regional association in Europe since the end of the war, was also taken with the proposal; along with the Netherlands government, which was still sceptical about unity, but even more enthusiastic about a 'third way' between East and West, they argued for the free convertibility of European currencies and for firmer co-operation in all areas concerned with currency, agriculture, industry and economic policy.[7]

Bevin, however, and consequently the British delegation under Sir Oliver Franks, did not agree with these integration proposals. The British Foreign Secretary entertained in the first instance only the idea of forming a 'club' in which the governments of Europe could consult together, and in time 'acquire the habit of practical co-operation'. Binding agreements were in any case only to be entered into if they had specific time-limits. A group of Foreign Office civil servants did in fact favour the customs union idea, in the hope of an independent Europe under British leadership, and Bevin, who had at first hoped for a continuation of the special relationship with the USA, endorsed this argument in September in the face of American pressure for unity initiatives. In the British Cabinet, however, Sir Stafford Cripps rejected the customs union as a hazard to the reconstruction programme for British industry, with the result that official British policy on the customs union question remained remarkably undecided. The customs union plan was jeopardised as a result of this British caution, and all more far-reaching unity proposals for the time being fell by the wayside. The Benelux countries delegation shrank from a rift with the British, whilst the Scandinavians felt justified in their own aversion to integration plans as a result of British caution. France and Italy decided to set up a study group on the preparation of a bilateral customs union, and thirteen of the sixteen participant countries initiated a study group for preliminary examination of the customs union question; no more than this was achieved.

This setback over integration plans made it more difficult for the French government to agree to the immediate incorporation of West German industry and the raising of production being called for by the representatives of the Benelux countries and Italy in the interests of the optimal use of all resources for European reconstruction, measures which were now inevitable after the Moscow agreements of Bevin and Marshall. The French particularly resisted the raising of annual German steel production to 10.7 million tons, as military governors Clay and Robertson had agreed, in execution of the Moscow resolutions. This increase meant the collapse of French plans to make France the leading European steel producer with German coal before German production could once again exhaust its full capacity. Not only this, a supremacy of German industry now threatened, but without bringing its joint exploitation by the Marshall Plan countries, or even a security control by means of European community organisations, any closer. Bidault thus now sought by means of a vigorous diplomatic campaign, extending even to threats of withdrawal, to achieve a revision of this aim, and meanwhile blocked all *rapprochement* over the question of Germany at the Paris Conference.[8]

Alarmed by the refusal of Great Britain to agree to an integration of the European economies, as well as by the opposition of France to the direct and full exploitation of German potential, the

US government now pressed for European agreement to the measures which in its view were indispensable for the success of the Marshall Plan. On 30 August William Clayton urged the CEEC for 'definite measures directed toward the progressive reduction and eventual elimination of barriers to trade within the area, priority ... (to) the reactivation of the most efficient existing productive facilities', the creation of a permanent joint organis-ation of participant countries, and a multilateral treaty commit-ting participant countries to a four-year plan for the economic recovery of Europe. The figure of 29,200 million dollars' worth of required American support reached by the delegates was mean-while rejected by Clayton as 'much too high'.[9] In order not to jeopardise the financing of the programme by the US Congress, the CEEC participants saw that it was necessary to revise the virtually completed response once again. In the report finally handed over to the US government on 22 September, they held to a figure of 19,300 million dollars, for which they declared them-selves committed to mutual help in the liberalisation of commerce and the co-ordination of certain basic industries, such as energy production and transport; they agreed to the establish-ment of a permanent community organisation, without conced-ing to it too extensive competence, and recognised the necessity for speedy German reconstruction, although combined with strict security precautions against any misuse of German indus-trial potential at the expense of the other participant countries. In terms of the integration concepts of the authors of the Marshall Plan and the European advocates of the 'third-force' concept, these were very modest, imprecise and to some extent contradic-tory pledges. Not without reason, Ramadier, the French Socialist Prime Minister, declared on 28 September that 'the Conference of the Sixteen had hardly laid the foundation stone' for a united Europe.[10]

During further discussions on the aid programme in the winter of 1947/8, US Congress representatives repeatedly called on the government not to be satisfied with these results. In the Administration, however, the view prevailed that ultimately one could not force an integration of the participant countries, includ-ing Great Britain, without striking a severe blow to the will for self-determination among Europeans (which it was intended to encourage in order to counter the Communist threat!). The French government made one more effort, urging the appoint-ment of a strong executive to the agreed community organisation, and equipping it with a series of competences to be understood as autonomous, among them in particular responsibility for the distribution of the aid funds. The British government was once again opposed, with the result that the OEEC (Organization of European Economic Co-operation) was provided in the convention signed on 6 April 1948 with only a weak General Secretariat dependent on a general assembly of government representatives working on the principle of unanimity. Jurisdiction over distribution was not out of the question.[11]

A significant opportunity to make use of the Marshall Plan in the sense of the third-force concept was thereby wasted. Certainly an institution had been created which rendered it possible for the first time for the economic problems of the European countries to be viewed not only from the perspective of individual states, but also from that of Europe as a whole, and it soon became the practice of the OEEC mutually to appraise national reconstruction programmes. Decisions for the solution of reconstruction problems nevertheless still remained dependent on the consensus of all participating governments, and as soon as a government saw short-term national interests in the slightest way affected, it shied out of the united front. A joint reconstruction programme, or what was more feasible, given the highly varied level of planning technique in the participant countries, a wide-ranging *rapprochement* over the priorities and division of labour in European reconstruction, could not arise in this way. Even less progress was made with attempts at integration within the OEEC; it took until September 1950 merely to bring about a 'European Payments Union' of participant countries. In view of such a meagre level of actual joint policy, it was bound to be extremely difficult for Europeans to implement their own interests in the face of those of the Americans, in the event of a conflict between the two.

American penetration of Western Europe

Disappointed by the lack of readiness for co-operation and integration of the Europeans, the US State Department now organised the Marshall Programme largely on the basis of its own ideas, with more regard for the demands of Congress and the other departments of the Administration than for the specific interests of the European states, thus involving the USA as a leading power in Western Europe to a much greater extent than had originally been considered either necessary or possible.

Instead of taking the report of the first CEEC conference as the binding basis of the aid programme as originally planned, the Truman Administration now sought to play down its importance and, in Kennan's words, 'to decide unilaterally what we finally wish to present to Congress'. In order to bridge the time gap until the passing of the legislation necessary for the establishment of the aid programme, it proposed initial immediate aid for countries at the greatest political risk. Congress thus approved on 17 December 1947 522 million dollars for France, Italy and Austria, and in March 1948 another 155 million dollars for overcoming immediate supply problems. For the long-term reconstruction programme, Truman presented Congress on 19 December, 1947 with a draft which envisaged the granting of a total of 17,000 million dollars (instead of the 19,300 million last requested by the Europeans) for four and a quarter years; this was still based on the CEEC report in its essential details. Even before official consultations had begun, however, the Administration altered its proposal under pressure from Vandenberg to the extent of deciding only on the principle of aid for four years, but not the level of aid, and it was in this form that the 'Foreign Assistance Act' came into effect, after many modifications of detail, on 3 April 1948. Aid funds now had to be proposed by the Europeans for each of the four years individually and approved each time by Congress, which increased the opportunities for American influence in general and for Congress in particular on the shaping of the programme, and which also made long-term independent planning virtually impossible for the Europeans. For 1948/9, 4,875 million dollars were granted in subsidies and loans. The payments of the following three years were each somewhat lower, so that the total aid up to 1952 ran to 12,992 million dollars, of which 9,290 million was in subsidies, 1,139 million in loans and 1,517 million in 'conditional aid'.[12]

Congress first implemented a range of specific individual interests of American economic groups which were detrimental to the efficiency of the reconstruction programme, and thus also to the general aims of American containment policy. Thus 50 per cent of all aid goods had to be transported on American ships and under the protection of American insurance companies — a stipulation which up to October 1948 alone cost 12 per cent of the payments so far granted. Agricultural products could only be bought with Marshall Plan funds out of American surplus (at half the US market price), even if they could be obtained more cheaply on other markets, for example those of the Third World. Plans for the establishment of European crude oil refineries were not approved; the Europeans had instead to import the oil of American firms at inflated prices. In the middle of 1950, the proportion of crude oil alone in the total Marshall Plan payments ran to 11 per cent. Instead of the 65,000 tractors requested, only 20,000 were supplied, although in the first fifteen months 65,000 trucks were supplied which no one had considered urgently necessary. In addition to all this there were a number of less spectacular irregularities.[13]

Of greater importance was the fact that Congress and the Administration organised the programme in such a way that it favoured American Open Door policy in its structure. The difficult task of distributing aid funds was left to the OEEC (against their resolution) and was subject to the definitive supervision of the American European Co-operation Agency (ECA) for the administration of Marshall Plan funds. At the same time, however, bilateral treaties were concluded with the individual participant countries that laid down principles for the liberalisation of foreign trade, the increase of commerce, European co-operation, preferential treatment for the USA, the protection of American property and private enterprise and American access to European sources of raw materials. Aid was granted mainly in the form of non-repayable dollar subsidies, which could be used for the importing of goods and capital goods. At the same time, however, the participant governments were obliged to pay the equivalent of the dollar amount issued to them into a special fund which was available up to a level of 95 per cent for the promotion of national reconstruction, while the remaining 5 per cent was intended to cover American administrative costs and propaganda and the acquisition of strategically important raw materials through the USA. Even the use of these 'equivalent means' was subject to the ultimate supervision of the ECA, so that the American government had considerable *de facto* opportunities at its disposal for influencing its national investments at that time.

It would certainly be an exaggeration to describe this Marshall Plan policy, with its varied deference to Congress, as dollar imperialism. The Europeans retained (against their will) the initiative in the formulation of individual programme phases, while the programme as a whole, in spite of its Open Door elements, was not aimed at a lasting structural dependence of the European

185

economies on the USA, but on the contrary was expressly aimed at the future superfluity of American aid and the restitution of European independence within the space of four years. Although the policy of high investment rates and export surpluses implemented by the ECA for the attainment of this goal entailed foregoing a direct massive increase in the buying power of the European masses, it nevertheless certainly allowed for a later increase in the general living standard. More than this, it was the indispensable precondition for the success of the reconstruction programme (which was being practised in a similar way by the Communists in the West and in the East). It should be emphasised, however, that the USA in its formulation of the Marshall Plan furthered its own national interests very effectively, whilst Europeans, not having understood how to equip themselves with effective instruments for joint trade, were left with few chances for furthering their own interests to the extent that these were not in accord with American concepts of European reconstruction.[14]

Decisions about the incorporation of the German Western zones clearly illustrate the degree of European dependence on the USA. After the failure of French plans to ensure that their own industrial production would be permanently ahead of German production with the Moscow agreements of Bevin and Marshall, and the OEEC had conceded under American pressure the necessity for using German potential directly and effectively for European reconstruction, the French government sought at least to prevent a lasting German dominance in the Europe of the future. During the drawing-up of the first OEEC distribution plan, France implemented a reduction of the dollar aid requested by the military governors for the bizone from 450 to 367 million dollars, as well as granting bizone credits to other participant countries to a figure of 90 million dollars. When Clay and the War Department, however, fearing a rapid reconstruction of West Germany, attacked this compromise in the distribution question, which was acceptable to all, the principle of European self-determination was breached in the face of considerable resistance from the State Department and the ECA. The OEEC had to transfer 414 million dollars to the bizone and forego bizone credits, so that of the total dollar aid of 1948, 28 per cent, went to West Germany alone. This was another of the first decisions leading to the later dominance of the German economy on the continent.[15]

The internationalisation of Ruhr industry, which the French government propounded to prevent German dominance and for the balanced use of German potential by all states in the region, collapsed under the united resistance of the British Labour government, the North Rhine Westphalian *Landtag* and the American government. A majority of the Labour government inclined towards a socialisation of the Ruhr complex in the national context; the German Socialist Party (SPD) in the British zone of occupation was preparing corresponding nationalisation plans, whilst the Christian Democrats (CDU) favoured 'communalisation' in the sense of decentralised public and private ownership (the *Landtag* then voted in August 1948 with the abstention of the CDU for the socialisation of Ruhr coal for the benefit of North Rhine Westphalia). In the USA, Republican speakers connected with John Foster Dulles favoured internationalisation in the French sense, whilst the State Department wanted to make the decision dependent on the vote of a representative, democratic and legitimised West German government, thus in fact taking socialisation in the national context completely into account, while Clay, the military governor, backed by 'free-enterprise' ideologues, formed a front against jeopardising West German reconstruction by socialisation experiments. Under Clay's pressure, the US government compelled the British in November 1947 to surrender responsibility for the ownership question to a future German government and to appoint in the meantime German trustees under Western supervision. In this way both internationalisation and nationalisation were for the time being rendered impossible, and the normative power of the situation worked towards the restitution of former private economic ownership relations. In lengthy negotiations lasting almost the whole of 1948, the creation of an international Ruhr authority, to supervise the distribution of Ruhr products and the economic policy of Ruhr enterprise, and consisting of representatives from the USA, Great Britain, France, the Benelux countries and West Germany, had been achieved due to the French. In 1951, when the fate of the enterprises was to be finally decided, as had been agreed, the remaining resistance to returning them to their original owners had been broken.[16]

The extensive 'restoration' of traditional private capitalist relations which thus proceeded in Europe was nevertheless not solely the result of the pragmatic containment policy of the US government, oriented towards the model of its own country, nor of the inability of Europeans, and in particular of the European Left, to organise themselves effectively, but at least equally as much the result of shifts in internal political power relations in European countries as a direct consequence of the Cold War. In France, the Communists had manoeuvred themselves out of centre field with Cominform policy, and anti-Communist hysteria, which was now becoming more and more widespread in the remaining parties, ensured that they remained out of things. In this way, the Socialists became the left wing of a coalition with Christian Democrats and conservatives, who moved increasingly further away from the reformist tendencies of the first post-war governments arising out of the Resistance. The more government policy increased in conservative characteristics, the more the Socialists lost the backing of their supporters, and vice versa. In Italy, the Socialists had split with the Communists in January 1947 over the question of action unity, thus unwittingly creating the precondition for a permanent polarisation of the political forces of their country under the influence of the Cold War. In the elections of April 1948, the Christian Democrats were clearly victorious (with massive American support) over the alliance of Communists and left-wing Socialists. This thus marked the foundation of the long-term rule of the *Democrazia Cristiana*, as well as the concentration of oppositional forces on the Communist Party. In Germany, the division between East and West reduced the previously very real chances the Social Democrats had of emerging from the elections as the strongest party. Within the Christian Democrat Party, conservative groups attained the leading positions, not least because their views corresponded most closely with the German policy concepts of the American leadership. After the narrowly won first parliamentary election of August 1949, the CDU decided equally narrowly in favour of the government without Social Democrat participation, so that even in the Federal Republic the more conservative groups were dominant. In Great Britain, the Labour government, consistent with the general shift in Europe, was under increasing pressure from the Conservatives. Not interested in too close an alliance with the continent in any case, they felt justified in their isolationism by the increasingly conservative developments taking place in the partner countries. Without the support of British socialists, the European unification movement, originally characterised by the hope for a socialist 'third force', became predominantly conservative.[17]

From 'third force' to Western integration

The trend towards the 'restoration' of political order and towards dependence on American leadership in Western Europe was strengthened not least by the fact that in reaction to the Soviet response to the Marshall Plan what had hitherto been the generally accepted theses of containment doctrine only in the USA now gained credence in Europe as well between the summer of 1947 and the spring of 1948, where they were understandably bound to acquire a more tangible dimension.

Until the summer of 1947, only a minority of European politicians could have been mustered for the formation of a Western bloc in the sense meant by the containment doctrine: Churchill, who swore by the Anglo-American partnership and encouraged a Franco-German reconciliation in the context of a unified (Western) Europe in order to be able to organise the 'West' against alleged Soviet expansion; Adenauer, who as early as 1945 regarded the Soviet occupation zone as lost in terms of a democratic reconstruction of Germany, and who was working towards the integration of the Western zone of Germany into the West European region; de Gaulle, who after his failed attempt towards a thoroughly impartial policy of equilibrium between East and West now preached from the opposition an internally and externally militant anti-Communism; and Bidault, for whom the end of all co-operation with the Soviet Union and his own Communists had come with the Moscow meeting of the Council of Foreign Ministers. The fact that the majority of Europeans thought differently not only shows the modification that had occurred in American strategy between the time of the Truman Doctrine and the Marshall Plan, but also European reaction to Marshall's offer. Bevin, who hoped for preferential treatment for Great Britain and who feared the negative effects of participation by the Soviet Union on both the extent and tempo of American aid, felt compelled out of regard for the feeling of this majority to invite his Soviet colleague as well as the French to a conference on the aid offer, and Bidault, as a result of pressure from his own Christian Democrat Party and from the ranks of his socialist coalition partners, was obliged to agree.[18]

Soviet rejection of the Marshall Plan reawakened traditional anti-Communist feeling in some quarters, which was voiced in increased doubts about the nature of Soviet policy. The majority of European cabinets nevertheless remained convinced of the necessity for an 'Open Door' policy towards Eastern Europe, and a course not dependent on the USA. The Communists in West European countries were still regarded entirely as opposition parties within the system. Only Cominform propaganda and the strike movements that followed in France and Italy in the late autumn of 1947 led the majority of Europeans to believe in the fundamental expansionist intentions of the Soviet Union and to the conviction arising among a growing proportion of the European public that the Soviet leadership would not shrink from engaging even military means to accomplish these ends.

On the brink of the London meeting of the Council of Foreign Ministers — at which from 25 November to 15 December 1947 Molotov tried in vain to polemicise against the resolve of the three Western foreign ministers to include the Western zone of Germany into the West European programme of reconstruction[19] — Bevin thus sought, backed vigorously by Bidault, to win his American colleague Marshall over to a plan for an alliance of Western powers which in particular would guarantee the Europeans military protection by the USA. 'We must devise some Western democratic system compromising the Americans, ourselves, France, Italy, etc., and of course the Dominions ... not a formal alliance, but an understanding backed by power, money and resolute action ... a sort of spiritual federation of the West.' 'As soon as circumstances permit,' read one British Cabinet paper of 2 January 1948, Spain and Germany should also be integrated into this defence system, 'without whom no Western system can be complete'. Marshall appeared to agree in principle, but made military engagement of the USA in Western Europe dependent on the prior intensification and co-ordination of European defence efforts. Without such an initiative from the European side, he maintained, such an engagement would be much more difficult to pass through Congress than economic aid. Bevin and Bidault therefore hastily worked on the establishment of a defence treaty between their countries and the Benelux countries as the first step towards the 'Western Union'. After unofficial preliminary talks between Bevin, Bidault and Churchill at the end of December in London, Bevin proclaimed the idea of the 'Western Union' on 22 January in a speech in the House of Commons. On 4 March the treaty negotiations began: as early as 17 March 1948 they were able to sign the 'Brussels Treaty', in which Great Britain, France, the Netherlands, Belgium and Luxemburg pledged themselves to mutual aid in the case of an armed attack on Europe, as well as to a stepping-up of political and economic co-operation.[20]

Meanwhile, at the beginning of 1948, hopes for a 'third force' independent of the USA were still sufficiently widespread for the initiators of the Brussels Treaty to conceal as far as possible the true function of the alliance in preparing the way for American military protection and American military aid for Europe, presenting it instead as the basis for a comprehensive political and military co-operation of Western Europe in the sense of the 'third-force' concept. Only in this way could it be successfully propounded internally in Europe. In Bevin's speech of 22 January in the House of Commons, which determined public discussion of the treaty, a Soviet threat was mentioned only covertly and American protection not at all, emphasis being much more on the 'consolidation' and 'spiritual Union' of Western Europe and on its potential economic power between the 'other two great powers, the United States and Soviet Russia'.[21] The Belgian Foreign Minister, Spaak, and the French Socialists at least did want the treaty to be put into effect in this sense, so that it was at first not easy to predict whether it would in fact lead to the formation of a bloc with the USA or to the formation of a relatively independent Europe.

A decisive shift in this situation was brought about with news of the elimination of non-Communist elements in Czechoslovakia at the end of February 1948. Almost all commentators in Western Europe now held that the thesis of the essentially expansionist character of the Soviet system had been vindicated. A fear of military aggression from the Soviet Union grew among the population, and the politicians in power, including most of the previous proponents of the 'third force', began to include at least the possibility of such an attack in their policies. Only an intellectual minority of the 'third-force' movement now continued to advocate a 'neutral' path between East and West.[22] The majority, like the fathers of the containment doctrine, saw the West European democracies as threatened by a combination of subversive activity at home and military threat from outside; the ability and willingness to distinguish between Communist movements and the Soviet Union, Communist ideology and real Soviet interests, diminished more and more. There was now no more doubt about the necessity for a military alliance with the USA, although the proponents of the 'third force' still hoped to be able to secure a *relatively* independent role for Europe within this alliance.

Bidault's and Bevin's earnest requests for American protection now found the necessary domestic political backing, with the result that one month after signing the treaty the Brussels powers were able to seek support officially from the USA.[23]

Considerable differences remained even after the Prague crisis between the Atlantic alliance policy in the sense meant by Churchill, for example, and European unity policy in the context of a Western alliance, such as was propounded by Blum. The former thought predominantly in military-strategic terms, whereas the latter regarded broad participation in general reconstruction as the best defensive measure. The former understood the integration of Western Europe exclusively as a defensive measure against the Soviet Union, whereas the latter viewed unification as security against American dominance, and was therefore far more interested in the self-sufficiency of European institutions. The former hoped to be able to regulate relations with Eastern Europe and the Soviet Union by a demonstration of strength; the latter relied in case of doubt on the reduction of tension as the precondition for gradual *rapprochement*. In the main, however, Europeans were no longer against and were more for the trend towards the formation of a Western bloc. The remaining special interests of the Europeans, such as the French interest in guarantees against a renewed strengthening of Germany, or the socialist interest in a transformation of the economic order of Europe, could now increasingly be overlooked in view of the exigencies of joint defence efforts. There was thus now little room left for independent European policy and a containment of the East–West conflict when measured against the ambitious 'third-force' plans.

Notes

1. The diverse 'third force' movement of the 1940s has not been adequately analysed by a long way. For the component which took up the idea of European unity, see the basic documentation of Walter Lipgens and Wilfried Loth (eds), *Documents on the history of European integration, 1939–1950*, vols. 1-4, (Berlin/New York 1984–1988). Of the socialist 'third force' concepts, those of the German Socialist Party in Hans-Peter Schwarz, *Vom Reich zur Bundesrepublik* (Neuwied, Berlin, 1966), pp. 483–588, and the French Left in Wilfried Loth, *Sozialismus und Internationalismus*, (Stuttgart, 1977); also ibid. for French postwar foreign policy in general.

2. Vincent Auriol, *Journal du septennat, 1947*, (Paris, 1970,) vol. 1, p. 380.

3. *L'Oeuvre de Léon Blum, 1947–1950*, (Paris, 1963) vol. 7, pp. 125–8.

4. Here in Blum's formulation of 6 Jan 1948, ibid., pp. 150f. On the 'third force' concept of the French Left in 1947 see the analysis in Loth, *Sozialismus*, pp. 156–66.

5. On the Paris CEEC conference, Harvey B. Price, *The Marshall Plan and its meaning*, (Ithaca, N.Y., 1955), pp. 26–55; as evidence of a course participant see Ernst H. van der Beugell, *From Marshall aid to Atlantic partnership, European integration as a concern of American foreign policy*, (Amsterdam, London, New York, 1966), pp. 68–82; the American documents in FRUS 1947, III, pp. 333–470; evaluation from the perspective of the Germany question in John Gimbel, *The origins of the Marshall Plan*, (Stanford, 1976), pp. 254–66; in general Wilfried Loth, 'The West European governments and the impulse given by the Marshall Plan', in *A History of European Integration*, Walter Lipgens et al., (ed), (Oxford, 1981), pp. 488–507; and Alan S. Milward, *The committee on European economic co-operation and the advent of the Customs Union*, ibid., pp. 507–71.

6. On the change of the French position see Claytons' report after a visit to Paris, FRUS, 1947, II, pp. 1022–4, and the analysis in Loth, *Sozialismus*, pp. 167–75. The text of the French customs union memorandum in A. and Fr. Boyd, *Western union, a study of the trend toward European unity*, (Washington, 1949), pp. 56f.

7. Sforza in a telegraphic directive to the most important Italian embassies on 16.6.1947, FRUS 1947, III, p. 254: compare generally Loth, *The West European governments*.

8. Compare Loth, *Sozialismus*, pp. 170–3; Gimbel, *Origins*, pp. 240–55, 252–4.

9. FRUS 1947, III, pp. 391–396; van der Beugel, *From Marshall Plan to Atlantic partnership*, pp. 79–81; Gimbel, *Origins*, pp. 255–9 and 262 (although with too one-sided emphasis of American interest in the reconstruction of West Germany).

10. Ramadier: speech in Mulhouse, *Le Populaire*, 29 Sept. 1947. Test of the report: *Committee of European Economic Co-operation, vol. I, General Report, vol. II, Technical Reports*, (Paris, London, 1947).

11. On Congress demands compare van der Beugel, *From Marshall aid to Atlantic partnership*, pp. 87–92 and 109–19; on the French initiative at the second CEEC conference of 15-18 March 1948 ibid., pp. 130–2; text of the OEEC convention in *Documents on American foreign relations*, (Washington, 1950), vol. X, pp. 244–50.

12. Kennan: memorandum of 4 Sept. 1947, FRUS 1947, III, pp. 397–405. On the following data compare Price, *The Marshall Plan and its meaning*, and van der Beugel, *From Marshall aid to Atlantic partnership*, as well as William Brown and Redvers Opie, *American foreign assistance*, (Washington, 1953), *passim*.

13. Compare this and the following Joyce and Gabriel Kolko, *The limits of power*, (New York, 1972), p. 428–52; Pierre Melandri, *Les États-Unis face à l'unification de l'Europe 1945–1954*, (Paris, 1980), pp. 108–44; Hardley Arkes, *Bureaucracy, the Marshall Plan and the national interest*, (Princeton, 1972).

14. Revisionist imperialism critique as a whole overestimates the decisiveness of American decision-makers, overlooks the ambivalence of

most decisions and underestimates the potential of Europeans for exerting an influence. The degree of American penetration in fact achieved in Western Europe is laid entirely at the door of the American desire for hegemony, whereas it was really at least equally an effect arising out of the inadequacies of European negotiating ability.

15. Compare Kolko, *Limits*, p. 430, van der Beugel, *From Marshall Aid to Atlantic partnership*, pp. 153–5.

16. Compare for the outcome of internationalisation plans Loth, *Sozialismus*, pp. 216–19 and 240f.; for the British and German attitudes to nationalisation see Wolfgang Rudzio, '*Die ausgebliebene Sozialisierung an Rhein und Ruhr*', in *Archiv für Sozialgeschichte* 18 (1978), pp. 1–39, and Rolf Steininger, 'Reform und Realität, Ruhrfrage und Sozialisierung in der anglo-amerikanischen Deutschlandpolitik 1947/48,' in *Vierteljahrshefte für Zeitgeschichte* 27 (1979), pp. 167–240; for discussion within America see Dörte Winkler, 'Die amerikanische Sozialisierungspolitik in Deutschland 1945–1948,' in Heinrich August Winkler, (ed), *Politische Weichenstellungen im Nachkriegsdeutschland 1945–1953*, (Göttingen, 1979), pp. 88–110; for decisions under Clay's influence see Gimbel, *Origins*, pp. 204–19.

17. Revisionist critics of the 'restoration' (e.g. Kolko, *Limits*, and for the West German region, where discussion is particularly intensive, Eberhardt Schmidt, *Die verhinderte Neuordnung 1945–1952*, 7th edn., 1977, (Frankfurt, 1970); Ute Schmidt and Tilman Fichter, *Der erzwungene Kapitalismus*, 2nd edn., 1975, (Berlin, 1971); Ernst-Ulrich Huster et al., *Determinanten der westdeutschen Restauration 1945–1949*, 2nd edn., 1973 (Frankfurt, 1972,) as a rule present American desire for hegemony as responsible for this development, even explaining it partly in terms of the objectives of the containment policy. In fact, as has been shown, it had diverse causes which cannot be understood as a whole without the prior onset of an East-West confrontation, firstly alleged and then actual. Ernst Nolte's thesis of the inevitability of a 'restoration' after all substantial political elements had rejected an unlimited state planned economy in 1945–46 (*Deutschland und der Kalte Krieg* (Munich, 1974), pp. 216–18) circumvents the essential problem: the decisions of political organisation within the mixed economy systems from 1947. On the relativity of the restoration concept see Theo Pirker, *Die verordnete Demokratie, Grundlagen und Entscheidungen der 'Restauration'*, (Berlin, 1977).

18. Compare Loth, *The West European governments*, pp. 490f. and p. 497. The reception of the containment doctrine in Western Europe outlined below has so far only been systematically researched in the case of France; compare Wilfried Loth, 'Frankreichs Kommunisten und der Beginn des Kalten Krieges', in *Vierteljahrshefte für Zeitgeschichte* 26 (1978), pp. 56–62; also *Sozialismus*, pp. 177-87; on the result of this reception see Klaus Hänsch, *Frankreich zwischen Ost und West* (Berlin, 1972), pp. 104–29, 189–96. The data available for the other countries point in the same direction, although parallel research would still be desirable.

19. Compare *FRUS 1947, II*, pp. 676–810.

20. On the attitudes of Bevin, Bidault and Marshall, see Georgette Elgey, *La République des illusions ou la vie secrète de la IV. République, 1945–1951*, vol. 1 (Paris, 1965), pp. 380–4, and Daniel Yergin, *Shattered peace*, (Boston, 1977), p. 334 and pp. 362f.; Bevin at the London council meeting

after *FRUS 1947, II*, pp. 815–17; paper of 2 Jan. 1948 in Attlee papers, after Yergin, *Shattered peace*, pp. 362f.; meeting of Bevin, Bidault and Churchill after *New York Times*, 25 Jan. 1948; about Spaak Jean Stengers, 'Paul-Henri Spaak et le traité de Bruxelles de 1948', in Raymond Poidevin (ed), *Histoire des débuts de la construction européenne*, (Bruxelles 1986), pp. 119–42.

21. Text in *Parliamentary Debates House of Commons*, 22 Jan. 1948, vol. 446, pp. 383–409.

22. Compare for France Loth, *Sozialismus*, pp. 188–201.

23. Text in *FRUS 1948, III*, p. 91.

9

The Formation of the Blocs

The re-orchestration of American containment policy and the Soviet and West European responses to the Marshall Plan together made 1947 the second year of change in the history of East–West relations. Only since the fruitless breakdown in the London Foreign Ministers' Council meeting in December 1947 were there no more signs of a solution to the differences between the two sides or to their joint problems. This possibility had been replaced by a fear on the part of all involved — the Americans since 1945–6, the Soviets since the summer/autumn of 1947 and the Europeans since the winter of 1947/8 — of an encroachment of greater or lesser violence by the other side on their own security zone. The conflict between East and West was no longer understood simply as a power-political struggle for spheres of influence and security requirements, but increasingly in terms of a battle for survival between two opposing social orders and life-styles. As a result of this ideological polarisation, the actual diversity of political life in East and West was increasingly lost to view, whilst as a result of this mutual fear the authoritarian forces intent upon the extension of the state security apparatus on both sides gained crucial reinforcement.

Against this background, the organisation of both camps — the founding of NATO, the Federal Republic of Germany and the first European institutions in the West, and the firmer grip of the Soviet Union on its allied countries, the founding of the GDR and COMECON in the East — was bound to take on the character of bloc formation as a consequence of this decision to divide. Although initially there was no lack of insecurity as to how each camp was to be organised and how protection from the other side was to be guaranteed, each crisis of mutual relations which resulted from this incipient organisation process — the Prague crisis of the spring of 1948, the Berlin crisis from the summer of 1948 and the autumn crisis of 1949 — all led to an intensification of this polarisation.

Discussion of the Atlantic Treaty

The US government was initially hesitant about European requests for military protection and aid. There could 'be no real question in the long term', as Marshall informed President Truman at the beginning of February 1948, as to what form the relations of the USA with the emerging Brussels Treaty would take: it had to be protected, if only in order not to destroy the investment of trust which the USA had meanwhile accumulated with Marshall aid in Western Europe, and not to drive the Europeans to resignation in the face of alleged overpowering Soviet pressure. On the other hand, officials of the State Department regarded an armed attack on the Western regions as extremely unlikely, if not out of the question. 'It is not Russian military power,' as Kennan never tired of emphasising, 'which is threatening us, it is Russian political power ... If it is not entirely a military threat, I doubt that it can be effectively met entirely by military means.'[1]

A massive stepping-up of defence efforts on the part of the West was, according to this interpretation, not only unnecessary, but even dangerous for the success of containment policy: every dollar invested in military defence would be lost to the more urgent need for the economic recovery of Europe. In addition, it was highly questionable whether Congress, which had presented obstacles even to the Economic Recovery Program, would pass long-term military engagement in Europe with the required three-quarters majority. At all costs, a collapse of this economic aid as a result of being linked with a military protection programme, however special, had to be prevented.

The efforts of the State Department towards 'containment' of the containment policy itself in the economic–political sphere were unsuccessful in preventing the fear that had arisen in Europe of military as well as other aggression from the Soviet Union being transferred to the USA. Nor could it prevent the American military, backed by the armaments industry, from exploiting this combination of factors, as well as out of general preventive strategic thinking, by urging a substantial extension of defence efforts. The central planning staff of the Joint Chiefs of Staff reflected generally widespread opinion when it asserted in a study completed on 11 December 1947 that there was no likelihood of a planned Soviet attack in the next five, or probably even in the next ten years, such an attack being precluded by Soviet reconstruction problems and the securing of hegemony in the Soviet Union and in Eastern Europe, as well as by US atomic superiority. An '"accidental" war', on the other hand, 'resulting perhaps from Soviet miscalculation as to how far one or more Western countries can be pushed without striking back, must be considered a continuing possibility'.[2] With the impact of the Prague crisis, this possibility seemed increasingly likely to observers, and for others a certainty. 'For many months,' wrote General Clay, for example, on 5 March 1948 from Berlin, his telegram hitting Washington like a bombshell, 'I have felt and held that war was unlikely for at least ten years. Within the last few weeks, I have felt a subtle change in Soviet attitude which I cannot define but which now gives me a feeling that it may come with dramatic suddenness.'[3]

To what extent officials in Washington in the spring of 1948 really believed in the potential danger of war it is difficult to say. Of Clay, it is known that he sent his alarm telegram to Washington in order to help the army in its struggle for a proportion of the budget in Congress, whilst in fact being convinced that 'there was (no) immediate danger of war with Russia'.[4] Many an official may have reverted after the initial excitement to a more differentiated way of looking at things, and the general view seems, for example, to have prevailed, after consultations with all departments of the Administration, in the formulation of the National Security Council on 30 March: there was no immediate danger of war, because the Soviet Union still had no prospect of being able to win a war; Soviet policy was aimed at 'domination of the world'; using to this end 'the complementary instruments of Soviet aggressive pressure from without and militant revolutionary subversion from within', both 'supported by the formidable material power of the USSR'; but it 'might ultimately resort to war if necessary to gain its ends'. A 'counteroffensive' on the part of the USA was thus desirable: 'first of all strengthening the military potential of the United States and secondly, mobilising and strengthening the potential of the non-Soviet world', both of these in order to secure the economic reconstruction programme psychologically, to be able to counter Soviet pressure with a credible military threat, and to be armed in the event of a conflict, however remote a possibility such a conflict might be.[5]

It is clear, on the other hand, that once again, as when they launched the Truman Doctrine a year earlier, members of the US government consciously presented the Soviet threat as being greater and more acute than they themselves actually estimated it to be, in order to push through Congress the measures they considered necessary for their long-term policy of containment: the Marshall Plan, a general military training, a partial reintroduction of military service, an extension of the air force budget, and a more psychological than material back-up for the Europeans. For President Truman there was another reason to seize on widespread warnings of Soviet aggression and demands for the extension of defence efforts: he had to demonstrate 'toughness' in the presidential election year of 1948 in order to validate his claim to lead the nation in the alleged crisis. On the day of the signing of the Brussels Treaty, he demanded in front of Congress 'assistance to other nations' and 'an adequate and balanced military strength'.[6] This tactic helped the Marshall Plan to overcome the last parliamentary hurdles, ensured an unforeseen extension of the military budget for the fiscal year 1948/9, in particular a doubling of air spending, and led to the passing of the Selective Service law on military service.

On the question of direct military engagement on the part of the USA in Europe, however, breakthrough was reached only at the end of May, when the French Foreign Minister, Bidault, made it clear to American negotiators that they would not obtain the agreement of the French National Assembly to the setting-up of a West German state without an American mutual assistance guarantee eliminating both the danger of a Soviet attack and offering long-term protection against a fresh threat to French security from the Germans. In view of this condition, the State Department struggled through to ratifying a formal alliance commitment, and since the French insisted on parliamentary backing for the American promise of support, Marshall and Lovett, the Under-Secretary of State, then also ensured a corresponding vote from the Senate. On 11 June, the Senate, thoroughly prepared by Senator Vandenberg and Lovett, voted by 64 to 4 in favour of a resolution approving the 'Association of the United States, by constitutional process, with such regional and other collective arrangements as are based on continuous and effective self-help and mutual aid, and as affect its national security' (the Vandenberg Resolution).[7]

This still left undecided, however, how substantial American engagement in Europe would turn out to be and how closely as a consequence the countries of the Western bloc would ally themselves. The idea in Washington was less that of a material military organisation than that of agreement to a formal guarantee by way of a psychological bolster to the European reconstruction programme. There was no particular hurry to conclude a treaty: nor was there readiness to participate to any significant degree financially in European armament; there was certainly hesitation, therefore, with regard to automatic support commitments.[8] In contrast to this, Europeans were urging just such an automatic commitment, as well as rapid back-up and an increased American presence in Europe. When these demands met with little response, they even began to doubt once again whether they should undertake the risk of an alliance which might provoke the Soviet Union, but which did not at the same time offer real protection against possible Soviet aggression. 'It seems,' a concerned Bidault announced on 16 July in the French Council of Ministers, 'that the American government is little inclined to undertake engagements in Europe at the present time.'[9] In fact, the next and so far the most serious crisis in East–West relations, the Berlin crisis, was to lay the whole of the European–American bloc formation momentarily open to question, although clearly only so that it would then be furthered all the more intensively.

The Berlin crisis

At the beginning of the Berlin crisis, the decision of the Western powers, after the end of the joint Germany policy of the Allies and in accordance with the logic of the Marshall Plan, was on the brink of the state organisation of West Germany. Bevin and Clay, in particular, had been pressing for such a step since the autumn of 1947, in order to overcome the still inadequate situation in the Western zones of Germany, and not least in order to free themselves of the burden of the occupation. The State Department likewise saw the necessity of securing the success of the Marshall Plan in West Germany by means of a reform of the currency system, which had been completely ruined by the inflationary policy of the National Socialists, as well as of a more pronounced involvement on the part of the Germans in the responsibility for reconstruction. It was aware, on the other hand, of not wanting to make the Western powers appear in the eyes of the Germans as responsible for the division of the nation, and of wanting to facilitate the diversion of the French from their hitherto 'tough' German policy. The French, for their part, oscillated between recognising the necessity of including West German potential in European reconstruction, or, in another version, viewing West Germany as a forefield to be consolidated against the Soviet Union, on the one hand, and, on the other, the fear of renewed German dominance, sometimes associated with remaining hopes for a leading role for France in Western Europe. The government, under pressure from the Socialists, was in the meantime prepared to agree to the founding of a West German state, but urged caution in proceeding with this and with concessions on questions of security, in order to be able to safeguard its change of course in internal politics.[10]

The result of these diverse interests was the cautious founding policy of the Western powers, safeguarding itself in stages, but ultimately also steadfast in purpose. On the eve of the London meeting of the Council of Foreign Ministers, Marshall and Bevin agreed on a final initiative for the creation of a unified German state in accordance with Western concepts and, should this fail, as it was expected to, on the consolidation of the bizone, combined with currency reform. When Western proposals for currency reform initially met with Soviet resistance in the Allied Control Council, the US representatives and those of the future Brussels Treaty consulted from 23 February onwards in London on the reorganisation of the three Western occupation zones, without waiting for a possible compromise with the Soviet Union. By way of an interim result, in order to test the reaction of the French and German public, they published on 6 March a resolution on the inclusion of the three Western zones in the European recovery programme, as well as the immediate merging of economic policy in the three zones. The final result came on 7 June in the 'London Recommendations', with the call to the Prime Minister of the West German *Länder* to 'convene a Constituent Assembly in order to prepare a constitution ... with provisions which will allow all the German states to subscribe as soon as circumstances permit'.[11]

The remaining disputed questions between France and the other powers, notably the internationalisation of the Ruhr and the proportion of federalist or centralist elements to be in the future state organisation, were masked with formal compromises. The first of these had in fact already been decided by the Anglo-American agreements of autumn 1947, whilst the second was largely left to the decision of the Germans themselves. After the French National Assembly had barely ratified the 'recommendations' at the end of a lively debate and with much reservation on 17 June, currency reform was announced in the three Western zones on 18 June. On 1 July, the West German prime ministers were notified of the tasks decided on in London.[12]

The Soviet leadership reacted to the incipient organisation of the West German state with the same mixture of conciliation and coercion which was to become typical of its policy with regard to Germany. Thus, after Molotov's polemics at the London Foreign Ministers' Council meeting, there ensued a number of conciliatory gestures: reparation payments from the East, negotiations on the settlement of lend–lease debts, a reduction in demands for reparations from Austria, and agreement to Austrian currency reform. From the end of January 1948, however, there were more provocations, this time in the Allied Control Council; and after these proved fruitless, there came the Soviet withdrawal from the Control Council on 20 March, and from the end of March/beginning of April a stepping-up of the control of railway traffic to Berlin, and after the lifting of this 'mini-blockade', there were repeated proposals from Molotov and Stalin to negotiate the disputed questions in Soviet–American summit talks. All this had the aim of preventing the formation of the Western state. With the conclusion of the Six Power Conference in London there followed new impediments to railway and road traffic, and with the announcement of currency reform in the Western zones the threat of incorporating the whole of Berlin into a currency reform of the Eastern zone. When the Western powers then extended the sphere of validity of the new currency on 23 June to include the Western zone of the former capital of the Reich, the Soviet authorities blocked the land links between Berlin and the Western zones on 24 June, and cut off the supplies of electricity and coal. At the same time, the already announced Eastern currency was introduced in the Soviet zone and the Soviet sector of Berlin. The blockade of West Berlin, which hit the Western powers at their only vulnerable point (and which had thus already been predicted as a possible consequence of the formation of the West German state by some American officials), was now intended to force the negotiations which had not previously been freely conceded, and thus prevent at the last minute the formation of the Western state. The prospect of coming to a negotiated solution with massive coercion of this kind could not be very great and augured, rather, a further entrenchment of the Western position, but the Soviet leadership had no other means left at its disposal, and the definitive installation of American capitalism, which showed every sign of being accompanied by a swift rearmament of Germany and the establishment of a US–European military alliance, seemed so dangerous that it was prepared deliberately to take the risk of a severe loss of prestige in order to avoid the situation. If it did not succeed in forcing the Western powers back to the All-German concept by means of the blockade, there was still some prospect of driving the Western Allies out of Berlin and thus being able to remove a substantial obstacle to the formation of a state on territory in its own zone of occupation.[13]

For some weeks it looked as though Stalin could really achieve the aim of his blockade policy. In spite of prior warnings from the experts, the Western governments had not been prepared for these Soviet measures, and although American fighting forces immediately improvised an airlift to West Berlin, it was not clear at first whether and for how long provision for over two million Berliners could be carried out from the air. In addition, there was a widespread fear that the Soviet Union could block even the air route. In fact this fear was unfounded, since Stalin was not prepared on account of the foundation of a Western state, however contrary to Soviet interests, to risk a war that would be bound to end with the destruction of the Soviet Union. The myth of Soviet strength, however, led most Western politicians to overlook how risky and how close to the limits of the feasible this Soviet manoeuvre really was. Clay, who did not share belief in this myth, repeatedly urged breaking through the blockade of the motorways with tanks, but was rebuffed by his government out of fear of an armed conflict. Hardly anyone wanted war on account of Berlin: not in the USA and definitely not in Europe (Churchill's demand for a preventive atomic war against the Soviet Union, conveyed to the British and American governments two months previously, had thus remained completely isolated). Viewed in the long term, therefore, the Western powers seemed to be in an untenable position, and the Soviet demand for suspension of the 'London Recommendations' and Four-Power negotiations on Germany were gaining increasing support in the West, particularly with the French, who were very dissatisfied with the London compromise anyway, and also among the Germans, whose prime ministers at first put up distinct resistance to the arranged step towards the formation of the West German state.[14]

Asked how the US government should act in the face of this looming dilemma, the political planning staff devised under Kennan the plan for a Soviet–Western agreement on the bilateral withdrawal of troops from Germany, to be followed by the restitution of a unified German state. 'We could then,' declared Kennan in a memorandum of 12 August, 'withdraw from Berlin without loss of prestige, and the people of the Western sectors would not be subjected to Soviet rule because the Russians would also be leaving the city.' Such a solution seemed to him, in spite of the risk of considerable complications for the European programme of reconstruction — including the Soviet zone — and the possibility of a unified Germany veering away from the West, still more acceptable than being permanently burdened with the Berlin problem, with an economically unviable West Germany without links with the East in the absence of a European federation, with the inclination of the West Germans towards reunification, and with the perpetuation of the division of Europe. If the Soviet leadership did not accept this solution, there was still time to carry out the 'London Recommendations', although now without being accused by the Germans and Europeans of dividing Europe. Kennan thus fought for that which he had already foreseen in 1945 as the consequence of containment policy, and indeed had even demanded. The Soviet threat to Berlin, which was intensified by his alarm at the incipient shift in American policy towards an intensively armed military alliance, and by disappointment at the lack of willingness on the part of the West Europeans to form a federation, had thus had a profound effect on him.[15]

In July and August 1948, the Washington Administration earnestly discussed the suspension of the foundation of the West German state in response to the blockade. Both Marshall and the US Ambassador in Moscow, Bedell Smith, were convinced that time would work in favour of the Soviet side and that Berlin could not be retained in the long term. They feared that, in spite of President Truman's strong words, they would not avoid suspending the 'London Recommendations'. Sir Brian Robertson, the

British Military Governor in Germany, argued along the same lines (without being acquainted with internal US discussion). In his case, Soviet conduct after the resolution on the establishment of a Western state aroused concern that the establishment of two German states would sooner or later lead to war with the Soviet Union. He thus wanted to make the All-German solution additionally attractive to the Soviet Union by offering participation in the control of Ruhr industry, which had so far always been refused.[16] However, in the US Administration there was a predominance of people who feared loss of confidence in the USA in Western Europe and a slow Finlandisation of Germany as a result of an East–West withdrawal from Germany. Moreover, Clay, still convinced of the weakness of the Soviet position and the necessity for a 'Western solution', strongly promoted the founding of the Western state, in order to establish dates on which the Western governments would subsequently not be able to retract.[17] Also, the spectacle of the blockade encouraged the anti-Communist consensus in West Germany, Western Europe and the USA to such an extent that withdrawal could no longer be considered feasible from the internal political viewpoint. The blockade appeared to the public as an attempt to incorporate Berlin and as much as possible of the rest of Germany into the sphere of Soviet hegemony. The fact that it was aimed specifically against the formation of the Western state was generally overlooked. The French government did not vote for a meeting of the Council of Foreign Ministers but, under pressure from the anti-Communist wave and because it now saw the lesser evil in the division of Germany, combined with the long-term presence of American troops on German soil, voted rather for the maintenance of the Western position. Around the end of August, the lasting success of the airlift began to emerge. On 26 August, Marshall formulated the maintenance of the Four-Power responsibility for Berlin and of the Western positions in West Germany as essential elements in every agreement on Berlin.[18] This marked the end of the critical phase of the Berlin crisis.

The institutionalisation of the division: FRG, NATO and GDR

What remained was an 'intermediate crisis', which made the Soviet threat seem sufficiently material in the West to encourage a consolidation of the *status quo* characterised by anti-Communism, without Western positions being seriously threatened, or the consensus of the West on the question of the agreed countermeasures being endangered. The Western side had withstood the trial of strength, and the blockade now emerged as the decisive psychological component in the formation of the Western bloc. Leading Western politicians lost all interest in a swift resolution of the crisis.[19] President Truman used the crisis to demonstrate his ability for 'leadership' and to bolster the seriously threatened Republican–Democrat consensus on foreign policy, all of which went a long way towards helping him in November 1948 to win the presidential elections against his Republican competitor Dewey, and towards completely isolating Henry Wallace, then a candidate for the Communist-supported Progressive Party.[20] Both on the question of the European–American military alliance, and on the question of the foundation of the West German state, the fear of Soviet aggression now prevailed over remaining resistance and misgivings. This thus strengthened the process of the formation of a Western bloc after it had been jeopardised by the blockade.

At their first meeting, from 8 to 10 July in Coblenz, the West German prime ministers had still rejected the task of forming a state and had demanded instead a joint and partly autonomous, but also a clearly provisional new administrative organisation for the three Western zones. Although no one now considered an attempt to incorporate the *Länder* of the Soviet zone of occupation, its dependence on the Soviet government having become in the meantime too great for this, and the social systems in East and West already too disparate, yet no one was ready to take responsibility for the division of the country. With the impact of the Berlin crisis, however, the inclination grew to submit to Clay's pressure. When during the second round of conferences on 15–16 and 21–22 July in Rüdesheim the Berlin Chief Burgermaster Ernst Reuter urged the swift establishment of a West German 'core state' with the inclusion of West Berlin, a majority of prime ministers voted for the calling of a constitutional assembly on 1 September 1948. In order to banish remaining misgivings, the military governors conceded the designation of the new constitution as a mere 'basic constitution', the discussion of which was to be undertaken by delegates of the *Länder* parliaments instead of by referendum. This thus enabled West German politicians to introduce the thesis of the provisional character of the formation of the Western state and the demand for reunification in 'free self-determination' to be written into the preamble of the basic constitution. The intensity and time-span of the integration of West Germany into the Western bloc was thus to remain open, although the fact of the foundation of a West German state could now no longer be doubted. The provisional thesis functioned mainly as a means to help the West Germans come to terms with their co-operation in the West German solution.[21]

The ensuing stages of the foundation of the West German state — the negotiations of the 'Parliamentary Council' of September 1948 until May 1949, parallel with the consultations of the Western Allies on the Ruhr statute and the occupation statute, the elections for the first *Bundestag* in August 1949 and the constituting of the first federal government in September 1949, and finally the partial concessions to West German sovereignty demands in the so-called 'Petersberg Agreement' between the Adenauer government and the high commissioners — were influenced by a balance of power broadly consisting of Anglo-American, French, Christian Democrat-Conservative and Social Democrat interests, in which the compromises made fell more in favour of the American and Conservative side. This was partly because this side had the greater resources at its disposal, and partly because its interests were in greater agreement. The constitutional consultations focused on questions of constitutional law: concessions on social and economic structures were not forthcoming. In practice, decisions were made more in favour of a competition-oriented market economy instead of welfare-state concepts of equalisation and participation. On the question of state apparatus, federal state concepts prevailed over state federalism. On the question of basic foreign policy, the tactically flexible Western integration policy of Konrad Adenauer prevailed over the principled loyalty to the claim to nationhood propounded by his Social Democrat counterpart Kurt Schumacher. All these factors together strengthened the conservative trends of incipient West European integration and the American leading role in Europe, thereby also increasing East–West polarisation.[22]

The only thing that at first remained out of the question was the inclusion of the Federal Republic of Germany in a Western military alliance. Such an inclusion would have been consistent with the logic of a defence organisation directed against Soviet expansion, and had therefore already been considered by British and American planning staffs in the spring of 1948, but could be as little expected of the West Germans, who were still hesitating as much about definitive integration into the West as the French, who were alarmed at the danger of a new German threat. In order not to jeopardise the stabilisation of the West, therefore, the American government deliberately put off discussion on the rearmament of Germany. In general, however, the negotiations on a US–European military treaty were furthered under the impact of the Berlin blockade. The thesis of the military threat from the Soviet Union was gaining credence among the American public, Kennan's fear of the economic reconstruction programme being damaged by superfluous efforts towards armament falling more and more into the background. Representatives of the Brussels Treaty states, Canada and the USA agreed on the thesis on 9 September 1948, after two months of negotiations in Washington, that 'peaceful coexistence' with the Soviet Union was not possible in the long term and that a joint defence alliance of the West must consequently be formed.[23] The American government liked to see in the Atlantic alliance a continuing concession to the over-anxious Europeans, whilst the French government wanted with the alliance plan, amongst other things, to pursue definitive protection against German aggression. Decisive, however, for overcoming the remaining contradictions in the question of the formation of an alliance was their shared conviction that Soviet aggression could now no longer definitely be ruled out. Likewise, a decisive factor in the parliamentary implementation of the treaty system was the fact that this conviction was also widespread among the American and European public.

After a series of further negotiations from October 1948 to March 1949, the North Atlantic Treaty was signed in Washington on 4 April 1949. Hesitantly, since they themselves did not feel threatened by Soviet aggression, a number of countries which had not been involved in the treaty negotiations joined in: Italy, under pressure from France, which did not want to take sole responsibility for territorial defence in the Mediterranean region; Norway, Denmark (with Greenland), Iceland and Portugal (with the Azores), because they formed important forefields of American and Canadian security. The American government agreed to the formation of a joint treaty organisation (later the North Atlantic Treaty Organization, abbreviated to NATO), but left open the scale and liability of the organisational structure. An automatic obligation for mutual support, as the Europeans had hoped for, was not agreed on; the signatories agreed solely, out of regard for the American Congress, to commit themselves to regarding an armed attack on one or more participant countries 'as an attack against them all' and to 'such action as it deems necessary, including the use of armed force, to restore and maintain the security of the North Atlantic area'.[24] The more restricted American interpretation of the treaty thus still predominated, and even a first military aid payment to the Europeans of 1.45 million dollars, which Truman announced in the US Congress even before the ratification of the treaty in July 1949, was mainly symbolically intended. A foundation stone was nevertheless thereby laid, from which strategic preventive thinking and the interests of the military–industrial complex were able to develop their own dynamic. The USA had become definitively engaged in Europe, and now had military obligations in addition to its economic and political ones: the era of American isolationism had finally come to an end.

The Soviet leadership nevertheless hoped into the winter of 1948/9 to be able to coerce the Western powers into relinquishing their position in West Berlin, and thus to reverse the process of formation of the Western bloc. When Western air fighting forces withstood the test of the winter, however, the leadership began to realise how the blockade was. in fact encouraging the formation of the Western bloc and thus began to seek a way of extricating itself from the crisis without too great a loss of face. The Western powers understandably were little inclined to make concessions, with the result that it took until May 1949 for the Soviet leadership to lift the blockade, in return for the sole concession of reconvening the Allied Council of Foreign Ministers. The Council thus met on 23 May 1949; Molotov's successor, Vishinsky, requested a Four-Power peace treaty with Germany and the establishment of a unified German state council on the basis of the zonal authorities in office in Frankfurt and East Berlin. Marshall's successor, Acheson, responded with a demand for prior free elections in the Soviet zone and the extension of the basic constitution to include the whole of Germany. Thus whilst the Soviet Union still favoured the administration of Germany on a unified basis, an administration which guaranteed the Soviet Union the right to consultation on Germany over and above its right of occupation, the USA insisted on the principle of self-determination, which in the natural course of events was bound to render the whole of Germany accessible to Western influence.

As expected, no *rapprochement* could be achieved on these contradictory positions, and the two delegations parted on 20 June,
although conducting themselves entirely in the proper manner.[25]
Without relinquishing its fundamental demand for a revision of
the 'London Recommendations', the Soviet Union had in fact
accepted the foundation of the Western state.

There was nothing left but to bring to completion the formation of a state in the Soviet zone of occupation, which had been
prepared for by the separate development of social systems in this
zone, but which had been for a long time held in suspension in
the hope of a unified German solution. In order to mobilise
German national sentiment against the move of the Western
powers to form a Western state, the Soviet leadership had
initiated through the German Socialist Unity Party (SED) in
November 1947 a 'German People's Congress for Unity and Just
Peace' composed of 'all democratic forces'. With only minimal
West German participation and manifest dominance of the SED,
this had supported Soviet demands for a unified German government. Still with a predominantly propagandist intention, but at
the same time nevertheless preparing the way for a separate and
substitute solution in the East, a second 'People's Congress' had
been introduced in March 1948, consisting of a permanent 'German People's Council' with 400 members and a number of
subcommittees. By July 1948, this council had worked out a draft
constitution for a (unified) German 'Democratic Republic' and
had passed this on 22 October 1948, but had then awaited further
developments of the Berlin crisis. Opponents of the People's
Congress Movement (such as Ernst Lemmer and Jakob Kaiser of
the Eastern CDU) had in the meantime been politically eliminated, and the SED reorganised more on the Soviet model. Only
after the definitive collapse of Soviet blockade policy was the
People's Congress movement mobilised to prepare the founding
of a separate state. On 19 March 1949, the People's Council
formally accepted the GDR constitution and announced at the
same time general elections for the third 'People's Congress' in
the *Länder* of the Soviet zone. This likewise approved the constitution, with a standard list of candidates and substantial manipulation, on 29 May and formed a new People's Council which then,
after awaiting the first elections, for the West German *Bundestag*
and the constituting of the first Federal government, formed the
'Provisional People's Chamber' of the GDR on 7 October 1949.
The salient characteristic of this new apparatus was its complete

dependence on the Soviet military government. After Soviet hopes for a neutral, unified Germany had been dashed, the Soviet zone was now to be drawn into the circle of the People's Democracies steadily being reorganised on the Soviet model. The 'Iron Curtain', which Churchill had already felt obliged to diagnose in March 1946, had now become a reality; however, it ran not 'from Stettin to Trieste', but along the frontier of the internal German zones of occupation.[26]

The universalisation of containment policy

Although the Berlin crisis had ended with a decided Soviet defeat, the American leadership once again believed itself to be threatened — in a way which was to intensify the formation of blocs even further. Three developments worked together to create a new crisis in Washington in the autumn of 1949.

Firstly, the Marshall Plan for Western Europe appeared to be threatening to collapse. Not only was European integration not proceeding, the West Germans making sovereignty demands, the French threatening to revert to unilateral nationalist positions, and unity of the OEEC countries on the distribution of the second annual payment of American aid occurring only with severe difficulties and at the last minute, but much more serious was the fact that the dollar deficit of the European countries was not decreasing, but increasing, thus postponing into the distant future the restitution of independence of the European economy. The British dollar deficit thus rose in the second quarter of 1949 to 157 million pounds sterling, as high as it had been in 1947 before Marshall aid, and twice as high as dollar payments through the Marshall Plan. France was able in the third quarter of 1949 to finance only one-tenth of its dollar imports out of its own imports. Whilst the ECA considered a total of European exports to a level of a 1,000 million dollars to be necessary for 1951–2, the OEEC only regarded 300 million as possible.[27] There was no way out in sight: integration as the basis for greater rationalisation and thus greater competitiveness of European production could not be coerced. American industry thus found itself from November 1948 onwards in its long-feared recession crisis, albeit substantially alleviated by the preventive measures of Open Door policy,[28] and it blocked every attempt to increase European imports, knowing that it had rather to reduce them. Congress showed itself less and less inclined to finance further subsidies and loans.

Secondly, the victory of Mao Tse Tung's troops in China in the course of the second half of 1949 (in December the last remaining Kuomintang troops of Chang Kai Shek left the Chinese mainland) seemed to extend substantially the influence of the Communist movement. This victory had in fact been predicted in Washington by the end of 1947 at the latest, after all American attempts had failed to move Chang Kai Shek to reform his infinitely corrupt, exploitative and dictatorial regime and to reach a peaceful solution with the Chinese Communists. Similarly, the Americans had only half-heartedly supported the Kuomintang troops without considering success possible (with 400 million instead of the requested 1,500 million dollars in 1948, for example). After victory occurred with a speed which surprised even Mao, however, the fear of a further strengthening of Communist movements in the Asian region (especially in Indo-China), and a realisation both of the untenability of Western positions and of massive Sino-Soviet differences began to predominate in the ruling circles of Washington. At the same time, a growing anti-Communist movement among the public (especially among right-wing Republicans) suspected the government of not having shown sufficient 'toughness' in its China policy, and was thus more prone to a negative interpretation of the Chinese revolution.[29]

Thirdly, news of the first Soviet atom bomb explosions at the end of August 1949 jeopardised the previous American security concept. Until that time the Administration, against the warnings of experts since 1945, had been confident that the American monopoly of atomic weapons would continue for a long time, and had consequently regarded a lower level of conventional armament as justifiable. Those circles which in the spring of 1948 had provided the first impetus for armament thus now received a substantial boost.

These three developments together brought about a crisis among the American leadership in the autumn and winter of 1949 comparable with the previous deep pessimism of the spring of 1947, but now leading to consequences extending far beyond the original containment policy. The total vision of a monolithic and expansive Soviet Communist movement, which had once been evoked in domestic politics for the promulgation of the containment programme, was now propounding itself. The aim of Soviet policy, as leading experts of the State Department and the War Department and atomic energy scientists wrote in a 'top secret' memorandum worked out for Truman in February– March 1950, was 'the complete subversion or forcible destruction of the machinery of government and structure of society in the countries of the non-Soviet world and their replacement by an apparatus and structure subservient to and controlled from the Kremlin. To that end Soviet efforts are now directed toward the domination of the Eurasian landmass.' The practice of Soviet policy was still highly selectively perceived, with hardly any distinction being made between the various factions of inter- national Communism, or a possible war in the foreseeable future. In order to evade this alleged all-embracing threat, the memoran- dum, initiated by Secretary of State Dean Acheson and approved by Truman on 25 April 1950 (with the registered number NSC 68), demanded 'a more rapid build-up of political, economic and military strength, and thereby the creation of confidence in the free world'. Particularly necessary for this in the unanimous view of the three groups of experts were 'the development of an ade- quate political and economic framework [over and above previ- ous treaties and organisations] ... a substantial increase in expenditures for military purposes [State Department planners thought in terms of 35,000–50,000 million dollars per annum instead of the 14,400 million allocated for 1950] ... a substantial increase in the military aid programe ... some increase in econ- omic assistance programs and recognition of the need to continue these programs until their purposes have been accomplished [thus beyond the foreseen end of Marshall Aid programme in 1952] ... the development of internal security and civilian defense ... [and last, but not least] increased taxes'.[30]

From the autumn of 1949 onwards, Secretary of State Acheson pursued a foreign policy more and more along the lines of this universalistic containment concept. The new government of China was not recognised; its entry into the UN was likewise blocked; advances on the part of the Chinese Prime Minister, Chou en Lai, towards a Sino-American settlement (viewed by the USA as a counterbalance to the Soviet threat) were rejected. In order to stop the Soviet advance in Asia and to bring French troops back to the European continent as soon as possible, the US government began to give financial support to the French intervention in Indo-China (starting with a sum of 10 million dollars approved on 1 May 1950). At the end of January 1950, Truman agreed to the much-disputed building of the hydrogen bomb. The resistance of Louis Johnson, the Secretary of Defense, who was conservative in terms of political finance, to an increase in military spending had been broken by the passing of NSC 68 in April 1950. From June 1950, therefore, the Korean War helped to convince Congress and the Europeans of the necessity of renewed defence efforts and a closer integration of the Western bloc.[31] The militancy, anti-Communist consensus and solidarity of the Western world were now greater than they had even been, almost comparable with the enforced solidarity of the more limited Soviet bloc.

With the formation of the blocs in 1948–9, the visions of the Truman Doctrine and the theses of Zhdanov were largely made a reality. Although political relations in the East and West, and certainly in the countries outside the alliance systems, were still far more intricate than the dichotomised world view of these two fundamental Cold War doctrines were prepared to admit, the two blocs now existed. Each lived in fear of the dominance of the other side, and each thus sought preventively to weaken the other, specifically by encouraging national differences and contradictions in the other camp, and strove to incorporate more and more regions of the world into its own side. It had now become infinitely difficult to reverse this process of bloc form-ation, not only because economic interests and social systems had meanwhile adapted to the polarisation between East and West, but above all because every retreat in terms of defence potential was now in fact bound to mean an advance to the other side. More feasible was the possibility of a partial balance between the blocs in the form of mutual recognition of security zones and *rap-prochement* on reciprocal or common interests. For good reason, both sides were ultimately afraid of an armed conflict and were otherwise scarcely prepared to undertake substantial costs or risks in order to achieve the hoped-for change in the *status quo* for their own benefit. Nevertheless these possibilities were not to be exhausted for a long time, since the ability to analyse the conflict in rational terms, at least on the Western side, had been lost, whilst the aggressive language of the Soviet leadership, like the brutal means used to secure its power, was not exactly calculated to encourage such a skill.

Notes

1. Marshall to Truman, 11 Feb. 1948, Truman papers, in Daniel Yergin, *Shattered peace*, (Boston, 1977), p. 363; Kennan to the National War College, 6 Oct. 1947, Kennan papers, in John L. Gaddis, 'Containment: a reassessment', in *Foreign Affairs* 55 (1976/7), p. 880. The following outline is based on hitherto unpublished sources (especially FRUS and in Yergin, *Shattered peace*, ch. XIII); now available in detail, Timothy P. Ireland, *Creating the entangling alliance. The origins of the North Atlantic Treaty Organization*, (London, 1981).

2. JSPC 814/3 of 11 Dec. 1947; published in excerpts in Thomas H. Etzold and John L. Gaddis (eds), *Containment, documents on American policy and strategy 1945–1950*, (New York, 1978) pp. 285–97, quotation p. 288.

3. Text in Jean Edward Smith (ed), *The papers of General Lucius D. Clay: Germany 1945–49*, (Bloomington, 1974), pp. 568f.

4. Thus on 3 March 1948 to the Department of State, likewise on 5 March to Lodge, Smith, *The papers of General Clay*, pp. 564–8; see also pp. 699–704.

5. NSC 7 of 30 March 1948, *FRUS* 1948, I, pp. 546–50. Dulles' statement of May 1949 to the external Senate committee that he 'know(s) of any responsible high official ... who believes that the Soviets now plan conquest by open military aggression' (*US Senate, Committee on Foreign Relations, Hearings: North Atlantic Treaty, April–May 1949*, (Washington, 1949), p. 343) thus contains, consciously or unconsciously, only half the truth; Joyce and Gabriel Kolko (*The limits of power* (New York, 1972), pp. 498–502) quite wrongly take this as the key document for their thesis that NATO was *not* founded primarily out of fear of the Soviet threat, and that it served predominantly as protection from Germany, and to prevent internal revolution and another European economic crisis.

6. See Yergin, *Shattered peace*, pp. 350–62. Truman's Congress in FRUS (1948), III, p. 54f.

7. See Ireland, *Creating*, pp. 57, 63, 69, 85–100 and Wilfried Loth, 'Die Deutsche Frage in französischer Perspektive', in Ludolf Herbst (ed), *Westdeutschland 1945–1955* (Munich, 1986), pp. 37–49, here p. 46f; text of the Vandenberg Resolution, in FRUS 1948, III, p. 135f.

8. See the recommendations of the National Security Council of 26 June 1948. FRUS (1948), III, p. 140f. and statements by Under Secretary of State Lovett at the first sitting of the Washington 'Exploratory Talks', ibid., pp. 149–51.

9. Vincent Auriol, *Journal du septennat*, Bd.2: 1948, (Paris, 1974), p. 318; see FRUS (1948), II, p. 233; Ireland, *Creating*, pp. 101–4; Escott Reid, *Time of fear and hope. The making of the North Atlantic Treaty 1947–1949*, (Toronto, 1977), pp. 114–18.

10. On Bevin see Feis, *From trust to terror*, p. 289; on Clay, John Gimbel, *Amerikanische Besatzungspolitik in Deutschland 1945–1949*, (Frankfurt, 1971), chs. 11-14; on the State Department, Yergin, *Shattered peace*, pp. 333f.; on France, Wilfried Loth, 'Die Deutsche Frage', pp. 44–7.

11. Text in *Documents on American foreign relations*, vol X, (Princeton, 1950), p. 110.

12. On the establishment process of the Federal Republic, which can

only be dealt with very briefly here, see finally Wolfgang Benz, *Die Gründung der Bundesrepublik. Von der Bizone zum souveränen Staat* (Munich, 1984).

13. See on Soviet fears the accounts by Maurice Thorez (in a report of autumn 1947; FRUS (1947), III, p. 813f, and Nikita Krushchev ('afraid of a new round of destruction', in Strobe Talbott (ed), *Kruschev remembers: the last testament*, (Boston, 1974), p. 191; on the aims of the action, Stalin's statements in conversation with Western Allied ambassadors 2 Aug. 1948 (that he had no intention of driving Western troops out of Berlin), the formation of a West German government being 'the only real issue': FRUS (1948), II, pp. 999–1006.

14. For American fears in general, Bohlen to Marshall, 4 Aug. 1948, see State Department Papers, given in Yergin, *Shattered peace*, pp. 385f., and Kennan's memorandum of 12 Aug. 1948, FRUS (1948), II, pp. 1288–96; for Clay, see Smith, *The papers of General Clay*, pp. 696f., 734–7, and FRUS (1948), II, p. 918, 957f. For the reaction of the West German Prime Minister, see Gimbel, *Amerikanische Besatzungspolitik*, pp. 271–92, and Thilo Vogelsang, 'Koblenz, Berlin und Rüdesheim, Die Option für den westdeutschen Staat im Juli 1948', in *Festschrift Hermann Heimpel*, vol. 1, (Göttingen, 1971), pp. 161–79. Kolko's thesis of a crisis calculated in advance in the interests of manipulating Congress (*Limits*, p. 491) is untenable.

15. Text of the memorandum PPS 37 loc. cit. (note 14) revised as PPS 37/1 of 15 Nov. 1948 (so-called 'Plan A') in FRUS (1948), II, pp. 1320–38; see also George F. Kennan, *Memoirs 1925–1950*, (Boston, 1967), pp. 421–6, with its somewhat misleading interpretation of his own motives; and Axel Frohn, *Deutschland zwischen Neutralisierung und Westintegration*, (Frankfurt/M, 1985), pp. 127–31.

16. See Bohlen to Marshall (14); Smith to Clay, FRUS (1948, II, p. 1006f. and 1032; on Robertson. Rolf Steininger, 'Wie die Teilung Deutschlands verhindert werden sollte — Der Robertson-Plan aus dem Jahre 1948', in *Militärgeschichtliche Mitteilungen* 33, (1983), pp. 49–89. On the whole issue see also Yergin, *Shattered peace*, pp. 367–392 and Avi Shlaim, *The United States and the Berlin Blockade, 1948–1949. A Study in Crisis Decision-making*, (Berkeley, Ca/London 1983).

17. To this extent, Clay had quite a substantial share in the emergence of the Federal Republic of Germany, a share as a rule underestimated in its significance by critics of his intervention policy towards the Prime Minister and later towards the Parliamentary Council. See John H. Baker, *Die deutschen Jahre des Generals Clay. Der Weg zur Bundesrepublik 1945–1949*, (Munich 1983), pp. 299–302.

18. FRUS (1948), II, pp. 1083–85. Kennan presented his plan once again in November 1948 (see note 15), but this time found no positive response.

19. Krushchev's criticism of the 'badly thought-out plan' of his predecessor (see Strobe Talbott (ed), *Krushchev remembers; the last testament*, (New York, 1976), p. 217f.) is also unjustified.

20. See Susan M. Hartmann, *Truman and the 80th Congress*, (Columbia, Mo., 1971); Robert Divine, 'The Cold War and the Election of 1948,' in *Journal of American History* 59 (1972), pp. 90–110; by the same author,

Foreign Policy and U.S. Presidential Elections, 1940–1948, (New York, 1974).

21. See Gimbel, *Amerikanische Besatzungspolitik*, pp. 271–92, and Vogelsang, *Koblenz, Berlin and Rüdesheim*.

22. On the course of internal decision-making in West Germany see particularly Werner Sörgel, *Konsensus und Interessen, Eine Studie zur Entstehung des Grundgesetzes für die Bundesrepublik Deutschland*, (Stuttgart, 1969); Volker Otto, *Das Staatsverständnis des Parlamentarischen Rates, Ein Beitrag zur Entstehungsgeschichte des Grundgesetzes für die Bundesrepublik Deutschland*, (Düsseldorf, 1971); Karlheinz Niclauß, *Demokratiegründung in Westdeutschland, Die Entstehung der Bundesrepublik 1945–1949*, (Munich, 1974); Hans-Hermann Hartwich, *Sozialstaatspostulat und gesellschaftlicher status quo*, 3rd edn, (Opladen, 1978).

23. Text of the memorandum of 9 Sept. 1948 (addressed to the participant governments) in FRUS (1948), II, pp. 237–48, ibid., pp. 148–236, for the Washington negotiations and pp. 249–351 as well as FRUS (1949), IV, pp. 1–281, on further negotiation phases in autumn/winter 1948/49.

24. Text of the North Atlantic Treaty in FRUS (1949), IV, pp. 281–5.

25. See American documents on the negotiations for a lifting of the blockade from January 1949 in FRUS (1949), III, pp. 594–840, as well as on the Paris Council meeting, ibid., pp. 856–1065.

26. See overviews in Karl-Dietrich Erdmann, *Das Zeitalter der Weltkriege*, (Stuttgart, 1976), pp. 780–9 (with overemphasis on systematic approach aimed at separation) and Dietrich Staritz, *Sozialismus in einem halben Land* (Berlin, 1976), pp. 155–74.

27. See Kolko, *Limits*, p. 457, 464, pp. 470f., as well as in general ibid., pp. 453–76. Kolko's attempt to present the deflationary policy of the ECA as responsible for the deterioration in the dollar crisis is unconvincing, however.

28. See Hans Günther Brauch, *Struktureller Wandel und Rüstungspolitik der USA (1940–1950)*, (Heidelberg, 1976), pp. 1089–104. The three-year delay in the crisis can be explained essentially in terms of the backlog of consumer goods immediately after the end of the war.

29. See the remarkable analyses of American policy towards China in Kolko, *Limits*, pp. 246–76 and pp. 534–62, and Ernest R. May, *The Truman Administration and China, 1945–1949*, (Philadelphia, 1975); William W. Stueck, Jr., *The road to confrontation: American policy toward China and Korea, 1947–1950*, (Chapel Hill, 1981).

30. Text of the NSC 68 memorandum in FRUS (1950), I, pp. 234–92, quotation in ibid., p. 238, 282 and 285, on its emergence Paul Y. Hammond, NSC 68: 'Prologue to rearmament', in Schilling, Hammond and Snyder, *Strategy, politics and defense budgets*, (New York, London, 1962), pp. 267–378; the data (not contained in the memorandum) on the military budget from Yergin, *Shattered peace*, p. 402. Kolko's thesis (*Limits*, p. 455, pp. 474ff., and p. 487), that armament plans took the place of the 'failed' Marshall economic aid, and that the European economic crisis was the real reason for the founding of NATO and its development is untenable: Acheson certainly used the technique of his predecessor Marshall in fuelling fear of Soviet expansion in order to mobilise aid funds, but in essence he demanded *both* economic and military aid

(although later both through NATO structures), and the still widespread view in 1948 that armament could damage economic aid (see above in note 1), was only displaced by the new fears of autumn 1949.

31. See Kolko, *Limits*, pp. 504–9, pp. 554–62; Yergin, *Shattered peace*, pp. 400–7; David A. Rosenberg, 'American atomic strategy and the hydrogen bomb decision' in *Journal of American History* 66 (1979), pp. 62–87; Michael H. Hunt, 'Mao Tsetung and the issue of accommodation with the United States, 1948–1950', in Dorothy Borg and Waldo Heinrichs (Hrsg.), *Uncertain years: Chinese-American relations, 1947–1950*, (New York 1980), pp. 181–233.

10

The Beginnings of West European Integration

Parallel with the formation of the Western bloc from 1948–50, the West European governments undertook the first steps towards the realisation of the concept of European unity. The beginnings of European unity policy were of a distinctly ambiguous nature: subjectively, they were sustained both by the 'third-force' movement, as well as by the increasingly numerous supporters of a Western defence bloc, converging in their efforts to strengthen Western Europe by integration along the lines of the original Marshall Plan. Most proponents of the 'third force' now wanted both European independence from the USA and protection from Soviet aggression. Objectively, however, incipient European integration contributed of course in the first instance to the consolidation of the Western camp, and was not least a means for solving the problems resulting from bloc formation, especially a settlement of Franco-German relations. At the same time, however, it formed a precondition for a relatively independent role for Europe within the Western alliance. The most disparate tendencies and interests were thus involved in the unity movement, and it was by no means clear at first which of these would prevail; a minimally integrated Europe as a palliative for the Western bloc, a strongly integrated liberal-conservative Europe as an equal power and political partner of the USA, or a united Europe moving in the democratic socialist direction and counteracting the world-wide trend towards polarisation.

The emergence of the Council of Europe

'Private' initiatives marked the beginning of the European

219

integration process, simultaneously highlighting lack of accord over the question of the future vision of Europe, and also leading to the first preliminary decisions before negotiations had even begun at the governmental level. Churchill, who wanted to use the concept of European unity to consolidate the Western bloc ideologically in Europe, and in particular to facilitate the Franco-German reconciliation, which would be indispensable to the cohesion of the Western alliance, had initiated in the spring of 1947 in Great Britain an informal 'club' of influential politicians and leading social circles known as the 'United Europe Movement' (UEM), which was intended to influence the governments of Western Europe along the lines of Churchill's European concept. Around the same time, a number of federation-oriented 'third-force' supporters formed the 'Union Européene des Fédéralistes' (UEF), the membership of which was politically relatively uninfluential, but comparatively strong in number (with 100,000 members in Western Europe). From July 1947, both planned a European manifestation of the unity concept, which was intended to initiate the basic impetus for the public and the Marshall Plan governments. On 14 December 1947 they agreed with a number of other groups on procedures for a Congress of this kind. The UEM prevailed on all essential points: what a united Europe should be like and by what means it was to be created were left deliberately vague. The presidency of the Congress was offered to Churchill.[1]

As preparations went ahead for the Congress, which had been set for May 1948 in The Hague, official delegations from the fourteen socialist and social democratic parties whose countries were involved in the Marshall Plan met in London from 20 to 22 March, and again in Paris on 24 and 25 April, to discuss a joint socialist European strategy in view of the Marshall Plan. In this instance it was the British Labour Party which dashed the hopes of third-force supporters (especially the French socialists and the Italian social democrats) for a joint commitment to the 'third-force' concept and energetic steps towards the setting-up of a supranational Europe. Although the parties were agreed in principle on the necessity for strengthening 'the true supranational authorities of the communities of the Five and the Sixteen [that is, the Brussels Treaty and the OEEC], they allowed themselves to be led by the Labour leadership into turning down the invitation to take part in the Congress at The Hague. Much as the socialists of the continent were interested in a swift and extensive integration of Europe, they did not want to break with the Labour Party: a socialist-governed Great Britain was ultimately intended to take on the leadership of the 'third-force' Europe.[2]

At the Congress in The Hague (7–10 May 1948), therefore, which was attended by over 700 European politicians and representatives from public life, international socialism and the 'third-force' movement consequently played only a secondary role. A minority of British and French socialists, the most prominent of whom was the former French Prime Minister, Ramadier, did take part in spite of the veto of their party leaderships, but were unable to prevent conservative and liberal politicians, ranging from Churchill to Paul Reynaud to Konrad Adenauer, from dominating the scene. Strictly market economy concepts prevailed in the resolutions of the Congress: the concept of Ruhr internationalisation was rejected, as was the demand for the participation of trade unions in European community organisations. Instead of calling for the immediate convocation of a constitutional assembly of the European federation, as 190 British and 130 French members of parliament had done on 18–19 March in resolutions proposed in parliament, the Congress settled for the convocation of a 'European Assembly' to develop plans for the unification of Europe and to be elected by national parliaments.[3]

The French socialists now attempted to transform at least this resolution into reality through the French government. They coerced Bidault, the Foreign Minister, into calling, at the second meeting of the consultative council of the Brussels Treaty states on 20 July, for the convocation of a 'European Parliamentary Assembly' for 'an exchange of opinion' on the problems of a European alliance. After one of the study groups set up under Ramadier at the Congress in The Hague had suggested to the governments of the Five the calling of a conference for the preparation of such a consultative parliament, they made sure on 18 August that the French government extended appropriate invitations to its allied governments.[4] Cautious as this initiative for the sake of the desired British participation was in its form, it was essentially aimed primarily at a European federation intended to extend beyond the formation of the Western bloc with the OEEC and the Brussels Treaty.

The initial treatment by the Labour government of this French effort was dilatory. On the one hand, it was not keen to see a unity extending beyond the intensification of inter-state relations, and on the other, it could not afford completely to snub those Europeans on the continent who wanted unity, in the interests of a consolidation of the Western alliance. Bidault's proposal was put off as 'unsuitable at the present moment' at the autumn sitting of the consultative council, and the Labour government reacted only unofficially to the second initiative of the French government, with a treatise by the party's Executive Committee which rejected all plans for the setting-up of a supranational authority as dangerous ventures endangering the solid construction of the 'Western Union'.[5] At the consultative council meeting of 25–26 October, Bevin finally agreed to negotiations on a European assembly, but initially wanted this to be understood only as a permanent Council of Ministers of the Brussels Treaty states. When the negotiation commission agreed in December on a double project for a 'council of Europe', composed of European ministers and open to all OEEC countries, and a 'European Consultative Assembly' of European parliamentary representatives with vaguely determined functions ('measures for the deepening of understanding'), he exercised his veto against an autonomous parliamentary assembly. Only when the new French Foreign Minister, Robert Schuman, had threatened on 13 January while on a visit to London that the French government would, if necessary, negotiate even without Great Britain, did Bevin relent. After further administrative preparations, a statute of the Council of Europe, Council of Ministers and the Consultative Assembly was announced on 5 May. An official discussion forum on the question of European unity was thus the price that Bevin had to pay to the continental Europeans in the interests of Western bloc formation.[6]

The collapse of the European Federation

The compromise reached did not satisfy the Europeans, however. The continental socialists in particular, under the leadership of the French SFIO, as well as a Labour minority led by Ronald Mackay and Richard Crossman, assailed the Labour leadership in the following months to persuade it to take part after all in swift measures towards European unity. In the first term of the Consultative Assembly of the Council of Europe (from 10 August to 5 September 1949 in Strasburg), they managed a few initial successes: going beyond the vague and restrictive guidelines of the Council of Europe, the first Euro MPs — the cream of their respective national political factions — initiated a standing committee to work outside the meagre allotted sittings of the Assembly and thus substantially to increase its political influence. A majority resolved that the '"aim and goal" of the Council of Europe was to create "an authority" invested with limited functions but real powers'. The standing committee was given the task of examining the question of political authority and arranging a special sitting of the Assembly for January 1950. The Council of Ministers was similarly requested to extend considerably the competence of the Assembly and to facilitate the entry of the Federal Republic of Germany before the beginning of the following term. In order to make it easier for the Labour leadership to agree, the pro-unity socialists made efforts towards a general recognition of socialist positions. In contrast with The Hague, a majority in Strasbourg was in favour of demanding a European economic community with 'central planning combined with a maximum degree of individual liberty'. The Ruhr issue and that of the co-ordination of European basic industries were considered worthwhile topics.[7]

These requirements and task allocations, however, overstepped what the Labour government was prepared to tolerate in the interests of the consolidation of the Western bloc. At the Council of Ministers meeting of 3–5 November, all recommendations of the Assembly for the extension of the statute were rejected under British pressure: the Council's resolutions had to be unanimous. All remaining recommendations and suggestions, including the plan for an early special sitting, were referred for further study to official administrative or international authorities, without obliging them to provide their reports by a specific date. Only the admission of the Federal Republic as associate member was approved and, subject to a final decision on its statute, the admission of the Saarland, the *de facto* autonomy of which the French government wanted to ensure. The path of the Council of Europe towards becoming a constituent assembly was thus stopped before it had even really begun in the work of the Commission of the Consultative Assembly. Pro-unity MPs who had made efforts to persuade the British at Strasburg felt snubbed and were bitterly disappointed.[8]

By now, pro-unity Europeans were faced with a fundamental decision: whether to hold back their initiatives in order to facilitate further co-operation from the British, thereby risking the collapse of the entire unity project, or to take substantial steps towards European unity without Great Britain, in the hope that the British would eventually be included in a successful European project, but taking the risk of driving them into even greater isolation. This was not a difficult decision for liberal and conservative groups on the continent: if the British did not want to participate, the necessary steps towards European reconstruction and the solution of the Germany issue would have to be taken without them. The socialists and other supporters of the 'third-force' idea, on the other hand, were faced with an impossible dilemma; without swift supranational solutions, what remained of European independence threatened to be subsumed within the general trend towards East–West polarisation, and without British participation there was the threat of a conservative Europe, possibly even led by a conservative West Germany, which was equally incompatible with the 'third force'. They could not have both supranationalism and be under British leadership. The rift over the question of how to proceed affected every faction of the Strasbourg Assembly. Characteristically, two politicians from the same party emerged as the spokesmen of these two positions: Guy Mollet, General Secretary of the French socialists, on the pro-British side and his political economy spokesman, André Philip, on the pro-federalist side.[9]

At the beginning of the second term of the Consultative Assembly (7–24 August and 18–24 November 1950), representatives of the Philip tendency presented a petition requesting the member states 'to create a political authority at the earliest possible moment' to decide on the majority principle on questions of 'human rights, foreign relations, economic policy and European security'. In addition, 'states desiring closer organisational links with one another' should conclude a federal treaty, with which they could then create a democratically elected parliament and a government which would be answerable to it.[10] Mollet, *rapporteur* of the political committee, proposed the maximum possible measures intended to strengthen the European Council in so far as they were feasible without jeopardising national sovereignty: among these were the integration of the OEEC, the Brussels Treaty and the Council of Europe, the co-ordination of foreign policy by means of preparatory consultative talks, separate agreements between individual Council members, the establishment of European sections in the affected ministries of member states, and regular consultative meetings of officials. He additionally requested conferring on the Consultative Assembly the right to draw up legislation that would acquire legality by ratification from the Council of Ministers, and the creation of 'administrative departments' for specific political areas of competence, thus in general equipping the Council with preliminary para-legislative and para-executive forms. Finally, he approved the creation of supranational separate associations of individual states for limited purposes along the lines of plans for the internationalisation of the basic European industries.

After dramatic disagreements between the two sides, the Strasbourg Assembly voted to the end of August with 68 votes to 19 and with 7 abstentions against the Philip resolutions, whilst Mollet's proposals obtained the necessary majority and were referred to the national parliaments for ratification: concern over the non-realisation of federal treaty plans in the absence of Great Britain had tipped the scales. Whilst in most parliaments of the member countries broad majorities were obtained in the weeks that followed for accepting the Strasbourg recommendations, the federalists, led by Philip, attempted to mobilise the European public for a revision of the resolutions in a spectacular 'federal treaty action', but with limited success. Occasional opinion polls had indeed always produced a basic West European inclination for a European federal state; at the same time, however, national governments and the decision-makers behind them felt obligated to the same population groups to represent specific national interests, which were often not compatible with the implications of a new European federation. As a result of this, it was not possible for any political pressure to emerge from hopes for European *rapprochement* and for a 'third force'. When the Strasbourg Assembly met again at the beginning of November, no one was surprised that the Philip proposals were defeated once again.

Meanwhile, however, even Mollet's apparently successful tactic for the gradual evolution of the Council of Europe was wrecked. In spite of agreement by the Labour MP James Callaghan in Strasbourg, the Labour majority in the British House of Commons rejected the Mollet proposals approved by the Council of Europe on 13 November. Now that the majority of the Assembly, out of regard for British difficulties in coming to terms with a supranational Europe, had brought the federal treaty movement to its demise, even the evolutionary path to the Council of Europe was blocked. The European Left was forced to face the fact that Great Britain was not interested in participating in binding community organisations, at least not for the time being.

The Schuman Plan

Whilst the French socialists had disagreed over the question of tactics towards Great Britain, thus foregoing the leading role they had hitherto enjoyed in unity politics, the initiative towards finding a way out of this impasse came from quite a different quarter. On 9 May 1950, Robert Schuman, the French Foreign Minister, who up to this time had kept a low profile, presented to the European public a proposal for the creation of a European Community for Coal and Steel.[11] The basic idea of the Schuman Plan, the transferral of competence for the guidelines and co-ordinated planning of the European basic industries to a supranational European committee, had also been in the forefront of socialist European policy since it had become clear in the autumn of 1948 that the ultimate socialist goal of European socialisation of all basic industries was no longer realisable in the foreseeable future. Appropriate initiatives to this end on the part of Philip in the Council of Europe had failed at the end of 1949 as a result of British opposition, the majority of socialists being unwilling to proceed without Great Britain. The decisive factor in Schuman's initiative was that he *was* prepared to take the risk of a break with Great Britain. By making it quite clear from the beginning that the French government would insist on the supranational competence of the coal, iron and steel authorities, he confronted the British unequivocally with a choice between either participating or not participating in the next steps towards the unification process.

Schuman was able to do this because, unlike the case of the socialists, both alternatives were compatible with the basic objectives of his policy. Schuman and Jean Monnet, chief of the planning department of the government and the actual instigator of the plan, were mainly concerned to prevent the collapse of the unification effort and consequent West German dominance of the European continent, and to secure a leading role for France in world politics, independent of the USA and over and above a unified Europe. In order to increase French competitiveness, French industrialists were to be exposed to direct external pressure, and thus to be forced to relinquish their traditional Malthusianism. French access to Ruhr coal was to be retained

226

beyond the foreseen end of the control and restriction measures towards West Germany, and German dominance of the coal, iron and steel industries was to be prevented. The 'third-force' idea was thus at the root of this initiative, but no longer linked with the hope for a socialist social order in Europe. On the contrary, Monnet could only envisage a prosperous and autonomous Europe as a liberal capitalist system with Keynesian state skeletal planning. A European Community without British participation, that is, on the basis of a Paris–Bonn axis, was far more acceptable in the light of these premises than a socialist vision of Europe. If the British, contrary to expectation, did participate after all, there would be optimal protection against German dominance, and if they did not participate, this protection would still be greater than in the case of competition without supranational supervision: France could possibly even achieve the leading political role in a unified Europe. In either case, the European position *vis-à-vis* the USA would be decisively strengthened.[12]

In order not to be suspected by the European Left of deliberately anti-British action, Monnet travelled to London five days after Schuman's official announcement, and tried to win over the British government, which, as expected, proved unwilling to enter into the conditions of supranationality, rejecting it definitively on 2 June, whilst the governments of France, the Netherlands, Belgium, Luxemburg, Italy and the Federal Republic of Germany announced, in a joint communiqué, negotiations on a coal, iron and steel union along the lines of Schuman's proposal. The French socialists again attempted by means of an international socialist conference in London to achieve a revision of the decision, but of course in vain. The Labour leadership in any case made it so abundantly clear that although it had no objection to closer union on the continent, it would 'never' take part in supranational solutions; thus the French socialists had no choice but reluctantly to join in Schuman's initiative. The Schuman Plan had thus overcome its first decisive hurdle: it had now been decided that a unified Europe in the closer sense would initially only come into being as a 'Europe of the Six', without British participation.

Clearly, however, the success of the plan was still not secure: on the contrary, in Germany and France there now emerged an ideologically heterogeneous opposition front, consisting of:

— the French Commumnists who saw in the plan only a means for the stabilisation of the Western bloc and of the cartel;

— most of French indistry, especially the steel industry, which was fearful of the consequences of unfettered competition in Europe;

— most of German industry, which for its part feared entering into competition after being weakened by prior decartelisation measures;

— the employers' federations and some liberals, who were opposed to the potential for intervention of a coal, iron and steel authority and feared a standardisation of social charges from above;

— the German Socialist Party, under the leadership of Kurt Schumacher, who saw in the plan a means for perpetuating French supervision of the German economy beyond the foreseen end of the occupation statute, and the establishment of a Europe of the 'four Cs'; capitalism, clericalism, conservatism and cartel, instead of a 'third-force' Europe;

— the Gaullists, who saw the plan both as the final relinquishment of French demands for leadership and as encouraging the danger of German dominance.

The plan found support in an equally heterogeneous coalition:

— among Christian Democrats on both the French and the German sides, who hoped for *rapprochement* under their leadership;

— among 'third-force' supporters, who saw in the 'Europe of the Six', in spite of the 'Four Cs', the sole remaining alternative to American dominance;

— among the majority of German unions and the non-Communist French trade unions, who expected positive effects from a common market on the employment situation and the standard of living;

— among entrepreneurs of the younger generation, who wanted to risk competition against higher chances of return in a common market;

— among German 'realists', such as Adenauer, who seized on the plan as a chance to break free of unilateral supervision of the Federal Republic by the Ruhr authorities and the occupation statute;

— by the French 'realists' who, like Monnet, saw in the plan the last chance to salvage something of French independence and supremacy.

In view of the conflicting hopes among those in favour, it constitutes a significant political achievement on the part of Adenauer, Schuman and (in the background) Monnet to have implemented the project in the face of an equally contradictory front of opponents, thus creating with a common market for the key industries of the continent the basis for a European community based on supranational co-operation. In the course of the treaty negotiations (June 1950–March 1951), the originally more reform-capitalist-technocratic-oriented project became more aligned with earlier 'third-force' plans. In addition to the Supreme Authority came parliamentary supervision by means of a two-chamber system, consisting of a parliamentary assembly and a Council of Ministers, as well as a judiciary in the form of a court of justice. Anti-trust and anti-cartel clauses were written into the treaty, these concessions securing the ratification of the treaty in the national parliaments, which ensued in the course of the second half of 1951, in France with a great majority. On 25 July 1952 the treaty on the 'European Community for Coal and Steel' came into effect: on the same date, the International Ruhr Authority transferred its distributive competence for Ruhr production to the new organisation.

The bases for a European policy

As is shown by the conflicting expectations and fears connected with the Schuman Plan, European integration was first a means of resolving internal European contradictions through compromise, and thus of strengthening the political influence of Europe as a whole in the world; and secondly, the Europe of the coal, iron and steel union was a compromise Europe which did not correspond entirely with any of the conceived European models which have been outlined above. As a consequence of British reticence, it was not so strong nor so nobly socialist-oriented as the 'third-force' movement had hoped, but neither was it, as a result of the initiative of the 'realists', which was supported by some of the European Left, so one-sidely oriented towards the American leadership as the originators of the 'Western Union' had envisaged. Even if the propects for realising concepts of a socialist order in a united Europe were visibly reduced, there was, on the other hand, also no majority for a completely integrated Western bloc. Although Bidault supporters attempted in the autumn of 1948 to incorporate the Brussels Treaty into the Atlantic Treaty, these attempts were successfully countered by the socialist Ramadier, by this time the French Minister of Defence. When on 16 April 1950, in accordance with the Western integration plans of Acheson and the NSC 68 programme, Bidault, now Prime Minister, launched the plan for a Supreme Atlantic Council, which was intended as a joint committee of states of the Western world to co-ordinate the defence efforts, the economy and later also the politics of the West, he encountered more rejection than acceptance. Fear of a perpetuation of the East–West division and of too great a dependence on the USA prevailed over the desire for greater American engagement in the interests of European security and greater financial support to extend beyond the end of the Marshall Plan.[13]

In spite of generalised anti-Communist feeling and pressure for American protection against Soviet aggression, therefore, a certain amount of interest in European independence within the Western alliance remained among the majority of Europeans. This was due to the 'neutralist' movement in Europe, that is the minority of the 'third-force' movement which agreed with the Marshall Plan, but not with the Atlantic Treaty and the founding of the West German state, and which now began, at the beginning of the 1950s, bitterly to oppose the armament trend in the West. Quite disparate groups can be mentioned in this connection: patriotic Protestants in Germany (Niemöller, Heinemann), reform-oriented Catholics in France (Gilson, the 'Esprit' group), part of the federalist 'Mouvement Socialiste pour les États-Unis de l'Europe' (MSEUE), the entirely nationalist left wing of the British Labour Party led by Aneurin Bevan, sceptical rationalists, such as groups led by *Le Monde* and *Observateur* in France and *Spiegel* in Germany, and romantic pacifists, won over to the Soviet-inspired 'Stockholm Peace Movement'.[14] These groups never achieved any positive effectiveness, first and mainly because they could never agree whether decisive nationalism or decisive European federalism was the best means of countering American dominance — they could not have both — and secondly, because they were successfully discredited as pro-Soviet sympathisers during the course of the general political polarisation. Nevertheless they did by their mere existence compel the established parties, especially the socialists, to show some regard for anti-American feeling, and gave them a permanently bad conscience about their earlier 'third-force' objectives.

In the meantime, tangible material preconditions for an independent policy had been created within the framework of the Western alliance. The crisis of the second half of 1949 had proved to be a transitory initial difficulty: in fact the reconstruction process of the West European political economies was proceeding remarkably well, on the basis of the potential which had remained in spite of war devastation and with additional support from Marshall Plan funds at the beginning of the 1950s.

Food imports from the USA reduced conspicuously. Compared with 1947, the increase in industrial production in 1951 was 35 per cent in Denmark, 33 per cent in Norway and Belgium, 31 per cent in Britain, 39 per cent in France, 54 per cent in Italy and 56 per cent in the Netherlands (in West Germany as high as 312 per cent). A free exchange of goods within the OEEC enabled internal trade to rise from 5.9 thousand million dollars in 1947 to 13.1 thousand million dollars in 1951, whilst imports from the USA decreased in both absolute and relative terms; 5.6 thousand million out of 15.2 thousand million in 1947, and 4.4 thousand million out of 20.6 thousand million in 1951. Exports to the USA increased in the same period from 0.73 to 1.81 thousand million dollars.

Even the European dollar deficit was replenished 'so rapidly that by 1951 the goods and services balance of most countries had been equalised, from 1950 onwards even showing surpluses'.[15]

To what extent the Europeans would make use of the remaining chances for an independent policy was another question. Each new crisis in East–West relations was bound to reduce the room for manoeuvre of European independence, whilst periods of *détente* in the East–West conflict could have the effect either of strengthening European self-assertion or increasing emphasis on divergent specific national interests. What remained at the beginning of the 1950s of the 'third force' was thus doubly threatened: on the one hand, by the tensions brought about by the Korean War from 1950, and on the other, by the 'destabilising' effect of the Soviet *détente* offensive from 1952 onwards.

Notes

1. See the precise and well-documented account of the European federations in Walter Lipgens, in English, not German translation: *A history of European integration 1945–1947* (Oxford, 1982), pp. 317–34 (UEM), 361–85 (UEF), 657–84 (Congress Issue).
2. Quotation from the Paris final resolution in *Le Populaire*, 27 April 1948; compare on this and the following Wilfried Loth, *Sozialismus und Internationalismus*, (Stuttgart, 1977), pp. 201–14.
3. Text of the resolution in *Europa-Archiv* 3 (1948), pp. 1443–46.
4. Ramadier memorandum and government resolutions of 18 Aug. 1948 in *L'Année politique 1948*, pp. 142f.; see also Vincent Auriol, *Journal du septennat, 1948*, vol. 2; (Paris, 1974), p. 368 and Marie-Thérèse Bitsch, 'La France et la naissance du Conseil de l'Europe' in: Raymond Poidevin (ed), *Histoire des débuts de la construction européenne*, (Bruxelles, 1986), pp. 165–98.
5. British Labour Party (ed), *Feet on the ground, a study of western union*, (London, 1948).
6. Compare Loth, *Sozialismus*, pp. 221–3, and Geoffrey Warner, *Die britische Labour Regierung und die Einheit Westeuropas 1949–1951*, in Vierteljahrshefte für Zeitgeschichte 28 (1980), pp. 310–30.
7. Council of Europe. Consultative Assembly. First ordinary Session, Documents No. 71 and 73.
8. Loth, *Sozialismus*, p. 248.
9. On this and the following see ibid., pp. 248–50, 257–60, 270–3.
10. Text in *Europa-Archiv* 5 (1950), p. 3360.
11. Schuman's declaration of 9 May 1950 in *Europa-Archiv* 5 (1950), pp. 3091f. See also Jean Monnet, *Erinnerungen eines Europäers* (Munich, 1978), pp. 349–469; Pierre Gerbet, '*Le genèse du plan Schuman*', in *Revue française de science politique* 6 (1956), pp. 525–53; William Diebold Jr., *The Schuman plan*, (New York, 1959), pp. 8–112; F. Roy Willis, *France, Germany and the new Europe, 1945–1967*, (Stanford, London, 1968), pp. 80–129; for interpretation see particularly Gilbert Ziebura, *Die deutsch-französischen Beziehungen seit 1945, Mythen und Realitäten*, (Pfullingen, 1970), pp. 50–56, and Loth, *Sozialismus*, pp. 262–70 and 379–81.
12. For the interpretation of the Schuman plan see Monnet's extremely informative memorandum of 3 May 1950 in *Le Monde*, 9 May 1970.
13. See Loth, *Sozialismus*, p. 187 and pp. 260f.
14. On France, see John T. Marcus, *Neutralism and nationalism in France*, (New York, 1958) (although it uses too schematised classification); Michel Winock, *Histoire politique de la revue 'Esprit' 1930–1950*, (Paris, 1975); Loth, *Sozialismus*, pp. 230–2, 278, 293, 358–60; Jean-Noel Jeanneney and Jaques Julliard, *Le Monde de Beuve-Méry ou le métier d'Alceste*, (Paris, 1979); on Germany see Rainer Dohse, *Der Dritte Weg. Neutralitätsbestrebungen in Westdeutschland zwischen 1945 und 1955*, (Hamburg, 1974); Dieter Koch, *Heinemann und die Deutschlandfrage*, (Munich, 1972); on Great Britain see Aneurin Bevan's own account, *In place of fear*, (Melbourne, 1952), and Leslie Hunter, *The road to Brighton Pier*, (London, 1959).

15. Quoted from the figures in Alfred Gosser, *Das Bündnis, Die westeuropäischen Lander und die USA seit dem Krieg*, (Munich, 1978), p. 119; figures for West Germany from Georges von Csernatony, *Le Plan Marshall et le redressement économique de L'Allemagne*, (Lausanne, 1973), p. 159. Joyce and Gabriel Kolko's thesis of the 'collapse of the Marshall Plan' (*The limits of power*, (New York, 1972), pp. 453ff.) is untenable; Kolko concentrates on the crisis of 1949 and neglects subsequent developments.

11

The Effects of the Korean War

The determination of the Truman Administration to give military, economic and political support to the Western alliance along the lines of the NSC 68 programme did not at first receive a positive response, either in Congress or among the West European allies. The Europeans did indeed have a strong interest in the USA's closer involvement in the European defence network, but did not regard themselves as being in a position appreciably to step up their own defence efforts. They feared that an increase in armaments spending would jeopardise the economic recovery which had only just begun, and have an adverse effect on the standard of living, which would not be feasible in domestic political terms. In Congress, particularly on the right wing of the Republican Party, a majority viewed the conduct of the Truman Administration in the Cold War as being decidedly too 'soft'; the same Republicans were nevertheless also fighting for a reduction in taxes and in the state budget, and were consequently not interested in supporting cost-intensive armament. At the Atlantic Council meeting in May 1950 in London, West European foreign ministers agreed in principle to Acheson's requests for reinforcement and intensified co-ordination of the Western alliance, but in tangible terms agreed only to 'examine' the question, and unanimously asserted that it would be 'premature' to consider a rearmament of Germany. After his return from London, Acheson wanted to present his reinforcement programme to Congress, which, however, refused to hold a joint sitting of both houses. The few representatives who did finally hear his report hardly appeared impressed by it. Even the current military aid project for Europe to the 'symbolic' level of 1,200 million dollars seemed endangered.[1] 'No one can say,' stated an anonymous top official of the Administration one year later, 'what would have come of these projects [of Acheson's], if the North Koreans had not marched south on 25th of June 1950.'[2] It was in fact only the Korean War which made the NSC 68 programme a reality.

The beginnings and escalation of the Korean War

In the same way that the Korean War acted as a catalyst in the Cold War, it was itself at first a product of the Cold War. None of those involved wanted it to turn out as it did, and had it not been for the general state of tension in the East and West, the course it took would be quite incomprehensible.

The beginnings of the Korean War can be traced to the middle of 1949. After American occupation troops had withdrawn in June 1949, leaving only 400 military advisers, the South Korean President, Syngman Rhee, ruler of a regime which in terms of corruption, arbitrary police conduct and anti-Communist aggression was in every way comparable with the China of Chang Kai Shek, pressed for an enforced reunification of the country. To this end he had considerably reinforced his army (from 60,000 men at the beginning of 1949 to 181,000 at the end of May 1950), and had sought to mobilise the USA for comprehensive military aid. The Truman Administration, however, had consistently refused such aid, and even the Republican opposition, among whom Rhee had hoped to find more sympathy for an aggressive policy, did not want to commit itself to supporting South Korean offensive plans; both sides considered the country sufficiently armed to repel a North Korean attack. The North Korean leadership had sought to mobilise the South Korean population against the President in order to counter the policy of Rhee, which was openly aimed at its demise, and had from January 1950 onwards likewise rearmed itself (to 135,000 men in June 1950). In the meantime, both more and less serious border incidents had been escalating on both sides of the 38th parallel, which divided the North from the South.[3]

Even the North Korean invasion of 25 June was at first not much more than one of these border incidents: the North Koreans advanced with just half their troops and a quarter of their tanks to the capital Seoul, just near the border, evidently in order to drive out Rhee and to unleash a swift general uprising against the regime. Directly prior to this, Rhee had visited the American Commander-in-Chief in Japan, General MacArthur, received John Foster Dulles in Seoul and begun to augment his troops again. This led the North Korean leadership (who of course could not have known of the Americans' negative response) to the decision to venture a decisive trial of strength in spite of the monsoon season, which was just beginning. The Soviet leadership, which had been supporting the North Korean armament effort since April 1950 in order to restore the military balance between North and South, had approved or at least tolerated this decision, in spite of the fact that it was not keen on the idea of an armed conflict with the USA, and since the Berlin blockade at least it was aware that every serious East–West crisis led to an increase in Western arms potential. The Soviet leadership clearly feared that Soviet non-involvement would over-enhance the position of China, and also counted on a swift victory without serious military involvement and without the intervention of the USA; it possibly also counted on the demoralising effect that Rhee's demise would have on Japan, which was allied with the USA. Three things spoke in favour of this calculation: the instability of the Rhee regime, American dislike of the 'dictator' and the fact that Korea had not been incorporated into the publicly declared 'Western defence perimeter'. Nevertheless some apprehension of American intervention did remain, and the Soviet leadership consequently took a back seat in diplomatic support of the North Koreans and took great care not to bring any Soviet military into the conflict.[4] Should the USA engage after all, there was still the prospect of decisively intensifying Sino-American tension in this way.

Members of the Truman government of course immediately saw in the North Korean offensive a 'Soviet provocation' of the free world, which the USA must repulse for the sake of its credibility.[5] They likewise hoped at first, however, to get away with very limited American engagement. The initial successes of the South Korean army seemed to justify this view: after two days they had halted the North Korean advance and the 'incident' seemed to be closed.

The fact that it did not remain so is due to a coalition of 'hawks' in the Western camp, for whom the Truman government was no longer a match. After an unsuccessful request for new airplanes and artillery guns in order to be able to launch a fresh offensive against North Korean troops across the 38th parallel,

Rhee withdrew his troops after the third day of action — whether defeated or undefeated can no longer be determined — surrendered Seoul on 28 June without a struggle, or at least without great efforts to defend it, and then proceeded to evacuate (in his own words): 'for tactical reasons we have been withdrawing from city to city in the hope that American reinforcements would arrive soon enough to launch an offensive'.[6] General MacArthur who, unlike his Washington superiors, was himself interested in a 'roll back' beyond the 38th parallel and in general in a repulsion of the Communist forces in the Asian region, supported this attempt to galvanise massive American aid by sending extremely pessimistic and imprecise evaluations of the situation to Washington. It is not clear whether this was deliberate, or whether they were the result of a false estimation of the situation, but at all events they differed substantially from all reports issuing from other sources. The Washington leadership team led by Truman and Acheson remained to some extent sceptical, but in order not to give the Republican opposition fresh cause for attack, and certainly also in order to maintain among the public the degree of crisis awareness necessary to implement their own armament plans, they decided on 27 June to instruct MacArthur to engage air and marine fighting forces south of the 38th parallel. Under pressure from the military, who did not want to rule out the possibility of Chinese intervention, they instructed the 7th US fleet to set up a marine blockade between Formosa and the Chinese mainland. Without waiting for the appropriate order, MacArthur also engaged his planes on 29 June, north of the 38th parallel: Truman issued the order a few hours later, and on the following day gave in to MacArthur's pressure for the engagement of American ground troops. Formally provided with a mandate from the UN to restore the old order (the Soviet Union had not attended the Security Council since January in protest against the exclusion of Red China, and even now had made no use of its right of veto), US and South Korean troops now fought under the supreme command of MacArthur. The civil war had turned into a global crisis.

Under MacArthur, the 'Western' troops executed the tactic of 'planned withdrawals and delaying actions to gain time' (MacArthur);[7] the general himself constantly demanded more troops, and American propaganda contributed to the thesis of the overpowering Communist aggressor, which acquired more and more the status of fact in the Western world. At the beginning of

September there was still only a small south-eastern corner of South Korean territory in 'Western' hands; MacArthur had over 180,000 men in ground fighting forces at his disposal and 70,000 members of the American Air Force and Fleet, whilst only 98,000 remained to the North Koreans, a third having only been recruited during the conflict. Meanwhile a bitter debate raged among the leaders of the West as to the aims of the war: the British government urged with great resolution for a localisation of the conflict, and agreed with the Soviet government on the offer of a return to the *status quo* in Korea in return for the concession of American neutrality over the Formosa question. The State Department rejected a proposal from Chang Kai Shek to send 33,000 national Chinese supplementary troops to Korea, and demanded a public commitment to keep UN troops at the 38th parallel, in both cases to prevent the intervention of the mainland Chinese. MacArthur, on the other hand (again exceeding his competence), proclaimed 'Sino-American military co-operation' in a communiqué signed by him and Chang Kai Shek until such time as there was a 'final victory' over the Communist threat; Dulles warned of a 'premature' commitment to the 38th parallel; the Defense Department argued for the reunification of Korea; and Rhee of course considered that 'this is the time to unify Korea'.[8]

On the whole the Truman government remained uncertain. On the one hand, it wanted to prevent a military conflict with China, but on the other believed that it could not afford to appear soft in the eyes of the public. MacArthur thus succeeded once again in taking the initiative, with the result that the hitherto uninvolved Chinese promptly intervened in order to prevent the establishment of the USA on their Manchurian border, and in addition perhaps also as a resumption of the Chinese civil war. On 9 September, MacArthur was empowered to extend his operations over the 38th parallel for the defeat of the North Korean army as long as no Soviet or Chinese intervention was announced, and in that case to engage only South Korean troops in border regions. On the strength of this, he had part of his troops land in Inchon (the harbour of Seoul) to the rear of the North Korean fighting forces, wiped this out within a few days — a full 30,000 men were able to save themselves by escaping over the 38th parallel to the North — and began an advance on North Korea. Although the Chinese leadership had warned three times of the consequences of an advance — on 2 October with an unequivocal threat of war, on 14 October with individual demonstrative air attacks, and at the beginning of November with an invasion by Chinese ground troops, which were nevertheless halted long before reaching the enemy lines — MacArthur succeeded, with a policy of *faits accomplis* on every occasion in implementing a continuation of the offensive. After he had reached the China-Korea border river at one spot on 24 November, the numerically slightly superior Chinese began a counter-offensive on 26 November. The 'Western' troops fled back over the 38th parallel, and MacArthur demanded the engagement of national Chinese troops and the atom bomb against the Chinese mainland.[9]

The Truman government was not prepared to go to the point of a 'major' war with China, which would have jeopardised once again the civil war decision of 1949; not only because the necessary expense seemed out of all proportion to the possible result — the restitution of pre-Communist conditions in Asia — but, above all, because a concentration in Asia would inevitably weaken Western defence potential in Europe, which was still more important. On the other hand, it was not able to find a rapid peace solution on the basis of the *status quo ante*: the ambitions of MacArthur and Rhee, as well as the concern of the militantly anti-Communist Republicans and the Democrats' own belief in the theory of unlimited Communist expansionism always stood in the way.[10] The 'limited' war in Korea thus shambled on for another two and a half years, in spite of ample opportunities for a peaceful conclusion, and without it being possible to state objectively for what purpose it was actually being waged. The armistice was not signed until 26 July, 1953 — under conditions which only slightly improved the *status quo ante* in favour of Rhee.

Dulles's 'policy of liberation'

The remarkably indecisive attitude of the Truman government during the Korean War only becomes comprehensible in the light of the militantly anti-Communist movement in the USA, which had been on the upswing even before the war, and which was on the point of becoming the dominant political factor in the country as a result of the war. The 'Attacks of the Primitives', as Acheson called this movement,[11] had begun in the winter of 1949/50 under the influence of the Communist victory in China.

With Mao's victory, the Communist threat acquired virtually demonic proportions in the eyes of many Americans, who were hardly at all aware of the global realities, but who had been hearing constant warnings of the expansive power of Soviet Communism from the Truman government since 1947. Their irrational fear now sought an outlet in accusations against their own government which, it seemed, had been unable to contain 'Communism' effectively, to prevent Communist expansion in Asia, even with the entire military and economic power of the USA, and which in addition appeared to have no effective protection against its dangerous opponent. Searching for an explanation for the 'failure' of the government, these hysterical anti-Communists seized on both alleged (according to a State official, Alger Hiss) and actual (according to the 'atomic spy' Klaus Fuchs) spying cases, and proceeded to suspect the entire Truman Administration more and more of being infiltrated with Communist spies and disloyal 'fellow travellers'. Dean Acheson in particular, who was working harder than anyone else towards an irrational universalisation of the containment policy, saw himself stranded in a sea of suspicion and attacks.

The militant core of the movement centred around the Republican Senator Joseph R. McCarthy, who began his campaign against the 'contaminated' government in February 1950 and who was able, in the wake of the fresh 'failure' of the Administration in the Korean War, to arouse a regular witch hunt of those politicans, artists and scientists who did not correspond totally to the ideal picture of the orthodox anti-Communist. Hundreds of liberals of all shades were named by McCarthy before the 'House Committee of Un-American Activities', without his having to carry the burden of proof for his incriminations. Denunciation and opportunistic 'self-supervision' spread, and many a person unjustly suspected (for example, the nuclear scientist Robert J. Oppenheimer) was only rehabilitated years later. McCarthy found backing from the traditionally anti-Communist trade union movement, the AFL, from official American Catholicism (particularly Cardinal Spellman), and from large sections of the Republican electorate. The Republican Party leadership consequently did not dare to oppose McCarthy's manifest extremism, preferring to make the 'failure' of the Democrat government in the face of the Communism, especially its 'failure' in the Chinese civil war, an electoral campaign platform for the Congressional elections of November 1950 and in the run-up to the presidential elections in 1952. The government was now put into a position of having to justify itself, having become a prisoner of its own mobilisation rhetoric.[12]

With this in the background, the high-handed conduct of General MacArthur in the Korean War was more than a contradiction between differing ideas as to the purpose of the war: it was also an attempt on the part of the ambitious General to become 'America's de Gaulle',[13] that is, to decide the race for the Republican presidential candidature for 1952 in his own favour and to move into the White House as popular hero of the anti-Communist movement. MacArthur was careful to ensure that the differences between himself and Truman, Acheson and the Pentagon became public knowledge. In the event of military success, he could then present himself as the victor who had fought 'Communism' *against* the resistance of the Democrat government; if success was not forthcoming, he could then cast himself in the role of victim of the machinations of Truman. The latter turned out to be the case: after he had publicly demanded an invasion of Chinese territory as an alternative to the strategy of his superior, Truman finally summoned the nerve in April 1951 to relieve him of his office. MacArthur returned to the USA and was given a hero's welcome. Before the assembled members of both Houses of Congress, he condemned in strong language the Asian policy of Truman in general and his Korean policy in particular. The danger of the established political groups being overrun by a populist movement led by MacArthur was greater than ever.

What followed ranks among the most bizarre events in the history of the Cold War. After it had become clear that the shift in the internal political climate now rendered a Democrat victory in the presidential elections of 1952 increasingly unlikely, Truman and the major industrial east-coast wing of the Republican Party worked together tactically in order to secure the continuity of foreign policy strategy even under a Republican President.[14] In December 1950, Truman appointed the extremely popular, though politically — in every respect — moderate Commander-in-Chief of the European Campaign of 1944–5, General Eisenhower, as Commander-in-Chief of the integrated NATO fighting forces in Europe, thus presenting the 'supra-partisan' Republican foreign policy-makers, led by Dulles and Vandenberg (who died in 1951), with a counter-hero to send into the campaign against MacArthur. They indeed succeeded, apparently with the active assistance of Truman, in winning Eisenhower as a candidate for nomination. Truman dispensed with a fresh candidate for the Democrats, whilst the Dulles group was able to offer the Republican Party Congress the candidate with the highest chance of winning, precisely because of his 'supra-partisan' quality. The presidential election itself produced no further surprises, particularly since Eisenhower, as a concession to populist circles, nominated the militantly anti-Communist Richard Nixon as Vice-President, whilst there was no question that Eisenhower would appoint Dulles as the new Secretary of State. Neither the composition of the Administration, its political conception, nor its practical foreign policy altered *substantially* in the Republican era from 1953 onwards; the 'Attack of the Primitives' had just been nipped in the bud, and finally ceased to be dangerous in the wake of the Soviet 'thaw' of 1954–5.

American policy altered in only two ways in the transition from Acheson to Dulles: in order to take the wind out of the sails of the anti-Communist movements and to ensure for Eisenhower the allegedly electorally-crucial support of Americans of East European origin, Dulles had fought the electoral campaign with attacks on the 'negative, pointless and immoral' policy of mere containment, and promised instead an 'active' and 'dynamic' 'policy of liberation' of countries ruled by Communism. He was not able to say what form such a liberation policy should take. He shrank from the idea of a forceful 'roll back' in the MacArthur sense, which could incite a Third World War, and as a result of his monolithic view of Communism did not know himself how to use peaceful means for weakening the coherence of the Eastern bloc, even when the Soviet structure tottered for a time after the death of Stalin in March 1953. An aggressive liberation rhetoric nevertheless developed out of the electoral campaign theme, which in the eyes of the Soviet leadership and its European allies was not always seen, and above all not always seen in the same way, as mere rhetoric, consequently leading in both cases to considerable unease regarding American policy. Similarly, Dulles had jumped onto the Republican thrift bandwagon and promised a reduction in defence spending. Even this promise could hardly be kept, least of all with supporters who schizophrenically demanded at the same time better protection from the 'Communist threat'. It nevertheless compelled Dulles not to increase proportionate expenditure on expensive conventional weapons and to rely instead on an expansion of comparably low-cost nuclear arms. The strategy of the Western alliance was thus aligned with the doctrine of 'massive retaliation', as Dulles publicly termed it on 12 January 1954. The potential aggressor was to be threatened with the use of the nuclear weapon even in the case of a limited conventional attack, not of course as an inevitable consequence, but certainly as a possibility — a threat which made Dulles's policy once again appear extremely aggressive, but which in fact lost credibility the longer it continued and which once again reduced the West's room for political manoeuvre. An aggressive disposition and a loss of remaining tactical flexibility were thus the lasting traces left in American foreign policy by the 'Attack of the Primitives'.[15]

The decisive step towards the universalisation of containment policy and towards this massive increase in defence spending had in fact already been taken before the Truman/Acheson Administration. The latter, as was to be expected, had used the hysteria unleashed by the Korean War to wrench from the still antagonistic Congress as much as possible in order to realise its own security concept, which centred on Europe. To this end, the Administration had once again used the technique of presenting conflicts in an over-dramatic light, a technique to which it eventually fell victim. From 13,100 million dollars in 1950, the American defence budget rose to 22,300 million dollars in 1951, 44,100 million in 1952 and 50,400 million in 1953.[16] The Soviet Union had been represented in the official rhetoric of the Truman as well as the Eisenhower government as the sole instigator of the 'Communist' aggression in Korea, and was considered fundamentally capable of undertaking similar aggressive military actions, if the opportunity arose in any other part of the world. If the experts of the Administration considered the probability of further Soviet aggression to be substantially more remote than was intoned in public, they were still themselves convinced of the monolithism of the 'Communist' movement and of the fundamental inherent nature of 'Communist' expansion. France's struggle against the National Communist Liberation Movement of Ho Chi Minh in Indo-China, initially condemned in 1946–7 as a neo-colonialist action, was now increasingly seen as a contribution to the containment of world Communism. Although violent disagreements continued to occur as to the objectives and methods of this war, the USA still contributed, between January 1950 and May 1954, 2,600 million dollars to support the French in Indo-China — 80 per cent of the total cost of the Indo-China

War.[17] Because of internal pressure and misinterpretation on their own part, which helped to increase that pressure, American foreign policy-makers lost not only the ability to assess realistically the dangers with which they were faced, but also — by sharp contrast with 'liberation' rhetoric — their opportunities for repelling Soviet claims to control, which presented themselves in the form of the diverse contradictions present within the 'Communist camp'. A containment of containment policy was thus under these conditions more to be expected from a Republican government: since it seemed in principle to be a reliable guarantee for an 'anti-Communist' policy, they were not under such great pressure to justify their foreign policy actions as the Democrats had been, and could therefore afford to give up what they deemed to be excessive engagement. It is no coincidence that the successful conclusion of the Korean War did not occur until the Eisenhower/Dulles Administration came into office.[18]

The decision to 're'-arm West Germany

In addition to the American defence budget, the reinforcement of conventional weapons and American engagement in Asia, the rearmament of West Germany and, inextricably linked with this, the creation of an integrated defence organisation of the Atlantic Treaty in Europe are also among the events which were decisively accelerated by the Korean War.[19] 'Whether one is prepared to admit it or not,' wrote the Paris daily newspaper *Le Monde*, after the signing of the Atlantic Treaty in April 1949, 'the rearmament of Germany is sitting in the Atlantic Treaty like the embryo in an egg', and although the French government immediately rejected all suggestions of an inclusion of the West German Federal Republic in the Western defence alliance, everyone in Europe knew that this was an accurate assessment. If one reckoned with the possibility of a Soviet invasion of Western Europe — and this calculation lay at the root of the Atlantic Treaty — then West German territory, as one could see from a glance at the map, was the most exposed forefield in Western security, so that Western defence could not begin only west of the Rhine. The fathers of the Atlantic Treaty had taken this fact into account when they included the Western occupation troops on German territory in the scope of the alliance agreements. In the long term, however, it seemed unwise to leave the protection of the Federal Republic only to Western troops. Such a unilateral division of the defence burden in Europe would lead to a unilateral increase in West Germany's economic power at the expense of the West European countries, which in addition to their own protection would also have to finance their West German competitors. There was nevertheless no question of a substantial increase in West European defence efforts: in spite of American pressure, in spite of the growing tendency for European governments to see in military rearmament a more effective protective measure than in a further rise in the living standard, and in spite of appropriate declarations of intention composed at regular intervals by the NATO Council of Ministers, the armaments programme proved internally open to implementation only to a limited degree. No European government could afford to pay for greater military security at the expense of a significant reduction in the standard of living — the fears unleashed by the Korean War were insufficient to warrant this. Alternatively, a West German defence programme could also serve the purpose not only of securing the protection of the Federal Republic, but in addition also of significantly reducing the notorious imbalance between Western and Eastern conventional arms. The still-vivid memory of the strike power of German troops in the Second World War led the Western Allies to expect benefits for the West from the German defence contribution which in fact far exceeded the current resources of the weak West German '*provisorium*'. Since the Eastern side shared this memory, West German rearmament was bound from the outset to have a considerable psychological deterrent effect. Now more than ever, German rearmament must to this extent have seemed urgent, since at the beginning of the Far East conflict no one could say — not even the American government — for how long and to what extent the USA would still be willing and able to station its own conventional fighting forces in Europe, particularly since France had already sent two-fifths of its troops to Indo-China, where in the meantime a real colonial war had developed from the guerrilla struggle of Ho Chi Minh's soldiers.

A number of political considerations, however, were put forward against the logic of the strategists and technocrats. Did remilitarisation not represent a substantial danger for the young and by no means stabilised West German democracy? Would it not inevitably lead to a strengthening of the political influence of the Federal Republic, which would reactivate the fears of European allied partners and thus threaten the cohesion of the alliance itself? Could it really be ruled out that a politically strong Federal Republic, ruled by national or very nationalist forces, would conduct its own independent foreign policy against the interests of the Western powers — be it the entanglement of its allied partners in a war for German unity or even its alliance with Soviet opponents in the interests of reunification? Finally, would West German troops not arouse Soviet unease and ultimately drive the East Europeans into the Soviet Union army, or in any case consolidate the division of Europe in such a way that any revision of it would become unthinkable — either in the sense of a 'third force' or in the sense of an anti-Communist 'roll back'?

Because the project for rearming the Federal Republic was bound to encourage considerations of this kind, the US State Department, since the beginning of the negotiations for the Atlantic Treaty in 1948, had taken care to exclude the problem. Even in the winter of 1949/50, when the Joint Chiefs of Staff in the course of the general universalisation of the containment concept of the American Administration decisively urged for the stationing of West German fighting forces, members of the State Department, although themselves primarily interested in a considerable extension of conventional armament in the West, spoke out against such a solution, 'unless the principal members of the Western European Defence system should, under some changed conditions not now predictable, reach the conclusion that some degree of rearmament of Germany would promote rather than impede the security of Western Europe as a whole'.[20] Out of similar concern for the cohesion of the Western alliance, Ernest Bevin, the British Foreign Secretary, had opposed the request of his colleague Shinwell in the Ministry of Defence for a German defence contribution. In the French government even a discussion of the problem had been stopped out of fear of a collapse of the government coalition. Even a West German defence contribution in the form of German membership of a supranational European defence community, as had already been proposed by Léon Blum in November 1949 as a solution to the conflict between the need for protection from the Soviet Union and for protection from Germany, seemed unacceptable to the overwhelming majority of West Europeans and Americans. When Winston Churchill called for a German troop contingent in the framework of such a European army before the House of Commons on 16 March 1950, he encountered more resistance than agreement.

The Korean War reversed the power ratio between those for and those opposed to German rearmament. Among the military, the fear was spreading that the events of Korea could repeat themselves on German soil, and they consequently pressed with greater urgency for the creation of a German army. Among politicians, who scarcely shared this fear (since they saw West German territory as protected in principle by the presence of the occupation troops), but who were almost without exception convinced of the necessity for strengthening conventional armament in Europe, the hope was growing that they could use the shock which had been unleashed among the Western public by the Korean War to implement their rearmament plans. During the second term of the Consultative Assembly of the Council of Europe, the project for an integrated European army — under the auspices of a European Minister of Defence, with appropriate European supervisory bodies and the possibility of German entry — was passed on 11 August with a majority of 89 representatives; only five representatives voted against, and 27 (most of whom were German Social Democrats and British Labour delegates) abstained. Over the heads of the State Department, General Hays, the acting American High Commissioner in the Federal Republic, held exploratory talks with representatives of the West German federal government. His superior, McCloy, in Washington was won over to the idea of a German defence contribution in the framework of a new European army; even in the State Department they worked their way round to the project (memorandum of 16 August) for an integrated 'European Defence Force', with American, Canadian and German participation consisting of national contingents, which was to include an international General staff and a single Commander-in-Chief, who was as far as possible always to be an American.[21]

By the end of August, public discussion of the rearmament question and the decision committees of the West had reached a stage where the West German *Bundeskanzler* could risk naming his conditions for a German defence contribution. Adenauer was aware that the Western powers were far more interested in German troops than in the Federal Republic itself, which was secured in principle by the presence of the occupation troops, and that negotiations on German rearmament therefore offered a unique opportunity for substantially smoothing the path of the Federal Republic from the status of occupied country, in which the victorious Western powers had retained decisive supreme powers, to equal partner of the Western alliance. The fact that the path to equality was linked with the rearmament issue and would in the way of things be through European and Atlantic integration — that is, through a partial relinquishment of sovereignty by the Western partners — and not through the restoration of the full national state sovereignty of the Federal Republic, was in his view an advantage rather than a disadvantage. For him, the anchoring of the Federal Republic in the Western alliance was a necessity both for political security and for social politics. In addition, he saw in this integration a means for making the Western powers settle on a political line towards Germany which would preclude any damage to the political and social achievements of the Federal Republic. Finally, he knew that the Federal Republic would sooner or later take on a leading role in an integrated European community on the basis of its economic potential, in spite of possible preliminary discrimination. Under these circumstances, rearmament seemed to him virtually the ideal means, in view of its socio-political implications, for securing in the long term the Western integration of the Federal Republic.

Shortly after the beginning of his chancellorship in November–December 1949, Adenauer had made sure with a series of ambiguous, non-committal interview statements that the theme of German rearmament remained a topic for international discussion (for both foreign and internal political reasons he himself could not appear to be the promoter of rearmament), and when as a consequence of the Korean War a majority emerged in favour of rearmament, he entered the debate again. The peak of this latest initiative consisted of two memoranda of 29 August 1950 to the High Commission. One offered a contribution in the form of a German contingent, 'in the case of the formation of an international West European army', once again ambiguously, thus leaving the decision as to the *form* of the German defence contribution entirely in the hands of the Western powers, but at the same being calculated to extract a decision as soon as possible, and it simultaneously called for a reinforcement of occupation troops as a guarantee of 'external security', as well as the formation of a police force for protection at the federal level to repulse internal Communist acts of violence, including encroachments by the People's Police of the Soviet zone. The second memorandum called for the improved regulation of 'relations between the occupation powers and the Federal Republic' by means of a system of treaty agreements, in particular by granting the High Commissioners the status of Ambassador, which implicitly presumed the abrogation of the occupation statute.[22]

This precipitate action on the part of the *Bundeskanzler* now rendered swift decisions unavoidable. At the New York Atlantic Treaty conference for the 'Big Three', Acheson called for the consent of his colleagues to the stationing of West German troops to a strength of perhaps ten divisions, as well as to the intensification of their own defence efforts, in return for an American pledge for the permanent stationing of troops on European soil, increased military aid and for taking on the chief command in an integrated NATO General Staff. Both Bevin and Schuman raised serious objections to this package: urgently as they desired an intensification of American engagement in Europe, they still saw themselves as hardly in a position in domestic political terms to consent to comprehensive German rearmament. The British government, which had hoped to be able to resolve the problem of the German defence contribution by means of a gradually expanding West German police troop, finally gave way in principle under Ameican pressure, but nevertheless insisted that West European units be set up *before* West German ones. The French government, which had to take into account opposition of varying degrees in the country, and which was itself divided in its opinion, sought at first to prevent any decision and finally, when pressure from the Americans and the other Allies was growing stronger, countered the American requests with a project for an integration of German troops at batallion or perhaps regiment level into a supranational European army (the Pleven Plan of 24 October).[23] Although this initiative was not least aimed at postponing the actual beginning of West German rearmament (by means of the necessary discussion of the project and the certainly time-consuming establishment of supranational institutions), the stationing of German troops and the establishment of an integrated Western fighting force had nevertheless been decided in principle. All that now remained to be decided were the questions of timing, whether these institutions should be at European or Atlantic level, and the question of German equality.

From the Pleven Plan to the EDC Treaty

The discussion of this question, however, was to last another full four years, within which time the basic decision of the Western governments was to be jeopardised on several occasions. It substantially affected the internal structure of the Western world and the outcome of the East–West confrontation, most deeply in France and in the Federal Republic itself.

At the level of government negotiations (which are discussed further below), it seemed at first as if the project for a European defence community such as had been proposed by Pleven would have little chance of success. The Pleven Plan contained a number of discriminatory elements against the Germans: the retention of a national General Staff and Defence Minister for all non-German participants for purposes outside the North Atlantic Treaty; substantial impediments to German access to an integrated General Staff, following the integration of troops at batallion level; a Europan Minister of Defence who, as matters stood, would be appointed by France, thus excluding the Germans from the decision-making centres of NATO; and possibly French supremacy within the organisation. These one-sided elements on the one hand secured for the plan a majority of 349 votes to 235 in the French parliament, but at the same time deprived it of all prospects for the necessary active co-operation of the West German government, thus leading to its rejection by the USA and most other NATO partners (with the exception of Belgium and Luxemburg). In addition, an integration at batallion level seemed entirely impracticable to the military experts of all Western countries, including France. Acheson, and a large number of Western politicians, thus saw in the plan nothing more than a French attempt at sabotage. In view of the danger of an appreciable reduction in American engagement in Europe following Chinese intervention in the Korean War, the French government felt obliged at the beginning of December to consent to the immediate posting of German 'fighting troops' (somewhere between batallions and divisions), without any decision being made as to their later incorporation into a European army. Only the abandonment of the idea of a German General Staff and the exclusion of German heavy weapons contingents were conceded. In return, the Americans consented at the Brussels meeting of foreign and defence ministers of the A⁴lantic Treaty on 18–19 December to the formation of an integrated NATO combat force, and had General Eisenhower appointed as its Commander-in-Chief.[24] Whether the German fighting troops would in future be integrated into the Atlantic combat force or into a European army now effectively depended on the conduct of the West

German government and Adenauer, who had been precisely informed only about the limitations connected with the Pleven Plan, and who initially of course favoured the Atlantic solution in expert talks with representatives of the High Commission on the posting of fighting troops which began on 9 January 1951. He hardly participated at all in negotiations on the Pleven Plan which were held from 15 February at the invitation of the French.[25]

Negotiations with the High Commission, however, soon reached deadlock, as the German representatives were not prepared to offer their defence potential without military equality from the outset, and the Allies, as a result of the limitations insisted upon by the French, were unable to guarantee this equality. In June 1951, the view prevailed among American decision-makers that the conflict between French security requirements and the German demand for equality could not be resolved without a supranational solution, and that German troops would thus not materialise without a European army. The French government, influenced by growing American concern about German demands for equality, found itself ready to surrender the most provocative discrimination of the Pleven Plan. Instead of the discrimination applying only to the recruitment of German troops by means of a European High Commissioner, the entire organisation of the European army was now to be regulated in the same way in the participant countries from the ranks upwards. This Franco-American compromise compelled the West German government to favour the European solution. When the French delegation, under American and German pressure, agreed to the omission of a transition period in which the Federal Republic was to have remained without its own Defence Minister, no longer insisted categorically on integration being below division level, and finally offered no more resistance to ₍ne subordination of the European army to the Commander-in-Chief of NATO, Adenauer decided at the end of August in favour of the supranational European army. The three Western foreign ministers were able at their Washington conference of 10–14 September to agree officially on a German defence contribution in the framework of a European Defence Community (EDC). The Federal government was informed that an abrogation of the occupation statute could only ensue in connection with German entry into the EDC.

More than eight months of relentless tug-of-war between the German demand for sovereignty and Western, especially French, reservations about security had to take place before the 'General Treaty' on the abrogation of the occupation statute could be signed on 26 May 1952 in Bonn, and the treaty on the founding of the European Defence Community was signed in Paris on 27 May.[26] The French side had had to make further concessions. In place of the supranational (that is, probably a French) Minister of Defence came a Commissariat of nine. Executive competence was not given over solely to this supranational Commissariat, but was staggered by means of a complex procedure involving the Council of Ministers, which could only pass unanimous decisions. The budget of the Community was to be subject to international regulations. Reductions in supranational status had been proposed by the Benelux countries, in the hope of greater readiness on the part of Great Britain to enter the EDC. Great Britain nevertheless remained outside under the new Conservative government of Churchill, which had succeeded the Labour Cabinet in November 1951, so that the new Community remained limited to the same six countries that participated in the coal and steel union. France was thus unable to balance the influence of the Federal Republic with the counter-influence of Britain. The British government was only willing to extend the pledge of mutual support agreed on in the Brussels Treaty to include the EDC, and therefore also the Federal Republic. The direct entry into NATO of the Federal Republic could in fact still be prevented, but a right of consultation on all political questions of the alliance had been conceded to it (inasmuch as it could call for joint sittings of the NATO and EDC councils at any time) by way of a transitional arrangement.

Adenauer, however, had also been obliged to accept some reductions to his maximum programme: the occupation statute was not to be abrogated by means of a security treaty between sovereign states; the three Western Allies granted the Federal Republic 'full authority' in domestic and foreign affairs only, retaining all rights pertaining to 'Germany as a whole', the right to proclaim a state of emergency and the right to station troops. The Federal Republic was still forbidden to manufacture war materials crucial to weapon technology or to conduct research in the field of such weapons; it likewise had no direct opportunity to affect the decisions of NATO bodies.

In relation to where the two sides had started, German interests had prevailed more successfully in terms of the logic of the armament question than those of the French, and it was no coincidence that French enthusiasm for the European Defence Community declined from the summer of 1951 to the same extent that the project gained support in the Federal Republic. The hopes for a leading role for France within the united continent had had to be buried, as had the possibilities contained in the Schuman and Pleven Plans for a relatively independent role for Europe in relation to the USA. The concept of the 'third force' had thus experienced yet another serious setback: American influence in Europe had stabilised beyond the end of Marshall aid.[27] Through the integration of the Federal Republic into the Western military alliance, moreover, the division of the continent had become several degrees more definite. In the Bonn Treaty, the Western Allies and the Federal Republic had each pledged themselves to a reunification model for Germany based on the continued existence of the internal order and its integration into the Western alliance system (reunification as the result of a 'policy of strength').[28] Not only had the Allies thereby secured themselves against a *rapprochement* between a strengthened Germany and the Soviet Union, but the Western powers had aligned themselves with the Federal Republic in their Germany policy. The Federal Republic, as a result of the state of tension unleashed by the Korean War, had become an important partner within the Western alliance. Its political leadership, therefore, was partly consciously and partly unconsciously aware, as long it could not be sure of its recent achievements and the Federal Republic was still subject to perceptible restrictions, that it had an interest in the continuance of this state of tension, and thus contributed to the further entrenchment of the Western bloc. German concepts of a reunification 'in freedom', part rhetoric, part earnest hope, were now supported more than ever by the Western powers, and even if Adenauer did not succeed in making the Western Allies commit themselves publicly in the Bonn Treaty to winning back the territories on the other side of the Oder and Neisse (which would have suited him very well in domestic political terms), the Allies would still have to pay heed to this claim of their new allied partner to speak for all Germans.

The essential achievement of the EDC project lay in the fact that by means of the conciliatory effect of the concept of supranational unification it banished the danger of a resurgence of nationalist, aggressive forces in the Federal Republic, which could have emerged for the Western world from German rearmament, and thus made available the maximum possible degree of defence potential. The price for this accomplishment was high, however: the prospects for German reunification receded into the unreachable distance, as did hopes for the autonomous self-determination of France, or for a 'third force' which could have overcome the contradictions between capitalism and Communism both internally and externally. Whether the majority of the political groupings in Europe were really prepared to pay this price also remained to be seen after the signing of the Treaties of Bonn and Paris.

Notes

1. London council meeting: FRUS (1950), III, pp. 94–125 and 828–1107, a summary of the discussions by Acheson on 14 May 1959, ibid., pp. 1061–67. Congress: Dean Acheson, *Present at the creation*, (New York, 1970), p. 400f.

2. *Atlantic Monthly*, June 1951, p. 22.

3. On the lead-up to the Korean War see Glenn D. Paige, *The Korean Decision: June 24–30, 1950*, (New York, London, 1968), pp. 66ff.; Joyce and Gabriel Kolko, *The Limits of Power*, (New York, 1972), pp. 565ff.; Robert R. Simmons, *The strained alliance, Peking, Pyongyang, Moscow and the politics of the Korean Civil War*, (New York, 1975), and Bruce Cummings, *The origins of the Korean War*, (Princeton, 1981).

4. In this case also we are led in the analysis of Soviet motives to indirect conclusions on the basis of observable events. It is difficult to imagine that Stalin was as surprised by the North Korean attack as the US government was (Kolko, *Limits*, p. 586), in view of the close links between the Korean CP leadership with Moscow. On the other hand, the 'traditional' thesis of a Soviet action prepared for long-term (e.g. David Rees, *Korea, The limited war*, (London, 1964)) corresponds neither to the lead-up nor to Soviet interests. See also Bernd Bonwetsch and Peter M. Kuhfus, 'Die Sowjetunion, China und der Koreakrieg', in *Vierteljahrshefte für Zeitgeschichte* 33 (1985), pp. 28–87, here pp. 46–52.

5. Ambassador Kirk from Moscow on 25 June, 1950, FRUS (1950), VII, pp. 139f.

6. Rhee to MacArthur, 12 Aug. 1950, MacArthur Papers, quoted after Kolko, *Limits*, p. 591; on the following see ibid., p. 578ff., Paige, *The Korean decision, passim*; Allen Guttman, *Korea: Cold War and limited war*, 2nd ed. (Lexington, 1972); FRUS (1950), VII, pp. 125–270.

7. MacArthur's situation report, Senate hearing, May 1951, quotes after Kolko, *Limits*, p. 591.

8. FRUS (1950), VII, pp. 271–730, esp. Dulles, pp. 386f., Bevin, pp. 396–9, Rhee, pp. 428–30, Department of Defense, pp. 502–10, State Department, pp. 617–23; Chang-MacArthur communiqué of 1 Aug. 1950 in *Documents on international affairs 1949–50*, p. 658.

9. See John W. Spanier, *The Truman-MacArthur controversy and the Korean War*, (Cambridge, 1959); Allen S. Whiting, *China crosses the Yalu: the decision to enter the Korean War*, (New York, 1960); Kolko, *Limits*, pp.

593–604; FRUS (1950), VII, pp. 731ff. The lead-up to Chinese intervention and the problem of American war objectives generally are likewise not illuminated by 'traditional' authors; China thus appears one-sidedly as an 'aggressor', whilst the remainder of the course of the war remains shrouded in mystery.

10. The motive emphasised by Kolko, *Limits*, p. 605–17, as being decisive, the artificial maintenance of a mood or crisis in the interests of the European reconstruction programme, in fact played only a small part in relation to this.

11. Acheson, *Present at the creation*, p. 462.

12. Next to the question of what was responsible for the 'turnabout of 1945', the causes of McCarthyism are the most disputed theme of the revisionism debate. Athan Theoharis, *The Yalta myths; an issue in U.S. politics, 1945–1955*, (Columbia, Mo., 1970); by the same author *Seeds of repression: Harry S. Truman and the origins of McCarthyism*, (Chicago, 1971) and Richard M. Freeland, *The Truman doctrine and the origins of McCarthyism* (see above ch. 6, note 8) draw attention in the first instance to the connection between the Truman Doctrine and the anti-Communist hysteria of the early fifties, thereby, however, wrenching the Truman administration entirely out of the context of its diverse dependence and attributing to it a deliberate and cynical production of McCarthyism. For a differentiated analysis of the various connections, such as is outlined here, compare Robert Griffith, *The politics of fear; Joseph R. McCarthy and the Senate*, (Lexington, 1970); also Richard M. Fried, *Men against McCarthy*, (New York, 1976). Contradictory interpretations are in Robert Griffith and Athan Theoharis (eds), *The specter: original essays on the Cold War and the origins of McCarthyism*, (New York, 1974).

13. Kolko, *Limits*, p. 571.

14. Whether and if so to what extent would still require explanation; compare provisionally Kolko, *Limits*, pp. 675–7 and Barton J. Bernstein, 'Election of 1952', in Arthur Schlesinger and Fred Israel (eds), *History of American Presidential Elections 1789–1968*, (New York, 1971), pp. 3215–340.

15. On Dulles's policy see Glenn H. Snyder, 'The "New Look" of 1953', in Schilling, Hammdon and Snyder, *Strategy, politics and defense budgets*, (New York, London, 1962), pp. 382–524; Michael Guhin, *John Foster Dulles: a statesman and his times*, (New York, London, 1972); Townsend Hoopes, *The devil and John Foster Dulles*, (Boston, Toronto, 1973); Martin Geiling, *Außenpolitik und Nuklearstrategie. Eine Analyse des konzeptionellen Wandels der amerikanischen Sicherheitspolitik gegenüber der Sowjetunion (1945–1963)* (Cologne, Vienna, pp. 96–167); Leonard Mosley, *Dulles. A biography of Eleanor, Allen and John Foster Dulles and their family network*, (London, 1978).

16. See Kolko, *Limits*, pp. 651–3; Daniel Yergin, *Shattered Peace*, (Boston, 1977), p. 408.

17. See account in Georgette Elgey, *Histoire de la IV République*, vol. 2: *La République des contradictions 1951–1954*, (Paris, 1968), p. 440. Basic reading on the war in Indochina is Philippe Devillers, *Histoire du Viet-nam 1940–1952*, (Paris, 1952).

18. The same applies to the Vietnam and China policies of the Nixon/Kissinger administration from 1969.

19. On the discussion about Federal German re-armament in 1949–50, see *Anfänge westdeutscher Sicherheitspolitik 1945–1956*, vol. 1: *Von der Kapitulation bis zum Pleven-Plan*, (Munich/Vienna, 1982); and Wilfried Loth, 'Der Koreakrieg und die Staatswerdung der Bundesrepublik', in Josef Foschepoth (ed)., *Kalter Krieg und Deutsche Frage*, (Göttingen, 1985), pp. 335–361.

20. FRUS (1949), III, p. 123.

21. FRUS (1950), III, pp. 212–19.

22. Extracts from the first memorandum in *Verhandlungen des Deutschen Bundestages, Stenographische Berichte*, 8 Feb. 1952, p. 8159 Af.; the second complete in Konrad Adenauer, *Erinnerungen 1945–1953*, (Stuttgart, 1965), pp. 358f.

23. Text in *Europa, Dokumente zur Frage der europäischen Einigung*, vol. 2, (Munich, 1962), pp. 812–815. See on the negotiations of autumn 1950 Wilfried Loth, *Sozialismus und internationalismus*, (Stuttgart 1977), pp. 282–89; and Norbert Wiggershaus, 'Die Entscheidung für einen westdeutschen Verteidigungsbeitrag 1950', in: *Anfänge westdeutscher Sicherheitspolitik*, vol. 1., pp. 325–402.

24. See FRUS, (1950), III, pp. 404–585; on the American position see memorandum of the US representative in the NATO Representative Council, Charles Spofford, 30 Nov. 1950, ibid., pp. 501–5.

25. On the negotiations with the Federal Republic until the conclusion of the treaties in May 1952 see Wettig, *Entmilitarisierung*, pp. 402–87, Baring, *Außenpolitik*, vol. 1, pp. 174–253, 262–281 and Edward Fursdon, *The european defense community, a history*, (London, 1980), pp. 105–188; Gerhard Wettig, *Entmilitarisierung und Wiederbewaffnung in Deutschland 1943–1955*, (Munich 1967); Arnulf Baring, *Außenpolitik in Adenauers Kanzlerdemokratie. Bonns Beitrag zur Europäischen Verteidigungsgemeinschaft*, 2nd ed., (Munich, 1971).

26. Trilingual text of the treaties in 'Die Vertragswerke von Bonn und Paris', *Dokumente und Berichte des Europa-Archiv*, vol. 10, (Frankfurt, 1952).

27. It contradicts, however, all the evidence of the sources to see at the same time in this unequivocal *result* of the debate on the rearmament of West Germany the primary aim of American rearmament policy, as is asserted by Kolko, *Limits*, p. 653–67. The Western ground fighting forces in Europe from 1950–52 were certainly insufficient for any serious defence concept against a Soviet invasion, but this was not because the Americans lacked the will for such a concept, but because as a result of the difficulties described here it could not be implemented militarily to the necessary extent.

28. In article 7 para. II the Federal Republic and the three Allies undertook to work together 'to the conclusion of the peace treaty regulation' in order to bring about their common goal by peaceful means: a reunited Germany possessing a free democratic constitution similar to that of the Federal Republic and integrated into the European community. Paragraph III (which was absent in the revised version of October 1954) declared the rights and duties resulting from the set of agreements for the Federal Republic, which were explicitly valid even for a reunited Germany, and even if agreements to other effect were to be reached by common understanding.

12

The Soviet *Détente* Offensive

From the Soviet point of view, the consolidation of Western bloc formation in the wake of the Korean War must have seemed threatening: the USA was committing itself to a long-term military presence on the European continent, and the West Europeans were gearing themselves both to overcoming the remaining contradictions among themselves with the aid of European integration and to reducing the gap in conventional armament. West German potential, as much overestimated in its significance by the Soviet leadership as by the Western public, threatened decisively to increase the military might of the West, and in addition the USA was continuing to prolong its engagement in Korea and in Indo-China. Whether and to what extent the Soviet leadership took seriously Western declarations of a 'policy of strength', and a 'policy of liberation', or its own propaganda theses of the aggressive, imperialistic character of Western bloc formation, it is difficult to judge. It is clear, however, that it saw a substantial weakening of its own position in Western measures towards armament and integration.[1] This danger emanating from the Western offensive must have seemed all the greater, since the Soviet Union was at that time faced with serious internal political problems: the one-sided forcing of heavy industry and the armaments industry in pursuit of building the Soviet Union into a bulwark once again had led to the productive workforce and labour becoming over-demanding and to a general economic and social misery which could jeopardise the continued existence of the Soviet system. Fear of Western expansion and a simultaneous need for an external political lull in order to master its internal political difficulties allowed a willingness to grow among the Soviet leadership to pay a high price in order to prevent West

257

German rearmament — the core of Western bloc consolidation. The Soviet *détente* offensive, which arose out of this situation, once again opened to question the general trend towards the entrenchment of bloc formation in Europe.

The Soviet notes on German policy of 1952

In response to Western plans for rearmament, the Soviet leadership at first drew attention to Four-Power responsibility for Germany and for the de-militarisation measures agreed upon in Potsdam; at the same time, the GDR leadership appealed to the West Germans to sit round 'a single table' with them. Neither of these measures was evidently enough to make any noticeable impact on the EDC negotiations. A Soviet initiative for a fresh Four-Power conference on Germany (note of 2 November 1950) had failed in June 1951, after weeks of preliminary negotiations on the question of the agenda: the GDR demand for the formation of a proportional All-Germany Council composed of representatives from both German states (first mooted in a letter from Grotewohl, the Prime Minister of the GDR, to Adenauer on 30 November 1950) had not met with a favourable response in the Federal Republic. It was only in the spring of 1952, when it became clear that a successful conclusion of the EDC negotiations was imminent, that the Soviet leadership worked its way round to a fundamental reorientation of its German policy.

On 10 March 1952, the Soviet leadership presented the three Western Allies with a note containing a concept for a peace treaty with Germany which on the decisive points went beyond the previous Soviet position on its German policy. Germany was not only to be reunited under the condition of ceding the territories east of the Oder and Neisse, and of pledging not to enter into any 'coalitions or military alliances' directed against any state that had 'participated in the war against Germany with its combat forces'; in addition, all occupation troops were to withdraw from the country one year after the conclusion of the peace treaty. They were to be replaced by national German combat forces 'which are necessary for the defence of the country'; even the production of armaments was to be permitted to the extent that they were required by these combat forces. Within a 'democratic' framework to be laid down in accordance with the Potsdam agreements, not only were all parties to be able to act freely, but also, as was expressly emphasised, all former members of the German *Wehrmacht*, including its officers and all 'former Nazis', were to have an opportunity to co-operate in the reconstruction of the new republic. Free elections for an All-German Parliament, specified the Soviet government in a second note on 9 April, should take place in the short term, albeit prepared by proportionally constituted FRG–GDR bodies under the supervision of the four Allies, and not, as the Western side had demanded, under the observation of the United Nations. The future status of Germany was to be established by the Allies before the assembly of the freely elected German government, but the peace treaty itself was only to be signed by this government. Two further notes of 24 May and 23 August 1952, more aggressive and impatient than the first two, but still showing a readiness to negotiate, urged the Western powers to take steps towards the solution of the German question on the basis of these proposals.[2]

In this way the Soviet leadership had, without realising it, arrived at almost the same concept of a neutralised and united Germany as the American Administration had reached two and a half years earlier under the pressure of the Berlin blockade and as an alternative to the cost-intensive road of the division of Germany and Europe. As in the American case, the Soviet offer entailed sacrificing an already attained degree of control over part of Germany, a sacrifice compelled by fear of the alternative — long-term burdening with a crisis-prone West Germany in the former case, and the fear of a heavily armed military bloc on the Western border of the Soviet sphere of influence in the latter. As in the earlier case, the concession of a neutral Germany free of Allied troops was associated with incalculable risks as far as its future domestic and foreign policy orientation and the cohesion of the other parts of its own camp were concerned. Those involved in the alternative solution nevertheless also reckoned on a good chance of ultimately being able to earmark German potential for the benefit of what had in the meantime become their own camp: the Americans by relying on the attractiveness of the Western social model in free elections; and the Soviets, on the one hand, by ostentatiously resuming the 'Rappallo line' of German–Soviet relations in the inter-war years, aiming for an alliance with national-conservative elements in Germany, and, on the other hand, by carrying out 'democratisation' measures on the basis of the agreements made in Potsdam, as well as by securing a minimum of permanent influence on the future policy of Germany as

259

a whole by the permanent presence of GDR and USSR representatives in the process leading up to free elections and the peace treaty.

What in the Soviet view constituted an acceptable minimum cannot clearly be discerned from the available documents, and it was not completely clear at the time of the Soviet initiative either. The formulation of the notes ('independent, democratic and peace-loving state') was as open to flexible interpretation as the Potsdam agreements had been in their time, and permitted the Soviet leadership a way out of its course, should it appear to be leading to Soviet disadvantage. Members of the Soviet government of course wished to secure the strongest possible position for Communist elements in a united Germany, but the decisive factor, as in their East European policy prior to the shift towards Cominform dogmatism, was the securing of foreign-policy loyalty and not the social form itself, for which in any case they had no fixed concept. What had in the meantime been achieved in the GDR by way of social transformation was certainly not simply to be sacrificed, but as far as possible safeguarded and transferred to West Germany. Since in the course proposed by the Soviet government the same also applied to the social system of the Federal Republic, there could, in view of the economic strength and ideological attractiveness of the Western system, be no doubt that an autonomous unified Germany would have a predominantly bourgeois structure after the peace treaty procedure came to an end.[3] To expect foreign-policy loyalty from such a Germany must, taking into account the great economic influence of the USA in West Germany, have seemed over-daring. The Soviet leaders, however, circumvented the danger of a drift of a unified Germany towards the West with the hope of increasing conflicts between Germany and the other capitalist states, as Stalin claimed to predict in his publication on *Economic problems of socialism in the USSR*, which appeared at the same time as the notes on Germany.[4]

The chances of success of the neutralisation project were nevertheless remote from the outset, as must have been apparent even from the Soviet viewpoint. Insistence on supervision of the entire peace treaty procedure robbed the proposal for free elections in the whole of Germany of much of its attractiveness, whilst commitment to the Oder–Neisse border robbed the appeal to national-conservative elements in Germany of much of its efficacy. A reunited Germany with a national army, albeit a

260

restricted one, was bound to be greeted with substantial misgivings by the West Europeans, especially the French. The question really was whether the advantages offered to the Western powers by the proposal — the opening of the former GDR to Western influence, a fall in armament costs, and a reduction of tension in Central Europe — would be able to outweigh these misgivings. Furthermore, it must have seemed doubtful whether the Western powers, after years of thinking and dealing in terms of the Cold War, would be at all capable of weighing up the advantages and disadvantages of the proposed project against one another. (In fact the US Administration had already decided against the neutralisation plans in 1948, under much less favourable Western basic conditions — which the Soviet leadership could not of course have known.) Fulfilment of the Western demand for free elections under UN supervision as a first step to reunification, which would have meant making more concessions and sacrificing unreservedly every possibility for influence in Germany, or a revision of the boundary situation created in Eastern Europe in 1945, such as would have been necessitated by a reunification extending beyond the Oder–Neisse boundary, seemed in the Soviet view more detrimental to its own security interests than the rearmament of the Federal Republic and the creation of an integrated Atlantic combat force, and could not therefore be offered as the price for the West giving up the EDC, however much these concessions would have increased the chances of the Soviet offer succeeding.[5] In order to deprive Western bloc formation of its central element, West Germany, the Soviet leadership was prepared to set aside the establishment of a 'socialist' GDR along Soviet lines, as it had been compelled to do after the failure of the joint Allied policy on Germany in 1948–9 in the course of Eastern bloc formation. It was not, however, prepared to sacrifice all opportunities for influencing German policy. Whether the Soviet Union was to proceed at all with the delicate brinkmanship between the completion of Western bloc formation and the incipient disintegration of its own security system was evidently disputed even among the Soviet leadership itself, as is indicated not only by the ambivalence of Soviet policy proposals, which permitted retreat without loss of face at any moment, but also by news of internal Soviet disagreements over German policy after Stalin's death in 1953, which did not permit the discernment of any clearly outlined positions or opinion groups, but which nevertheless bear witness to the existence of two schools of thought in Soviet German policy: a more dogmatic one giving preference to the 'building of socialism' in the GDR, and a more adventurous one, which augured great advantages for the Soviet Union with a reunification under certain conditions.[6] The fact that Stalin, who was undoubtedly, in the last years of his life, the final authority on all domestic and foreign-policy questions, decided on the second alternative in the spring of 1952 seems to have been contingent, as far as we can tell, on somewhat irrational ideological reasons. An intensified anti-Semitism (which can be discerned, for example, in the argumentation of the trials against Slanský and other 'Titoists' and in the vigorous criticism of Israel)[7] led Stalin to show more sympathy towards national-conservative Germans and to overestimate their influ-ence on West German politics. Alternatively, the fact that the neutralisation project, even if it only had a remote chance of being brought about, could still be used as a superb tactic, may also have played a part in the decision: it is possible that Stalin hoped to delay the conclusion of the EDC project with the peace treaty proposal, perhaps leading internal Western conflicts to shatter the painstakingly achieved compromise and to pass the responsibility for the definitive division of Germany on to the Western side.[8]

Decision in the Federal Republic

The decision on the outcome of the Soviet initiative fell primarily to the Federal Republic. The prospects for German reunification, perhaps even linked with the hope for a future independent role for a united Germany between the world powers was, if at all, primarily attractive to the West Germans, without whose free consent the EDC project could not be accomplished. A positive response on the part of the Western powers could thus only be contemplated in the event of a positive reaction from the West Germans.

At first glance, the prospects for such a positive reaction may not have seemed bad: the forced Western integration policy of Adenauer had after all met with considerable internal resistance.[9] However much rearmament suggested itself out of fear of the Soviet threat and interest in the achievement of equality, it was fundamentally opposed to everything that had been stated and taught in West Germany since 1945 in terms of the renunciation of militarism and power politics, thus clearly making the path to reunification more difficult, to such an extent that it was certain to provoke a broad front of opponents. Democrats feared the resurgence of traditional anti-democratic elements; patriots and expellées were concerned about the chances for reunification; pacifists and socialists were horrified at the intensification of East–West tension; apolitical also-rans shrank from their experience of National Socialism; and the Allies from the new engagement which was being called for; nationalist maximalists regarded as insupportable the restrictions connected with the EDC project. All these positions were represented in diverse combinations and angles, and since the debate about rearmament was not only concerned with the future foreign-policy orientation of the Federal Republic, but was inextricably linked with the Republic's identity, it was conducted with great vigour.

Thus Gustav Heinemann, along with a sizeable proportion of political Protestantism, Ulrich Noack's pacifist 'Nauheim circle', Rudolf Augstein in *Spiegel*, and Paul Sethe in the *Frankfurter Allgemeiner Zeitung*, partly out of nationalist, partly out of Christian-pacifist-determined motives (in various combinations), opposed Western integration in the Catholic-conservative style and urged the safeguarding of every opportunity to be free of blocs. Kurt Schumacher and the great majority of the SPD were at first strongly averse to such hopes for a neutralised, unified Germany, but at the same time equally averse to any long-term link with the Western powers before a solution to the reunification question had been reached. The more defined the conservative stamp of the integrated Europe became, the more the concept of neutralisation found support, even among the SPD.[10] Even parts of the government coalition, the all-German wing of the CDU and Jakob Kaiser and some among the FDP (Reinhold Maier, Karl-Georg Pfleiderer)[11] were concerned about the loss of West German manoeuvrability in relation to the Soviet Union. Economic circles represented in the coalition hoped for the opening-up of East European markets. They all argued, with varying degrees of optimism regarding Soviet intentions, but all with equal vigour, for a serious examination of the Soviet government's negotiation offer.

Certainly there was from the outset no lack of strong political elements in favour of the EDC project: the overwhelming majority of political Catholicism, together with large groups of the Rhineland and south German bourgeoisie; representatives of the traditional political Right and expellées, who set their hopes for reunification on the 'policy of strength' propounded by Adenauer; a minority of industrial groups, who saw their chances lying mainly in an integrated West European market; the European unity movement, which had captured the greater proportion of the pro-reform younger generation and which saw the EDC as a crucial, if not exactly an ideal means for bringing about European unity. Much as their commitment to the EDC was related to the degree of economic involvement with the West that had in the meantime been achieved and with the predominant orientation towards the model of Western democracies (including their anti-Communist basic consensus), it was equally under permanent pressure to justify itself on the question of reunification, and it was thus by no means certain whether it would survive a serious reunification proposal from the Soviet Union.

At all events Konrad Adenauer definitely feared a crumbling of the EDC front even among his own ranks in the face of the Soviet notes on Germany, and he consequently endeavoured to formulate on his own the Federal German response to the Soviet initiative, circumventing not only the opposition, but even his own government. Although on the day the first Soviet note was conveyed to the Western powers Jakob Kaiser urged in the cabinet the forcing of a serious dialogue with the Soviet Union, and others also spoke in favour of an examination of it in the same cabinet meeting, Adenauer subsequently had his press spokesman announce that the Federal government did not regard the note as a reliable basis for negotiation. When the High Commissioners informed him on the same day that their governments wished the EDC negotiations to be continued without regard to the Soviet note, he expressed his positive satisfaction and relief at this decision, without further consultation with his cabinet or with the higher echelons of the government coalition. In the same way, he took care in the following months to represent the Federal government to the High Commissioners as far as possible alone. This seemed to him the only way of avoiding the danger of the neutralisation of Germany, which in his view would inevitably lead either to a weakening of the West and to the advance of Communist elements or, no less dangerous, to a lapse into traditional national state rivalry on the European continent and thus to a strengthening of traditional war-mongering elements in Germany and among its European neighbours.[12]

This caution was to prove unfounded, however. Among public

opinion in the Federal Republic, in so far as it was articulated in press commentaries, hopes of a chance for reunification were outweighed by the fear of a Soviet take-over nourished by anti-Communist generalisations, and Western integration seemed to the majority to be the safer road, not only to the safeguarding and stabilisation of the socio-political *status quo*, but even towards a revision of the state of affairs in the Red Army's sphere of influence. Adenauer's policy of non-negotiation already had a majority behind it in 1952, even if the declarations of his opponents were more spectacular.[13] Even most of those in favour of negotiation with the Soviet government, moreover, insisted out of anti-Communist or nationalist rigour entirely as a matter of course on conditions which the Soviets were not in fact ready to concede: on free elections without any possibility for Soviet supervision and a revision of the Oder–Neisse boundary. Since the Soviet leadership showed no sign (and indeed could show no sign) in the course of discussion of any willingness to make concessions on these two points, the line of argument of those in favour of negotiation increasingly lost support — the more so since Adenauer knew how to direct discussion precisely towards these sensitive issues, and since the GDR leadership, for contrasting, although equally comprehensible reasons, feared a serious exploration of the Soviet negotiation offer, a factor which contributed to its demonstrating inadequate willingness of the Eastern bloc to negotiate. A powerful 'reunification party' against Adenauer's policy, such as was encouraged by Rudolf Augstein from March 1951, was not able to emerge under these conditions. Rather the convinced supporters of the EDC were now joined by the resigned proponents of a reunification 'in freedom' and of a 'new', non-capitalist Europe. Even in the SPD, which continued to fight for acceptance of the Soviet negotiation offer, the neutralisation idea did not remain uncontested, and rearmament was accepted in principle, in spite of all criticism of procedure.

Basically, therefore, almost no one among the leading political circles of the Federal Republic was prepared during the years after the end of the war to risk the established economic, social and constitutional-political priorities of West Germany for the benefit of a fresh, all-German start. Where such a willingness did exist because people were dissatisfied with the decisions of the previous years, the basic anti-Communist consensus, which had been crucial for the founding of the Federal Republic, allowed the ability to make compromises with the Soviet side, which paid heed to the minimal interests of all those concerned, to be lost. Reunification was therefore for the majority of West Germans ultimately only to be contemplated in terms of a transferral of the social system of the Federal Republic to the GDR, and since the Soviet leadership, under the conditions of its specific security system, was unable to agree to such a withdrawal from Germany without any opportunity for supervision, the West Germans in fact moved in their line of argument and in their political dealings away from reunification and towards the 'Western integration before reunification' order of priorities which Adenauer had already reached at the end of the war. If they had been hesitant and only followed with great reservation in 1948 the initiatives of the Western powers for the founding of the Western state, when faced with the decision themselves, they now ratified the lines laid down at that time. Instead of halting the founding process of the West German state, therefore, the Soviet neutralisation proposal had in fact quite definitely accelerated it.

Under these circumstances, there could hardly be any more doubt as to the Western reaction to the Soviet notes. In France and Great Britain, the Soviet proposal awakened vague hopes for a dismantling of the East–West confrontation in Central Europe and, linked with this, hopes for a prevention of problematic West German rearmament at the last moment, so that both governments were for a time under strong internal pressure to examine the notes seriously. Their initiatives nevertheless lacked the necessary backing, since the majority of the French saw an even greater security risk in a united Germany equipped with a national army than they did in the East–West tension in Europe and in West German combat forces integrated into the EDC. In addition, the British did not wish once again, as in the inter-war years, to be committed to the protection of France from a potentially strong Germany, and both France and Britain remained essentially convinced of the necessity for a military strengthening of the West in relation to the Soviet Union. The American government, which had in the meantime shifted towards an increasingly universal containment practice and was also under mounting pressure from militant anti-Communism among the American public, was unable to draw any positive benefits from the Soviet proposal, which was directly aimed at striking the American containment apparatus at its economic, military and political heart in Europe. Acheson consequently rejected a Four-Power conference on the proposal as resolutely as Adenauer, and

Eden and Schuman were unable to offer any resistance to this US–German alliance.[14]

In their notes of reply, the Western powers placed at the heart of their argument the demand for free elections *before* any establishment of the future status of Germany — in the reasonable hope that this would provoke the Soviet government into a rejection of the demand, thus enabling themselves to flaunt the inadequate substance of the Soviet proposal to the people of the Federal Republic. On Adenauer's advice there was no lack of effort to expose the Soviet position in relation to the Oder–Neisse issue and to discredit the Soviet proposal as an attempt to return to the Control Council regime. With the demand that a future German government must be conceded the right to enter into treaties and alliances in accordance with the principles of the United Nations, the aim of the Soviet initiative — the neutralisation of Germany — was unequivocally rejected in the very first note of reply of 25 March 1952. The general treaty and the EDC treaty were signed respectively two and three days after the third Soviet note of 24 May, after the 'all-German' wings of the FDP and the CDU had been conceded at the last minute a qualification (by no means, however, the removal) of what was known as the 'binding clause', in which the rights and duties undertaken in connection with Western integration were to extend to a reunited Germany. When the British and French governments proved willing after all in June–July at least to entertain the suggestion of a new Four-Power conference on Germany, this initiative collapsed at the outset with the resistance of the Americans and the Germans.

17 June 1953

The lack of willingness of the Western powers to accept the Soviet neutralisation proposal, or even to take it seriously, at first strengthened the position in the Soviet power zone of the opponents of a risky new policy orientation towards Germany. Stalin allowed the campaign for the neutralisation proposal to continue, but otherwise concentrated his efforts towards overcoming internal difficulties by means of a renewed exertion on all sides. The GDR leadership found under these conditions opportunities for stabilising its own position by creating *faits accomplis*. On the day on which the general treaty was signed, the hitherto largely permeable zone borders between the FRG and the GDR were closed off: of the 200 or so crossing points between East and West Berlin, 120 were closed. At the second party conference of the SED, from 9 to 12 July 1952, the beginning of the 'planned building of socialism' was proclaimed in the GDR and an intensification of the 'class struggle' was announced. In the following months the collectivisation of agriculture, trade and industry was systematically carried out, the 'barracked *Volkspolizei*' better armed, the administrative structure centralised by means of the abolition of the five *Länder* in favour of fourteen districts, required production levels raised, and consumer goods neglected in favour of the creation of new capital goods. In the Soviet Union, for the first time in thirteen years, a meeting of the Communist Party was called for 5 October 1952, at which new and ambitious plan targets were announced and Stalin was placed more firmly than ever at the centre of all decisions. Three months after the party meeting, the arrest of a group of nine doctors was announced who had allegedly sought the lives of the higher echelons of the state and army. At the same time, a campaign to increase vigilance against 'negligence', 'gullibility' and 'anti-Marxist opportunism' was staged. A fresh wave of purges was evidently intended to secure Stalin's rule and thus overcome the tensions which had manifested themselves.[15]

Stalin's death on 5 March 1953 nevertheless reduced to nought all hope of being able to solve the problem of the loyalty of Soviet citizens and the coherence of the Soviet bloc in this way. The regime slid into greater difficulties than before, since in addition to the system of production and distribution, which had become unbalanced, there was now also the problem of who was to rule. In the struggle for the successor to the Generalissimo, this could bring out the various power conclaves and apparatuses of the regime more than had been the case under the authority of the dictator. The leading triad, consisting of Malenkov (the Prime Minister), Beria (the Chief of Police and Minister of the Interior), and Khrushchev (the *de facto* Party Chief), which had emerged ten days after the death of the dictator, not only introduced a relaxation of the coercive state system with an amnesty for Stalin's political victims and the rehabilitation of the 'murderer doctors', also aiming for greater encouragement of the consumer-goods industry and agriculture, but they also renewed with great vigour the *détente* offensive introduced by Stalin. A reduction in the pressure issuing from the Western powers outside was more necessary than ever for the continuance of the Soviet system.[16] Even at Stalin's funeral ceremony on 9 March, Malenkov spoke emphatically of the 'possibility for a lasting coexistence and for peaceful competition between the two different systems', whilst Beria announced a 'policy of securing peace, a struggle against the preparation and unleashing of another war, a policy of international co-operation and the development of practical links with all countries on the basis of reciprocity'.[17] The vigorous anti-Western polemic in the Soviet press was dropped, Western diplomats in the Soviet Union acquired greater room for manoeuvre; in the armistice talks in Korea, Communist representatives showed great willingness to make concessions, so that finally on 23 June the conclusion of an armistice on the basis of the *status quo ante* became possible, and the Western powers were once again invited to a Four-Power conference on the reunification of Germany.

The most far-reaching moves towards the revision of internal and foreign-policy guidelines in the first months after Stalin's death were made by Beria, perhaps in order to pre-empt a general revision movement which would affect him most as long-time chief of the police apparatus, since he had no base of his own among the population, but perhaps also because he was, through his secret service, best informed about the current internal and foreign political situation of the regime. Whether he was really prepared in this regard 'to liquidate the German Democratic Republic as a socialist state' in order to prevent the formation of the EDC and to release a reunited Germany *entirely* from Soviet control, as Khrushchev subsequently accused him in 1963 of having been,[18] cannot be precisely ascertained. At all events, supported by Malenkov, he did immediately attempt to deprive the GDR of the chance of blocking itself off from a reunification at the expense of its unlimited hegemony by means of the forced extension of a social and ruling system on Soviet lines. In so doing, he in fact created the preconditions for a greater degree of willingness to make concessions, which brought about after all, negotiations with the Western powers on the neutralisation of Germany.

On 15 April 1953, the SED leadership was instructed by the Soviet Politburo to reduce the pace and specifications for the 'building of socialism' in order to take the edge off the meanwhile considerable dissatisfaction and agitation of the GDR population, discernible in a rapidly increasing flow of refugees. At the end of

May, after a testing of opinion implemented by the Moscow Control Commission, and carried out against the will of the SED leadership, had informed Moscow leaders of the full extent of unrest in the GDR, the Control Commission was dissolved, the office of a Soviet High Commissioner was created in Germany in accordance with the Western pattern, and Vladimir Semyonov, who had worked towards a change of policy as political adviser to the Control Commission and who had been ordered back to Moscow a few weeks earlier, was entrusted with the safeguarding of this office. Back in East Berlin as High Commissioner in the first weeks of June, Semyonov demanded in drastic language that the SED leadership make a fundamental revision of its German policy. He was supported in this by Wilhelm Zaisser, the GDR Minister for State Security, who was in a similar political position to that of Beria and who was directly subordinate to him, as well as by Rudolf Herrnstadt, Editor-in-Chief of the SED mouthpiece *Neues Deutschland*. In accordance with their concepts, the political bureau of the SED decided on the withdrawal of numerous measures against the existence of private farmers and craftsmen, as well as against the freedom of cultural activity and of the churches, on the lifting of certain restrictions on inter-zone traffic, the withdrawal of embargo orders and expulsions, and a series of amnesties and tax exemptions. The decision, published without comment two days later in *Neues Deutschland*, contained the admission that the party and government had 'made a series of errors', as well as the announcement of a comprehensive reorientation of the entire policy towards the middle classes, culture and agriculture. The grounds for this policy change were expressly stated as being 'the great aim of bringing about the unity of Germany, which calls on both sides for measures practically facilitating the reconciliation of both sides'.[19]

In fact, in reaching these decisions, the political bureau of the SED also had in mind, in addition to the dissatisfaction produced by the enforced 'building of socialism', those bourgeois elements in the Federal Republic which, as the experience of 1952 had taught, had had to be won over to the idea of reunification with considerable assurances regarding civil rights and social forms. For workers, who were just as exposed to the pressure of Sovietisation policy as the other groups within the GDR population, and who had been burdened in the course of policy as recently as 29 May with a rise in work norms of an average of 10 per cent, no alleviating measures were announced. In terms of the development of opinion in West Germany, this did not seem to be urgent. It can be understood from accounts known so far of the background to the new policy that the SED was to be transformed into a people's party of all classes, which could hold its own even in the event of all-German free elections. At the same time, the Western powers were to be presented with an effective negotiating partner in the High Commissioner for the joint solution of the German question. The replacement of the former SED leaders' group, led by Walter Ulbricht, the First Secretary, which had borne the brunt of the responsibility for delineation and Sovietisation policy since the middle of 1952, now seemed only a matter of time. It did not escape the attention of careful observers that the otherwise customary signature of Ulbricht was missing from the published congratulatory greetings for the birthday of a high party functionary.

In the meantime, these preparations for a more specific Soviet reunification proposal were immediately forestalled by co-operation among those opposed to a compromise between East and West. The American and Federal German governments disregarded the reorientation in East Berlin and again treated the Soviet *détente* offers as purely tactical manoeuvres. President Eisenhower demanded as 'proof of the peaceful intentions of the Soviet Union' and as a precondition for the termination of the Cold War not only free elections in the whole of Korea and the conclusion of a state treaty with Austria, but also the reunification of Germany in the framework of the West European community, and in addition the release of the East European countries in complete independence — in other words, the retreat of the Soviet Union from all the positions it had achieved since the Second World War.[20] Through the Western powers, the population of the GDR was thus left without a realistic leadership in the regime's crisis. Pent-up anger, linked with the hopes stirred by the announcement of the new policy, immediately led to a broad movement of uprising against the SED regime, which no longer heeded the international basic conditions of German policy. Beginning with the protests of East Berliner construction workers on 16 June against the raising of norms, unrest had spread by the morning of 17 June to a national general strike for the removal of the government and for free elections. In Berlin, Halle, Magdeburg, Leipzig and a number of smaller towns, enterprises were hit by strikes; state shops, SED offices and police stations were set on fire; prisoners were released; and the resignation of Ulbricht and Grotewohl was repeatedly demanded in demonstrations. Ulbricht left Berlin and the SED leadership began to crumble, *without* the Western powers having proved ready to make any concessions.

The point had now definitely been reached in the Soviet view when the palpable disadvantages of the all-German neutralisation policy outweighed the possible advantages. The collapse of the SED regime made it brutally apparent to the Soviet leadership just how unstable the basis of its influence in Central Europe really was, and how little a neutralised Germany, in which the Western powers in addition showed no sign of interest, could be relied upon. The uprising in the GDR was thus not only contained and finally put down by the engagement of Soviet troops on the afternoon of 17 June (apparently with no discussion at all); but after some hesitation a majority in Moscow showed themselves in favour of a decision not to prolong the announced liberalisation of the GDR, firmly to re-establish Ulbricht and no longer to send the SED regime into temporary retirement for the sake of an all-German solution. After Soviet tanks had quashed the uprising movement and the withdrawal of the raising of norms had been conceded, Ulbricht was able to re-stabilise his position (albeit without resorting to the enforced 'building of socialism'). Beria was removed from his posts on 26 June (and then shot on 24 December); two weeks later, Zaisser and Herrnstadt lost their posts. In the official Germany policy statements of East Berlin and Moscow, the demand for a proportionally composed all-German council surfaced once again: on 15 August the Soviet government even asserted that the two German governments should not only participate in the settlement of the peace treaty, but continue into the reunification process[21] — an offer which in view of the recently demonstrated weakness of the SED regime seemed to the Western powers even less acceptable than ever, and now really intended more for propaganda than any real purpose. On 22 August, the Soviet leadership agreed with a GDR delegation on the cancellation of all reparation payments and post-war debts within one year, as well as a drastic reduction in occupation costs, the handing over of 'mixed' enterprises to GDR ownership, and Soviet goods supplies and credit to a level of 485 million roubles. The diplomatic missions of both sides were given embassy status.[22] The GDR was no longer a bargaining chip for Soviet Western policy, but a partner in its own security system, and thus worthy of consolidation.

Thus 17 June 1953 marked the end of Soviet willingness to withdraw from its zone of occupation and any prospect of a German reunification in equal accordance with the interests of East and West. It was indicative of the degree of alienation between East and West that this of all days was immediately celebrated in the Federal Republic as the 'Day of German Unity'.

The break-up of the Western bloc

In spite of the collapse of Beria's German policy, the Soviet Union's need for *détente* in the East–West confrontation continued. The immediate danger of a disintegration of the Soviet system now seemed over, and all groups in the party and state apparatus were in agreement regarding the necessity for increased encouragement of consumer-goods production and a dismantling of coercive measures. The power struggle between the party and state apparatuses, however, personified in Khrushchev and Malenkov, had by no means yet been resolved. Malenkov, who had been able to distance himself from Beria in time, steered towards a uniform encouragement of the consumer-goods sector, whereas Khrushchev gave priority to the development of agriculture, so that at the same time there would be prospects for fresh investment in the heavy industrial sector (that is, agricultural machine-building) and thus he would gradually be able to win over to his side those elements that had encouraged the earlier policy. Until the choice between these two apparatuses had been made, the need of the Soviet state for peace in its external relations would continue to be great, even though now, as a result of an increased awareness of danger after Beria's fall, and to some extent a partial paralysis on both sides, the ability to take decisive foreign-policy initiatives had diminished.[23] The first successful hydrogen-bomb explosion on 13 August 1953, with which the Soviet Union in principle, if not quantitatively, caught up with the American lead in the arms race, robbed German rearmament of much of its danger, whilst Western inactivity on 17 June shook the credibility of the 'policy of liberation'. Seen in the long term, however, a Western bloc firmly integrated with the aid of the supranational EDC must have seemed as threatening as before. Without entirely giving up hope for an all-German arrangement (that is, without deciding definitively between the advocates of a cementing of the GDR and those in

273

favour of a flexible German policy), the Soviet leadership therefore centred its efforts on the encouragement of centrifugal forces
within the Western alliance.

Points of departure for such a strategy were readily available to
the extent that obvious Soviet gestures of *détente* had meanwhile
aroused doubts in Western Europe about the dogma of the Soviet
Union's unshakeable urge for expansion. On the other hand,
with the gradual transition of the Soviet Union towards strategic
armament and the concentration of the USA on the strategy of
'massive retaliation', the danger was increasing that an armed
conflict between East and West could proliferate into a nuclear
war on European soil. At the same time, an economic upswing
was manifesting itself in all countries of the Western alliance such
as had not been experienced for forty years. The necessity of
being incorporated into a military–political organisation of the
West dominated by the USA was consequently never again so
intensely felt as it was at the beginning of the 1950s. Awareness of
the necessity of ultimately reaching some understanding with the
Soviet Union was also growing, and hopes of mediation between
East and West also arose.

In Great Britain, Churchill, as Prime Minister, along with a
large proportion of the British public, interpreted Soviet actions
after Stalin's death, in contrast with the ideologically trapped
American government, as a sign of genuine willingness to negotiate on the part of the Soviet government and — not without some
hope of a mediating role for Britain, which could only improve
the influence and independence of the kingdom, which was now
being towed along by the USA — was aiming towards an examination of the Soviet offers. Churchill went here so far as to accept
the idea of a neutralisation of Germany, as had been proposed by
the Soviet leadership, as an acceptable compromise for all parties.
On 11 May 1953, he publicly demanded a fresh Four-Power
summit conference on all disputed questions between East and
West, thereby recognising for the first time the satisfaction of
Soviet security interests in the face of West German rearmament
as a precondition for real *détente*.[24] In France, the fear of the Soviet
threat subsided and the fear of German dominance within the
European community grew proportionately. This was felt all the
more keenly since in the course of the treaty negotiations the
EDC project changed from being an instrument for containing
the German recovery into a guarantee of future German equality,
whilst the first signs of the Federal German 'economic miracle'

were making the unbroken dynamism of France's old adversary glaringly apparent. Even in the Federal Republic, the population of which approved Adenauer's policy of Western integration with a surprisingly high majority in the *Bundestag* elections of 6 September 1953, EDC opponents created out of the Soviet initiatives vague hopes for a collective security order for the whole of Europe. The opposition's line of argument was becoming visibly more radical.

These diverse interests of East and West manifested themselves in a protracted tussle over the project of the Four-Power conference. Dulles and Adenauer, whose political agreement had been clear since the first state visit of the *Bundeskanzler* to the USA at the beginning of April 1953, at first blocked all Churchill's initiatives. Only when the phase of comprehensive Soviet willingness to negotiate had come to an end with the events of 17 June did Dulles prove prepared, at a conference of the three Western foreign ministers held in Washington from 10 to 14 July 1953, to agree to the suggestion of a Four-Power conference of foreign ministers for 'discussion' of the German question — by no means to sacrifice the EDC, but rather to demonstrate to the British the impossibility of an understanding with the Soviet Union and to play off Soviet conduct on 17 June against Soviet reunification propaganda. The Soviet leadership, whom in the meantime it no longer suited to make an unequivocal declaration of its position on Germany, responded with an ambiguously worded reiteration of all its previous plans for Germany, which was consequently immediately rejected by the Western powers. With the intention of making an arrangement with France for a solution to the Indo-China problem, they additionally called for an extension of the conference agenda to include all problems of the East–West conflict and the inclusion of China as a conference participant. The last point was acceptable to the British government, which had given diplomatic recognition to Mao Tse Tung's regime in 1950, but was not to the American government, which still saw in an upgrading of Peking only a dangerous strengthening of Moscow. After months of plotting on all sides, Churchill finally managed to achieve a minimum compromise: a conference of foreign ministers of the Soviet Union and the three Western powers (not a summit conference of heads of government) would take place, with the themes of Germany and Austria without greater specification of the agenda, although with the possibility towards the end of consulting on a proposal for a possible conference of Five with China on Korea and Indo-China.

In Berlin, where the four foreign ministers finally met from 25 January to 18 February,[25] each side presented its maximum position in relation to German policy, without showing any willingness to make substantial concessions. Eden, the British Foreign Secretary, and Bidault, his French counterpart, were — in spite of all hopes for a general *détente* — not prepared to take on the risk of a neutralised, united Germany. Western negotiation proposals, condensed into the so-called Eden Plan, thus fell entirely within the guidelines of Dulles and Adenauer: free elections were to take place in the whole of Germany as a first step to the settlement of a peace treaty with the co-operation of the freely elected all-German government, as well as the freedom of this future government not only to take over the international rights and duties of the FRG and the GDR, but also to reject them — in other words, the opportunity to integrate the whole of Germany into NATO and the EDC. By contrast with this, Malenkov called not only for guarantees for the lasting neutrality of Germany, but also the transferring of responsibility for the elections to a 'provisional all-German government' to be composed of the parliaments of the FRG and the GDR 'with the broad participation of democratic organisations', and the conclusion of a collective security treaty for the whole of Europe at which the USA was to have only observer status — as was China.[26] The outcome of the conference was thus simply an entrenchment of positions on both sides, or more precisely a strengthening of those of Dulles and Adenauer on German policy, and the reinforcement of the regime of the GDR in the Soviet power zone.

Only in one respect did the conference produce a positive result: the four foreign ministers agreed on the calling of a conference in Geneva on 26 April 1954 on Korea and Indo-China to which, in addition to other 'interested states', the People's Republic of China was also to be invited. Since the beginning of 1953, French governments had been trying to internationalise the Indo-China war, which was costing France more and more energy — that is, either to make it a Western campaign financed by the USA in order to achieve a decisive military breakthrough, or to find an internationally supported peace settlement which would permit France to withdraw from military engagement without great loss of face. In view of this, Dulles, in the interests of an early return of French troops to the European continent and in the hope of French ratification of the EDC in return, had raised the level of US financial commitment to the French campaign, although he refused a US military intervention out of regard for Congress, which was determined to save money, and also out of fear of a direct Chinese intervention. The Soviet offer of mediation, made by Molotov to Bidault on the eve of the Berlin conference, was thus very welcome to the French government, and since at that moment a dramatic deterioration in the French position in Indo-China was in the offing, Dulles had no choice but to yield to the pressure of his West European Allies and agree to negotiations at least in principle.[27]

None the less there was serious tension between the USA and its European Allies in subsequent weeks. On the one hand, Dulles and Eisenhower warned of the consequence of a Western withdrawal from Indo-China, but, on the other, they refused to come to the aid of the main French forces, which numbered 10,000 men and were surrounded near Dien Bien Phu, 300 km from Hanoi, with a massive bombardment from the air, as the French government was ever more urgently demanding in order to improve its negotiating position for Geneva. Dien Bien Phu thus fell to North Vietnamese troops on 7 May. The French position at the Indo-China conference, which was meanwhile under way, was further weakened by Eisenhower's public declaration on 10 June that he did not intend to ask Congress to approve an American bombardment. When as a result of these events the Laniel–Bidault government in Paris collapsed and Pierre Mendès-France, a long-standing critic of French Indo-China policy, took over the office of Prime Minister, Dulles, out of fear of a negotiated solution that unilaterally sacrificed Western interests, did not want to send his chief negotiator Bedell Smith, who had been recalled to Washington for consultation, back to the negotiating table. The fact that during the night of 21 July a settlement of the Indo-China problem, precisely in accordance with what the American and British governments had regarded as an acceptable solution, emerged at all, bordered under these circumstances on a political miracle. Eden, who regarded a continuation of the conflict as being as catastrophic as a split among the Western negotiating partners, mediated between Dulles and Mendès-France. Molotov, who received no assurances from Mendès-France on the EDC question, but who could nevertheless only expect from a continuation of the conflict an even firmer reliance of France on the USA,[28] urged Ho Chi Minh to be compliant. Even Chou en Lai the Chinese Prime Minister, who still did not want to rule out completely the possibility of

277

American intervention, denied the North Vietnamese unconditional support. The result was a division of Vietnam along the 17th parallel — that is, closer to the 18th parallel, which the French had first demanded as a demarcation line, than the 13th parallel, which had formed the basis of North Vietnamese demands. Additionally, in an unsigned concluding declaration, free elections for the reunification of the country were announced for July 1956.

Mendès-France, who in spite of American suspicions to the contrary was not prepared to permit a weakening of the Western position in Indo-China beyond the militarily inevitable level, now immediately called on the American government to take part in a protection of South Vietnam from possible aggression from the North. To crown the degree of contradiction in American Indo-China policy, Dulles responded not only with a proposal for a South-East Asian defence treaty against Communist expansion (which came into being on 8 September 1954 with the Treaty of Manila), but also with the despatching of American military and advisers to South Vietnam, who shortly entirely replaced their French colleagues and soon intervened in the fate of the country even more markedly than before. In the meantime, however, a rift occurred in Franco-American relations which could no longer be patched up even by the mutually firm conviction of the necessity for containing 'Communism'.

By the middle of 1954, the Soviet *détente* offensive had not in effect led to the originally hoped-for revision of bloc formation in Central Europe, but, on the contrary, to the strengthening and consolidation of those relations which had been created since the beginning of the division process in East and West, and which the majority of decision-makers on both sides were not prepared to disturb. Not least due to the reluctant co-operation of the American government, the contradictions remaining between the Western powers had emerged in even starker relief, a further concentration of Western forces under American leadership consequently seeming increasingly less likely. Long after the expansion of the Soviet sphere of influence, the American capacity for expansion had also reached its limits, thus creating the conditions in which a certain equilibrium could be reached between the two blocs — a balance which facilitated the reduction of tension on both sides, as long as the essential security interests of one or the other were not thereby disturbed. This shift in the character of East–West relations was nevertheless not perceived by all those involved: it was to take some time for them to adjust their political course accordingly.

Notes

1. At the end of 1950, in conversation with the Italian Communist leaders Togliatti, Longo and Secchia, Stalin described the world situation as 'serious', 'tense' and 'perilous'; their committee colleague Giorgio Amendola reports from this conversation the view was held 'that the Cold War was heading both internally and externally for a parting of the ways (...) The hypothesis of a general conflict no longer appeared to be something plucked from thin air.' Documented in *Osteuropa-Archiv* 20 (1970), pp. A703–18.

2. Published with the corresponding Western notes of reply *inter alia* in Eberhard Jäckel (ed), *Die Deutsche Frage 1952–1956, Notenwechsel und Konferenzdokumente der vier Mächte*, (Frankfurt, 1957). The notes have been as controversially discussed in recent historical literature as among the contemporary public. 'Traditional' authors see in the Soviet initiative simply an attempt to wreck the founding of the EDC by encouraging internal Western conflicts; thus amongst others Gerhard Wettig, *Entmilitisierung und Wiederbewaffnung in Deutschland 1943–1955*, (Munich 1967), pp. 497–522; by the same author 'Die sowjetischen Deutschland-Noten vom 10. März 1952', in: *Deutschland-Archiv* 15 (1982), pp. 130–48; Hermann Graml, 'Nationalstaat oder westdeutscher Teilstaat. Die sowjetischen Noten vom Jahre 1952 und die öffentliche Meinung in der Bundesrepublik Deutschland', in: *Vierteljahrshefte für Zeitgeschichte* 25 (1977), pp. 821–64; by the same author 'Die Legende von der verpaßten Gelegenheit', in *Vierteljahrshefte für Zeitgeschichte* 29 (1981), pp. 307–41. By contrast with this, Klaus Erdmenger, *Das folgenschwere Mißverständnis. Bonn und die sowjetische Deutschlandpolitik 1949–1955*, (Freiburg 1967), pp. 132–61, and Gerd Meyer, *Die sowjetische Deutschlandpolitik im Jahre 1952* (Tübingen 1970), emphasise with differing evaluations of Soviet motives the seriousness of the negotiation proposal. Rolf Steininger, *Eine vertane Chance. Die Stalin Note vom 10. März 1952 und die Wiedervereinigung* (Berlin/Bonn, 1985) offers additional evidence for the second thesis, particularly the account of a conversation on 26 July 1952 between Stalin and the Italian Socialist leader Pietro Nenni. After this, the Soviet leadership was apparently in the first note 'really prepared to make sacrifices in order to achieve reunification'.

3. The idea that the essential forces of the Federal Republic were to be kept from political power, as Meyer assumes in his scenario for the right wing and perhaps even the centre parties of the former government coalition (CDU/CSU, FDP, DP) (p. 78), which attaches too much importance in general to the ideological, propagandist statements of East German rulers, can be regarded as excluded from the procedure proposed by the Soviet government. The Soviets could not seriously suppose that the political leadership of the Federal Republic would sign its own death warrant.

4. 'The question arises, what guarantees are there that Germany

and Japan will not rise to their feet again, that they will not try to break free from American servitude and to lead an independent life? I think there are no such guarantees', Joseph W. Stalin, *Ökonomische Probleme des Sozialismus in der UdSSR*, (Berlin (East), 1952), p. 36. Whether Stalin is referring here to the 'Germany' of the Federal Republic or a unified Germany in the sense of the notes is disputed, but in the context of the argument presented here this is not crucial.

5. In contrast with Graml, *Nationalstaat oder westdeutscher Teilstaat*, pp. 830–840, I see precisely in this lack of attractiveness evidence of the seriousness of the Soviet proposals: merely a show offer for propaganda purposes which remained unbinding could have been formulated in a more appealing way. The forbidding wording observed by Graml in the notes in the DDR commentaries seems to have been a concealed attempt to take the edge off the Soviet initiative.

6. See below, pp. 268–73.

7. The emphasised motive, overestimated, however, as the virtually exclusive motive for the shift in Germany policy in Ernst Nolte, *Deutschland und der Kalte Krieg*, (Munich, 1974), pp. 294f. and 341–4.

8. Thus, Wettig, and Graml respectively. If one takes the Soviet interests of the time into account, this can obviously not have been the *only* purpose of the initiative. The fact that at the point of the Soviet offer Germany was already irrevocably divided had been realised by virtually no-one at the time. Such perspicacity cannot, therefore, be attributed to Stalin and taken as proof of the purely propagandist character of the proposal, as it is by Graml, *Nationalstaat oder westdeutscher Teilstaat*, pp. 830f.

9. See Erdmenger, *Mißverständnis*, and Klaus von Schubert, *Wiederbewaffnung und Westintegration*, 2nd ed., (Stuttgart, 1972), *passim*; Nolte, *Deutschland*, pp. 289–330; Hans-Adolf Jacobsen, 'Zur Rolle der öffentlichen Meinung bei der Debatte um die Wiederbewaffnung 1950–1955', in: *Aspekte der deutschen Wiederbewaffnung bis 1955* (Boppard, 1975), pp. 61–117; Graml, *Nationalstaat*, pp. 845–64; and Knud Dittman, *Adenauer und die deutsche Wiedervereinigung. Die politische Diskussion des Jahres 1952*, (Düsseldorf, 1981).

10. On this see also Udo F. Löwke, *'Für den Fall, daß ...' SPD und Wehrfrage 1949–1955*, (Hanover, 1969); by the same author, *Der SPD und die Wehrfrage 1949–1955*, (Bonn-Bad Godesberg, 1976); Kurt Thomas Schmitz, *Deutsche Einheit und Europäische Integration, Der sozialdemokratische Beitrag zur Außenpolitik der Bundesrepublik Deutschland unter besonderer Berücksichtigung des programmatischen Wandels einer Oppositionspartei*, (Bonn-Bad Godesberg, 1978), pp. 61–118.

11. On this Dietrich Wagner, *FDP und Wiederbewaffnung. Die wehrpolitische Orientierung der Liberalen in der Bundesrepublik Deutschland 1949–1955*, (Boppard, 1978).

12. As well as Graml, *Nationalstaat*, see also Andreas Hillgruber, 'Adenauer und die Stalin-note vom 10, März 1952', in Dieter Blumenwitz et al, (eds), *Konrad Adenauer und seine Zeit*, vol. 2: *Beiträge der Wissenschaft*, (Stuttgart, 1976), pp. 111–30.

13. This being a substantial finding by Graml, *Nationalstaat*.

14. See on this now the impressive documented edition of Rolf Steininger (ed), *Eine Chance zur Wiedervereinigung? Die Stalin–Note vom 10.*

März 1952, (Berlin/Bonn, 1985) p. 297.

15. See Adam B. Ulam, *Stalin Koloß der Macht*, (Esslingen, 1977), pp. 677–694.

16. On this and the following see Hans Wassmund, *Kontinuität im Wandel. Bestimmungsfaktoren sowjetischer Deutschlandpolitik in der Nach-Stalin-Zeit*, (Cologne, Vienna, 1974); Arnulf Baring, *Der 17. Juni 1953*, (Cologne, Berlin, 1965); Wettig, *Entmilitarisierung*, pp. 620–34; Ilse Spittman and Karl Wilhelm Fricke (eds), *17. Juni 1953. Arbeiteraufstand in der DDR*, (Cologne, 1982).

17. *Pravda*, 10 March 1953, quoted after Wettig, *Entmilitarisierung*, p. 620.

18. Speech of 8 March 1963, quoted after *Neues Deutschland*, 14 March 1963.

19. *Neues Deutschland*, 11 June 1953.

20. Speech of 16 April 1953, in *Europa-Archiv* 8 (1953), pp. 5731–34.

21. Text of the note in Jäckel, *Die deutsche Frage*, pp. 43–6.

22. Communiqué and proceedings in *Europa-Archiv* 8 (1953), pp. 5973ff.

23. Seminal on the connection between internal policy and détente initiatives in the post-Stalin era, if also in many ways unmethodical, is Wassmund, *Kontinuität im Wandel*.

24. See Josef Foschepoth, 'Churchill, Adenauer und die Neutralisierung Deutschlands', in *Deutschland-Archiv* 12 (1984), pp. 1286–1301; Rolf Steininger, 'Ein vereintes, unabhängiges Deutschland? Winston Churchill, der Kalte Krieg und die deutsche Frage im Jahre 1983', in: *Militärgeschichtliche Mitteilungen* 34 (1984), pp. 105–44.

25. The most complete documentation on the conference so far is in the *Europa-Archiv* 9 (1954); pp. 6372ff. (on the course of the conference); pp. 6489ff (on the European security problem) and pp. 6526ff. (draft treaties); 'Aufschlußreiche Gespräche am Rande der offiziellen Sitzungen dokumentiert Hermann-Josef Rupieper, Die Berliner Außenministerkonferenz von 1954', in: *Vierteljahrshefte für Zeitgeschichte* 34 (1986), pp. 427–53. Illuminating talks on the eve of the official sittings are documented by Hermann-Josef Rupieper. 'Die Berliner Außenministerkonferenz von 1954', in: *Vierteljahrshefte für Zeitgeschichte* 34 (1986), pp. 427–53.

26. Responsibility for the failure of détente attempts during this phase of East–West relations cannot be attributed solely to the Soviet side (Wettig, *Entmilitarisierung*, pp. 635f.) any more than solely to the American side (Joyce and Gabriel Kolko, *The limits of power*, (New York, 1972), pp. 701–704).

27. Basic reading on this and the following is Philippe Devillers and Jean Lacouture, *Vietnam: de la guerre française à la guerre américaine*, (Paris, 1969), also Georgette Elgey, *Histoire de la IV République*, vol. 2; *La République des contradictions 1951–1954*, (Paris, 1968), pp. 473–550; Bernard Fall, *Dien-Bien-Phuh. Un coin d'enfer* (Paris, 1968).

28. Not, however, further complaisance towards the Soviet Union, as Ulam, *Rivals*, pp. 215f. asserts, consequently underestimating the Soviet role in the emergence of the Indochina Agreement and overestimating the Chinese role.

13

The Ratification of Bloc Formation

The tensions between the Western Allies, unleashed by the convergence of the economic upswing in Western Europe, Soviet *détente* initiatives, the creation of a Soviet arsenal of hydrogen bombs, and the change-over of the USA to a strategy of 'massive retaliation', and which had first manifested themselves in the tussle over the project of a Four-Power conference and the settlement of the Indo-China problem, only emerged with full force in the conflict over the EDC. Conceived at a time when the European states were economically weak, the Soviet Union was seen as militarily aggressive, and the most urgent security problem for West Europeans appeared to be the strengthening of conventional armaments. The EDC project no longer answered to the same extent the interests of all those involved under these changed circumstances, and was thus looked upon with increasing antagonism by both supporters and opponents. Since under changed conditions the relationship of the Western powers among themselves needed to be rearranged, a protracted struggle developed in connection with the EDC project. Outstanding decisions on future priorities in both Soviet Germany and Western policy depended on the outcome of this struggle.

The collapse of the EDC

Although it had been proposed by the French government in October 1950 and implemented against the initial resistance of the other Allies, the EDC project in time encountered the stiffest resistance in France itself.[1] Behind the French proposal were from the outset not only convinced Europeans, who saw in the

EDC a decisive step towards realising the concept of integration, as well as committed anti-Communists, who regarded a German defence contribution as inevitable out of fear of the Soviet Union, but also resigned proponents of the traditional French German policy, who hoped with the launching of the complex treaty project at first to prolong German rearmament, and later to prevent German equality in the form of integration. To the extent that German diplomacy succeeded in eliminating the discriminatory elements against the Federal Republic from the original French draft in the course of treaty negotiations, the majority in favour of the EDC treaty in France began to waver. When, subsequent to the signing of the treaty in the spring of 1952, world political conditions began gradually to change, the opponents of German rearmament (Communists and traditional right-wingers) and of its supranational form (Gaullists, those representing large portions of French industry) were joined by more and more supporters of an East–West *détente* policy, a policy of independence in relation to the USA and of a 'third-force' Europe. The Socialists, radical socialists and moderate right-wingers in particular, who had as a rule supported the foreign policy of the French government, fell into serious internal party disagreements over the EDC problem. For fear of a collapse in parliament the government protracted ratification, with the result that the prospects for an acceptance of the project became increasingly remote.

In order to render the set of agreements acceptable to a majority of the French parliament, or to shift the blame for a failure of the project onto the treaty partners, the government of René Mayer (among which were a number of independent Gaullists) called in February 1953 for agreement on a series of additional protocols, which were said to make the treaty more 'precise', but which in fact were intended to alter it substantially. France was thus to retain the right to decide freely how many soldiers to put at the disposal of the EDC, and how many were to be used in national overseas units. For the purposes of these national units, unrestricted national armaments production was to be retained. Joint mobilisation plans were to stay strictly limited to the sphere of European combat forces; national military schools were to continue. American allocations should only be made to the EDC, and not to individual member states (that is, not to the Federal Republic). From the British government, the Mayer government called for binding agreements on the stationing of strong British divisions on the continent for the duration of the EDC treaty and the transferral of responsibility for the use of these troops to the EDC. From the Federal German government, it called for agreement to the definitive integration of the Saarland into France as a precondition for ratification of the EDC treaty.

France's European partners, however, were not prepared to agree to these demands, partly because they did not believe French warnings of an opposed chamber majority, and partly because they saw the project endangered in their own countries in the event of deviation from the compromise reached in May 1952. Churchill was not willing to limit the British freedom to negotiate so extensively as was now being demanded of him by the French government. He committed himself solely to the close military co-operation of British European units with the EDC and to the consultation of the EDC countries prior to a withdrawal of British troops. The governments of Belgium, Italy and the Netherlands rejected the additional French demands out of fear of French dominance in the European community and out of justified concern at a negative reaction from the Federal Republic. The latter saw even less reason to agree to special French wishes, since the American protective power allowed no doubt to arise as to its interest in seeing the EDC coming about in its original form.

The American Administration under Dulles clung resolutely to the EDC — not only because it had meanwhile come to regard the project as the best form of Western defence organisation against the Soviet Union, and in view of its financial needs even hoped that a strong European defence community would one day be able to render the large-scale presence of American troops on European soil superfluous, but also because an integrated, supranational defence organisation seemed the best means of committing the West Europeans to them. The first signs of West European efforts towards *détente* made Dulles and those groups represented by him uneasy. British efforts towards an arrangement with the Soviet Union were seen as immoral and dangerous, while France with its strong Communist Party and unresolved colonial problem seemed liable to succumb to Soviet coercion; even the Federal Republic was suspected after the departure of Adenauer of possibly wanting to abandon its course towards Western integration. In the long term, therefore, not only East–West equilibrium seemed jeopardised by a failure of the EDC, but moreover the long-term political and economic influence of the USA in Western Europe. This explains why American commitment to the EDC became all the more stubborn the more that the EDC was questioned in Europe.

At the end of January 1953, only a week after entering office, Dulles had informed his European Allies that his government adhered to the EDC as the only possible form of German rearmament, and that a delay in its ratification would be bound to have repercussions on future American foreign aid, even on future American policy in general. On 13 December 1953, he announced in Paris a 'painful examination' of American European policy as a whole in the event of West European countries not uniting as a military, economic and political unit. In the course of the first half of 1954, he threatened more or less openly with the release of the Federal Republic into full national state sovereignty in the case of further procrastination over the treaty, and with a direct inclusion of the West Germans in NATO in the event of the treaty failing. On 29 August 1954, one day before the deciding vote in the French National Assembly, he went so far as to announce the possibility of an Eight-Power conference of West European states: the USA and Canada could consult on the settlement of the German defence contribution without the participation of France.

American coercive tactics, however, achieved the opposite of what was intended. The EDC appeared less and less as a freely chosen instrument for European self-determination, and more and more as a means dictated by the USA for pulling France into line with a Western world unilaterally aligned with American interests. The concern of 'right-wing' EDC opponents to avoid a sell-out of national interests, and fear on the part of 'left-wing' treaty opponents of an escalation of the East–West conflict were thus expressed in a vigorous anti-Americanism which fed daily on the conduct of the American ruling circles. Coercion on the matter of the EDC, the refusal to give military support to France in Indo-China, as well as the obstruction of a negotiated settlement to the Indo-China question, and the excesses of McCarthyism, the limited role of which belied the domestic political purpose — of Dulles's aggressive liberation rhetoric — all this led to increasing political conflations rejecting a united Europe. Encouraged by the USA, such a Europe seemed likely to be dominated by it, with the Federal Republic, France's long-time enemy, occupying the role of privileged partner within it. Reservations about the American leadership were further intensified when the American secret service staged the downfall in Iran in August 1953 of Mossadegh, the Iranian Prime Minister, who had dared to nationalise the oil deposits in his country, as well as when the Washington government had President Guzmán exiled from Guatemala in June 1954, after he had begun to expropriate the United Fruit Company. The majority of the French people now lined up in 1953–4 against this alleged Americanisation of France with the aid of the EDC, wanting to be sure that the power of military decision remained in their own country, being alarmed at the idea of too broad a political communalisation in Europe, as well as hoping to be able to restore the former 'greatness' of France with a policy of *rapprochement* between East and West.[2]

The fact that the EDC could no longer be brought about in its original form under these conditions is indicated (although contemporaries were not fully aware of it at the time) by the fate of the project for a European Political Community (EPC), which was intended in the first instance to secure the connection between the coal and steel industries and the EDC, and then to be developed into a supranational, political corporation along the lines of European federalism. In article 38 of the EDC treaty, the negotiating partners had aimed for the creation of such a political community as the logical consequence of military and (beginning with the coal and steel community) economic integration. Anticipating the coming into force of the EDC treaty, one of the *ad hoc* assemblies of the coal and steel community called into being by the parliamentary assembly and consisting of 75 European representatives had worked out between September 1952 and March 1953 a proposal on the EPC.[3] Although the *ad hoc* assembly had passed its draft on 10 March 1953 with 50 votes in favour and five abstentions (in the absence of the SPD representatives), it was not discussed further by the foreign ministers of the six partner states. No one was prepared to risk any longer taking the first step towards the political federalisation of Europe which could possibly prove to be the kiss of death to the EDC. A conference of foreign ministers set for 30 March 1954, which was to discuss the EPC project after all, was temporarily postponed a week before the start. Thereafter the EPC was never again a subject for official debate. Under the circumstances, no further efforts were necessary from Moscow in order to bring down the EDC. French EDC opponents naturally introduced the prospect for such an exchange deal into their line of argument and the Soviet leadership also showed its willingness to exert an appropriate influence on Vietminh, if France were to drop the EDC treaty. Nevertheless Molotov found neither in Bidault, the French Foreign Minister, nor in his successor and new Prime Minister, Pierre Mendès-France, a partner who would have been willing to enter into this proposal. The proposal likewise altered nothing in terms of internal French power relations. Mendès-France merely completed the cosmetic act of allowing the Soviet leadership to pay for something it basically already had: on the one hand, he announced the definitive clarification of the EDC question after the conclusion of the Geneva Indo-China conference; and on the other hand, he threatened to resign, if a satisfactory solution to the Indo-China question were not reached within few weeks, thus offering the Soviet side sufficient motivation to accept in Geneva a division of Vietnam that in no way corresponded to the military and political strength of Vietminh.

After the foreign affairs and defence committees of the French National Assembly had shown themselves on 9 and 18 June 1954, albeit with a small majority, to be against the ratification of the EDC treaty, Mendès-France, who had just become Prime Minister in the midst of the negotiating crisis of the Geneva Indo-China conference, decided to bring the EDC crisis to a head. By no means disposed to being anti-European, and ultimately convinced of the necessity for posting German troops within the framework of the Western defence alliance, he nevertheless had little sympathy for a supranational European community without Great Britain and with an anti-Soviet stance, and he was above all concerned to overcome the deep division that the EDC had created in France, which threatened to weaken the country in the long term.[4] When the Belgian Foreign Minister, Spaak, in accordance with an arrangement with Dulles, urged at the end of June a fresh foreign ministers' conference of the six negotiating partners to clarify the French position on the EDC, Mendès-France thus presented, like René Mayer before him, additional demands for modification of the treaty, but was prepared, in the case of a rejection of the modifications, to leave the set of agreements to its parliamentary fate — as long as the guarantee remained that France would not lose all influence on the arrangement of German rearmament.

The modification proposals presented by Mendès-France to his cabinet on 13 August envisaged, in particular, a suspension of the supranational elements of the treaty for a period of eight years.[5] Important decisions were only to be possible at NATO level, not at the level of the EDC; member states were to have a right of veto against the decisions of the EDC Commissariat; the envisaged election of a European Parliament and the creation of the EPC were to be dropped. Besides this, NATO and the EDC were to support each other more; their terms (hitherto 20 years for NATO and 50 years for the EDC) should be balanced out; Great Britain was to take part in the sittings of the EDC Council of Ministers as soon as questions of mutual co-operation were to be discussed and a future revision of the treaty could be jointly discussed; American and British fighting forces on German soil were to be included in the integration of EDC units; as soon as these commitments of remaining NATO partners failed to be kept or Germany was reunited, every EDC member was to have the right to leave the community. Finally, the Federal Republic was again to accept unilateral discrimination: only the fighting forces stationed on its territory were to be integrated; the manufacture of heavy war materials, including nuclear production, was not to be permitted on its territory, whereas it was to be permitted in France, even if the materials were not to be distributed there; the expansion of troops in the Federal Republic was to take place under European direction for at least the first four years. Mendès-France was fully aware that it would be difficult to win the negotiating partners over to such far-reaching modifications after the ratification process had already been completed in the Federal Republic and the Benelux countries. On the other hand, he did not exclude the possibility of success, and above all saw no other chance of winning back the majority in France which had previously backed the original Pleven Plan. He also hoped with these modifications to be able to spur Great Britain into entering the EDC, and possibly within the eight-year trial period to achieve a far-reaching East–West *détente* of such a kind that the treaty agreements as a whole would lose their point.

The rejection of the French proposals, however, was much harsher than Mendès-France had feared; French EDC supporters such as Robert Schuman, André Philip and Guy Mollet made it abundantly and publicly clear to the negotiating partners that they rejected the modification proposals, and that these proposals were therefore much less capable of carrying a majority in parliament than the original EDC treaty. Dulles, who was now more prepared to risk a collapse of the EDC than a further postponement of German rearmament, urged the Five through his special emissary Bruce not to make any concessions. The Five, especially Adenauer, were fundamentally suspicious of the intentions of the new French Prime Minister, who did not yet belong to the 'European circle', and allowed themselves to be persuaded by French proponents of the EDC that a majority for the original treaty could still be carried. In Brussels, where the foreign ministers of the Six finally met from 19 to 22 August, France's negotiating partners only proved willing to be consulted on secondary issues, such as on the question of the adjustment of the EDC and NATO treaty terms, or in connection with the suspension of the community regulations for the internal structure of EDC troop units, but not on the finality of a supranational political community, and certainly not on discrimination against the Federal Republic. They conceded that the EDC was not to make any political decisions, and also a veto right, although this was only to occur in the case of the Council of Ministers previously determining the existence of a 'vital' interest. The conference was broken off without the Six establishing more than their lack of agreement.

Churchill provided the final impetus for the collapse of the EDC; sought out by Mendès-France directly after the Brussels conference, he urged the latter to do everything in his power to carry the EDC treaty through the French parliament after all. Mendès-France, however, omitted from his statements that in the event of the failure of the EDC the British government would instigate another attempt to reach an agreement with France on German rearmament.[6] After the danger thereby seemed to be reduced of a fresh arrangement being reached without consultation with the French, Mendès-France worked with renewed vigour towards the failure of the treaties, not leaving the French public in the dark as to the isolation and 'humiliation' of France at the Brussels conference and avoiding a definite statement on the treaty agreements in parliament. The fate of the EDC was thus sealed. When the committee spokesmen and the Prime Minister presented their reports to the French National Assembly on 28 and 29 August, it soon became clear to EDC supporters that they no longer had a majority behind them, and they thus aimed for a postponement of the debate; a majority of 319 against 264 representatives, however, refused on 30 August to enter into any discussion of the treaty at all. The number of treaty opponents was even greater, some of them wanting at least to permit a parliamentary division over the EDC.

The Paris Treaties

Western bloc formation reached its limits with the collapse of the EDC. The West European states obviously did not (yet) permit themselves to merge with one another and become subordinated to American hegemony to the extent that would have been in the interests of a true offensive policy of strength. The Soviet *détente* offensive had achieved an initial victory, and Dulles and Adenauer had been obliged to accept bitter defeat. The concept of German reunification in the sense of an annexation of the Eastern territories to Western Germany now wholly lost all realistic political basis, whilst the idea of European unity lost much of its former fascination — so much so that with the EDC even the idea of a 'third-force' Europe was lost to memory, the realisation of independence from the USA being sought only in the much less effective form of national state independence. The more far-reaching fears associated by EDC supporters with a failure of the project did not prove justified. The USA did not reach an understanding with the Federal Republic at France's expense, nor with the Soviet Union at the expense of the Federal Republic, nor did the West European nations return to the old rivalries of the interwar years, nor reach an understanding with the Soviet Union at the expense of the USA. On the contrary, the crisis triggered by the failure of the EDC made it clear to all involved that apart from the special ambitions of the USA, France and the Federal Republic there was a basic level of common 'Western' interest. Since, moreover, none of those involved could afford to damage these interests, agreement on a substitute for the EDC solution to German rearmament was reached remarkably quickly.

The fact that the Western powers immediately agreed on a solution that overlooked none of the participants was due in the first instance to Adenauer. Whilst the French as well as the British and American governments now at first wanted to offer the Federal Republic the early implementation of the general treaty without the EDC treaty, Adenauer rejected all separation of the sovereignty and rearmament questions, calling instead for the direct guaranteeing of sovereignty, including military sovereignty, and thus compelled the Allies to accept both a completely new and a swift solution extending beyond previous treaties.[7] The idea for this solution, which now had to come under Adenauer's pressure in the first weeks of September 1954, emerged from the contact between Eden and Mendès-France.[8] It consisted of reactivating the Brussels Treaty of 1948 by inviting the participation of the Federal Republic and Italy, and transferring the security decisions envisaged in the framework of the EDC treaty, in so far as this was possible without the introduction of supranational elements, to the thus extended Five-Power treaty. In this way, although the treaty guarantees against a resurgence of German militarism were more limited, the French were no longer expected to accept *both* German rearmament and their own renunciation of sovereignty, and above all France now had Great Britain on its side within the alliance to balance out a possible top-heavy German influence.

A number of concessions were necessary before this solution was to appear acceptable to all those involved, and these were often made only after dramatic disagreements: Mendès-France accepted after a visit from Eden on 16 September the principle of the membership of the Federal Rpublic in NATO (beyond the Brussels Treaty); on the same day, Adenauer persuaded Dulles, who had hastened to Bonn on a lightning visit, that the Brussels Treaty solution contained the maximum which was at that time attainable in terms of European integration, thus diverting him from continuing to foil the plan as an attempt to neutralise Europe. Dulles then agreed to a conference on the new proposed solution, at which (the London Nine-Power conference from 28 September to 3 October) he extended the guarantee for American troop presence which had been valid for the EDC to the new 'West European Union' (WEU). Eden likewise guaranteed not to withdraw troops from the continent against the will of the majority of the WEU, whilst Adenauer relinquished at the last minute the right of the Federal Republic to manufacture ABC (advanced ballistic) weapons, guided missiles, large warships and bombers. The way was thus now open for the signing of the 'Paris Treaties' on 23 October 1954; a protocol on the lifting of the occupation statute for the Federal Republic; a revised general treaty which emphasised the sovereignty of the Federal Republic more strongly than the Bonn Treaty of 1952 and which scrapped the 'binding clause' of Article 7 for a reunited Germany; an agreement on the extension of the Brussels Treaty into the West European Union; a resolution of the NATO Council of Ministers to accept the Federal Republic and to increase the competence of NATO Commanders-in-Chief; and finally a protocol on voluntary arms limitation to which the Federal Republic acquiesced.[9]

In order to secure an adequate majority for the treaty agreements in the French parliament, Mendès-France had made two further requests: the definitive recognition of a politically autonomous Saarland economically linked with France and the creation of a *de facto* supranational arms agency of the WEU to decide on the distribution of American arms supplies and the investment of the European armaments industry. On the first issue, Mendès-France largely had his way: in order not to jeopardise the WEU solution, Adenauer agreed in the concluding negotiations in Paris (from 19 to 23 October) to a Saar statute transferring foreign-policy jurisdiction to a Commissioner of the WEU and which transferred monetary and economic links of the Saarland to France — not indefinitely, however, but only until final settlement in a peace treaty, this being the major concession which Adenauer managed to achieve. Clearly this was rather a hypothetical proviso: although Adenauer could be certain that time would work in his favour for a solution more in the Federal German interest, a peace treaty was still far from being in the offing. (No one could have foreseen that the referendum of the Saar population carried out by Mendès-France on this statute, in order to give the envisaged solution a lasting character, would lead to the opposite outcome.) In fact on 25 October 1955, 67.7 per cent of Saarlanders rejected the statute decided on in Paris, and since the position of the Federal Republic had in the meantime become more secure, and Franco-German relations had at the same time become more relaxed, Adenauer was able on 5 June 1956 to obtain the agreement of Mollet's government to the annexation of the Saarland to the Federal Republic, in return for a number of financial compensations.

On the question of the armaments agency, Mendès-France at first obtained Adenauer's agreement, to whom it seemed after all to salvage a vestige of European supranationality. The smaller European partners, however, immediately opposed the project, assuming — rightly! — that the British government would never submit to the arms control envisaged, which would thus lead to French dominance of the arms sector. The American government also made it clear that it was not willing to be deprived of jurisdiction over the distribution of its arms supplies by a European authority. Nevertheless the Allies did not reject this unusual demand of the French outright, but postponed it until the extra conference, which had been called in Paris for 17 January 1955 — this was early enough to demonstrate to the French public their interest in French wishes for arms control, and late enough not to endanger the ratification of the WEU treaty package in the Paris parliament in the event of a negative outcome of the negotiations. After the French National Assembly had approved the WEU on 30 December 1954 with 287 votes to 260 (with 79 abstentions), the market economy-oriented group, which had a pragmatic approach to foreign policy and was led by Erhard, the Minister for Economic Affairs, began to prevail within the Adenauer Administration, opposing the arms authority as an encroachment on freedom of enterprise. As leader of the delegation in Paris, Erhard sought to protract the problem, and when the French Council of the Republic also ratified the treaty agreements on 28 March 1955 (with 184 votes to 110), the WEU Council agreed on 7 May to the creation of a 'standing arms committee' to be entrusted with the task of consulting with member states on questions of arms standardisation and production. The French demand was thereby turned down, although in a way which successfully aimed at not injuring French national feeling once again, as before 30 August 1954.

In the meantime, however, the treaty agreements had to undergo one more serious crisis in the Federal Republic, where opponents to Western integration were becoming increasingly radicalised as the final contractual securing of the West German defence contribution drew near. Not only did the SPD attack the Paris Treaties and demand another Four-Power conference on reunification before definitive inclusion in the Western bloc, vigorously backed by a fresh round of notes from the Soviet government, which declared such a conference represented the last chance for German reunification: more decisive even than this was the fact that towards the end of 1954 an extra-parliamentary resistance movement against the Western integration policy now formed. The federal congress of the German Trade Unions (FGTU) turned against the incorporation of the Federal Republic into the Western alliance system, and the Federal Youth Conference of the FGTU in addition categorically rejected any form of rearmament, whilst among social groups linked with the SPD and the FGTU referenda and strikes against the passing of the Paris Treaty agreements were increasingly being demanded. In order not to lose control entirely of this movement, the SPD and the FGTU leadership placed themselves at its head. With their co-operation, a manifesto was passed on 29 January 1955 in St Paul's Church in Frankfurt by leading anti-rearmament people, who saw in the Paris Treaties a blow against the 'right of reunification'. In the weeks that followed, the Federal government found so much support that it was in danger of slipping into serious difficulties, if the SPD and FGTU had decided to call a general strike. Ultimately they did not do this alone, however — out of respect for the parliamentary decision process, for fear of lasting disturbance to the reconstruction process, due to a disinclination to have the GDR leadership as an ally, and because they themselves had no clear alternative concept at their disposal after the rejection of neutralism.[10] The St Paul's Church movement thus collapsed as a result of its own internal contradictions, and the German *Bundestag* ratified the Paris Treaties on 27 February 1955 with a safe majority. When the treaties came into effect on 5 May, the Federal Republic acquired sovereignty, and four days later took part for the first time in a NATO session.

The effect of the crisis triggered by the collapse of the EDC was thus a fundamental consolidation of the Western camp. The West Germans decided once again with an even larger majority (an overwhelming one, if one adds those who were undecided) in favour of Western integration; the French struggled their way through with an equally large majority to recognition of the existence of a virtually sovereign West German state as a consequence of bloc formation; the British and the Americans intensified their interest in lasting ties with Western Europe. All these decisions were made in spite of the Soviet Union continuing its *détente* offensive, proving not only the vigour of the basic anti-Communist consensus in Western societies, but also the strength of those social and economic interests that had meanwhile adjusted themselves to the structures of the Cold War. As the fate of the EDC had shown, there certainly remained a whole range of tensions and contradictions within the Western camp, but precisely because there was now no attempt to overcome them in accordance with a unified schema, the structure of internal Western relations discovered through the WEU acquired a lasting character.

The founding of the Warsaw Pact

The Soviet leadership was unable to offer any further significant resistance to this completion of the Western bloc's formation. It did continue its *détente* offensive: on 24 July 1954, a few days after the conclusion of the Geneva Indo-China conference, it offered the Western powers another all-European security conference, at which the peaceful coexistence and economic co-operation of the European states, without regard to differences in their social systems, were to be secured by means of a treaty into a collective security system.[11] Fresh negotiations of the four Allied foreign ministers on the German question in preparation for this conference were similarly motivated. Their proposals at this time nevertheless remained remarkably imprecise and open in terms of content: the USA was invited to the security conference, but was evidently not to be directly involved in the security system itself; the prospects for a united Germany within this system were upheld, but the FRG and the GDR were at first to be equally involved in its creation. These proposals were probably aimed at bringing the EDC to an indirect collapse through the removal of Western fears, but were not enough fundamentally to threaten the basic Western consensus. After the failure of the EDC, every attempt to deepen the crisis of the Western alliance system by means of attractive *détente* offers was discontinued. The three Western powers were able unanimously to reject the Soviet offer of 10 September with the comment that the Austrian state treaty must first be signed, free elections held in the whole of Germany and concessions be forthcoming on the arms question.

The fact that the Soviet leadership lost a chance to weaken the Western alliance at the moment of failure of the EDC can be traced to internal Soviet power struggles. After the demise of Beria, neither Malenkov nor Khrushchev, the state bureaucracy nor the party apparatus could afford risky foreign policy initiatives affecting the interests of noteworthy groups in Moscow or East Berlin. By the middle of August 1954, Khrushchev had been able to score important partial successes — his Virgin Lands programme was intensified at the expense of other investment areas, and the party attained general predominance over the state authorities. In order to secure his rise, however, he had become more dependent on the dogmatic party circles around Molotov, who were for fundamental reasons distrustful of an arrangement with the Western powers. He likewise had to obtain the loyalty of the army and of heavy industry, who hoped for growth rates in armaments from his policy. The position of Malenkov, who had committed himself more unequivocally than Khrushchev to a dismantling of the military blocs subsequent to the nuclear 'balance of horror', was further weakened when the Western powers reached a surprisingly swift agreement on an alternative to the failed EDC solution — with the result that Khrushchev was increasingly able to formulate the offers to the Western side that Malenkov had previously lacked to confirm the success of his policy. On 23 October, the day the Paris Treaties were signed, the Soviet government reiterated its call for the working out of a collective security treaty for Europe; this time, however, it was linked with an offer with regard to the procedure for free elections in Germany, namely that Soviet delegates wished to 'discuss' the Eden Plan presented by the Western powers at the Berlin conference in January 1954. On 13 November, they invited 23 European states and the USA to a conference on collective security (at which, however, only representatives from the Eastern bloc countries met in Moscow from 29 November to 2 December). On 15 January 1955, the Federal Republic was again offered an agreement 'on the holding of all-German free elections', it being indicated this time, in addition to previous offers, that they could agree 'on the setting-up of appropriate international observation'.[12] These offers came too late, however, to cause any serious disturbance to the consolidation process of the Western bloc; by the time the Soviet leadership formulated its hitherto furthest-reaching concession with the intimation of the international control of all-German elections, the Paris Treaties had already overcome the decisive hurdle in the French National Assembly.

After the failure to prevent the rearmament of the Federal Republic, advocates of a stabilisation of GDR hegemony were finally able to have their way. Ten days after the declaration of 15 January, which for its part had already conspicuously intoned the 'good relations' between the Soviet Union and the GDR, and had made the establishment of an international system of supervision for the holding of free elections independent of the consent of the 'governments of the German Democratic Republic and the German Federal Republic', the Presidium of the Supreme Soviet declared the 'state of war between the Soviet Union and Germany' to be 'at an end', and the propaganda for the all-German plans of the Soviet leadership was adjusted accordingly. On 8 February, Malenkov resigned from the office of Prime Minister, without however, losing his seat in the Party Presidium. Bulganin was his successor — a concession of Khrushchev to the military. During the following weeks, bilateral relations between the GDR and the Soviet Union were intensified, the integration of the GDR into the Eastern bloc system was pushed ahead, and the upgrading of its international position was encouraged.

Détente over the German question was in future only to be possible on the basis of international recognition of the SED leadership, indicating the degree to which GDR proponents had prevailed with Khrushchev.

Closely linked with the consolidation of SED rule were the efforts of the new leading circle around Khrushchev to place relations with the East European satellite states on a permanent footing. Under Stalin, the Soviet system of control over the East European regimes had ultimately rested on informal ties between the dictator and national Communist leaders and on the principle of divide and rule. Such methods could no longer be maintained under a collectively determined Soviet leadership, and as soon as internal Soviet power struggles had become less explosive, Khrushchev set out to reorganise the Eastern bloc. One means to this end was to grant somewhat greater political autonomy to East European Communist leaders in order to strengthen their position in their respective countries and to enable their ties with the Soviet Union to appear more tolerable. The unilateral alignment of East European economies was dropped and a degree of flexibility permitted in the formulation of respective national 'Roads to Socialism', whilst recommending the adoption of the diversification in production which had taken place in the Soviet Union. Another means was the institutionalisation of bloc formation, which was implemented by using the rearmament of the Federal Republic as an impetus for mobilising the continuing fear of the German threat among East Europeans, notably the Poles and Czechs, for the creation of a collective military alliance of the Eastern bloc. In the final communiqué of the Moscow security conference, the Eastern bloc countries announced on 2 December 1954 'joint measures ... necessary for the strengthening of their defence capability' in the event of it not being possible to bring about a collective security system for the whole of Europe. On 21 March 1955, the Soviet news agency announced plans for the conclusion of a mutual assistance pact and that the establishment of a United Supreme Command of the Soviet Union and the People's Democracies had reached a decisive stage. On 14 May, nine days after the Paris Treaties came into effect, representatives of the East European governments and the Soviet government signed in Warsaw a 'treaty of friendship, co-operation and mutual assistance'; the GDR was among the signatories.[13]

With the founding of the Warsaw Pact, Eastern bloc formation clearly also reached its internal limit. The initially envisaged creation of an international military command of Warsaw Pact states was not forthcoming, since the Soviet leadership believed it could not afford to include East European leaders in military planning and decisions. The Consultative Political Committee of the pact was likewise not permitted to develop into a self-sufficient decision-making body. Although decisions on the posting and engagement of troops were to take place on the mutual understanding of the participant governments, the Supreme Command was none the less always reserved for a Soviet officer. How precarious the balance between control and autonomy remained, both of which when they went too far threatened the Soviet demand for control, was shown by Khrushchev's attempt to normalise relations with Yugoslavia (which of course had stayed out of the new pact). Together with Bulganin, he travelled at the end of May 1955 to Belgrade and on 2 June concluded with Tito an agreement on the extension of economic, cultural and political relations on the principle of mutual non-interference and equality. Back in the Kremlin, however, he was obliged to face serious criticism from the traditionalist group, led by Molotov, whose members feared substantial upsets in their relations with other national Communist leaders from a reconciliation with the 'heretic' Tito, and consequently pursued Khrushchev's policy of reconcilation only very reluctantly, at times with a resistance which held it back: they had all either reached or strengthened their power positions in the struggle against 'Titoism' and were therefore bound to fear an intensification of opposition forces from a revision of their position. This and the continuing determination of the Yugoslavs to be independent led to reconciliation being restricted to the level of a tension-ridden 'peaceful coexistence' and to the break of 1948 never being completely reversed.[14]

Similarly linked with GDR consolidation was the recognition of the Federal Republic by the Soviet Union. On 7 June 1955, the Soviet government invited Adenauer to Moscow for talks on the taking-up of diplomatic relations with Moscow. This represented not only an indication of Soviet willingness to come to terms with the reality of West German NATO integration, but also an extremely clever move towards the international upgrading of the GDR. In view of the continuing hope for unification among the Federal German public, Adenauer could hardly distance himself from this 'proposal', even if he thereby lastingly damaged the claim of the Federal Republic to be sole German representative and denied his own demand for overcoming the division of Germany as a precondition for *détente*. Although moving towards this step of strengthening the *status quo* only reluctantly and full of dark forebodings, when the Soviet leader held back at the last moment during his visit in Moscow (9–13 September), the lure of agreement and the return of the last 10,000 German prisoners-of-war from the Soviet Union, he finally agreed, against the resistance of his colleagues von Brentano and Hallstein, to establish diplomatic relations. He felt he could not afford the glory of the return of the prisoners-of-war to go to the SPD or even the SED, in view of his internal political position.[15]

In this way, the Soviet leadership assisted Adenauer to great internal political success and at the same time did a great deal to stabilise the GDR. On the very day of Adenauer's departure, the GDR leadership was invited to talks in Moscow in a show of parallel status, concluding a treaty on bilateral relations with the GDR on 20 September 1955 which declared the GDR to be 'free to make decisions on questions concerning its domestic and foreign policy', with the sole reservation of the Four-Power agreement on 'Germany as a whole'. At a conference of the four Allied foreign ministers on the German problem, which took place from 27 October to 16 November 1955 in Geneva, the Soviet government called once again for the recognition of the GDR by the Western powers, and responded to Western reunification plans with the observation that the time was not yet 'ripe' for a joining of the two German states.[16]

The 'spirit of Geneva'

Once the disagreement over West German rearmament had yet again confirmed the division between East and West, but at the same time bloc formation had reached its own internal limits on both sides, a reduction of tension again became possible *in principle*. Both sides had secured their spheres of influence and neither was able to coerce the other against its will on important issues, so that a relative equilibrium had been achieved from which a gradual and parallel reduction of threat potential in relation to each other could be undertaken. The *détente* process could obviously only make progress to the extent that this equilibrium was maintained, that both sides were aware of it, that no side undertook large-scale interference in the interests of the other side, and that no side interpreted the actions of the opposite side as a large-scale attack on its own security sphere. Since these conditions were not present in the same way and certainly only rarely in this combination, the thawing of the Cold War became a protracted process constantly threatened with setbacks. This process did nevertheless begin at the moment when bloc formation on both sides had reached its ultimate point.

The Soviet leadership continued its *détente* offensive even after defeat over the rearmament question, since it was concerned to prevent a greater concentration of Western forces and to conceal its own weaknesses. At the end of March 1955, members of the Soviet government indicated their willingness to withdraw their occupation troops from Austria in return for certain economic concessions and a guarantee of lasting neutrality. After years of fruitless negotiations, it was thus possible to sign the Austrian state treaty within a short time on 15 May. One of the conditions on which the Western powers had made talks on a collective security system contingent had thereby been fulfilled, and since no further danger threatened the Western integration of the Federal Republic, the Western governments neither wished nor were wholly able to shut themselves off from Soviet *détente* initiatives. In order to satisfy widespread hopes in the country for *détente*, the French government proposed another summit conference of the heads of government and foreign ministers of the four victorious powers. The British government joined in, in the hope of successfully continuing its mediating role; the American government saw no further reason to resist, and the Soviet government took the opportunity to demonstrate its co-operativeness.

Thus Eisenhower, Bulganin/Khrushchev, Faure, the French Prime Minister, and Eden, who had replaced Churchill in April, met from 18 to 23 July 1955 in Geneva with large staffs and extensive participation on the part of the public;[17] however, no substantial *rapprochement* was achieved. The Western powers did not go along with Adenauer's request to discuss disarmament questions and a collective security system in general, linked only with progress on the question of German reunification,[18] but accorded the German question great urgency in all their remarks, whereas the Soviet delegation was concerned from the outset directly to negotiate the creation of a collective security system with a maintenance of the *status quo* in Germany. The Soviet delegates presented a disarmament plan transferring control of nuclear production to a UN organisation without a right of veto, but which overlooked the crucial places of production and transport systems. Eisenhower responded with a proposal for mutual air inspection of all military installations ('open sky'), which promised the USA far more information on the Soviet arms situation than could additionally be known about US arms. Both sides baulked at the risk of entertaining the proposals of their opposite number. Dulles attempted in vain to bring the situation of the East European countries into the discussion; Bulganin attempted, also in vain, to persuade the American delegation to negotiate on recognition of China and the settlement of the Formosa question. On the German question, the Western powers made a gesture towards the Soviet government by including in the Eden Plan the idea of a demilitarised zone in the border territory between East and West and an international military control in Central Europe, although, in line here with Adenauer, they were not prepared to recognise the *status quo* in the GDR. The government leaders could only resolve to have the disputed proposals 'examined' in detail by their foreign ministers, who could not avoid admitting their lack of agreement when they met in Geneva again in October/November.

The Geneva summit meeting did not pass off entirely without results, however; for the first time since the beginning of the open confrontation between East and West, the heads of government of the 'Big Four' had consulted in a polite manner, as well as emphasising their fundamental willingness to co-operate, and had not only acted according to the maxim of not wanting the Cold War to turn into a real war, but had also articulated this publicly. From now on, the Truman Doctrine and Cominform theses could not be presented as the sole basic ideologies of the Cold War: they now had to reckon with the 'spirit of Geneva', that is, with the conviction that the conflict between East and West was not inevitable, and did not necessarily have to end in the victory or defeat of one side. Although hopes for a convergence of the systems in East and West associated by *détente* proponents with this 'spirit of Geneva' were exaggerated, and opponents of *détente* in East and West co-operated on more than one occasion to prevent a reduction in the confrontation, the de-ideologising of the Cold War had nevertheless begun and the first dispositions towards East–West crisis management been found.

Notes

1. Basic reading on the collapse of the EDC is Raymond Aron and Daniel Lerner (eds), *La querelle de la C.E.D*, (Paris, 1956); Gerhard Wettig, *Entmilitarisierung und Wiederbewaffnung in Deutschland 1943–1955*, (Munich, 1967), pp. 523–89; a sound overview in F. Roy Willis, *France, Germany and the New Europe (1945–1967)*, (Stanford, London, 1968), pp. 157–84. Some additional information and interpretations, unfortunately without a systematic, extensive analysis of the previous state of research, is offered by Paul Noack, *Das Scheitern der Europäischen Verteidigungsgemeinschaft. Entscheidungsprozesse vor und nach dem 30. August 1954*, (Düsseldorf, 1977).

2. The role of anti-Americanism and the directly related role of American conduct during the collapse of the EDC have in my opinion been underestimated in accounts so far. In fact there emerged in France during the months of the concluding discussion on the EDC a basic foreign policy attitude of distancing from the USA and towards a supranational Europe which was to prove crucial for the foreign policy of the Fifth Republic.

3. Text of the draft treaty in *Europa, Dokumente zur Frage der europäischen Einigung*, (vol. 2, pp. 947–82).

4. On the position of Mendès-France, *Choisir, Conversations avec Jean Bothorel*, (Paris, 1974), paperback edition 1976, pp. 84–96, as well as the authorised account of Pierre Rouanet, *Mendès-France au pouvoir*, (Paris, 1965).

5. Published in *Le Monde*, 24 Aug. 1954.

6. There is no evidence for Noack's thesis as described here (*Scheitern*, p. 14) that 'the British share in the collapse of the EDC is greater than has previously been supposed'.

7. This being a far-reaching finding of Noack, *Scheitern*, pp. 94–101, pp. 188f.

8. Both disputing its authorship: see Eden *Memoiren*, (Cologne, 1960), p. 181, and Mendès-France *Choisir*, pp. 94f.

9. Text of the Paris proceedings in *Bundesgesetzblatt*, vol. 2, (1955), pp. 305ff; on negotiations on the ratification of the resolutions, in detail, Wettig, *Entmilitarisierung*, pp. 590–619; Willis, *France*, pp. 185–209; Noack, *Scheitern*, pp. 93–138 and pp. 151–63 as on the basis of British documents Rolf Steininger, 'Das Scheitern der EVG und der Beitritt der Bundesrepublik zur NATO in: *Aus Politik und Zeitgeschichte* B 17, (1985), pp. 3–18.

10. See Udo F. Lowke, *Die SPD und die Wehrfrage 1949–1955*, (Bonn-Bad Godesberg, 1976) pp. 119–23.

11. Text in *Europa-Archiv* 9 (1954), pp. 6942ff.; see on this and the following Hans Wassmund, *Kontinuität im Wandel*, (Cologne, Vienna, 1974), pp. 67–97.

12. Text in *Europa-Archiv* 10 (1955), pp. 7206ff., 7209, 7345f. Once again I cannot agree that the Soviet offers were purely tactically intended, as is asserted by most 'traditional' authors. Wettig, *Entmilitarisierung*, p. 634.

13. Treaty text and interpretation in Boris Meissner (ed), *Der Warschauer Pakt*, (Cologne, 1962); on the lead-up also Jörg K. Hoensch,

Sowjetische Osteuropapolitik 1945–1975 (Kronberg, 1977), pp. 88–100.

14. Ibid., pp. 100-5; in more detail Zbigniew Brzezinski, *Der Sowjetblock. Einheit und Konflikt*, (Cologne, 1962), pp. 195–215.

15. See Adenauer's detailed account in: *Erinnerungen 1953–1955*, (Stuttgart 1966), pp. 487–556, in contrast with the information from British diplomacy in Josef Foschepoth, 'Adenauers Moskaureise 1955', in *Aus Politik und Zeitgeschichte* B 22/1986, pp. 30–46.

16. Conference documents in *Europa-Archiv* 10 (1955), pp. 8429–37.

17. See public conference documents in *Europa-Archiv* 10 (1955), pp. 8098–8120.

18. See Adenauer, *Erinnerungen 1953–1955*, pp. 437–86; also *Erinnerungen 1955–1959*, (Stuttgart, 1967), pp. 31–63, 92–103.

What Was the 'Cold War'?
An Assessment

The Cold War did not come to an end with the Geneva conference, at least not in the minds of people at the time. Among the
leading circles of the Western alliance, those elements now
gained the upper hand that misinterpreted Soviet *détente* efforts as
a pause for breath prior to the next wave of expansion, and that
consequently rejected all recognition of the *status quo* and
certainly any far-reaching agreement. The Soviet *détente* offensive
reached the limits of what it could achieve at this point and
Khrushchev attempted, after he had realised this in 1958, to halt
the constant increase in American superiority in strategic arms,
particularly the deployment of nuclear weapons in the Central
European region, with a policy of open threat. With the aim of
reaching a comprehensive treaty settlement, he demanded in an
ultimatum, from November 1958, using the threat of a fresh
blockade, the withdrawal of the Western Allies from Berlin and
the conclusion of a peace treaty with a neutralised Germany.
When the Western side responded to this threat only with verbal
reinforcements of its position, he installed Soviet missile bases on
Cuba. When the Kennedy Administration responded to this
provocation with a blockade of the island, however, Khrushchev
was obliged to face the seriousness of the Western deterrent
threat. This means of persuading the West to recognise the *status
quo* thus also failed: as a result of the Khrushchev war of nerves
(linked with the 'Sputnik shock'), American strategic arms levels
rose rapidly.

What was by now the quite obvious vital interest of the two
world powers in the prevention of a nuclear war led in July 1963
to an agreement to stop nuclear testing and five years later to the
non-transmission treaty on nuclear weapons. At the same time,
the ideological dimensions of the conflict diminished more and
more. In the Soviet Union, recovery from the drop in the standard of living and the development of civil technology had become
the primary political goals; at the same time, the realisation
increased that this goal could not be achieved without comprehensive co-operation with Western industrial nations. Among the
USA and its allies, the spectacle of the Sino-Soviet conflict shattered the illusion of the monolithic unity of the Communist bloc.
At the same time the basic domestic political anti-Communist

consensus broke up in shock at the catastrophic effects of an over-sized containment concept in the Vietnam War. At the end of the 1960s the rapid reinforcement of Soviet nuclear arms led to a nuclear stalemate: both sides from then on had available an extensive second-strike capacity. In the Federal Republic, a majority of political groupings proved willing under the Brandt/ Scheel government to recognise the *status quo*. The Chinese leadership endeavoured to form a counterbalance to the pressure of the Soviet Union. In the USA, the Nixon/Kissinger Administration entered office prepared to pull out of Vietnam and to reach an agreement with China. Only the convergence of these factors permitted at the beginning of the 1970s an extensive limitation and defusing of the East–West conflict, although not its elimination.

What came to an end in 1955 was the process of bloc formation in East and West — that is, the process of establishing a new international order after the collapse of the European state system following National Socialist expansion — a process dominated by the power-political and ideological contradictions of the USA and the USSR. This process stemmed from the social predispositions of the states involved and had a polarising effect on the USSR, since it was influenced by the mutual fear of an encroachment by the opposite side on its own security sphere; it thereby lead to the division of Germany and Europe, to a permanent siege state in mentalities and practice, and to world-wide competition for spheres of influence. Whether one sees the whole of the Cold War in this light or not is a matter of convention. If one takes the way people saw themselves and the modes of speech they used at the time as the decisive criteria, the Cold War would then begin in 1947 and end after the Cuban crisis of 1962. If one places the system conflict between the USA and the Soviet Union and its effects on the European continent at the centre of the analysis, then the beginning of the conflict would date from 1917 at the latest and still be without a discernible end. If one defines the Cold War as that period in which the antagonism between the two world powers of the USA and the USSR dominated the international system, then 1943 would mark the beginning and the end would likewise remain open, although Soviet–American antagonism has since been overlaid by a number of other conflict areas. None the less, these uses of the term 'Cold War' are so imprecise in terms of content that in the interests of precise conceptualisation it would be advisable to limit the term to the

305

central process from 1941 to 1955, as described here.[1]

The fact that the establishment of a new international order after the Second World War occurred in the form of a Cold War and led to bloc formation was, as has repeatedly been made clear in the course of the analysis, a probable, but by no means an inevitable development. A fundamental power-political contradiction did predominate between the two new world powers that met in the centre of the European continent, a contradiction inextricably linked with palpable differences in their social structures and ideological exigencies. The liberal-capitalist system of the USA, in accordance with its liberal principles, was set on establishing a tendentious world-wide system of free trade in order to avoid profound economic crises and secure its socio-political *status-quo*, being at the same time set on the unlimited economic expansion of the USA, which had meanwhile become the strongest world power. The Soviet mobilisation dictatorship oriented itself according to its claim to be centre of a world revolutionary movement, and could only survive by protecting itself from these liberal principles, by opposing the forward economic march of the USA with a counteracting force and by freeing itself from the pressure of aggressive neighbouring states in its Western forefield. Both Soviet and American universalism were none the less restricted, both in terms of means and of the will to prevail. At the same time there were a number of important reasons in favour of continuing the peaceful co-operation that had begun with the anti-Hitler coalition, or more precisely for each side pursuing its respective national objectives using co-operative means. Economically the American interest in new outlets and establishing new sources of raw materials complemented the Soviet interest in capital assistance, and politically a majority of decision-makers in both systems were initially interested in a reduction in military engagement and international tension. Even ideologically there was no lack of convergence between the revolutionary traditions of 1776 and 1917 in general, or Rooseveltian progressivism and Stalinist people's democracy in particular. All conflicts over spheres of influence and social-order concepts notwithstanding, the vital interests of the two powers were never threatened by the other side to such an extent that a far-reaching arrangement was out of the question. An expansion of the Soviet power zone towards Western Europe was not a threat, any more than American capitalism had a particularly enduring interest in the economic penetration of Eastern Europe. In the preventive deflection

306

of feared expansion by the other side, the American government and the Soviet leadership in fact pursued (without knowing it) the same stabilisation strategy in Europe.

The crucial impetus for the escalation of the conflict was given by the USA, in its refusal to recognise the Soviet security zone which had implicitly already come into being; it was likewise the USA which more emphatically determined the course of the conflict, being structurally and, in terms of the means of power at its disposal, far superior to its opponent at all times. The reason for the USA's unwillingness for *rapprochement* was not the economically-determined Open Door interest *per se*. Although the latter was drawn into the formulation of foreign policy strategy and finally prevailed in a diversity of political decisions, it inclined more towards an open system type of competition unhampered by political barriers,[2] as propagated by Henry Wallace in 1946, than towards bloc formation. Decisive for the form of Open Door policy which led to confrontation was in fact the foreign policy idealism which dominated the political culture of the country, manifesting itself sometimes as isolationism and sometimes as aggressive moralism. This idealism prevented the Roosevelt Administration from impressing the realities arising out of the war on American society, and helped leading groups to attain key positions at the beginning of the Truman Administration that equated the situation in Europe at the end of the war with the world economic crisis, and Soviet Communism with National Socialism. It also made it necessary for these leading groups to present the alleged Soviet threat in an exaggerated form in order to be able to stave it off and to secure the Open Door policy, which was in fact essential to their social system. Finally, it compelled American foreign policy under Acheson and Dulles to make large-scale adaptations to this exaggerated containment concept.

The inability of the USA to come to terms with the imperialist forms for securing Soviet interests in Eastern Europe, or to perceive the actual objectives of Soviet policy, in turn reinforced those dogmatic elements and tendencies within the Soviet leadership which assumed that an economic expansion of the USA towards Europe would take on an imperialist character, and which therefore deemed necessary, and implemented in 1947, an enforced alignment of the European countries with the Soviet model, breaking off the remaining ties with the Western powers by rejecting the Marshall Plan and switching to an aggressive propaganda language. Soviet policy thus for its part strengthened the position of those opposed to co-operation in the USA, and in particular positively forced the 'Western bloc' option onto West Europeans, in spite of the fact that the Soviet Union, because of its structural inferiority and the internal weakness of its power framework, was well disposed to a co-operative relationship with the non-Communist world. The realists were soon no longer able to prevail over this unavowed, but all the more effective coalition of the dogmatists. When the Soviet leadership began to realise its strategic mistakes in 1952, a coalition of *détente* supporters did come into existence, taking much of the militancy from the confrontation, but it was still unable to overcome the coalition of the dogmatists for a long time.

The bloc-formation process thus occurred on the principle of 'self-fulfilling prophecy', the Western policy of refusal to co-operate and of coercion provoking the closing-off and uniform alignment of the Soviet bloc, which the anti-Communist dogmatists had asserted would happen, the monolithisation of Eastern Europe and the obstruction of the Marshall Plan giving rise to the formation of the Western bloc, against the alleged effects of which it was in fact aimed. Each side found cause in the formation of the opposite bloc to see confirmation of its overestimation of the strength of the opponent, however little justification there had ever actually been for theses of the fundamental imperialism of the other side. The division of Germany was an inevitable consequence of this process. Although not pursued by any side as a primary political aim, no side was prepared to abandon the whole of Germany to the other side, and indeed could not be prepared to do so, given the significance of German potential. While fear of dominance by the other side (and, on the American side, an additional fear of the incorporation of France into the Soviet sphere of influence) blocked a joint German solution, there arose in occupied Germany two disparate social systems aligned with the interests of the respective occupying power. When bloc formation had reached a stage where *rapprochement* could only be considered in terms of a neutralisation of Germany, not only did the risk of such a neutralisation seem too high to the majority of decision-makers in East and West, but, in addition, most West Germans, as well as the new power elites in the Soviet zone, voted to retain the *status quo* that had meanwhile been attained.

The nature and scope of Western bloc formation was largely determined by the West Europeans themselves. Compelled as a result of the fundamentally isolationist-idealist attitude in American society to secure trading partners and outlets without paying any appreciable price for them in terms of political commitment, American policy was oriented towards co-operation with the power elites of Western Europe, which thus gave the West Europeans an opportunity for determining the inter-relationship between themselves and America, and also therefore the character of East–West relations. It fell to them to counteract the trend towards East–West polarisation by emphasising and securing European autonomy in relation to the USA. In fact they did succeed, in so far as they did not share the American thesis of the expansive character of Soviet policy, in preventing or mitigating bloc formation until 1947, showing similar signs again from 1953 onwards. In the meantime, however, they did not avail themselves of the chance for autonomy offered them with European integration, strengthening instead the political influence of the USA on the European continent and in effect provoking the latter's military engagement, with the result that the years from 1947 to 1952 became the crucial phase in the Cold War and the formative phase for the blocs. This decision was likewise probable, but by no means inevitable; whereas, on the one hand, basic 'Western' concepts of a pluralistic political order linked the old continent with the new, and Soviet conduct was bound to awaken fear among the West Europeans, on the other hand, the contradictions in sentiment and ideological claims between American progressivism and European conservatism, American 'free enterprise' ideology and European socialism were great, as were those of the economic interests of the mixed-economy systems in European countries — sometimes for, sometimes against European integration, sometimes for co-operation with the American defenders of free enterprise, sometimes for protection against the superior power of American capital. Central factors in the decision against the 'third-force' concept were first, the degree of vestigial nationalism in Great Britain and also, to a lesser extent, in France; secondly, an entirely genuine fear of Soviet expansion; and thirdly (albeit in fact only in third place!), the fact that this fear allowed itself to be manipulated for the purposes of maintaining the social *status quo* in Western Europe.

The process of bloc formation was furthered by a broad coalition of political elements that directly or indirectly exploited it: the military–industrial complexes in the USA and (to a more limited degree) in the USSR, which activated concepts of threat on both sides in order to expand their proportion of the social product; the traditional power elites in Western Europe, who, largely discredited after the war and threatened by the upsurge of the West European Left, found in the argumentation models of the Cold War and in confederacy with the USA an appropriate means at least partially to salvage their faltering positions; leading political elements in Eastern Europe, which instigated their struggle against 'Titoism' from 1948 onwards; and those belonging to the leading groups in East and West generally, who attained their positions by means of anti-Communist or anti-Western arguments respectively, and were dependent on the continuance of the conflict situation for their legitimacy. All these were thus 'secondary causes' of the Cold War; neither alone nor together sufficient to initiate the conflict, they worked towards it, partly consciously, partly unconsciously, and once the escalation mechanism had been set in motion, allowed it to become a lasting reality firmly rooted in domestic politics and persisting beyond its own causes.

The European Left became the chief victim of the at first only alleged and then actual confrontation, or, more precisely, those political forces in Europe pressing unequivocally for an overthrow of the capitalist system. In Western Europe, the national emancipatory elements of the Communist Parties were neutralised by the Soviet stabilisation strategy, falling into isolation as a result of pseudo-revolutionary Cominform policy; the social democrats and socialist parties were permanently weakened by the separation of the Communists, whereas their conservative and liberal counterparts achieved substantial and proportional advantages in co-operation with the American leading power. In Eastern Europe, indigenous socialist elements, which had played a substantial part in the first phase of 'people's democratic' transformation, were increasingly obliged in the course of bloc formation to give way to those who conformed dogmatically to the Soviet model. Western Europe organised itself, inasmuch as it organised itself at all, along majority conservative lines. Of the 'third-force' Europe, only the rudiments of Keynesian structural planning remained. Within the two power zones, therefore, the Cold War proliferated into a conflict of political organisation — though in this case not, as was maintained by the basic official doctrines of the two sides, between the American and Soviet 'ways of life' but, in a more significant relativisation of the fundamental socio-ideological contradiction between East and West,

310

between liberal-capitalist and democratic-socialist concepts of social organisation on the Western side and between autonomy and Soviet penetration within the Soviet security zone.

The fact that the fundamental principles of the 'Western' way of life within the Western hemisphere were not seriously threatened at any stage of the conflict, and that the Soviet need for control was constantly threatened within the Soviet security zone (this in fact less on account of American 'imperialisation', however, than as a consequence of the internal weakness of the Soviet system itself) makes it clear that the conflict of systems between the 'Eastern' and 'Western' ways of life, which lies at the root of the Cold War, but by no means made it inevitable that it would happen, was (and is) not a conflict between two basically equal great powers. It is, rather, a conflict between a Western system, which in principle permits a diversity of ways of life and power configurations, and the tendentially totalitarian absolutisation of one of these possibilities in the Eastern bloc. There was thus nothing to fear in terms of 'Western' principles from an 'open' competition of systems — that is, a co-operative one making use of every chance for *détente* — but, on the contrary, everything to gain. The fact that the great majority of relevant political elements in the 'West' ultimately decided in favour of the opposite conception is what constitutes the tragedy of the Cold War.

Notes

1. The process of transition from Cold War to *détente* likewise urgently requires comprehensive historical analysis; in this case, however, preliminary work is understandably much less advanced than in the case of the bloc formation process. See for a preliminary overview Wilfried Loth, 'Europa in der Weltpolitik', in Wolfgang Benz and Hermann Graml (eds), *Das Zwanzigste Jahrhundert II. Europa nach dem Zweiten Weltkrieg* (Frankfurt M 1983), pp. 469–512 and pp. 535–538.

2. Speech of 12 Sept. 1946, *Vital Speeches of the Day*, vol. 12, pp. 738–741, in extract form in Walter LaFeber (ed), *The Origins of the Cold War, 1941–1947. A historical problem with interpretations and documents* (New York, 1971), pp. 144–148.

Sources and Bibliography

For orientation on the progress of research discussion, see Wilfried Loth, 'Der "Kalte Krieg" in der historischen Forschung', in Gottfried Niedhardt (ed.), *Der Westen und die Sowjetunion* (Paderborn, 1983), pp. 155–75; for information on new publications at the beginning of the 1980s, see Wolfgang Michalka (ed.), *Ost-West-Konflikt und Friedensunsicherung*, (Stuttgart, 1985).

Sources

Acheson, Dean *Present at the creation: my years in the State Department* (New York, 1970)

Adenauer, Konrad *Erinnerungen*, 4 vols. (Stuttgart, 1965–8)

Auriol, Vincent *Journal du septennat*, 7 vols. (Paris, 1970–9)

Bailey, Thomas A. *The Marshall Plan summer, an eyewitness report on Europe and the Russians in 1947* (Stanford, Ca., 1977)

Blum, John Morton *From the Morgenthau diaries: years of war 1941–1945* (Boston, 1967)

Blum, Léon *L'Œuvre de Léon Blum*, 7 vols, in 9 parts (Paris, 1954–72)

Bohlen, Charles *Witness to history 1929–69* (New York, 1973)

Byrnes, James F. *All in one lifetime* (New York, 1958)

Churchill, Winston *Triumph and tragedy* (Boston, 1953)

Djilas, Milovan *Conversation with Stalin* (New York, 1962) Documents on American foreign relations, vol. 1–13 (1938/9–51) (Princeton, NJ)

Eden, Anthony *The Eden memoirs. The reckoning* (London, 1965)

Etzold, Thomas H. and John Lewis Gaddis (ed.) *Containment: documents on American policy and strategy 1945–1950* (New York, 1978)

Foreign relations of the United States (FRUS), edited by the Department of State, Washington. See the review of volumes published so far in Hans. R. Guggisberg, 'Dokumente zur amerikanischen Außenpolitik von 1940 bis 1950, Das Quellenwerk Foreign Relations of the United States', *Historische Zeitschrift*, 226 (1978), pp. 622–35

Gasteyger, Curt (ed.) *Einigung und Spaltung Europas 1942–1965* (Frankfurt, 1965)

de Gaulle, Charles *Memoires de guerre*, vol. 3: *Le Salut, 1944–46* (Paris, 1959)

Harriman, W. Averell and Elie Abel, *Special envoy to Churchill and Stalin 1941–1946* (New York, 1975)

Hull, Cordell *The memoirs of Cordell Hull*, 2 vols. (New York, 1948)

Jäckel, Eberhard (ed.) *Die deutsche Frage 1952–1956. Notenwechsel und Konferenzdokumente der vier Mächte* (Frankfurt, 1957)

Kennan, George F. *Memoirs 1925–1950* (Boston, 1967)

LaFeber, Walter (ed.) *The origins of the Cold War 1941–1947. A historical problem with interpretations and documents* (New York, 1971)

Lipgens, Walter and Wilfried Loth (eds.) *Documents on the history of Euro-*

pean integration, vols. *1–4, 1934–50* (Berlin/New York, 1984–8)

Loewenheim, Francis L., Harold D. Langley and Manfred Jonas (eds) *Roosevelt and Churchill. Their secret wartime correspondence* (London, 1975)

Meissner, Boris (eds.) *Das Ostpakt-System* (Frankfurt Berlin, 1955)

—— (ed.) *Der Warschauer Pakt* (Cologne, 1962)

Mendès-France, Pierre, *Choisir. Conservations avec Jean Bothorel* (2nd edn, Paris, 1976)

Millis, Walter (ed.) *The Forrestal diaries* (New York, 1951)

Molotov, Vyacheslav M. *Fragen der Außenpolitik, Reden und Erklärungen* (Moscow, 1949)

Roosevelt, Elliott (ed.) *Franklin D. Roosevelt: his personal letters 1928–1945,* 2 vols. (New York, 1950)

Smith, Jean Edward (ed.) *The papers of General Lucius D. Clay: Germany 1945–49,* (Bloomington, Ind., 1974)

Steininger, Rolf (ed.) *Eine Chance zur Wiedervereinigung? Die Stalin-Note vom 10. Marz 1952* (Berlin/Bonn, 1985)

Talbot, Strobe (ed.) *Krushchev remembers* (Boston, 1970)

—— *Khrushchev remembers: the last testament* (Boston, 1976)

Truman, Harry S. *Memoirs. Years of decisions* (Garden City, NY, 1955)

Vandenberg, Arthur Jr (ed.) *The private papers of Senator Vandenberg* (Boston, 1972)

Bibliography

Alperowitz, Gar *Atomic diplomacy: Hiroshima and Potsdam* (New York, 1965)

Amen, Michael Mark *American foreign policy in Greece 1944–49* (London, 1979)

Anderson, Terry H. *The United States, Great Britain and the Cold War, 1944–1947* (Columbia/London, 1981)

Anfänge westdeutscher Sicherheitspolitik 1945–1956, vol. 1: *Von der Kapitulation bis zum Pleven-Plan* (Munich/Vienna, 1982)

Arkes, Hardley *Bureaucracy, the Marshall Plan and the national interest,* (Princeton, NJ, 1972)

Aron, Raymond and Daniel Lerner (eds.) *La querelle de la CED* (Paris, 1956)

Backer, John H. *The decision to divide Germany. American foreign policy in Transition* (Durham, 1978)

—— *Die deutschen Jahre des Generals Clay. Den Weg zur Bundesrepublik 1945–1949* (Munich, 1983)

Baring, Arnulf *Der 17. Juni 1953,* (Cologne/Berlin, 1965); (2nd edn, Stuttgart, 1983)

—— *Außenpolitik in Adenauers Kanzlerdemokratie. Bonns Beitrag zur Europäischen Verteidigungsgemeinschaft,* 2 vols. (Munich, 1971)

Benz, Wolfgang *Die Gründung der Bundesrepublik. Von der Bizone zum souveränen Staat* (Munich, 1984)

Bernstein, Barton J. (ed.), *Politics and policies of the Truman administration* (Chicago, 1970)

—— *The atomic bomb, the critical issues* (Boston/Toronto, 1976)

313

Birke, Ernst and Rudolf Neumann (eds.) *Die Sowjetisierung Ost-Mitteleuropas. Untersuchungen zu ihrem Ablauf in den einzelnen Ländern*, vol. 1 (Frankfurt/Berlin, 1959)

Brauch, Hans Günter 'Struktureller Wandel und Rüstüngspolitik der USA (1940–1950). Zur Weltführungsrolle und ihren innenpolitischen Bedingungen' dissertation (Heidelberg, 1976)

Brzezinski, Zbigniew *The Soviet bloc* (Cambridge, 1969)

Buhite, Russel D. *Soviet–American relations in Asia, 1945–1954* (Norman, 1981)

Clemens, Diane S. *Yalta* (New York, 1970)

von Csernatony, Georges 'Le plan Marshall et le redressement économique de l'Allemagne', dissertation (Lausanne, 1973)

Cumings, Bruce, *The origins of the Korean War* (Princeton, NJ, 1981)

Dallek, Robert *Franklin D. Roosevelt and American foreign policy, 1932–1945* (New York, 1979)

Davis, Lynn Etheridge *The Cold War begins. Soviet–American conflict over Eastern Europe*, (Princeton, NJ, 1974)

Deuerlein, Ernst *Deklamation oder Ersatzfrieden? Die Konferenz von Potsdam 1945*, (Stuttgart, 1970)

Diebold, William Jr *The Schuman Plan* (New York, 1959)

Diepenthal, Wolfgang, *Drei Volksdemokratien. Ein Konzept der kommunistischen Machtstabilisierung und seine Verwirklichung in Polen, der Tschechoslowakei und der Sowjetischen Besatzungszone Deutschlands 1944–1948* (Cologne, 1974)

Divine, Robert A. *Roosevelt and World War II* (Baltimore, Md, 1969)

—— *Foreign policy and US presidential elections 1940–1948* (New York, 1974)

Douglas, Roy *From war to Cold War 1942–48* (London, 1981)

Elgey, Georgette *Histoire de la IVe République*, 2 vols. (Paris, 1965–8)

Erdmenger, Klaus *Das folgenschwere Mißverständnis. Bonn und die sowjetische Deutschlandpolitik 1949–1955* (Freiburg, 1967)

Fainsod, Merle *How Russia is ruled*, 2nd edn. (Cambridge, Mass., 1963)

Fauvet, Jaques *Histoire du parti communiste français*, 2nd edn, (Paris, 1977)

Feis, Herbert *Churchill, Roosevelt, Stalin. The war they waged and the peace they sought* (Princeton, NJ, 1957)

—— *Zwischen Krieg und Frieden. Das Potsdamer Abkommen* (Frankfurt, Bonn, 1962;)

—— *The atomic bomb and the end of World War II*, 2nd edn, (Princeton, NJ, 1966)

—— *From trust to terror, the onset of the Cold War 1945–1950* (New York, 1970)

Fischer, Alexander *Sowjetische Deutschlandpolitik im Zweiten Weltkrieg 1941–1945* (Stuttgart, 1975)

Fischer, Louis *The road to Yalta. Soviet foreign relations 1941–1945* (New York, 1972)

Fleming, Donna F. *The Cold War and its origins, 1917–1960*, 2 vols (Garden City, NY, 1961)

Fontaine, André, *Histoire de la guerre froide*, 2 vols. (Paris, 1965–7)

Foschepoth, Josef (ed.) *Kalter Krieg und deutsche Frage* (Göttingen, 1985)

Freeland, Richard M. *The Truman doctrine and the origins of McCarthyism.*

Foreign policy, domestic politics and internal security 1946–1948 (New York, 1972)

Fried, Richard M. *Men against McCarthy* (New York, 1976)

Frohn, Axel *Deutschland zwischen Neutralisierung und Westintegration. Die deutschlandpolitischen Planungen und die Deutschlandpolitik der Vereinigten Staaten von Amerika 1945–1949* (Frankfurt, 1985)

Gaddis, John L. *The United States and the origins of the Cold War 1941–1947* (2nd edn, New York, 1976)

—— *Strategies of containment. A critical appraisal of postwar American national security policy* (New York/Oxford, 1982)

Gardner, Lloyd C. *Economic aspects of new deal diplomacy* (Madison, 1964)

—— *Architects of illusion. Men and ideas in American foreign policy 1941–1949* (Chicago, 1970)

—— Arthur Schlesinger, Jr and Hans J Morgenthau *The origins of the Cold War* (Waltham, Mass., Toronto, 1970)

Gardner, Richard N. *Sterling–Dollar diplomacy: Anglo-American collaboration in the reconstruction of the multilateral trade,* (Oxford, 1956; 2nd edn, New York, 1969)

Geiling, Martin *Außenpolitik und Nuklearstrategie. Eine Analyse des Konzeptionellen Wandels der amerikanischen Sicherheitspolitik gegenüber der Sowjetunion (1945–1963)* (Cologne/Vienna, 1975)

Geyer, Dietrich *Von der Kriegskoalition zum Kalten Krieg,* in *Sowjetunion Außenpolitik,* vol. 1, 1917–1955 (Osteuropa-Handbuch series) (Cologne/Vienna, 1972)

Gimbel, John *Amerikanische Besatzungspolitik in Deutschland 1945–1949* (Frankfurt, 1971)

—— *The origins of the Marshall Plan (Stanford, Ca, 1976)*

Graml, Hermann 'Nationalstaat oder westdeutscher Teilstaat. Die sowjetischen Noten vom Jahre 1952 und die öffentliche Meinung in der Bundesrepublik Deutschland', in *Vierteljahrshefte für Zeitgeschichte,* 25 (1977), pp. 821–64

—— 'Die Legende von der verpaßten Gelegenheit', *Vierteljahrshefte für Zeitgeschichte,* 29 (1981), pp. 307–41

—— *Die Alliierten und die Teilung Deutschlands. Konflikte und Entscheidungen 1941–1948* (Frankfurt, 1985)

Griffith, Robert *The politics of fear: Joseph R. McCarthy and the Senate,* (Lexington, 1970)

—— and Athan Theoharis (eds), *The specter: original essays on the Cold War and the origins of McCarthyism* (New York, 1974)

Grosser, Alfred *Das Bündnis. Die westeuropäischen Länder und die USA seit dem Krieg* (Munich 1978)

Hacker, Jens *Der Ostblock: Enstehung, Entwicklung und Struktur 1939–1980* (Baden-Baden, 1983)

Hahn, Werner G. *Postwar Soviet politics. The fall of Zhdanov and the defeat of moderation, 1946–1953* (New York, 1982)

Halle, Louis J. *Der Kalte Krieg, Ursachen, Verlauf, Abschluß* (Frankfurt, 1969)

Hammond, Paul Y. 'Directives for the occupation of Germany: The Washington controversy', in Harold Stein (ed.), *American civil-military decisions* (Birmingham, Ala., 1963)

——— 'NSC 68: prologue to rearmament', in Schilling, Hammond, Snyder (eds), *Strategy, politics and defense budgets* (New York/London, 1962)

Hammond, Thomas T. (ed.) *Witnesses to the origins of the Cold War* (Seattle, 1982)

Hathaway, Robert M. *Ambiguous partnership: Britain and America, 1944–1947* (New York, 1981)

Heiter, Heinrich *Vom friedlichen Weg zum Sozialismus zur Diktatur des Proletariats. Wandlungen der sowjetischen Konzeption der Volksdemokratie 1945–1949* (Frankfurt, 1977)

Herken, Gregg F. *The winning weapon. The atomic bomb in the Cold War 1945–1950* (New York, 1981)

Herring, George C. *Aid to Russia 1941–1946. Strategy, diplomacy, the origins of the Cold War* (New York, 1973)

Hillgruber, Andreas *Sowjetische Außenpolitik im Zweiten Weltkreig* (Königstein, 1979)

——— *Europa in der Weltpolitik der Nachkriegszeit 1945–1963* (Munich, Vienna, 1979; 2nd edn, 1981)

Hoensch, Jörg K. *Sowjetische Osteuropapolitik 1945–1975* (Kronberg, 1977)

Horowitz, David, *Kalter Krieg. Hintergründe der US-Außenpolitik von Jalta bis Vietnam*, 2 vols. (Berlin, 1969)

Ireland, Timothy P. *Creating the entangling Alliance. The origins of the North Atlantic Treaty Organization* (London, 1981)

Issraelian, Viktor *Die Antihitlerkoalition. Die diplomatische Zusammenarbeit zwischen der UdSSR, den USA und England während des Zweiten Weltkrieges 1941–1945* (Moscow, 1975)

Jones, Joseph M. *The fifteen weeks (February 21–June 5, 1947)* (2nd edn, New York, 1964)

Kimball, Warren F. (ed) *Franklin D. Roosevelt and the world crisis 1937–1945*, (Lexington, 1973)

——— *Swords or ploughshares? The Morgenthau plan for defeated Nazi Germany, 1943–1946* (Philadelphia, 1976)

Kirkendall, Richard S (ed.) *The Truman period as a research field. A reappraisal 1972* (Columbia, Mo., 1974)

Kolko, Gabriel *The politics of war. The world and United States policy 1943–1945* (New York, 1968)

Kolko, Joyce and Gabriel *The limits of power. The world and United States Policy 1945–1954* (New York, 1972)

Kuklick, Bruce *American policy and the division of Germany. The clash with Russia over reparations* (Ithaca, NY/London, 1972)

Kuniholm, Bruce R. *The origins of the Cold War in the Near East* (Princeton, NJ, 1980)

LaFeber, Walter, *America, Russia and the Cold War* (New York, 1967: 3rd edn, 1976)

Leffler, Melvin P. 'The American conception of national security and the beginnings of the Cold War, 1945–1948', *American Historical Review*, 89 (1984), pp. 346–81

Link, Werner 'Die amerikanische Außenpolitik aus revisionistischer Sicht', *Neue Politische Literatur*, 16 (1971), pp. 202–20

——— *Das Konzept der friedlichen Kooperation und der Beginn des Kalten*

Krieges (Düsseldorf, 1971)

Lipgens, Walter *History of European integration 1945–1947* (Oxford, 1982)

Lorenz, Richard *Sozialgeschichte der Sowjetunion I 1917–1945* (Frankfurt, 1976)

Loth, Wilfried 'Der "Kalte Krieg" in deutscher Sicht', *Deutschland-Archiv*, 9 (1976), pp. 204–13

—— *Sozialismus und Internationalismus. Die französischen Sozialisten und die Nachkriegsordnung Europas 1940–1950* (Stuttgart, 1977)

—— 'The West European governments and the impulse given by the Marshall Plan', in W. Lipgens et al. (eds.), *A history of European integration*, vol. 1 (Oxford, 1982), pp. 488–507

—— 'Frankreichs Kommunisten und der Beginn des Kalten Krieges', *Vierteljahrshefte für Zeitgeschichte*, 26 (1978), pp. 7–65

—— 'Die doppelte Eindämmung, Überlegungen zur Genesis des Kalten Krieges 1945–1947', *Historische Zeitschrift*, 238 (1984), pp. 611–31

—— 'Die deutsche Frage in französischer Perspektive', in Rudolf Herbst (ed.), *Westdeutschland 1945–1955. Unterwerfung, Kontrolle, Integration* (Munich, 1986), pp. 37–49

Löwke, Udo F. *Die SPD und die Wehrfrage 1949–1955* (Bonn-Bad Godesberg, 1976)

Lundestad, Geir *The American non-policy towards Eastern Europe 1943–1947* (Tromsö/New York, 1975; 2nd edn, 1978)

Maddox, Robert J. *The New Left and the origins of the Cold War* (New York, 1973)

Marcou, Lilly *Le Kominform* (Paris, 1977)

Martin, Bernd 'Verhandlungen über separate Friedenschlüsse 1942–1945. Ein Beitrag zur Entstehung des Kalten Krieges', *Militärgeschichtliche Mitteilungen*, 7 (1976), pp. 95–113

Mastný, Vojtěch, 'Stalin and the prospects of a separate peace in World War II', *American Historical Review*, 77 (1972), pp. 43–66

—— *Russia's road to the Cold War. Diplomacy, warfare and communism 1941–1945* (New York, 1979)

Matloff, Maurice and Edward L. Snell, *Strategic planning for coalition warfare: 1943–1944* (Washington, DC, 1959)

May, Ernest R. *The Truman administration and China 1945–1949* (Philadelphia, Pa, 1975)

McCagg, William O. Jr. *Stalin embattled 1943–1948* (Detroit, 1978)

McNeill, William H. *America, Britain and Russia, their cooperation and conflict 1941–1946* (London, 1953)

Meissner, Boris *Rußland, die Westmächte und Deutschland* (2nd edn, Hamburg, 1954)

Melandri, Pierre *Les Etats-Unis face à l'unification de l'Europe 1945–1954* (Paris, 1980)

Messer, Robert L. *The end of an alliance: James F. Byrnes, Roosevelt, Truman, and the origins of the Cold War* (Chapel Hill, 1982)

Meyer, Gerd *Die sowjetische Deutschland-Politik im Jahre 1952* (Tübingen, 1970)

Morgan, Roger *The unsettled peace. A study of the Cold War in Europe* (London, 1974)

Myant, Martin *Socialism and democracy in Czechoslovakia, 1945–1948* (New York, 1981)

Niedhart, Gottfried *Der Westen und die Sowjetunion. Einstellungen und Politik gegenüber der UdSSR in Europa und in den USA seit 1917* (Paderborn, 1983)

Noack, Paul *Das Scheitern der Europäischen Verteidigungsgemeinschaft. Entscheidungsprozesse vor und nach dem 30. August 1954* (Düsseldorf, 1977)

Nolte, Ernst *Deutschland und der Kalte Krieg* (Munich, 1974; 2nd edn, Stuttgart, 1985)

Notter, Harley *Postwar foreign policy preparation 1939–1949* (Washington, DC, 1949)

Nove, Alex, *An economic history of the USSR* (Harmondsworth, 1972)

Paige, Glenn D. *The Korean decision: June 24–30, 1950* (New York/London, 1968)

Paterson, Thomas G. *Soviet–American confrontation, postwar reconstruction and the origins of the Cold War*, (Baltimore, Md/London, 1973)

—— *On every front: the making of the Cold War* (New York, 1979)

Penrose, Ernest F. *Economic planning for peace* (Princeton, NJ, 1953)

Pirker, Theo *Die verordnete Demokratie. Grundlagen und Entscheidungen der 'Restauration'* (Berlin, 1977)

Poidevin, Raymond (ed.) *Histoire des débuts de la construction européenne* (Brussels, 1986)

Price, Harvey B. *The Marshall Plan and its meaning* (Ithaca, NY, 1955)

Roberts, Walter R. *Tito, Mihailović and the Allies 1941–1945* (New Brunswick, NJ, 1973)

Rose, Lisle A. *After Yalta* (New York, 1973)

Sandford, Gregory W. *From Hitler to Ulbricht. The Communist reconstruction of East Germany, 1945–46* (Princeton, NJ, 1982)

Schmitt, Hans A. *US occupation in Europe after World War II* (Lawrence, 1978)

von Schubert, Klaus *Wiederbewaffnung und Westintegration. Die innere Auseinandersetzung um die militärische und außenpolitische Orientierung der Bundesrepublik 1950–1952* (Stuttgart, 1970; 2nd edn, 1972)

Schwabe, Klaus 'Die amerikanische Besatzungspolitik in Deutschland und der Beginn des "Kalten Krieges" (1945–46)', in *Rußland-Deutschland-Amerika*, commemorative volume for 80th birthday of Fritz T. Epstein (Wiesbaden, 1978), pp. 311–32

Schwarz, Hans-Peter *Vom Reich zur Bundesrepublik. Deutschland im Widerstreit der außenpolitischen Konzeptionen in den Jahren der Besatzungsherrschaft 1945–1949* (Neuwied, Berlin, 1966; 2nd edn, Stuttgart, 1980)

—— 'Adenauer und Europa', *Vierteljahrshefte für Zeitgeschichte*, 27 (1979), pp. 471–523

Sharp, Tony *The wartime alliance and the zonal division of Germany* (Oxford, 1975)

Sherwin, Martin J. *A world destroyed. The atomic bomb and the Grand Alliance*, (New York, 1975)

Sherwood, Robert E. *Roosevelt and Hopkins*, (Hamburg, 1950)

Simmons, Robert R. *The strained alliance, Peking, Pyongyang, Moscow and the politics of the Korean civil war* (New York, 1975)

Snell, John L. *Wartime origins of the East–West dilemma over Germany* (New

Orleans, 1959)

Snyder, Glenn H. 'The "New Look" of 1953', in Schilling, Hammond and Snyder, *Strategy, politics and defense budgets* (New York/London, 1962), pp. 382–54

Spittman, Ilse and Karl Wilhelm Fricke (eds.) *17 Juni 1953. Arbeiteraufstand in der DDR* (Cologne, 1982)

Staritz, Dietrich *Sozialismus in einem halben Land. Zur Problematik und Politik der KPD/SED in der Phase der antifaschistisch-demokratischen Umwälzung in der DDR* (Berlin, 1976)

—— *Die Gründung der DDR. Von der Sowjetischen Besatzungsherrschaft zum sozialistischen Staat,* (Munich, 1984)

Steininger, Rolf 'Reform und Realität. Ruhrfrage und Sozialisierung in der anglo-amerikanischen Deutschlandpolitik 1947–48', *Vierteljahrshefte für Zeitgeschichte,* 27 (1979), pp. 167–240

—— *Eine vertane Chance. Die Stalin-Note von 10. März 1952 und die Wiedervereinigung,* (Berlin/Bonn, 1985)

Taubmann, William *Stalin's American policy: from entente to détente to Cold War* (New York, 1982)

Theoharis, Athan *The Yalta myths: an issue in US politics, 1945–1955* (Columbia, Mo., 1970)

—— *Seeds of repression: Harry S. Truman and the origins of McCarthyism* (Chicago, 1971)

Thompson, Kenneth W. *Cold War theories: vol. 1: World polarization 1944–1953* (Chapel Hill, 1982)

Tucker, Robert W. *The radical left and American foreign policy* (Baltimore, Md/London, 1971)

Ulam, Adam B. *Expansion and coexistence. The history of Soviet foreign policy 1917–1967* (London, 1968; 2nd edn, 1974)

—— *The rivals. America and Russia since World War II* (New York, 1971; 2nd edn, London, 1973)

—— *Stalin Koloß der Macht* (Esslingen, 1977)

Ullman, Walter *The United States in Prague 1945–1948* (New York, 1978)

Van der Beugel, Ernst H. *From Marshall aid to Atlantic partnership. European integration as a concern of American foreign policy* (Amsterdam/London/New York, 1966)

Walton, Richard J. *Henry Wallace, Harry Truman and the Cold War,* (New York, 1976)

Wassmund, Hans *Kontinuität im Wandel. Bestimmungsfaktoren sowjetischer Deutschlandpolitik in der Nach-Stalin-Zeit* (Cologne/Vienna, 1974)

—— *Der Weg nach Potsdam. Zur Gründungsgeschichte der DDR* (Munich/Vienna, 1980)

Wettig, Gerhard *Entmilitarisierung und Wiederbewaffnung in Deutschland 1943–1955* (Munich, 1967)

Wexler, Imanuel *The Marshall Plan revisited. The European recovery program in economic perspective* (Westport, Conn., 1983)

Wheeler-Bennet, John and Anthony Nicholls *The semblance of peace. The political settlement after the Second World War* (London, 1972)

Williams, William A. *Die Tragödie der amerikanischen Diplomatie* (Frankfurt, 1973)

Willis, F. Roy *France, Germany and the New Europe (1945–1967)* (Stanford,

Ca/London, 1968)

Winkler, Heinrich August (ed.) *Politische Weichenstellungen im Nachkriegs-deutschland 1945–1953* (Göttingen, 1979)

Wittner, Lawrence S., *American intervention in Greece, 1943–1949* (New York, 1982)

Yergin, Daniel *Shattered peace. The origins of the Cold War and the national security state* (Boston, 1977)

Index